# MATH for AUTOMOTIVE TECHNICIANS

### LUKE D. THOMPSON

Publisher
**The Goodheart-Willcox Company, Inc.**
Tinley Park, Illinois
www.g-w.com

Copyright © 2019
by
The Goodheart-Willcox Company, Inc.

All rights reserved. No part of this work may be reproduced, stored, or transmitted in any form or by any electronic or mechanical means, including information storage and retrieval systems, without the prior written permission of The Goodheart-Willcox Company, Inc.

Manufactured in the United States of America.

ISBN 978-1-63563-222-4

3 4 5 6 7 8 9 – 19 – 23

**The Goodheart-Willcox Company, Inc. Brand Disclaimer:** Brand names, company names, and illustrations for products and services included in this text are provided for educational purposes only and do not represent or imply endorsement or recommendation by the author or the publisher.

**The Goodheart-Willcox Company, Inc. Safety Notice:** The reader is expressly advised to carefully read, understand, and apply all safety precautions and warnings described in this book or that might also be indicated in undertaking the activities and exercises described herein to minimize risk of personal injury or injury to others. Common sense and good judgment should also be exercised and applied to help avoid all potential hazards. The reader should always refer to the appropriate manufacturer's technical information, directions, and recommendations; then proceed with care to follow specific equipment operating instructions. The reader should understand these notices and cautions are not exhaustive.

The publisher makes no warranty or representation whatsoever, either expressed or implied, including but not limited to equipment, procedures, and applications described or referred to herein, their quality, performance, merchantability, or fitness for a particular purpose. The publisher assumes no responsibility for any changes, errors, or omissions in this book. The publisher specifically disclaims any liability whatsoever, including any direct, indirect, incidental, consequential, special, or exemplary damages resulting, in whole or in part, from the reader's use or reliance upon the information, instructions, procedures, warnings, cautions, applications, or other matter contained in this book. The publisher assumes no responsibility for the activities of the reader.

**The Goodheart-Willcox Company, Inc. Internet Disclaimer:** The Internet resources and listings in this Goodheart-Willcox Publisher product are provided solely as a convenience to you. These resources and listings were reviewed at the time of publication to provide you with accurate, safe, and appropriate information. Goodheart-Willcox Publisher has no control over the referenced websites and, due to the dynamic nature of the Internet, is not responsible or liable for the content, products, or performance of links to other websites or resources. Goodheart-Willcox Publisher makes no representation, either expressed or implied, regarding the content of these websites, and such references do not constitute an endorsement or recommendation of the information or content presented. It is your responsibility to take all protective measures to guard against inappropriate content, viruses, or other destructive elements.

# PREFACE

*Math for Automotive Technicians* is designed to help students learn and apply basic math skills. The first part of this text provides 12 lessons that develop a mastery of basic math skills in the context of automotive service. Coverage includes whole number operations, decimals, greater than/less than, fractions, conversion, graphs and tables, formulas, measurement, and specifications. The second part consists of 96 case studies that apply and extend the basic math skills with actual vehicle procedures, data, and specifications. For ease of integration with curricula based on the NATEF standards, the case studies are grouped into automotive service areas, including chassis systems, engine mechanical, and electrical. Answers to odd-numbered practice problems are listed in the back of the text.

Most CTE students take standard math courses taught by math instructors who may find it challenging to demonstrate specific applications in a field such as automotive technology and thus show why learning math is essential to career success. While these students may have received instruction in basic math previously, many of them cannot perform simple calculations or measurements and will not be motivated to improve their math skills without seeing direct applications to their areas of interest.

*Math for Automotive Technicians* fits an applied math course that covers whole numbers, fractions, decimals, measurements, and basic concepts of algebra and geometry. The most significant distinguishing feature of this text is the scaffolding of basic math skills into case studies that are specifically related to instruction in standard automotive areas, such as vehicle maintenance, chassis systems, electrical, and others. This approach allows for a true integration of math and skilled trade instruction.

This text can also be used in programs where the automotive technology instructors provide supplemental math lessons in their classes. This has become a very common phenomenon because of the expectation that instruction in mathematics will pervade the curriculum and because many or most automotive technology students need additional instruction in basic math.

# ABOUT THE AUTHOR

Luke D. Thompson is passionate about teaching math as it relates to automotive technology. He believes math instruction for automotive technicians should be immersed in the context of automotive technology and reflect what actually occurs in the automotive shop. *Math for Automotive Technicians* is the culmination of Mr. Thompson's efforts to create a product in which mathematical thinking and problem solving is structured around the NATEF tasks.

Mr. Thompson teaches automotive technology at Tahoma High School in Maple Valley, WA, where he achieved NATEF accreditation for his program. He previously taught at NATEF-accredited high schools in Washington and Michigan. His automotive industry experience includes working as a prototype technician at Ford Motor Company's Research and Development Division. Mr. Thompson holds an A.A.S. in Automotive Technology from Henry Ford College, a B.S. in Secondary Career and Technical Education from Wayne State University, and a M.Ed. in Curriculum and Instruction with a focus on math and science from the University of Washington. He is a recipient of the ASE Industry Education Alliance "Outstanding Instructor Award" and holds various ASE certifications, including Master Certified Automobile Technician.

# REVIEWERS

The author and publisher wish to thank the following industry and teaching professionals for their valuable input into the development of *Math for Automotive Technicians*.

**Jasper Adams**
Niagara Career & Technical Center
Sanborn, NY

**Louis Bramante**
Vineland Senior High School
Vineland, NJ

**James Chastain**
Autry Technology Center
Enid, OK

**Alan Darr**
Kathleen Senior High School
Lakeland, FL

**Shawn P. Day**
Center of Applied Technology North
Severn, MD

**Ray Dove**
Weaver Academy
Greensboro, NC

**Brian Noel**
Consumnes River College
Sacramento, CA

**Gary Wilfong**
Frederick County Career and Technology
Frederick, MD

# ACKNOWLEDGMENTS

The author and publisher would like to thank the following individuals for their contribution in the development of *Math for Automotive Technicians*.

Neal Strausbaugh, assistant crew chief, US Army Top Fuel Team, Don Schumacher Racing.

Bryan Kelly, owner, Valley Automotive Repair and Electric, Maple Valley, Washington.

Jordan Paster, lube technician/Ford ASSET student, Scarff Ford, Auburn, Washington.

Kirk Tobel, sales and service technician, Les Schwab Tire Centers, Maple Valley, Washington.

Sinh Bui, engine builder and machinist, Action Machine, Seattle, Washington.

Daniel Addie, service technician, Porsche Bellevue, Bellevue, Washington.

John Dascher, diagnostic specialist, Lexus of Bellevue, Bellevue, Washington.

Amber Avery, technician, Toyota of Kirkland, Kirkland, Washington.

Amandeep Singh, technician and Mopar CAP student, Rairdon's Chrysler-Dodge-Jeep, Arlington, Washington.

# G-W INTEGRATED LEARNING SOLUTION

## Together, We Build Careers

At Goodheart-Willcox, we take our mission seriously. Since 1921, G-W has been serving the career and technical education (CTE) community. Our employee-owners are driven to deliver exceptional learning solutions to CTE students to help prepare them for careers. Our authors and subject matter experts have years of experience in the classroom and industry. We combine their wisdom with our expertise to create content and tools to help students achieve success. Our products start with theory and applied content based on a strong foundation of accepted standards and curriculum. To that base, we add student-focused learning features and tools designed to help students make connections between knowledge and skills. G-W recognizes the crucial role instructors play in preparing students for careers. We support educators' efforts by providing time-saving tools that help them plan, present, assess, and engage students with traditional and digital activities and assets. We provide an entire program of learning in a variety of print, digital, and online formats, including economic bundles, allowing educators to select the right mix for their classroom.

## Student-Focused Curated Content

Goodheart-Willcox believes that student-focused content should be built from standards and/or accepted curriculum coverage. *Math for Automotive Technicians* purposefully scaffolds critical math skills across the spectrum of automotive technician service areas. This approach, which is deeply grounded in the NATEF task list, helps ensure that meaningful content is taught side-by-side with the mathematics. We call on industry experts and teachers from across the country to review and comment on our content, presentation, and pedagogy. Finally, in our refinement of curated content, our editors are immersed in content checking, securing and sometimes creating figures that convey key information, and revising language and pedagogy.

# FEATURES OF THE TEXTBOOK

Features are student-focused learning tools designed to help you get the most out of your studies. This visual guide highlights the features designed for the textbook.

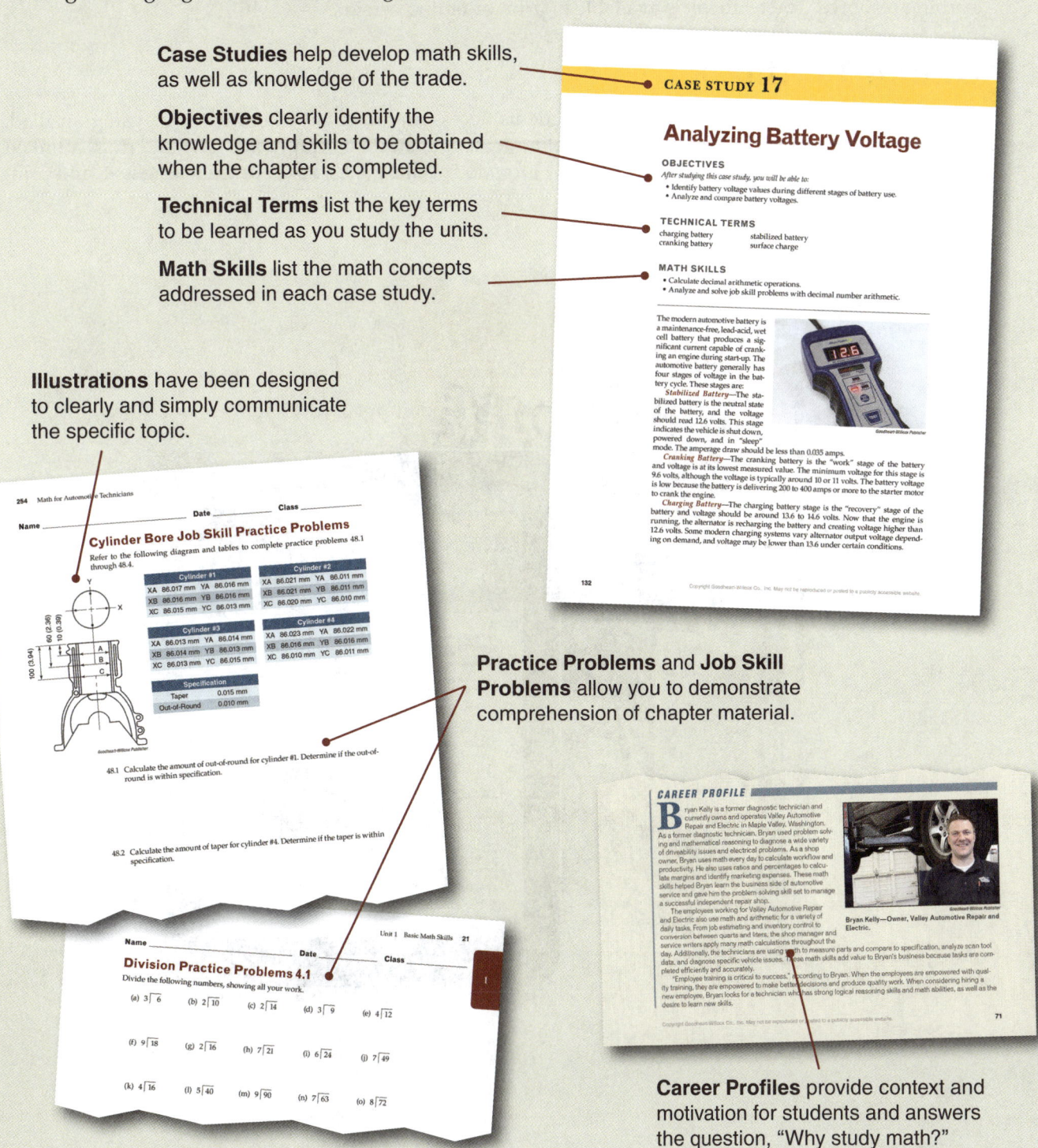

**Case Studies** help develop math skills, as well as knowledge of the trade.

**Objectives** clearly identify the knowledge and skills to be obtained when the chapter is completed.

**Technical Terms** list the key terms to be learned as you study the units.

**Math Skills** list the math concepts addressed in each case study.

**Illustrations** have been designed to clearly and simply communicate the specific topic.

**Practice Problems** and **Job Skill Problems** allow you to demonstrate comprehension of chapter material.

**Career Profiles** provide context and motivation for students and answers the question, "Why study math?"

# STUDENT RESOURCES

## Textbook

The *Math for Automotive Technicians* textbook provides an exciting, full-color, and highly illustrated learning resource. The textbook is available in print or online versions.

## Online Textbook

This online version of the textbook gives students access anytime, anywhere whether using an iPad, netbook, PC, or Mac computer. Using the online textbook, students can easily navigate from a linked table of contents, search specific topics, quickly jump to specific pages, zoom in to enlarge text, and print selected pages for offline reading.

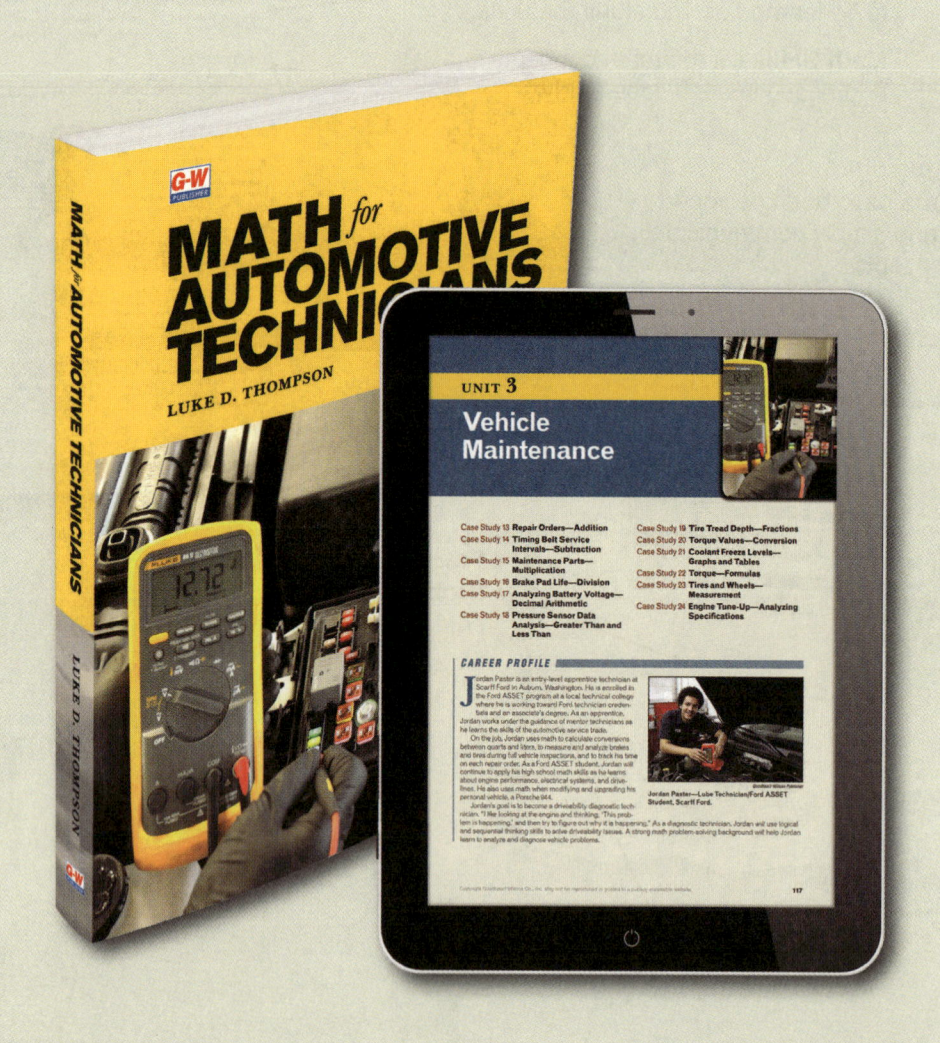

# INSTRUCTOR RESOURCES

Instructor resources provide information and tools to support teaching, grading, and planning; class presentations; and assessment.

## ExamView® Assessment Suite

The ExamView® Assessment Suite allows instructors to quickly and easily create, administer, and score tests, both in print and online. Create many versions of formative and summative exams, multiple versions of a single test, and automatically generate answer keys. For additional versatility, instructors can easily modify existing questions and add new questions to fit course needs.

## Instructor's Resource CD

A variety of time-saving teaching support tools are provided in the Instructor's Resource for *Math for Automotive Technicians*. Answer keys are included for textbook questions. Customizable lesson plans provide chapter-specific instructional resources, tools for practice and assessment, and other resources available for teaching the chapter content. An overview of the products in the teaching package is provided, as well as any correlation charts that may apply to the course.

## Online Instructor Resources

Online Instructor Resources are comprehensive, time-saving teaching tools organized in a convenient, easy-to-use online bookshelf. Lesson plans, answer keys, ExamView® Assessment Suite software, and other resources are available on demand, 24/7 from home or school.

# CONTENTS

## Unit 1–Basic Math Skills ........................... 1
Lesson 1–Addition.................................2
Lesson 2–Subtraction ..............................7
Lesson 3–Multiplication...........................11
Lesson 4–Division................................17
Lesson 5–Decimal Arithmetic.......................23
Lesson 6–Greater Than and Less Than ..............31
Lesson 7–Fractions ...............................37
Lesson 8–Conversion .............................43
Lesson 9–Graphs and Tables.......................47
Lesson 10–Formulas ..............................53
Lesson 11–Measurement ..........................59
Lesson 12–Analyzing Specifications.................65

*[handwritten in margin: Week 1 / 7, 5, 11]*

## Unit 2–Around the Shop ......................... 71
Case Study 1–Work Uniforms–Addition ..............72
Case Study 2–Shop Inventory–Subtraction ...........75
Case Study 3–Scrap Metal Pricing–Multiplication.....78
Case Study 4–Paying for Professional Tools–Division..82
Case Study 5–Flat-Rate Labor Times–Decimal Arithmetic....85
Case Study 6–Customer Service Surveys–Greater Than and Less Than ....91
Case Study 7–Hose Length Calculations–Fractions....95
Case Study 8–Fluid Volume–Conversion .............98
Case Study 9–Workplace Productivity–Graphs and Tables ....101
Case Study 10–Wage Earnings–Formulas............106
Case Study 11–Shop Equipment–Measurement.......110
Case Study 12–Vehicle Identification Number–Analyzing Specifications .......113

## Unit 3–Vehicle Maintenance ......................117
Case Study 13–Repair Orders–Addition .............118
Case Study 14–Timing Belt Service Intervals–Subtraction ....123
Case Study 15–Maintenance Parts–Multiplication....126
Case Study 16–Brake Pad Life–Division.............129
Case Study 17–Analyzing Battery Voltage–Decimal Arithmetic.....132
Case Study 18–Pressure Sensor Data Analysis–Greater Than and Less Than ....136
Case Study 19–Tire Tread Depth–Fractions..........139
Case Study 20–Torque Values–Conversion ..........143
Case Study 21–Coolant Freeze Levels–Graphs and Tables....147
Case Study 22–Torque–Formulas ..................151
Case Study 23–Tires and Wheels–Measurement .....155
Case Study 24–Engine Tune-Up–Analyzing Specifications....159

## Unit 4–Chassis ... 163
- Case Study 25–Unsprung Weight–Addition ... 164
- Case Study 26–Service Intervals–Subtraction ... 169
- Case Study 27–Tire Size Aspect Ratio–Multiplication ... 172
- Case Study 28–Stopping Distance Factors–Division ... 175
- Case Study 29–Alignment Angles–Decimal Arithmetic ... 178
- Case Study 30–Analyzing Tires–Greater Than and Less Than ... 182
- Case Study 31–Ride Height Measurements–Fractions ... 187
- Case Study 32–Linear Measurement–Conversion ... 190
- Case Study 33–Brake Fluid Testing–Graphs and Tables ... 194
- Case Study 34–Tire Diameter–Formulas ... 199
- Case Study 35–Disc Brake Micrometer–Measurement ... 203
- Case Study 36–Brake System–Analyzing Specifications ... 205

## Unit 5–Engine Mechanical ... 209
- Case Study 37–Valve Overlap and Duration–Addition ... 210
- Case Study 38–Camshaft Lobe–Subtraction ... 215
- Case Study 39–Rocker Arm Ratio–Multiplication ... 218
- Case Study 40–Compression Ratio–Division ... 222
- Case Study 41–Engine Block Calculations–Decimal Arithmetic ... 226
- Case Study 42–Piston Bore Clearance–Greater Than and Less Than ... 230
- Case Study 43–Engine Parts–Fractions ... 233
- Case Study 44–Engine Size–Conversion ... 236
- Case Study 45–Cooling System–Graphs and Tables ... 239
- Case Study 46–Engine Power and Efficiency–Formulas ... 244
- Case Study 47–Cam and Crank Journal–Measurement ... 248
- Case Study 48–Cylinder Bore–Analyzing Specifications ... 252

## Unit 6–Electrical ... 257
- Case Study 49–Voltage Drop–Addition ... 258
- Case Study 50–Reference Voltage–Subtraction ... 262
- Case Study 51–Ohm's Law Part 1–Multiplication ... 265
- Case Study 52–Ohm's Law Part 2–Division ... 268
- Case Study 53–Applying Ohm's Law–Decimal Arithmetic ... 271
- Case Study 54–Wire Gage Sizes–Greater Than and Less Than ... 275
- Case Study 55–Wire Length–Fractions ... 279
- Case Study 56–Temperature–Conversion ... 282
- Case Study 57–Graphing Ohm's Law–Graphs and Tables ... 286
- Case Study 58–Electrical Circuit Resistance–Formulas ... 291
- Case Study 59–Digital Multimeter–Measurement ... 295
- Case Study 60–Electrical System Specifications–Analyzing Specifications ... 300

## Unit 7–Engine Performance ... 305
- Case Study 61–Electronic Throttle Controls–Addition ... 306
- Case Study 62–Mass Airflow–Subtraction ... 309

Case Study 63–Ignition Coil Voltage–Multiplication . . . . . . . . . . . . . . . . . . . . . . . . . . .311
Case Study 64–Analyzing Compression Tests–Division . . . . . . . . . . . . . . . . . . . . . . .315
Case Study 65–Fuel Trim–Decimal Arithmetic . . . . . . . . . . . . . . . . . . . . . . . . . . . . . .320
Case Study 66–Spark Plug Gap–Greater Than and Less Than . . . . . . . . . . . . . . . .323
Case Study 67–Fuel Tank Capacity–Fractions. . . . . . . . . . . . . . . . . . . . . . . . . . . . . . .327
Case Study 68–Pressure–Conversions . . . . . . . . . . . . . . . . . . . . . . . . . . . . . . . . . . . .329
Case Study 69–Engine Sensors–Graphs and Tables. . . . . . . . . . . . . . . . . . . . . . . . . .332
Case Study 70–Lambda–Formulas . . . . . . . . . . . . . . . . . . . . . . . . . . . . . . . . . . . . . . .337
Case Study 71–Vacuum/Pressure Gauge Reading–Measurement . . . . . . . . . . . . . .341
Case Study 72–Module Pinout Diagrams–Analyzing Specifications . . . . . . . . . . .345

## Unit 8–Driveline . . . . . . . . . . . . . . . . . . . . . . . . . . . . . . . . . . . . 349
Case Study 73–Multi-Disc Clutch Adjustments–Addition . . . . . . . . . . . . . . . . . . . .350
Case Study 74–Driveline Angle Calculation–Subtraction. . . . . . . . . . . . . . . . . . . . .354
Case Study 75–Gear Ratio Torque–Multiplication . . . . . . . . . . . . . . . . . . . . . . . . . .357
Case Study 76–Differential Gear Ratios–Division . . . . . . . . . . . . . . . . . . . . . . . . . .361
Case Study 77–Hydraulic Pressure–Decimal Arithmetic . . . . . . . . . . . . . . . . . . . . .365
Case Study 78–Planetary Gear Set Ratios–Greater Than and Less Than. . . . . . . .369
Case Study 79–Manual Gear Set Ratios–Fractions. . . . . . . . . . . . . . . . . . . . . . . . . .373
Case Study 80–Odometer Distance Values–Conversions . . . . . . . . . . . . . . . . . . . .376
Case Study 81–Shift Solenoids–Graphs and Tables . . . . . . . . . . . . . . . . . . . . . . . . .379
Case Study 82–Driveline Speed–Formulas . . . . . . . . . . . . . . . . . . . . . . . . . . . . . . . .383
Case Study 83–Gear Backlash–Measurement. . . . . . . . . . . . . . . . . . . . . . . . . . . . . .387
Case Study 84–Differential Backlash–Analyzing Specifications . . . . . . . . . . . . . . .390

## Unit 9–Air Conditioning and Hybrid Technology . . . . . . 395
Case Study 85–Air Conditioning System Oil–Addition . . . . . . . . . . . . . . . . . . . . . .396
Case Study 86–Compressor Clutch Air Gap–Subtraction. . . . . . . . . . . . . . . . . . . . .399
Case Study 87–Hybrid Vehicle High-Voltage Battery–Multiplication . . . . . . . . . . .402
Case Study 88–Electric Car Speed and Acceleration–Division . . . . . . . . . . . . . . . .404
Case Study 89–Cooling System Boiling Point–Decimal Arithmetic . . . . . . . . . . . .408
Case Study 90–Hybrid Vehicle Payback–Greater Than and Less Than . . . . . . . . .412
Case Study 91–Evaporator and Condenser Area–Fractions . . . . . . . . . . . . . . . . . . .416
Case Study 92–Refrigerant Weight–Conversions . . . . . . . . . . . . . . . . . . . . . . . . . . .419
Case Study 93–Air Conditioning System Pressures–Graphs and Tables . . . . . . . .423
Case Study 94–Miles per Gallon Equivalent–Formulas . . . . . . . . . . . . . . . . . . . . . .427
Case Study 95–Air Conditioning Gauge Reading–Measurement . . . . . . . . . . . . . .430
Case Study 96–Hybrid Electric Fuel Economy–Analyzing Specifications . . . . . . .434

Reference . . . . . . . . . . . . . . . . . . . . . . . . . . . . . . . . . . . . . . . . . . . . . . . . . . . . . . . . . . .439
Glossary . . . . . . . . . . . . . . . . . . . . . . . . . . . . . . . . . . . . . . . . . . . . . . . . . . . . . . . . . . . .446
Index . . . . . . . . . . . . . . . . . . . . . . . . . . . . . . . . . . . . . . . . . . . . . . . . . . . . . . . . . . . . . . .449
Answers to Odd-Numbered Questions . . . . . . . . . . . . . . . . . . . . . . . . . . . . . . . . . . .455

# UNIT 1
# Basic Math Skills

| Lesson 1 | Addition | Lesson 7 | Fractions |
| --- | --- | --- | --- |
| Lesson 2 | Subtraction | Lesson 8 | Conversion |
| Lesson 3 | Multiplication | Lesson 9 | Graphs and Tables |
| Lesson 4 | Division | Lesson 10 | Formulas |
| Lesson 5 | Decimal Arithmetic | Lesson 11 | Measurement |
| Lesson 6 | Greater Than and Less Than | Lesson 12 | Analyzing Specifications |

## CAREER PROFILE

With a high school small gas engine class and a passion for drag racing under his belt, Neal Strausbaugh sent out almost 100 résumés to drag racing teams after high school. With only one reply, he became a crew member of a small team, working as a parts cleaner, bottom end engine builder, and tire technician. After 16 years of race technician experience, Neal is now an assistant crew chief for a world-class drag racing organization, Don Schumacher Racing.

Every crew member who works on the organization's 11,000+ horsepower top fuel dragsters must use math when building and repairing a car. From basic tape measures and micrometers to buret gauges and data acquisition sensors, math and logical analytic problem solving is part of every racing setup procedure. The team has even fabricated specialty measurement tools designed for unique measurements.

Goodheart-Willcox Publisher

Neal Strausbaugh—Assistant Crew Chief, US Army Top Fuel Team, Don Schumacher Racing.

"It is never too late to kick yourself in gear," says Neal. "Even if you are behind, it does not mean you are not going to make it." After a difficult time with math classes early in high school, Neal was motivated to get to work and be successful. Now, as a team leader, Neal uses his math and logical reasoning skills to make crucial decisions that affect the outcome of a Top Fuel race, where fractions of a second make the difference between winning and losing. Neal has found the value in surrounding himself with great people, and everyone contributes to the team effort.

# LESSON 1

# Addition

## OBJECTIVES

*After studying this lesson, you will be able to:*
- Identify the addend and sum components of a basic addition problem.
- Compute addition problems with a variety of addends.
- Analyze and solve word problems using addition.

## TECHNICAL TERMS

addends          addition          sum

---

*Addition* is the process of combining two or more separate values to form a total value. The total value, or *sum*, is determined when the separate values, or *addends*, are combined.

$$\text{Addend} + \text{Addend} = \text{Sum} \qquad \begin{array}{r} \text{Addend} \\ + \text{Addend} \\ \hline \text{Sum} \end{array}$$

Basic addition is a counting operation, and can be expressed as a visual representation and expressed with points on a number line.

A visual representation of the addition operation follows:

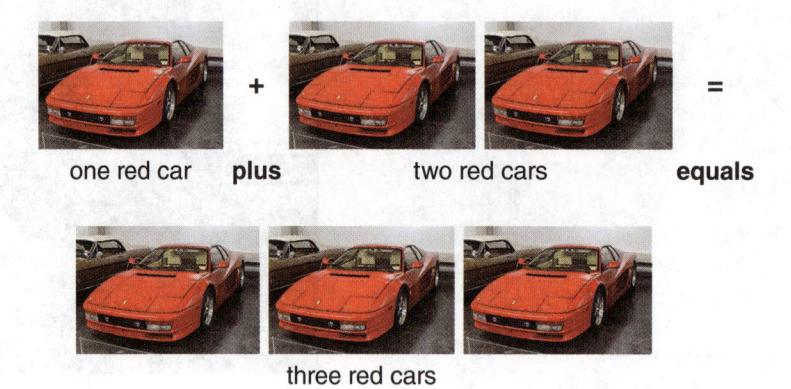

one red car    **plus**    two red cars    **equals**

three red cars

A number line representation of the addition operation follows:

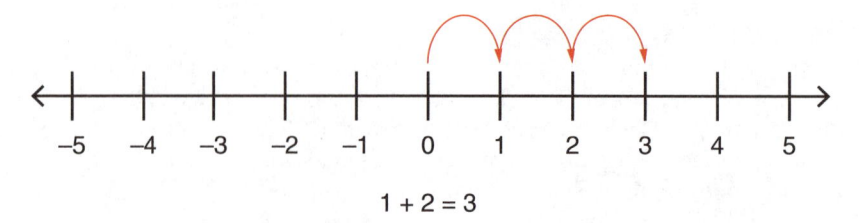

$1 + 2 = 3$

In these basic addition examples, 6 plus 2 equals 8. The problem can be written vertically or horizontally, as shown. Generally, the vertical format (on the left) is easier to solve than the horizontal format, and will be useful when adding numbers with larger values.

$$\begin{array}{r} 6 \\ +\,2 \\ \hline 8 \end{array} \qquad 6 + 2 = 8$$

**Complete addition practice problems 1.1.**

Addition problems with larger addends may require the process of carrying. In this mathematical process, when a column sum equals 10 or more, the 1 must be "carried" to the next column and included in the next step of the addition problem. Review the following examples.

$$\begin{array}{r} {}^{1}1\,2 \\ +\;\;9 \\ \hline 2\,1 \end{array} \qquad \begin{array}{r} {}^{1}1\,4 \\ +\;\;8 \\ \hline 2\,2 \end{array} \qquad \begin{array}{r} {}^{1}2\,8 \\ +\;\;6 \\ \hline 3\,4 \end{array}$$

**Complete addition practice problems 1.2.**

Addition problems may include larger addends and may include more than two addends. The carrying process remains the same, but may be required in multiple columns. Review the examples.

$$\begin{array}{r} 2 \\ 3 \\ 1 \\ 2 \\ +\,1 \\ \hline 9 \end{array} \qquad \begin{array}{r} 1\,4\,2\,2 \\ +2\,3\,5\,7 \\ \hline 3\,7\,7\,9 \end{array} \qquad \begin{array}{r} {}^{1\;1\;1}2\,4\,7\,9 \\ 3\,4\,5\,7 \\ +1\,1\,2\,3 \\ \hline 7\,0\,5\,9 \end{array}$$

**Complete addition practice problems 1.3.**

Addition problems may also be presented as *word problems*. This type of math problem requires reading through a written problem and extracting the critical information required to solve the problem. When reading the problem, read carefully to determine the question being asked by the problem.

**Example:** An automotive repair shop performed 3 oil changes on Monday, 6 oil changes on Tuesday, and 4 oil changes on Wednesday. How many oil changes has the shop performed so far this week?

Monday oil changes + Tuesday oil changes + Wednesday oil changes = total oil changes

3 oil changes + 6 oil changes + 4 oil changes = 13 oil changes

13 oil changes have been performed so far this week.

Often, word problems will include distracting information that is not part of the math operation needed to solve the problem. Notice in the following example that the engine size information is not part of the word problem, and is distracting information. A good strategy for this type of problem is to underline the necessary information.

**Example:** A technician is replacing the spark plugs on two different engines. One engine is a 1.9-liter engine with 4 spark plugs. Another engine is a 4.6-liter engine with 8 spark plugs. Calculate the number of spark plugs the technician is changing.

$$\text{spark plugs changed in engine 1} + \text{spark plugs changed in engine 2} = \text{total number of spark plugs changed}$$

$$4 \text{ spark plugs} + 8 \text{ spark plugs} = 12 \text{ spark plugs}$$

12 spark plugs were changed by the technician.

**Complete addition practice problems 1.4.**

Name _____  Date _____  Class _____

## Addition Practice Problems 1.1

Add the following numbers, showing all your work.

(a)  4
    +3

(b)  5
    +2

(c)  1
    +7

(d)  6
    +6

(e)  4
    +1

(f)  1
    +2

(g)  8
    +5

(h)  9
    +3

(i)  5
    +9

(j)  3
    +8

(k)  7
    +3

(l)  9
    +8

## Addition Practice Problems 1.2

Add the following numbers, showing all your work.

(a)  17
    + 5

(b)  18
    + 6

(c)  14
    + 9

(d)  25
    + 8

(e)  18
    + 9

(f)  48
    + 7

(g)  38
    + 8

(h)  58
    +13

(i)  23
    + 7

(j)  28
    + 7

(k)  38
    +17

(l)  48
    +29

## Addition Practice Problems 1.3

Add the following numbers, showing all your work.

(a)  4
     8
     2
    +1

(b)  346
    +126

(c)  19
     48
    +23

(d)   814
     3524
    +2719

(e)  3
     5
     7
     9
    +2

(f)  2945
    +1319

(g)  44
     70
     96
    + 25

(h)    680
      1642
    +25879

Unit 1  Basic Math Skills  5

(i)  2
     9
     8
     5
    +6

(j)     2 5
      6 8 6 1
     +4 3 5 8

(k)  7 9
     8 1
     2 3
    +4 3

(l)   4 2 2 1 5
      1 9 3 6 7
     +5 3 2 9 1

## Addition Practice Problems 1.4

(a) An independent repair shop performed service on 6 trucks, 12 cars, and 1 motorcycle this week. Calculate how many total vehicles were serviced.

(b) A technician is performing three oil changes this morning. All of the vehicles use 5W-20 engine oil. One vehicle requires 4 quarts of oil, one vehicle requires 5 quarts of oil, and one vehicle requires 7 quarts of oil. Calculate how many quarts of oil the technician will need to perform these three oil changes.

(c) In January, a technician serviced 37 vehicles. In February, the technician serviced 41 vehicles. In March, the technician serviced 39 vehicles. In April, the technician serviced 14 vehicles. Calculate how many vehicles the technician has serviced so far this year.

(d) Each week, a technician buys new tools required to perform vehicle service. The first week of the month the technician bought $237 worth of tools, the second week $458 worth of tools, the third week $187 worth of tools, and the fourth week $97 worth of tools. Calculate how much the technician spent on tools this month.

(e) An independent repair shop replaced 129 car batteries in 2014, 143 car batteries in 2015, and 134 car batteries in 2016. Calculate how many car batteries they replaced in this three-year span.

# LESSON 2

# Subtraction

## OBJECTIVES

*After studying this lesson, you will be able to:*
- Identify the minuend, subtrahend, and the difference components of a basic subtraction problem.
- Compute subtraction problems with a variety of minuends and subtrahends.
- Analyze and solve word problems using subtraction.

## TECHNICAL TERMS

difference
minuend
subtraction
subtrahend

---

*Subtraction* is the process of removing one value from another value to form a difference value. The new value, or *difference*, is determined when the *subtrahend* is removed from the *minuend*.

$$\text{Minuend} - \text{Subtrahend} = \text{Difference}$$

$$\begin{array}{r} \text{Minuend} \\ - \text{Subtrahend} \\ \hline \text{Difference} \end{array}$$

Basic subtraction is a counting operation, and can be expressed as a visual representation and expressed with points on a number line.

A visual representation of the subtraction operation follows:

three yellow cars     **minus**

two yellow cars     **equals**     one yellow car

A number line representation of the subtraction operation follows:

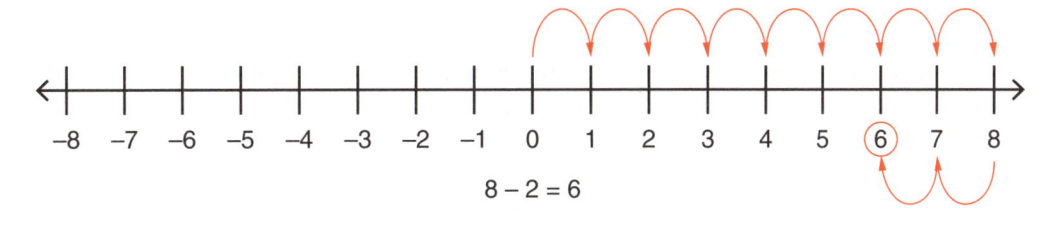

$$8 - 2 = 6$$

In these basic subtraction examples, 8 minus 2 equals 6. The problem can be written vertically or horizontally, as shown. Generally, the vertical format is easier to solve, and will be useful when the number values are larger.

$$\begin{array}{r} 8 \\ -2 \\ \hline 6 \end{array} \qquad 8 - 2 = 6$$

**Complete subtraction practice problems 2.1.**

Subtraction problems with larger minuend and subtrahend values may require borrowing value from the next column in order to complete the operation. Review the examples.

$$\begin{array}{r} {}^{2}\,{}^{17} \\ \cancel{3}\,\cancel{7} \\ -1\,9 \\ \hline 1\,8 \end{array} \qquad \begin{array}{r} {}^{11} \\ 3\,\cancel{\rlap{\,1}}\,\cancel{1} \\ 4\,2\,1 \\ -2\,8\,9 \\ \hline 1\,3\,2 \end{array}$$

**Complete subtraction practice problems 2.2.**

Subtraction problems may result in a difference that is a negative number. This occurs when a larger number is subtracted from a smaller number. To calculate these problems, subtract the smaller number from the larger number, and then use the sign (+ or –) of the larger number for the answer. Review the examples.

$$\begin{array}{r} 4 \\ -9 \\ \hline -5 \end{array} \qquad \begin{array}{r} 5 \\ -1\,5 \\ \hline -1\,0 \end{array}$$

**Complete subtraction practice problems 2.3.**

Subtraction problems may also be presented as *word problems*. This type of math problem requires reading through a written problem and extracting the critical information required to solve the problem.

**Example:** An auto repair shop earns a promotional rebate from an auto parts supplier once they replace 20 sets of brake pads. So far they have replaced 9 sets of brake pads. Calculate how many more sets of brake pads must be replaced to earn the promotional rebate.

brake pad set replacements needed for rebate − brake pad sets replaced = remaining brake pad sets

20 brake pad sets − 9 brake pad sets = 11 brake pad sets

11 more sets of brake pads need to be replaced.

Often, word problems will include distracting information that is not part of the math operation needed to solve the problem. Notice in the following example that the engine size information is not part of the math problem, and is distracting information. Review the example.

**Example:** A technician is performing a compression test on a 3.8-liter V6 engine. The lowest cylinder has a compression of 129 psi and the highest cylinder has a compression of 145 psi. Calculate the difference between the highest and lowest cylinders.

compression in highest cylinder − compression in lowest cylinder = difference

145 psi − 129 psi = 16 psi

16 psi is the difference between the highest and lowest cylinders.

**Complete subtraction practice problems 2.4.**

Name _____ Date _____ Class _____

# Subtraction Practice Problems 2.1

Subtract the following numbers, showing all your work.

(a)  9     (b)  6     (c)  4     (d)  7     (e)  9     (f)  4
    −2         −3         −1         −2         −8         −1

(g)  8     (h)  9     (i)  8     (j)  3     (k)  9     (l)  7
    −5         −3         −4         −2         −6         −4

# Subtraction Practice Problems 2.2

Subtract the following numbers, showing all your work.

(a)  23      (b)  242     (c)  457     (d)  2356
    −16          − 27         −252         − 579

(e)  87      (f)  827     (g)  665     (h)  1342
    −29          − 52         −489         − 894

(i)  64      (j)  945     (k)  129     (l)  4569
    −37          −565         − 90         −3128

# Subtraction Practice Problems 2.3

Subtract the following numbers, showing all your work.

(a)  3     (b)  8     (c)  4     (d)   6     (e)   5
    −8         −9         −7         −13         −20

(f)  2     (g)  4     (h)  2     (i)   4     (j)   9
    −7         −6         −8         −19         −31

# Subtraction Practice Problems 2.4

(a) A technician owes $437 for professional mechanic's tools. He plans to pay $205 this week toward his tool bill. Calculate how much he will owe after this payment is applied to his account.

(b) A repair shop has 43 quarts of 5W-20 oil in stock. This week, they have four oil changes scheduled that will use a total of 19 quarts of 5W-20 oil. Calculate how many quarts of oil will be in stock after this week.

(c) A technician is measuring radiator efficiency. The upper radiator hose measures 209°F. The lower radiator hose measures 167°F. Calculate the change in temperature from the upper radiator hose to the lower radiator hose.

(d) A cooling system flush is recommended at 90,000 miles on a vehicle with 78,432 miles. Calculate how many miles until the cooling system flush is recommended.

(e) A customer is comparing two sets of brake pads based on price. The premium brake pads cost $67. The economy brake pads cost $39. Calculate the difference in price between the premium and economy brake pads.

# LESSON 3

# Multiplication

## OBJECTIVES

*After studying this lesson, you will be able to:*
- Identify the factors and product components of a basic multiplication problem.
- Compute multiplication problems with a variety of factors.
- Analyze and solve word problems using multiplication.

## TECHNICAL TERMS

factor          multiplication          product

---

*Multiplication* is the process of combining sets of a value into a total, or *product*, where one *factor* is the quantity in each set and the other factor is the number of sets.

$$\text{Factor} \times \text{Factor} = \text{Product} \qquad \begin{array}{r} \text{Factor} \\ \times \text{Factor} \\ \hline \text{Product} \end{array}$$

Multiplication can be expressed as a visual representation and expressed with values in a table.

A visual representation of the multiplication operation follows:

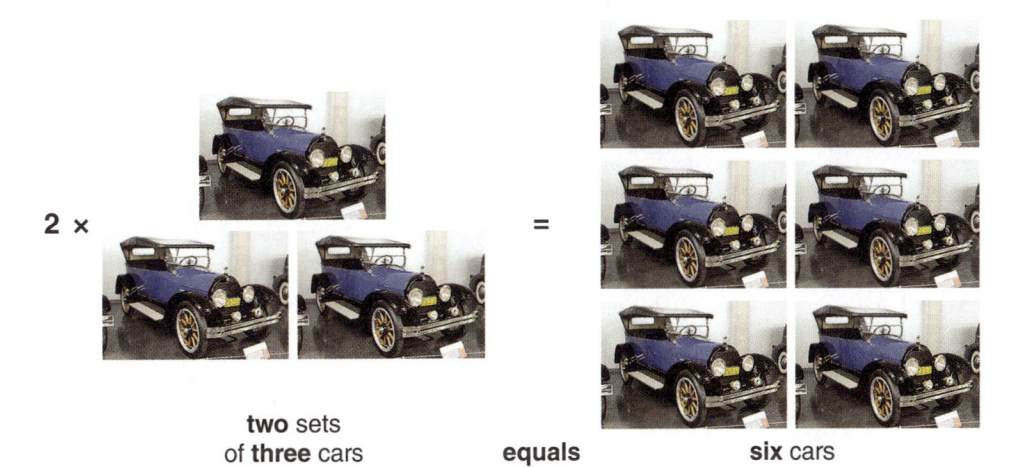

2 × **two** sets of **three** cars **equals** **six** cars

A table representation of the multiplication operation follows. This example shows 7 × 6 = 42.

|   | 0 | 1 | 2 | 3 | 4 | 5 | 6 | 7 | 8 | 9 |
|---|---|---|---|---|---|---|---|---|---|---|
| 0 | 0 | 0 | 0 | 0 | 0 | 0 | 0 | 0 | 0 | 0 |
| 1 | 0 | 1 | 2 | 3 | 4 | 5 | 6 | 7 | 8 | 9 |
| 2 | 0 | 2 | 4 | 6 | 8 | 10 | 12 | 14 | 16 | 18 |
| 3 | 0 | 3 | 6 | 9 | 12 | 15 | 18 | 21 | 24 | 27 |
| 4 | 0 | 4 | 8 | 12 | 16 | 20 | 24 | 28 | 32 | 36 |
| 5 | 0 | 5 | 10 | 15 | 20 | 25 | 30 | 35 | 40 | 45 |
| 6 | 0 | 6 | 12 | 18 | 24 | 30 | 36 | 42 | 48 | 54 |
| 7 | 0 | 7 | 14 | 21 | 28 | 35 | 42 | 49 | 56 | 63 |
| 8 | 0 | 8 | 16 | 24 | 32 | 40 | 48 | 56 | 64 | 72 |
| 9 | 0 | 9 | 18 | 27 | 36 | 45 | 54 | 63 | 72 | 81 |

In these basic multiplication examples, 6 times 2 equals 12. The problem can be written in two formats, as shown. Generally, the vertical format is easier to solve, and will be useful when the number values are larger.

$$\begin{array}{r} 6 \\ \times\ 2 \\ \hline 12 \end{array} \qquad 6 \times 2 = 12$$

**Complete multiplication practice problems 3.1.**

Multiplication of factors larger than 9 require an additional step to complete the problem. Analyze the steps shown.

**Step 1**
9 × 8

$$\begin{array}{r} ^{7} \\ 1\,8 \\ \times\ 9 \\ \hline 2 \end{array}$$

**Step 2**
(9 × 1) + 7

$$\begin{array}{r} ^{7} \\ 1\,8 \\ \times\ 9 \\ \hline 1\,6\,2 \end{array}$$

**Step 1**
8 × 7

$$\begin{array}{r} ^{5} \\ 4\,8 \\ \times 1\,7 \\ \hline 6 \end{array}$$

**Step 2**
(7 × 4) + 5

$$\begin{array}{r} 4\,8 \\ \times 1\,7 \\ \hline 3\,3\,6 \end{array}$$

**Step 3**
1 × 8 *and* 1 × 4

$$\begin{array}{r} 4\,8 \\ \times 1\,7 \\ \hline 3\,3\,6 \\ +4\,8\,0 \end{array}$$

**Step 4**
336 + 480

$$\begin{array}{r} 4\,8 \\ \times 1\,7 \\ \hline 3\,3\,6 \\ +4\,8\,0 \\ \hline 8\,1\,6 \end{array}$$

**Complete multiplication practice problems 3.2.**

Multiplication problems may also be presented as *word problems*. This type of math problem requires reading through a written problem and extracting the critical information required to solve the problem.

**Example:** A tire technician has 8 cars scheduled for new tires today. All of the cars are replacing all 4 tires. Calculate how many tires the technician is replacing today.

$$\text{number of cars} \times \frac{\text{number of tires}}{\text{replaced per car}} = \frac{\text{total number of}}{\text{tires replaced}}$$

$$8 \text{ cars} \times 4 \text{ tires per car} = 32 \text{ total tires}$$

32 tires are being replaced today.

Often, word problems will include distracting information that is not part of the math operation needed to solve the problem. Notice in the following example that the cost per shirt information is not part of the math problem, and is distracting information.

**Example:** A repair shop manager is ordering new work uniforms for all of the technicians. The work uniforms are a flat fee of $18 per shirt, for M, L, and XL. There are 12 technicians and each will be getting 6 uniform shirts. Calculate how many total uniform shirts will be ordered.

$$\frac{\text{number of}}{\text{technicians}} \times \frac{\text{number of uniform}}{\text{shirts per technician}} = \frac{\text{total number of}}{\text{uniform shirts}}$$

$$12 \text{ technicians} \times 6 \text{ shirts per technician} = 72 \text{ total shirts}$$

72 uniform shirts will be ordered.

**Complete multiplication practice problems 3.3.**

**Work Space/Notes**

Name _____  Date _____  Class _____

## Multiplication Practice Problems 3.1

Multiply the following numbers, showing all your work.

(a)   4    (b)   2    (c)   6    (d)   4    (e)   8    (f)   2
    × 3        × 6        × 7        × 9        × 0        × 1

(g)   7    (h)   9    (i)   7    (j)   2    (k)   4    (l)   9
    × 4        × 3        × 5        × 9        × 6        × 8

## Multiplication Practice Problems 3.2

Multiply the following numbers, showing all your work.

(a)   3 4    (b)   4 7    (c)   2 9    (d)  1 3 5    (e)  4 2 8
    ×   5        ×   8        ×   3        ×   2 1        ×   1 9

(f)   5 7    (g)   6 3    (h)   8 9    (i)  1 3 5    (j)  5 6 3
    × 1 3        × 1 8        × 2 3        ×   2 1        ×   2 4

## Multiplication Practice Problems 3.3

(a) A technician earns $20 per hour and worked 38 hours during the most recent pay period. Calculate how much the technician will earn for this pay period.

(b) A technician has elected to have $35 from each weekly paycheck saved in a retirement account. Calculate how much will be taken out over the course of one year (52 weeks).

**Name** _____  **Date** _____  **Class** _____

(c) A customer has selected a set of 4 new tires that cost $67 per tire. Calculate how much the customer will spend to purchase this set of new tires.

(d) An independent repair shop manager has decided to stock cases of common grades of engine oil. Each case contains 12 bottles of oil. The manager ordered 7 cases of 5W-20 engine oil. Calculate how many total bottles of 5W-20 engine oil the repair shop will have in stock.

(e) A service manager has ordered more quarter-fold shop towels. Each package of shop towels has 90 towels. A case of shop towels includes 15 packages of shop towels. Calculate how many shop towels are in a case.

(f) The technicians in a repair shop use 15 cans of brake clean spray per month. Calculate how many cans they use in 12 months.

# LESSON 4

# Division

## OBJECTIVES

*After studying this lesson, you will be able to:*
- Identify the dividend, divisor, and the quotient components of a basic division problem.
- Compute division problems with a variety of dividends and divisors.
- Analyze and solve word problems using division.

## TECHNICAL TERMS

dividend
division
divisor
quotient

---

*Division* is the process of separating a single quantity into smaller groups of an equal, lesser quantity. The *quotient* is determined by separating the *dividend* into groups based on the *divisor*.

$$\text{Dividend} \div \text{Divisor} = \text{Quotient} \qquad \text{Divisor} \overline{\smash{)}\text{Dividend}}^{\text{Quotient}}$$

Division can be expressed as a visual representation and as an inverse operation to multiplication.

A visual representation of the division operation follows:

Six cars **divided** into three groups **equals** two cars in each group.

Division is an inverse operation to multiplication:

If:
$a = b \times c$
then,
$a \div b = c$

If:
$6 = 2 \times 3$
then,
$6 \div 2 = 3$

In these basic division examples, 6 divided by 2 equals 3. The problem can be written in two formats as shown below. Generally, the format shown on the right is easier to solve, and will be useful when the number values are larger and long division operations are required.

$$6 \div 2 = 3 \qquad 2\overline{)6}^{\,3}$$

**Complete division practice problems 4.1.**

When solving division problems, the divisor may not always go into the dividend evenly. When this happens, a remainder is part of the answer. To solve, think how many times this number will go into the other number. Analyze the example for the process to determine the remainder.

| **Step 1** | **Step 2** | **Step 3** |
|---|---|---|
| 3 *into* 17 *is* 5 | 5 × 3 | 17 − 15 |
| $3\overline{)17}^{\,5}$ | $\begin{array}{r}5\phantom{0}\\3\overline{)17}\\-15\end{array}$ | $\begin{array}{r}5\,r\,2\\5\overline{)17}\\-15\\\hline 2\end{array}$ |

**Complete division practice problems 4.2.**

Division problems with larger dividends and divisors require additional steps to complete the problem. This method is commonly known as "long division." Analyze the example shown.

| **Step 1** | **Step 2** | **Step 3** |
|---|---|---|
| 8 *into* 42, 5 *times* | 5 × 8 | 42 − 40, *bring down* 9 |
| $8\overline{)429}^{\,5}$ | $\begin{array}{r}5\phantom{00}\\8\overline{)429}\\-40\phantom{0}\end{array}$ | $\begin{array}{r}53\phantom{0}\\8\overline{)429}\\-40\phantom{0}\\\hline 29\end{array}$ |

| **Step 4** | **Step 5** | **Step 6** |
|---|---|---|
| 3 × 8 | 29 − 24, r 5 | 53 r 5 = 53 5/8 |
| $\begin{array}{r}53\phantom{0}\\8\overline{)429}\\-40\phantom{0}\\\hline 29\\-24\end{array}$ | $\begin{array}{r}53\,r\,5\\8\overline{)429}\\-40\phantom{0}\\\hline 29\\-24\\\hline 5\end{array}$ | $r\,5 = \dfrac{5}{8}$ |

**Complete division practice problems 4.3.**

Division problems may also be presented as *word problems*. This type of math problem requires reading through a written problem and extracting the critical information required to solve the problem. Review the example.

**Example:** A rental car fleet shop has 210 oil changes scheduled for today. There are 7 technicians assigned to perform these oil changes. Calculate how many oil changes each technician is expected to complete.

$$\frac{\text{total number of}}{\text{oil changes performed}} \div \frac{\text{number of technicians}}{\text{performing oil changes}} = \frac{\text{number of oil changes}}{\text{per technician}}$$

210 total oil changes ÷ 7 technicians = 30 oil changes per technician

Each technician is expected to complete 30 oil changes today.

Often, word problems will include distracting information that is not part of the math operation needed to solve the problem. Notice in the following example that some of the engine size information is not part of the math problem, and is distracting information. Also, notice how the remainder can be written as a fraction, with the divisor as the denominator of the fraction.

**Example:** A 5.7-liter engine has 351 cubic inches of displacement and 8 cylinders. Calculate how many cubic inches of displacement each cylinder has.

$$\frac{\text{total engine displacement}}{\text{(in cubic inches)}} \div \frac{\text{number of}}{\text{cylinders}} = \frac{\text{displacement (in cubic inches)}}{\text{per cylinder}}$$

351 cubic inches ÷ 8 cylinders = 43 r 7

351 cubic inches ÷ 8 cylinders = 43 7/8 cubic inches per cylinder

Each cylinder has a displacement of 43 7/8 cubic inches.

**Complete division practice problems 4.4.**

**Work Space/Notes**

Name _____ Date _____ Class _____

## Division Practice Problems 4.1

Divide the following numbers, showing all your work.

(a) $3\overline{)6}$  (b) $2\overline{)10}$  (c) $2\overline{)14}$  (d) $3\overline{)9}$  (e) $4\overline{)12}$

(f) $9\overline{)18}$  (g) $2\overline{)16}$  (h) $7\overline{)21}$  (i) $6\overline{)24}$  (j) $7\overline{)49}$

(k) $4\overline{)16}$  (l) $5\overline{)40}$  (m) $9\overline{)90}$  (n) $7\overline{)63}$  (o) $8\overline{)72}$

## Division Practice Problems 4.2

Divide the following numbers, showing all your work.

(a) $2\overline{)7}$  (b) $2\overline{)13}$  (c) $3\overline{)11}$  (d) $3\overline{)14}$  (e) $4\overline{)17}$

(f) $9\overline{)23}$  (g) $4\overline{)29}$  (h) $7\overline{)22}$  (i) $6\overline{)27}$  (j) $7\overline{)53}$

## Division Practice Problems 4.3

Divide the following numbers, showing all your work.

(a) $5\overline{)129}$  (b) $7\overline{)145}$  (c) $7\overline{)456}$  (d) $3\overline{)387}$

(e) $6\overline{)560}$  (f) $4\overline{)350}$  (g) $7\overline{)243}$  (h) $8\overline{)454}$

Name _____  Date _____  Class _____

# Division Practice Problems 4.4

(a) An independent repair shop purchased a new diagnostic scan tool for $3,768. The scan tool will be paid back in 12 equal monthly payments. Calculate the amount of each monthly payment.

(b) A shop owner has allocated $9,000 total for year-end bonuses. The bonus money will be split evenly among 5 employees. Calculate how much each employee will receive as a bonus.

(c) A V6 engine is advertised to produce 222 horsepower at 5,200 rpm. Calculate the amount of advertised horsepower in each cylinder.

(d) Three technicians are driving from Butte, Montana, to Las Vegas, Nevada, for a major aftermarket parts convention. The distance between the two cities is 870 miles. If they agree to split the driving evenly, calculate how many miles each technician will drive to get there.

(e) A hybrid vehicle high-voltage battery produces 318 volts. The high-voltage battery pack is made up of 159 cells wired in series. Calculate the amount of voltage each cell produces.

(f) A technician earned $64,360 while working in an independent repair shop in 2016. Calculate how much the technician earned per month during 2016.

(g) A 15-year-old pickup truck has 134,540 miles on the odometer. Calculate the number of miles on the odometer per year of the truck.

# LESSON 5

# Decimal Arithmetic

## OBJECTIVES

*After studying this lesson, you will be able to:*
- Identify place value of whole and decimal numbers.
- Calculate addition, subtraction, multiplication, and division operations using decimal numbers.
- Analyze and solve word problems with decimal numbers.

## TECHNICAL TERMS

decimal numbers    decimal point

---

*Decimal numbers* are used to distinguish the number values that are between whole numbers. For example, the number 4.7 is between whole numbers 4 and 5. The *decimal point* locates the place value of the whole number and indicates the value on the right side of the decimal point.

Refer to the table regarding place value on both sides of the decimal point.

| | |
|---:|:---|
| 1,000,000.0 | millions |
| 100,000.0 | hundred thousands |
| 10,000.0 | ten thousands |
| 1,000.0 | thousands |
| 100.0 | hundreds |
| 10.0 | tens |
| 1.0 | ones |
| 0.0 | zero |
| tenths | 0.1 |
| hundredths | 0.01 |
| thousandths | 0.001 |
| ten thousandths | 0.0001 |

It is common practice for a technician to discuss numbers, especially decimal numbers, with high levels of precision. Refer to the place value table to determine the place value examples.

0.008

eight thousandths

nine thousand four hundred and sixty-three

9,463

**Complete decimal arithmetic practice problems 5.1.**

*Rounding* is the process of simplifying a number to a larger or a smaller value that makes calculations easier. When rounding, if the digit to the right of the place you are rounding to is 0, 1, 2, 3, or 4, round down. For example, 19.2 rounded to the nearest whole number would be rounded down to 19.0 or 19. If the digit to the right of the place you are rounding to is 5, 6, 7, 8, or 9, round up. For example, 14.8 rounded to the nearest whole number would be rounded up to 15.0 or 15.

**Complete decimal arithmetic practice problems 5.2.**

Addition and subtraction of decimal numbers is nearly identical to whole number operations. The decimal point remains in the same location and carrying or borrowing is unaffected. Review the examples shown.

$$\begin{array}{r} \overset{1\,1\,1\;\;\;1}{196.46} \\ +237.59 \\ \hline 434.05 \end{array} \qquad \begin{array}{r} 895.35 \\ -574.12 \\ \hline 321.23 \end{array}$$

**Complete decimal arithmetic practice problems 5.3.**

Multiplication of decimal numbers requires careful placement of the decimal point once the multiplication problem is solved. This is determined by counting the number of places to the right of the decimal point in the numbers being multiplied, and positioning the decimal point accordingly. In this example, two numbers are to the right of the decimal point, so the decimal point is placed two digits to the left in the answer. Review the example.

$$\begin{array}{r} 73.7 \\ \times 45.3 \\ \hline 221\;\;1 \\ 3685\;\;0 \\ +2948\;0 \\ \hline 33386\;1 \end{array} \qquad 3338.61$$

**Complete decimal arithmetic practice problems 5.4.**

Division of decimal numbers requires moving the decimal point in the divisor to the right until the number is a whole number. Then, move the decimal point to the right in the dividend the same number of places. After moving the decimal points in both the divisor and dividend, complete the long division problem. The decimal point will remain in the same location once the division is completed. Review the example.

| Starting Point | Decimal Point Shifted | Division Complete |
|---|---|---|
| 23.5⟌152.75 | 235.⟌1527.5 | 235.⟌1527.5 → 6.5, −1410, 117 5, −117 5, 0 0 |

**Complete decimal arithmetic practice problems 5.5.**

Decimal arithmetic problems may also be presented as *word problems*. This type of math problem requires reading through a written problem and extracting the critical information required to solve the problem. A word problem may also require two or more arithmetic operations to reach the final answer.

**Example:** A V8 engine has 56.75 cubic inches of displacement in each cylinder. Calculate the total amount of displacement in the engine.

number of cylinders × cubic inches per cylinder = total displacement

8 cylinders × 56.75 cubic inches per cylinder = 454 total cubic inches

The engine has 454 cubic inches of displacement.

**Complete decimal arithmetic practice problems 5.6.**

**Work Space/Notes**

Name _____ Date _____ Class _____

# Decimal Arithmetic Practice Problems 5.1

Use the place value table to determine the value of the given number. If the number is given, write the words describing the number. If the words are given, write the number.

(a) 0.4 _____

(b) 237 _____

(c) 0.0003 _____

(d) 2,800,000 _____

(e) 4,879 _____

(f) 0.045 _____

(g) Three hundred and fifty _____

(h) Fifty-six hundredths _____

(i) Two hundred and one thousandths _____

# Decimal Arithmetic Practice Problems 5.2

Round the numbers given in (a) through (f) to the nearest whole number.

(a) 0.7 _____  (b) 2.3 _____  (c) 45.9 _____

(d) 81.2 _____  (e) 351.5 _____  (f) 14.6 _____

Round the numbers given in (g) through (l) to the nearest ten.

(g) 71 _____  (h) 43 _____  (i) 49 _____

(j) 99 _____  (k) 132 _____  (l) 564 _____

# Decimal Arithmetic Practice Problems 5.3

Add the following numbers, showing all your work.

(a)   7.7
      2.6
    +4.3

(b)  92.47
    +23.65

(c)   46.78
     356.48
    +372.05

(d)   8.9
     -3.7

(e)  98.35
    - 7.79

(f)  453.25
    - 79.79

(g)   9.6
     +7.4

(h)  53.55
    - 9.69

(i)  858.98
    +610.07

Copyright Goodheart-Willcox Co., Inc. May not be reproduced or posted to a publicly accessible website.

## Decimal Arithmetic Practice Problems 5.4

Multiply the following numbers, showing all your work.

(a) 3.5 × 4.5

(b) 8.2 × 9.4

(c) 5.54 × 8.06

(d) 3.44 × 2.89

(e) 10.45 × 7.67

(f) 24.78 × 6.96

(g) 15.88 × 6.70

(h) 34.89 × 6.99

## Decimal Arithmetic Practice Problems 5.5

Divide the following numbers, showing all your work.

(a) 2.75 ⟌ 9.625

(b) 3.65 ⟌ 16.425

## Decimal Arithmetic Practice Problems 5.6

(a) An inline 6 engine needs new spark plugs. The copper core spark plugs cost $1.67 each and the iridium spark plugs cost $7.39 each. Calculate the cost of the iridium spark plugs for this engine.

(b) A technician is performing three cooling system flushes. The coolant capacity of the first vehicle is 5.59 liters, the second vehicle 6.50 liters, and the third vehicle 9.80 liters. Calculate the total amount of coolant capacity for these three vehicles.

**Name** _____ **Date** _____ **Class** _____

(c) A piston diameter measures 93.971 mm and the cylinder bore measures 94.008 mm. Calculate the difference between the piston diameter and the cylinder bore.

(d) A service writer is preparing an estimate for a customer to rebuild a worn parallelogram steering system. The pitman arm costs $21.79, the idler arm costs $19.67, the center link costs $57.89, the inner tie rods cost $14.50 each, and the outer tie rods cost $16.35 each. Calculate the total cost for a new pitman arm, idler arm, center link, two inner tie rods, and two outer tie rods.

(e) The intake lobe height on a camshaft is 43.890 mm. The exhaust lobe height on a camshaft is 44.262 mm. Calculate how much larger the exhaust lobe is compared to the intake lobe.

(f) A key-off battery draw measures 0.015 amps. The minimum allowable amount of key-off battery draw is 0.003 amps. Calculate how far above specification this battery amperage draw is.

**Work Space/Notes**

# LESSON 6

# Greater Than and Less Than

## OBJECTIVES

*After studying this lesson, you will be able to:*
- Identify greater than, less than, and equal symbols.
- Compare whole numbers, decimal numbers, and fractions.
- Analyze and solve word problems by comparing numbers.

## TECHNICAL TERMS

equal
greater than
less than
plus or minus symbol

---

The process of analyzing numbers includes determining inequalities. When a number value is the exact same as another number, they are considered *equal*. If numbers are unequal when compared, they are labeled as *greater than* or *less than*.

$$= \text{Equal To}$$
$$> \text{Greater Than}$$
$$< \text{Less Than}$$

Whole numbers and decimal numbers can be compared as equal to, greater than, or less than. Review the examples.

$$7 = 7 \qquad 4 < 9 \qquad 6.2 > 4.2 \qquad 0.099 < 0.103$$

**Complete greater than and less than practice problems 6.1.**

Fractions and mixed numbers can be compared as equal to, greater than, or less than. Review the examples.

$$\frac{1}{4} = \frac{1}{4} \qquad \frac{3}{8} < \frac{5}{8} \qquad \frac{27}{64} > \frac{7}{64} \qquad 3\frac{7}{8} < 5\frac{3}{8}$$

**Complete greater than and less than practice problems 6.2.**

Greater than and less than problems also include a plus or minus range symbol, shown in the following example.

$$5 \pm 2$$

The *plus or minus symbol* indicates a range of values. In this example, the range of values is 2 more and 2 less than 5. The range would be 3 to 7.

**Complete greater than and less than practice problems 6.3.**

Greater than and less than problems may also be presented as *word problems*. This type of math problem requires reading through a written problem and extracting the critical information required to solve the problem. Multiple arithmetic operations may be required to solve word problems.

**Example:** A 2013 Chevrolet Camaro produces 323 horsepower at 6,500 rpm. A 2013 Ford Mustang produces 305 horsepower at 6,500 rpm. Determine which engine produces more horsepower.

$$323 \text{ horsepower} > 305 \text{ horsepower}$$

The Camaro produces more horsepower.

**Complete greater than and less than practice problems 6.4.**

Name _____ Date _____ Class _____

## Greater Than and Less Than Practice Problems 6.1

Compare the numbers and fill in the blank with <, >, or =.

(a) 27 ___ 35
(b) 17 ___ 19
(c) 45 ___ 45
(d) 1,690 ___ 689
(e) 629 ___ 345
(f) 3,457 ___ 4,329
(g) 0.13 ___ 0.09
(h) 1.23 ___ 1.32
(i) 4.67 ___ 46.93
(j) 21 ___ 21
(k) 347 ___ 473
(l) 1.89 ___ 1.09
(m) 0.03 ___ 0.05
(n) 3.35 ___ 3.36
(o) 43.2 ___ 34.2

## Greater Than and Less Than Practice Problems 6.2

Compare the fractions and fill in the blank with <, >, or =.

(a) $\frac{5}{16}$ ___ $\frac{9}{16}$
(b) $\frac{13}{16}$ ___ $\frac{5}{16}$
(c) $\frac{3}{8}$ ___ $\frac{7}{8}$
(d) $\frac{7}{32}$ ___ $\frac{15}{32}$
(e) $\frac{3}{4}$ ___ $\frac{3}{4}$
(f) $\frac{37}{64}$ ___ $\frac{27}{64}$

## Greater Than and Less Than Practice Problems 6.3

Identify the range of the values given.

(a) 4±3 _____

(b) 19±6 _____

(c) 25±6.5 _____

(d) 0.9±0.3 _____

(e) 1.75±0.25 _____

(f) 1.354±0.027 _____

**Name** _____ **Date** _____ **Class** _____

## Greater Than and Less Than
## Practice Problems 6.4

(a) In the month of January, Technician A installed 7 new car batteries and Technician B installed 4 new car batteries. In February, Technician A installed 8 new car batteries and Technician B installed 5 new car batteries. Determine if more batteries were installed in January or in February.

(b) A technician is comparing professional tool sets. Set 1 has 65 sockets and 39 wrenches. Set 2 has 47 sockets and 43 wrenches. Determine which set has more individual tools.

(c) A customer is comparing replacement brake pad options. Premium ceramic brake pads cost $67.49 per set. Economy semimetallic brake pads cost $34.89 per set. Determine which brake pad set costs less.

(d) The left front tire tread depth is 5/32". The right front tire tread depth is 7/32". Determine which tire has a greater tread depth.

(e) So far this week, Technician A has completed 7 oil changes, 4 tire rotations, and 3 full service brake jobs. Also this week, Technician B has completed 6 oil changes, 6 tire rotations, and 2 full service brake jobs. Determine which technician has completed more total jobs this week.

Name _____ Date _____ Class _____

(f) A customer is comparing the cost of four replacement shock absorbers. Brand K shocks cost $34.89 each for front and $40.39 each for rear. Brand R shocks cost $38.29 each for front and $38.59 each for rear. If replacing two front and two rear shocks, determine which brand costs more.

(g) A customer is comparing two oil change options. Option 1 is a full service oil and filter change for $57.99. Option 2 is a full service oil change for $8.57 per quart of oil and $12.45 for a new filter. If the vehicle requires 5 quarts of oil, determine which oil change option costs less.

(h) In the month of July, a technician performed 7 full brake jobs, 9 alignments, and 15 front suspension service jobs. In August, the same technician performed 9 full brake jobs, 3 alignments, and 17 front suspension service jobs. Determine in which month the technician completed fewer total jobs.

(i) A technician is performing a wheel alignment. The front camber specification is 1.3° ± 0.4°. Calculate the range of values acceptable for the front camber angle.

**Work Space/Notes**

# LESSON 7

# Fractions

## OBJECTIVES

*After studying this lesson, you will be able to:*
- Identify the numerator and denominator parts of a fraction.
- Identify fraction values based on a shaded figure.
- Convert improper fractions, reduce fractions to lowest terms, and convert to common denominators.
- Calculate addition and subtraction of fractions in standard problems and word problems.

## TECHNICAL TERMS

denominator improper fraction mixed number
fraction lowest terms numerator

---

A *fraction* is a numerical representation of a part of a whole. The *numerator* is the part and the *denominator* is the whole. A *mixed number* is a whole number followed directly with a fraction.

$$\frac{\text{Numerator}}{\text{Denominator}} \qquad \frac{\text{(Part)}}{\text{(Whole)}}$$

Shown is a visual representation of parts of a whole, with the shaded areas representing fractions becoming a whole number.

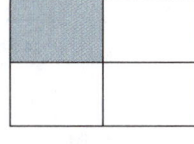

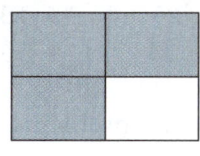

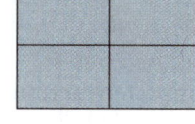

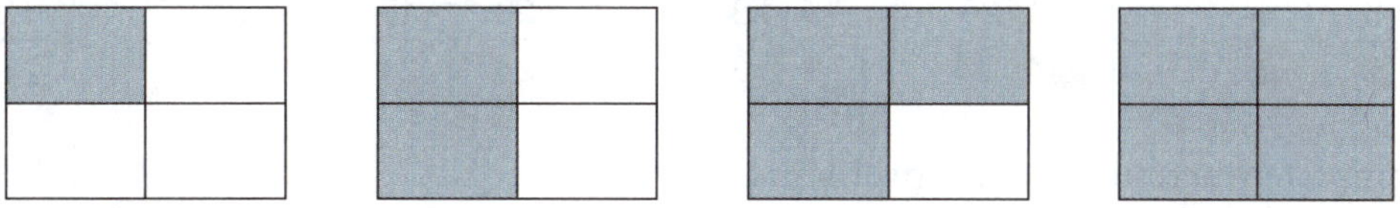

1/4 2/4 or 1/2 3/4 4/4 or 1

**Complete fractions practice problems 7.1.**

A fraction is considered an *improper fraction* when the numerator is a larger number than the denominator. When this occurs, the fraction can be converted to a mixed number. Divide the numerator by the denominator, and then create a mixed number. Use the remainder as the numerator for the new fraction. Review the example.

$$\frac{16}{9} \qquad 16 \div 9 = 1 \text{ r } 7 \qquad 1\frac{7}{9}$$

**Complete fractions practice problems 7.2.**

A fraction can be reduced to *lowest terms* when the terms can both be divided evenly by the same number. If the numerator and the denominator can both be divided by the same number evenly, the fraction can be reduced by that factor. Review the example.

$$\frac{10 \div 10}{20 \div 10} = \frac{1}{2} \qquad \frac{36 \div 9}{81 \div 9} = \frac{4}{9}$$

**Complete fractions practice problems 7.3.**

A standard (customary) tape measure divides one inch into fractions, to one-sixteenth of an inch. Addition and subtraction of these tape measure fractions is common, and requires a common denominator. Review the table and the following examples.

| 1 |||||||||||||||| 
|---|---|---|---|---|---|---|---|---|---|---|---|---|---|---|---|
| 1/2 |||||||| 1/2 ||||||||
| 1/4 |||| 1/4 |||| 1/4 |||| 1/4 ||||
| 1/8 || 1/8 || 1/8 || 1/8 || 1/8 || 1/8 || 1/8 || 1/8 ||
| 1/16 | 1/16 | 1/16 | 1/16 | 1/16 | 1/16 | 1/16 | 1/16 | 1/16 | 1/16 | 1/16 | 1/16 | 1/16 | 1/16 | 1/16 | 1/16 |

$$\frac{3}{8} + \frac{1}{8} = \frac{4}{8} = \frac{1}{4} \qquad \frac{7}{16} + \frac{13}{16} = \frac{20}{16} = 1\frac{1}{4} \qquad \frac{11}{16} - \frac{3}{16} = \frac{8}{16} = \frac{1}{2}$$

**Complete fractions practice problems 7.4.**

Fractions with uncommon denominators must be changed so they have common denominators before they can be added or subtracted. One way to make denominators the same is to multiply the top and bottom of one fraction by the denominator of the other fraction. Do this for both fractions. Review the following examples.

$$\frac{1}{4} + \frac{3}{8} = \frac{1 \times 8}{4 \times 8} \; \frac{8}{32} \qquad \frac{3 \times 4}{8 \times 4} \; \frac{12}{32} \qquad \frac{8}{32} + \frac{12}{32} = \frac{20}{32} = \frac{5}{8}$$

$$\frac{5}{6} + \frac{5}{8} = \frac{5 \times 4}{6 \times 4} \; \frac{20}{24} \qquad \frac{5 \times 3}{8 \times 3} \; \frac{15}{24} \qquad \frac{20}{24} + \frac{15}{24} = \frac{35}{24} = 1\frac{11}{24}$$

**Complete fractions practice problems 7.5.**

Fraction arithmetic problems may also be presented as *word problems*. This type of math problem requires reading through a written problem and extracting the critical information required to solve the problem.

**Example:** A technician is measuring the length of two torque-to-yield cylinder head bolts. The unused bolt is 7 5/8″. The used bolt is 7 7/8″. Calculate how much the used bolt stretched compared to the new bolt.

$$\text{length of used bolt} - \text{length of unused bolt} = \text{amount used bolt has been stretched}$$

$$7\,7/8'' - 7\,5/8'' = 2/8'' = 1/4''$$

The bolt stretched 1/4″.

**Complete fractions practice problems 7.6.**

Name _____ Date _____ Class _____

## Fractions Practice Problems 7.1

Determine the fraction based on the shaded area.

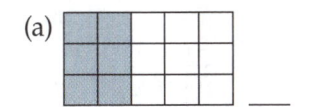

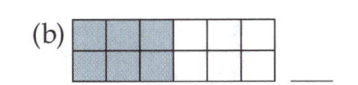

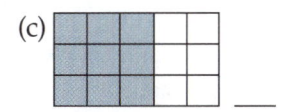

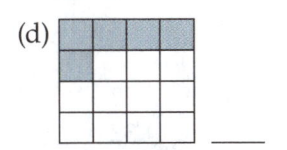

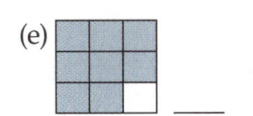

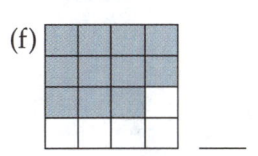

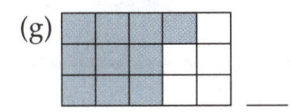

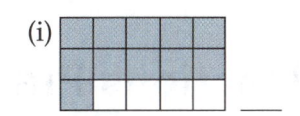

(a) ____   (b) ____   (c) ____

(d) ____   (e) ____   (f) ____

(g) ____   (h) ____   (i) ____

## Fractions Practice Problems 7.2

Convert each fraction from improper to a mixed number.

(a) $\dfrac{15}{7}$   (b) $\dfrac{23}{9}$   (c) $\dfrac{35}{4}$   (d) $\dfrac{21}{6}$   (e) $\dfrac{25}{4}$

## Fractions Practice Problems 7.3

Reduce each fraction to lowest terms.

(a) $\dfrac{6}{8}$   (b) $\dfrac{12}{16}$   (c) $\dfrac{16}{32}$   (d) $\dfrac{38}{64}$   (e) $\dfrac{24}{32}$

(f) $\dfrac{15}{45}$   (g) $\dfrac{21}{49}$   (h) $\dfrac{27}{63}$   (i) $\dfrac{20}{90}$   (j) $\dfrac{5}{25}$

## Fractions Practice Problems 7.4

Add and subtract the fractions. Write answers in lowest terms.

(a) $\dfrac{1}{4} + \dfrac{1}{4} =$ _____

(b) $\dfrac{5}{16} + \dfrac{7}{16} =$ _____

(c) $\dfrac{27}{32} - \dfrac{13}{32} =$ _____

Copyright Goodheart-Willcox Co., Inc. May not be reproduced or posted to a publicly accessible website.

Name _____ Date _____ Class _____

(d) $\dfrac{5}{16} + \dfrac{5}{16} =$ _____

(e) $\dfrac{1}{16} + \dfrac{13}{16} =$ _____

(f) $\dfrac{15}{16} - \dfrac{3}{16} =$ _____

(g) $\dfrac{9}{16} + \dfrac{11}{16} =$ _____

(h) $\dfrac{5}{8} + \dfrac{7}{8} =$ _____

(i) $\dfrac{31}{32} - \dfrac{27}{32} =$ _____

(j) $\dfrac{7}{8} + \dfrac{7}{8} =$ _____

(k) $\dfrac{3}{4} + \dfrac{3}{4} =$ _____

(l) $\dfrac{29}{32} - \dfrac{23}{32} =$ _____

## Fractions Practice Problems 7.5

Find a common denominator and then add or subtract the fractions.

(a) $\dfrac{5}{16} + \dfrac{17}{32} =$ _____

(b) $\dfrac{3}{8} + \dfrac{7}{16} =$ _____

(c) $\dfrac{3}{4} - \dfrac{9}{32} =$ _____

## Fractions Practice Problems 7.6

(a) A technician is analyzing brake pedal height. With the brake pedal not pushed, the brake pedal height measures 8 7/8". With the brake pedal pushed, the brake pedal height measures 3 5/8". Calculate the brake pedal movement distance.

(b) A lift kit is being installed on a pickup truck. The current ride height of the rear axle is 38 5/16". The lift kit will raise the rear axle 4 1/2". Calculate the new ride height of the rear axle.

**Name** _____ **Date** _____ **Class** _____

(c) A new tire has a tread depth of 13/32″. A tire is worn down to 4/32″. Calculate how much tire has worn away.

(d) A technician is replacing corroded vacuum lines on an engine. One vacuum line is 21 5/16″ long. The other vacuum line is 7 7/8″ long. Calculate how much vacuum line is needed to replace both vacuum lines.

(e) A technician is replacing heater hoses on an engine with bulk heater hose. One heater hose is 38 5/8″ and the other heater hose is 36 1/16″. Calculate how much heater hose is needed to replace both heater hoses.

(f) A fuel tank is 7/8 full. It must be less than 1/4 full so that the fuel pump can be removed. What fraction of this fuel tank needs to be emptied so the tank is 1/4 full?

# Work Space/Notes

# LESSON 8

# Conversion

## OBJECTIVES

*After studying this lesson, you will be able to:*
- Identify unit designations for length, area, weight, pressure, volume, temperature, speed, torque, and electricity.
- Identify the conversion factor multiplication process.
- Calculate conversions between unit designations for length, area, weight, pressure, volume, temperature, speed, torque, and electricity.

## TECHNICAL TERMS

conversion factor      unit conversion

---

Units of measurement have unique labels depending on the type of measurement. *Unit conversion* is converting between different units of measurement. The quantity remains the same, but the unit is changed through a conversion factor, typically by multiplication.

Review the table showing the common automotive-related unit designation labels.

| Length | | Volume | | Weight | |
|---|---|---|---|---|---|
| inch | millimeter | quart | milliliter | ounce | milligram |
| foot | centimeter | gallon | liter | pound | gram |
| yard | meter | cubic inch | cubic centimeter | ton | kilogram |
| mile | kilometer | cubic foot | cubic meter | | |
| **Pressure** | | **Area** | | **Temperature** | |
| pounds per square inch | bar | square inch | square centimeter | Fahrenheit | Celsius |
| | | square foot | square meter | | |
| **Speed** | | **Torque** | | **Electricity Prefix** | |
| miles per hour | kilometers per hour | inch-pounds | Newton-meters | milli | 0.001 |
| | | foot-pounds | | kilo | 1,000 |
| | meters per second | | | mega | 1,000,000 |

The process of converting a value from one unit to another typically requires multiplication or division by the *conversion factor*. For example, if 1 inch is equal to 2.54 centimeters, the conversion factor is 2.54.

**Example:** Convert 7 inches to centimeters.

$$7 \text{ inches} \times \frac{2.54 \text{ cm}}{1 \text{ inch}} = 17.78 \text{ cm}$$

$$7 \text{ inches} = 17.78 \text{ centimeters}$$

Since multiplication and division are inverse operations, use division to convert back to inches.

**Example:** Convert 17.78 centimeters to inches.

$$17.78 \text{ cm} \times \frac{1 \text{ inch}}{2.54 \text{ cm}} = 7 \text{ inches}$$

$$17.78 \text{ centimeters} = 7 \text{ inches}$$

Refer to the Length Conversion Factors table to complete the length conversion problems.

| Length Conversion Factors |||||
|---|---|---|---|---|
| 1 inch | = 25.4 mm | | 1 mile | = 5,280 feet |
| 1 inch | = 2.54 cm | | 1 meter | = 1000 mm |
| 1 foot | = 30.48 cm | | 1 kilometer | = 1000 meters |
| 1 foot | = 0.3048 meter | | 1 mile | = 1609.3 meters |
| 1 yard | = 0.9144 meter | | 1 mile | = 1.60 kilometers |

**Example:** Convert 3 feet to centimeters.

$$3 \text{ feet} \times \frac{30.48 \text{ cm}}{1 \text{ foot}} = 91.44 \text{ cm}$$

$$3 \text{ feet} = 91.44 \text{ centimeters}$$

**Complete conversion practice problems 8.1.**

Refer to the Weight Conversion Factors table to complete the weight conversion problems.

| Weight Conversion Factors |||||
|---|---|---|---|---|
| 1 ounce | = 28.35 grams | | 1 kilogram | = 2.20 pounds |
| 1 pound | = 16 ounces | | 1 US ton | = 2,000 pounds |
| 1 pound | = 453.6 grams | | 1 metric ton | = 1000 kilograms |
| 1 pound | = 0.453 kilograms | | 1 metric ton | = 2,204.6 pounds |

**Example:** Convert 4 pounds to ounces.

$$4 \text{ pounds} \times \frac{16 \text{ ounces}}{1 \text{ pound}} = 64 \text{ ounces}$$

$$4 \text{ pounds} = 64 \text{ ounces}$$

**Complete conversion practice problems 8.2.**

Name _____  Date _____  Class _____

## Conversion Practice Problems 8.1

Complete the length conversion problems.

(a) Convert 4 miles to meters.

(b) Convert 8 inches to cm.

(c) Convert 3 miles to feet.

(d) Convert 12 yards to meters.

(e) Convert 385 mm to inches.

## Conversion Practice Problems 8.2

Complete the weight conversion problems.

(a) Convert 12 ounces to grams.

(b) Convert 4 metric tons to pounds.

(c) Convert 985 grams to pounds.

(d) Convert 356 pounds to kilograms.

(e) Convert 85 kilograms to pounds.

(f) Convert 134 ounces to pounds.

(g) Convert 5 US tons to metric tons.

# LESSON 9

# Graphs and Tables

## OBJECTIVES

*After studying this lesson, you will be able to:*

- Identify data found in graphs and tables.
- Analyze and create graphs based on data.
- Compute arithmetic word problems based on data found in graphs and tables.

## TECHNICAL TERMS

bar graph  graph

---

A *graph* is a visual representation of a relationship between multiple sets of data. A graph is used to analyze a large data set, and can offer a visual perspective of the information. Typically, data is located in a table and then used to create a chart or graph showing the data.

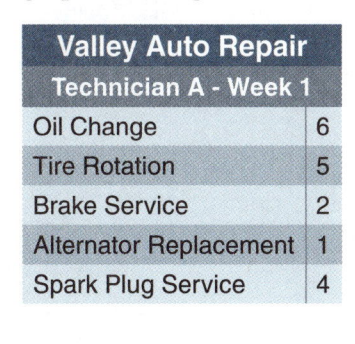

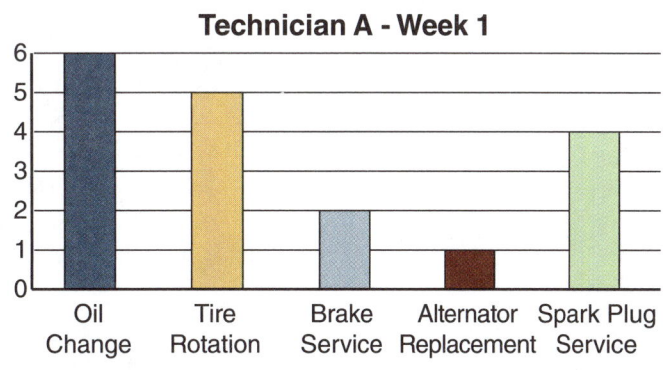

| Valley Auto Repair | |
|---|---|
| **Technician A - Week 1** | |
| Oil Change | 6 |
| Tire Rotation | 5 |
| Brake Service | 2 |
| Alternator Replacement | 1 |
| Spark Plug Service | 4 |

**Technician A - Week 1**

The *bar graph* is a visual representation of the data given in the table. A bar graph is the simplest and most common form of graph. In this example, the visual representation of the data shows the quantity and types of jobs that Technician A has completed during Week 1. The same data can also be shown in a pie chart.

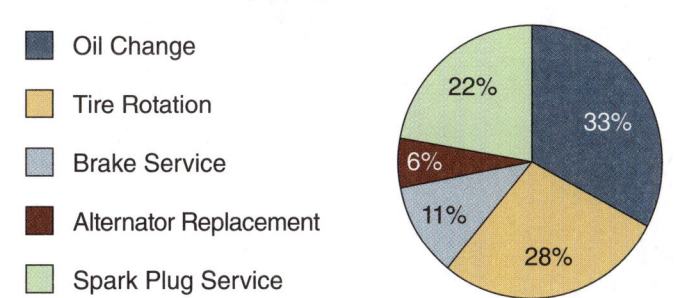

**Technician A - Week 1**

- Oil Change — 33%
- Tire Rotation — 28%
- Brake Service — 11%
- Alternator Replacement — 6%
- Spark Plug Service — 22%

**Complete graphs and tables practice problems 9.1.**

When data changes based on another variable, such as time or speed, a line graph is often used. This type of graph can be used to analyze changes to the variables of the data.

| Month | Oil Changes |
|---|---|
| January | 7 |
| February | 10 |
| March | 9 |
| April | 8 |
| May | 11 |
| June | 12 |
| July | 15 |
| August | 12 |
| September | 7 |
| October | 9 |
| November | 11 |
| December | 10 |

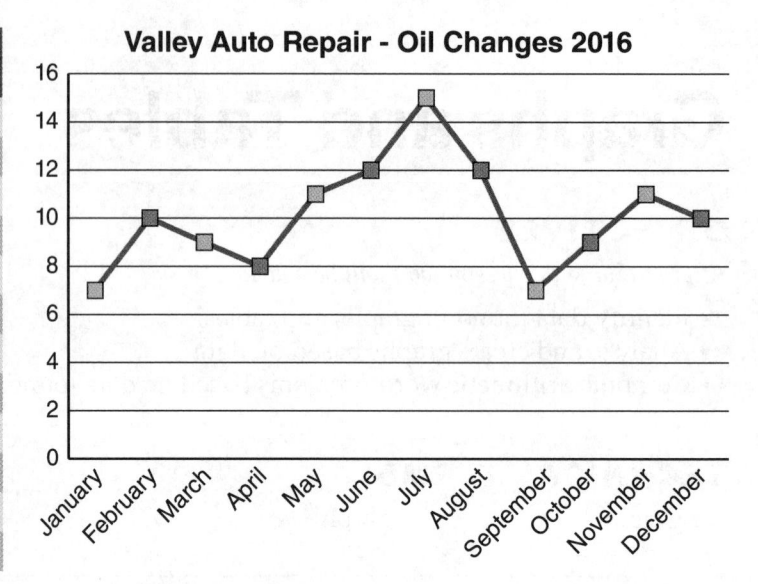

**Complete graphs and tables practice problems 9.2. and 9.3.**

Name _____ Date _____ Class _____

## Graphs and Tables Practice Problems 9.1

Use the following graph to complete problem 9.1 (a).

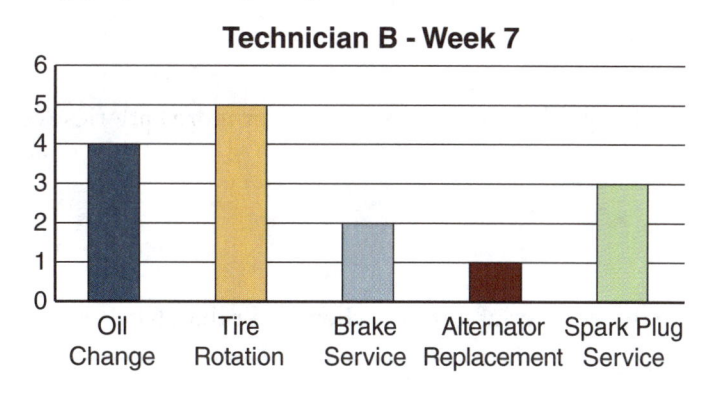

**Technician B - Week 7**

(Bar graph showing: Oil Change = 4, Tire Rotation = 5, Brake Service = 2, Alternator Replacement = 1, Spark Plug Service = 3)

(a) Analyze the graph above. Determine the work performed by Technician B during Week 7. Complete the following table.

| Oil Change | Tire Rotation | Brake Service | Alternator Replacement | Spark Plug Service |
|---|---|---|---|---|
|  |  |  |  |  |

## Graphs and Tables Practice Problems 9.2

Use the following Batteries Replaced graph to complete problems 9.2 (a) to 9.2 (f).

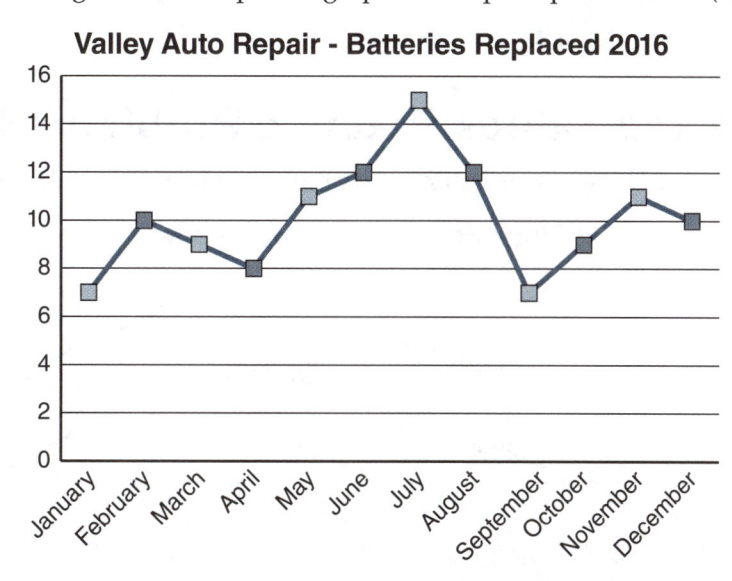

**Valley Auto Repair - Batteries Replaced 2016**

(Line graph showing monthly batteries replaced: January = 7, February = 10, March = 9, April = 8, May = 11, June = 12, July = 15, August = 12, September = 7, October = 9, November = 11, December = 10)

(a) Determine the month when the most batteries were replaced.

(b) Determine the month(s) when 9 batteries were replaced.

(c) Determine the number of months when 10 or more batteries were replaced.

(d) Determine the number of months when fewer than 6 batteries were replaced.

(e) Calculate how many batteries were changed in January, February, and March.

(f) Calculate how many batteries were changed in June, July, and August.

# Graphs and Tables Practice Problems 9.3

Use the following Horsepower graph to complete problems 9.3 (a) through 9.3 (f).

**Big Block Engine Dyno (Horsepower)**

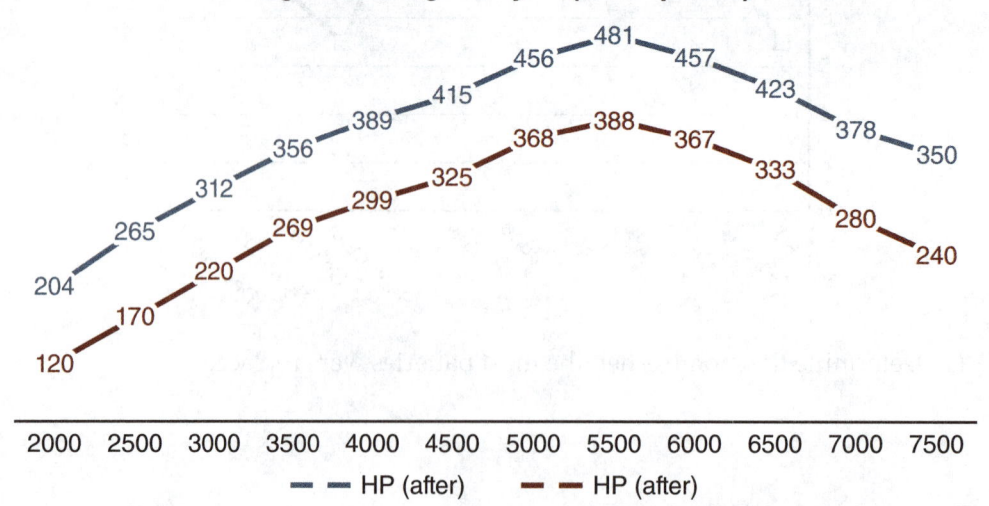

HP (before): 204, 265, 312, 356, 389, 415, 456, 481, 457, 423, 378, 350
HP (after): 120, 170, 220, 269, 299, 325, 368, 388, 367, 333, 280, 240

RPM: 2000, 2500, 3000, 3500, 4000, 4500, 5000, 5500, 6000, 6500, 7000, 7500

— — HP (after)    — — HP (after)

**Name** _____  **Date** _____  **Class** _____

(a) Identify the HP (before) at 4,500 rpm.

(b) Calculate the HP gain at 3,500 rpm.

(c) Identify the rpm of the highest HP (before).

(d) Calculate the HP gain at 5,500 rpm.

(e) Determine which is greater, HP (before) at 6,500 rpm or HP (after) at 3,000 rpm.

(f) Determine which HP gain is greater, 3,000 rpm or 6,500 rpm.

**Work Space/Notes**

# LESSON 10

# Formulas

## OBJECTIVES

*After studying this lesson, you will be able to:*
- Identify the basic structure of a formula.
- Determine order of operations for solving formula equations.
- Calculate word problems using basic formulas.

## TECHNICAL TERMS

formula           order of operations

---

A *formula* is a mathematical sentence that can be used to determine the results based on the inputs. When different inputs are entered into the formula, a unique result is given. The formula does not change, but the variety of input values create a variety of output values.

**Example:**

$x = a + b + c$

Solve for $x$, if…

$a$ = Julie ate 4 slices of pizza.
$b$ = Russel ate 3 slices of pizza.
$c$ = Tom ate 5 slices of pizza.

$$x = 4 \text{ slices} + 3 \text{ slices} + 5 \text{ slices}$$
$$x = 12 \text{ total slices}$$

Together, Julie, Russel, and Tom ate 12 slices of pizza.

New data can be applied to the same formula, with different results.

**Example:**

$x = a + b + c$

Solve for $x$, if…

$a$ = Eli ate 6 slices of pizza.
$b$ = Peyton ate 2 slices of pizza.
$c$ = Matthew ate 7 slices of pizza.

$$x = 6 \text{ slices} + 2 \text{ slices} + 7 \text{ slices}$$
$$x = 15 \text{ total slices}$$

Together, Eli, Peyton, and Matthew ate 15 slices of pizza.

**Complete formulas practice problems 10.1.**

A formula may include multiple mathematic operations, such as addition and multiplication and division. When this type of formula is used, the *order of operations* must be followed when solving the formula. The order of operations is the sequence in which different math operations must be performed. Review the formula below, in which all four basic arithmetic operations are included.

$$x = \frac{(a - b) \times c}{d} + e^2$$

Solve arithmetic operations in the order shown in the table below.

| Order of Operations P E [M D] [A S] | |
|---|---|
| Parentheses | (4 + 3) |
| Exponents | $\sqrt{}$ or $5^2$ |
| Multiply or Divide<br>**Left to Right** | $5 \times 6$<br>$8 \div 4$ |
| Add or Subtract<br>**Left to Right** | $9 + 5$<br>$6 - 3$ |

NOTE: If a problem includes a fraction bar, perform all calculations above and below the bar before dividing the numerator by the denominator.

**Example:**

$$x = \frac{(6 - 3) \times 2}{3} + 4^2$$

$$x = \frac{3 \times 2}{3} + 16$$

$$x = \frac{6}{3} + 16$$

$$x = 2 + 16$$

$$x = 18$$

**Complete formulas practice problems 10.2.**

Formula problems may also be presented as *word problems*. This type of math problem requires reading through a written problem and extracting the critical information required to solve the problem. Review the following examples.

**Example:** A 2003 sedan was driven 347 miles on 14 gallons of gas. Use the formula to calculate the fuel mileage from this data. Round the answer to the nearest tenth.

fuel mileage = miles driven ÷ gallons of gas used

The miles per gallon fuel economy of the sedan is 347 ÷ 14.

347 ÷ 14 = 24.8

The fuel mileage is 24.8 miles per gallon.

**Example:** A shop owner offers a $0.55 raise for each ASE certification test passed, up to eight tests. Use the formula to calculate the new hourly wage for a technician who was making $16.35/hour and passed 4 ASE certification tests.

$$\text{new hourly wage} = (\text{number of ASE tests} \times 0.55) + \text{prior hourly wage}$$
$$(4 \times 0.55) + 16.35 = \text{new hourly wage}$$
$$2.20 + 16.35 = 18.55$$

The new hourly wage is $18.55.

**Complete formulas practice problems 10.3.**

**Work Space/Notes**

Name _____ Date _____ Class _____

## Formulas Practice Problems 10.1

$x = a + b + c + d$

Use the formula above to complete problem 10.1 (a).

(a) Complete the table with the different data sets.

|   | Set 1 | Set 2 | Set 3 |
|---|---|---|---|
| a | 4 | 200 | 13 |
| b | 5 | 300 | 15 |
| c | 8 | 700 | 18 |
| d | 4 | 900 | 19 |
| x = | | | |

## Formulas Practice Problems 10.2

Use the order of operations to solve the following equations.

(a) $x = 4^2 + (12 - 3) + \dfrac{9}{18}$

(b) $x = 7(15 - 4) + 9(4 + 3)$

(c) $x = \dfrac{9(4 + 6)}{3(7 + 3)} + 50^2$

## Formulas Practice Problems 10.3

(a) A 2012 convertible was driven 297 miles on 16 gallons of gas. Use the formula to calculate the fuel mileage from this data. Round the answer to the nearest tenth.

(b) A 2015 luxury car was driven 337 miles on 15 gallons of gas. Use the formula to calculate the fuel mileage from this data. Round the answer to the nearest tenth.

**Name** _____ **Date** _____ **Class** _____

(c) A 2009 minivan was driven 287 miles on 13 gallons of gas. Use the formula to calculate the fuel mileage from this data. Round the answer to the nearest tenth.

(d) A 2014 pickup truck was driven 304 miles on 17 gallons of gas. Use the formula to calculate the fuel mileage from this data. Round the answer to the nearest tenth.

(e) A technician earns $14.67/hour. If she passes 5 ASE certification tests and receives $0.55 raise per test, calculate her new hourly wage.

(f) A technician earns $16.70/hour. If he passes 7 ASE certification tests and receives $0.55 raise per test, calculate his new hourly wage.

(g) A technician earns $19.34/hour. If she passes 2 ASE certification tests and receives $0.55 raise per test, calculate her new hourly wage.

(h) A technician earns $15.17/hour. If he passes 8 ASE certification tests and receives $0.55 raise per test, calculate his new hourly wage.

# LESSON 11

# Measurement

## OBJECTIVES

*After studying this lesson, you will be able to:*
- Identify common measurement tools.
- Determine the process to interpret measurement tools.
- Analyze measurement tools to determine the measurement value.

## TECHNICAL TERMS

dial caliper
dial indicator
digital dial caliper
feeler gauge
micrometer
steel ruler
tape measure
tire pressure gauge
tire tread depth gauge

---

Automotive maintenance and light repair requires a variety of measurements and measurement tools. The ability to identify the correct measurement tool to use and to make consistent, accurate measurements, are critical skills for any technician. Review the common measurement tools.

**Tape Measure**
General purpose measurement tool used for low precision measurements, accurate to 1/16 of an inch.

**Steel Ruler**
General purpose heavy-duty ruler with precision to 1/32 of an inch or 0.5 mm.

**Dial Caliper**
Precision measurement tool capable of measuring inside diameter, outside diameter, and depth to 1/1,000 of an inch.

**Micrometer**
Precision measurement tool capable of measuring outside diameter to 1/1,000 of an inch or 0.01 mm.

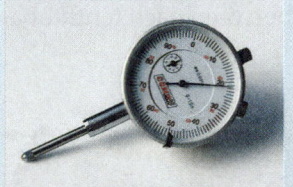

**Dial Indicator**
Precision measurement tool designed to measure round or moving surfaces or end-play to 1/1,000 of an inch.

**Tire Gauges**
Tire pressure and tread depth measurement gauges, used to measure tire pressure and tread depth.

**Digital Dial Caliper**
Digital precision measurement tool capable of measuring inside diameter, outside diameter, and depth in metric and standard.

**Feeler Gauges**
A precision metal tab-style set of gauges designed to measure the gap between parts.

*Goodheart-Willcox Publisher*

## Reading a Tape Measure

A *tape measure* is designed to measure from 1/16 inch to 12 feet or greater, depending on the length of the tape measure. Some tape measures include an inch scale and a metric scale. A tape measure typically indicates inches and feet along the tape, so at 36″, both 36″ and 3′ are marked. To measure with a tape measure, identify which marking line on the tape matches up with the item being measured. The graduated scale on the tape uses different length lines to identify positions on the scale. Review the following examples.

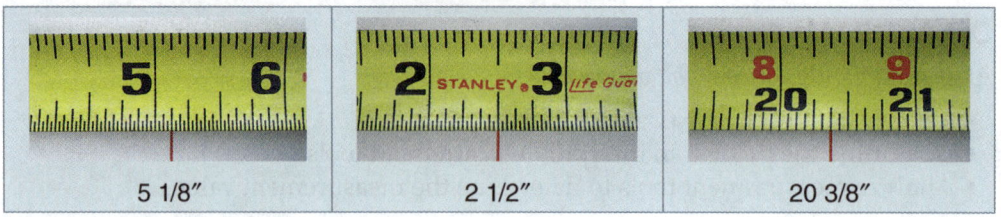

| 5 1/8″ | 2 1/2″ | 20 3/8″ |

Goodheart-Willcox Publisher

## Reading a Steel Ruler

A *steel ruler* is a more precise type of tape measure, typically only six or twelve inches long. A steel ruler, also known as a machinist ruler, can be divided into 32nds and 64ths of an inch, as well as 0.5 mm. Since a steel ruler is a more solid tool than a tape measure, the steel ruler can be used with more accuracy. Use the graduated scale on the steel ruler to determine the length of the object being measured. Review the following examples.

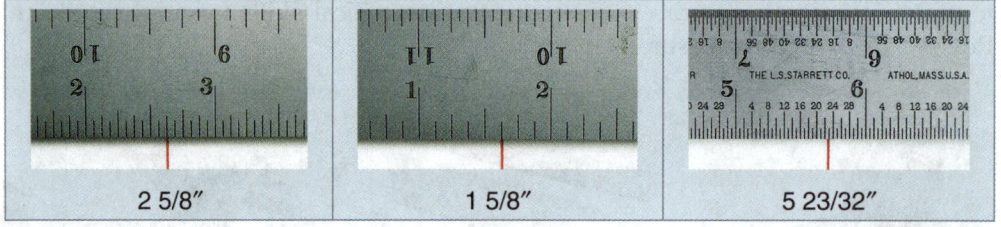

| 2 5/8″ | 1 5/8″ | 5 23/32″ |

Goodheart-Willcox Publisher

Complete measurement practice problems 11.1.

## Reading a Dial Caliper

A standard *dial caliper* typically divides ten inches into 1/1,000 of an inch. The jaws of the dial caliper can be used to measure inside diameter (I.D.) and outside diameter (O.D.). The extending tab on the end of the dial caliper can also be used to measure depth. The scale on the body of the dial caliper indicates inches and tenths of an inch. The dial scale indicates hundredths of an inch between each tenth of an inch. Review the following examples.

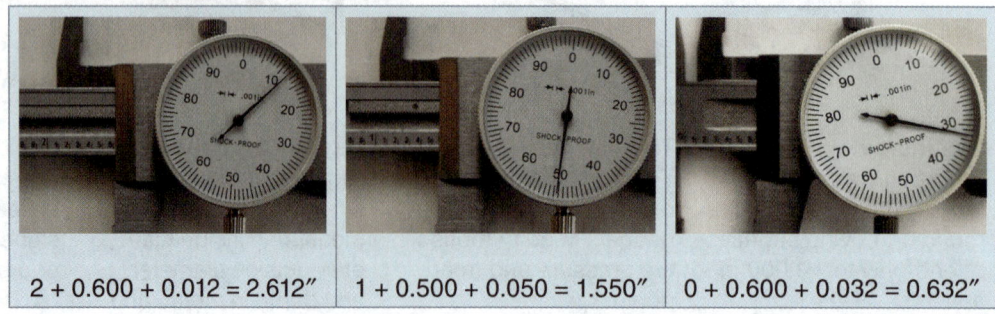

| 2 + 0.600 + 0.012 = 2.612″ | 1 + 0.500 + 0.050 = 1.550″ | 0 + 0.600 + 0.032 = 0.632″ |

Goodheart-Willcox Publisher

Complete measurement practice problems 11.2.

## Reading a Micrometer

A *micrometer* can be used to measure outside diameter in inches and metric. The micrometer has accuracy to 0.001″ or 0.01 mm. A micrometer uses a thimble that rotates to open the measurement gap. A typical inch micrometer opens the gap 0.025″ per rotation. As the thimble rotates, a scale is exposed showing the number of rotations. Use the scale on the body and the thimble to determine the measurement of the gap. Review the following examples.

Metric (0 mm–25 mm)

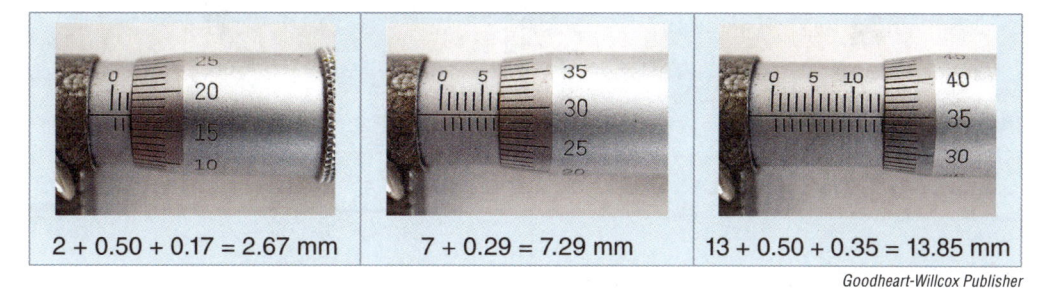

| 2 + 0.50 + 0.17 = 2.67 mm | 7 + 0.29 = 7.29 mm | 13 + 0.50 + 0.35 = 13.85 mm |

*Goodheart-Willcox Publisher*

Standard (0″–1″)

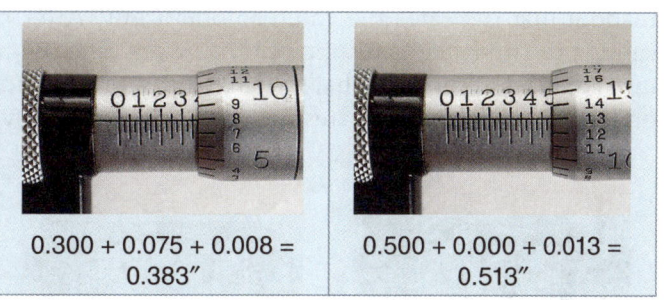

| 0.200 + 0.025 + 0.010 = 0.235″ | 0.300 + 0.075 + 0.008 = 0.383″ | 0.500 + 0.000 + 0.013 = 0.513″ |

*Goodheart-Willcox Publisher*

**Complete measurement practice problems 11.3.**

## Reading a Dial Indicator

A *dial indicator* is a compound gauge used to measure round or rotating items, such as crankshafts and brake discs, and to measure end play. The dial indicator has a plunger that moves 1 inch and rotates the dials on the gauge face. The compound gauge uses a small gauge in the center to count each 0.100 of an inch. The large, outer gauge counts the 0.001 of an inch within each number of the small gauge. Review the following examples.

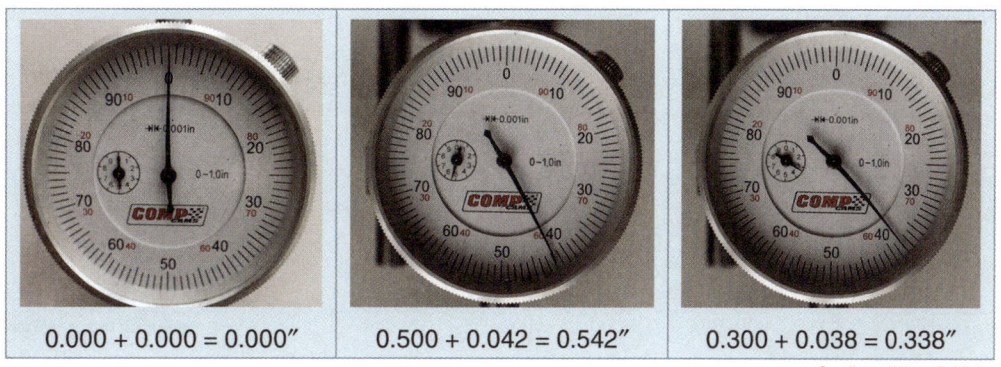

| 0.000 + 0.000 = 0.000″ | 0.500 + 0.042 = 0.542″ | 0.300 + 0.038 = 0.338″ |

*Goodheart-Willcox Publisher*

## Tire Gauges

A *tire pressure gauge* is used to measure tire pressure, and a *tire tread depth gauge* is used to measure tire tread depth. The scales on the gauges are similar, and typically include inch and metric designations. The pressure gauge indicates psi and kPa. The tread depth gauge indicates millimeters and 32nds of an inch. Review the following examples.

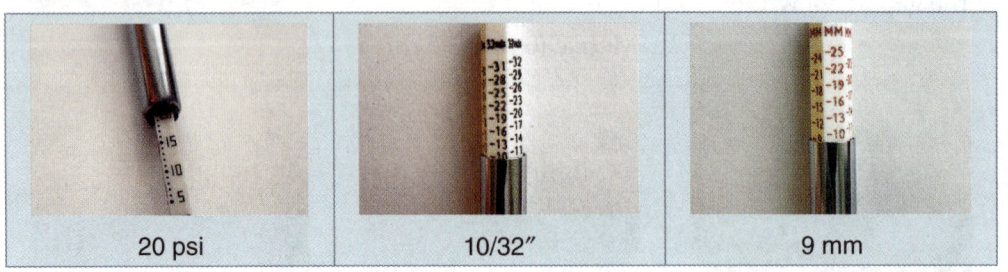

| 20 psi | 10/32" | 9 mm |

Goodheart-Willcox Publisher

## Digital Dial Calipers

A *digital dial caliper* is the same as an analog dial caliper but uses a digital readout that indicates the value automatically. After powering on the digital dial caliper, the first step is to zero out the gauge. The digital readout also has an inch/mm conversion function that switches between inch and metric scales. The reading on the digital screen indicates the value measured. Review the following examples.

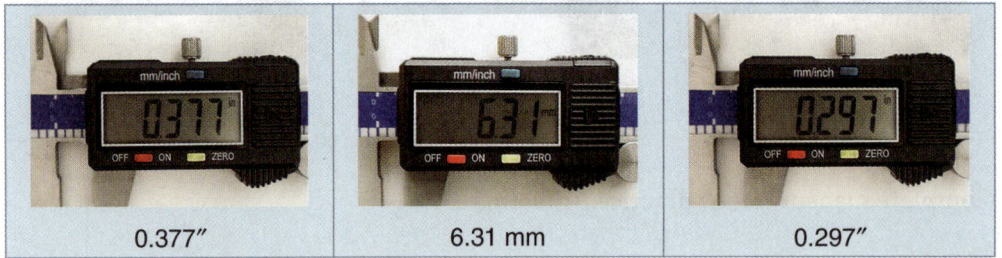

| 0.377" | 6.31 mm | 0.297" |

Goodheart-Willcox Publisher

## Feeler Gauges

A *feeler gauge* is designed to compare the thickness of a metal tab gauge to the gap being measured. A set of feeler gauges typically has 25 or more metal tabs starting around 0.001" thick, and each tab is 0.001" thicker than the previous one. Often, each tab includes the inch and metric value on the tab. If a gap is designed to be set at 0.008", use the 0.008" gauge tab to set the gap to that exact thickness. Review the following examples.

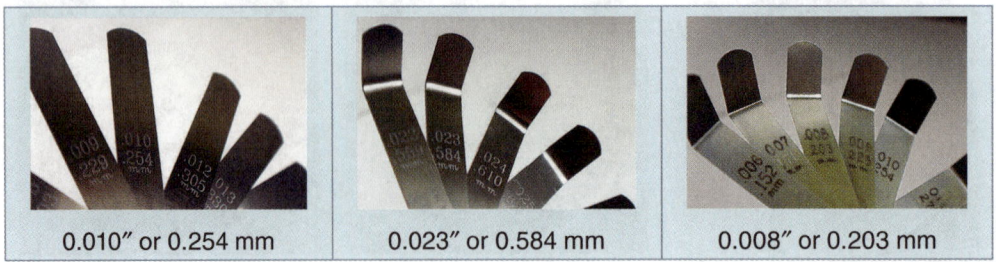

| 0.010" or 0.254 mm | 0.023" or 0.584 mm | 0.008" or 0.203 mm |

Goodheart-Willcox Publisher

**Complete measurement practice problems 11.4.**

Name _____ Date _____ Class _____

## Measurement Practice Problems 11.1

Record the measurements shown on the following tape measures and steel rulers.

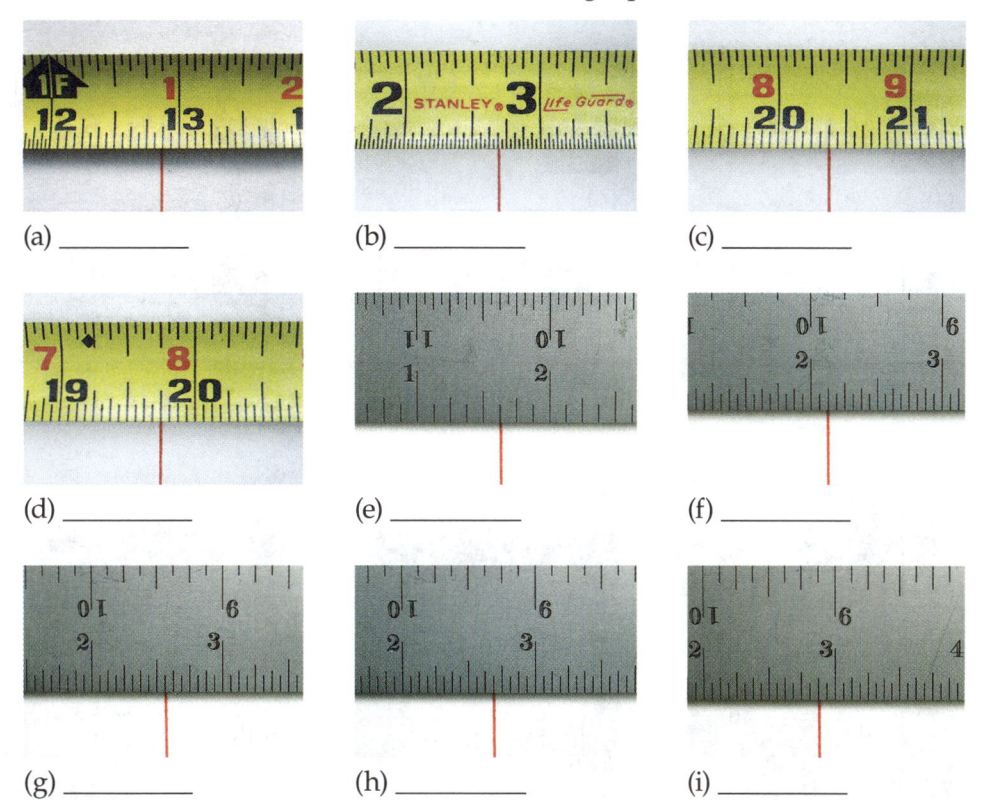

(a) _____   (b) _____   (c) _____

(d) _____   (e) _____   (f) _____

(g) _____   (h) _____   (i) _____

## Measurement Practice Problems 11.2

Record the measurements shown on the following dial calipers.

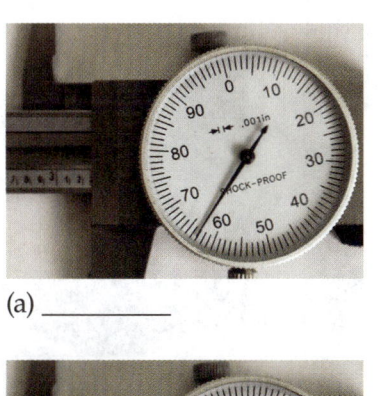

(a) 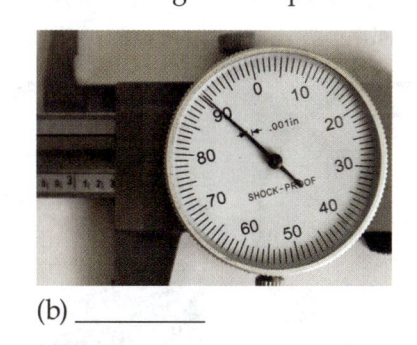 _____   (b)  _____   (c) _____

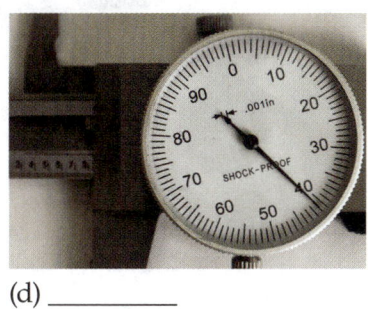

(d) 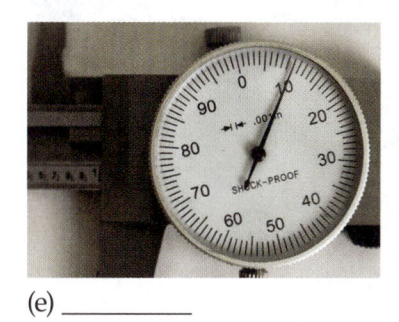 _____   (e)  _____   (f) _____

Copyright Goodheart-Willcox Co., Inc. May not be reproduced or posted to a publicly accessible website.

# Math for Automotive Technicians

Name _____  Date _____  Class _____

## Measurement Practice Problems 11.3

Record the measurements shown on the following metric and standard micrometers.

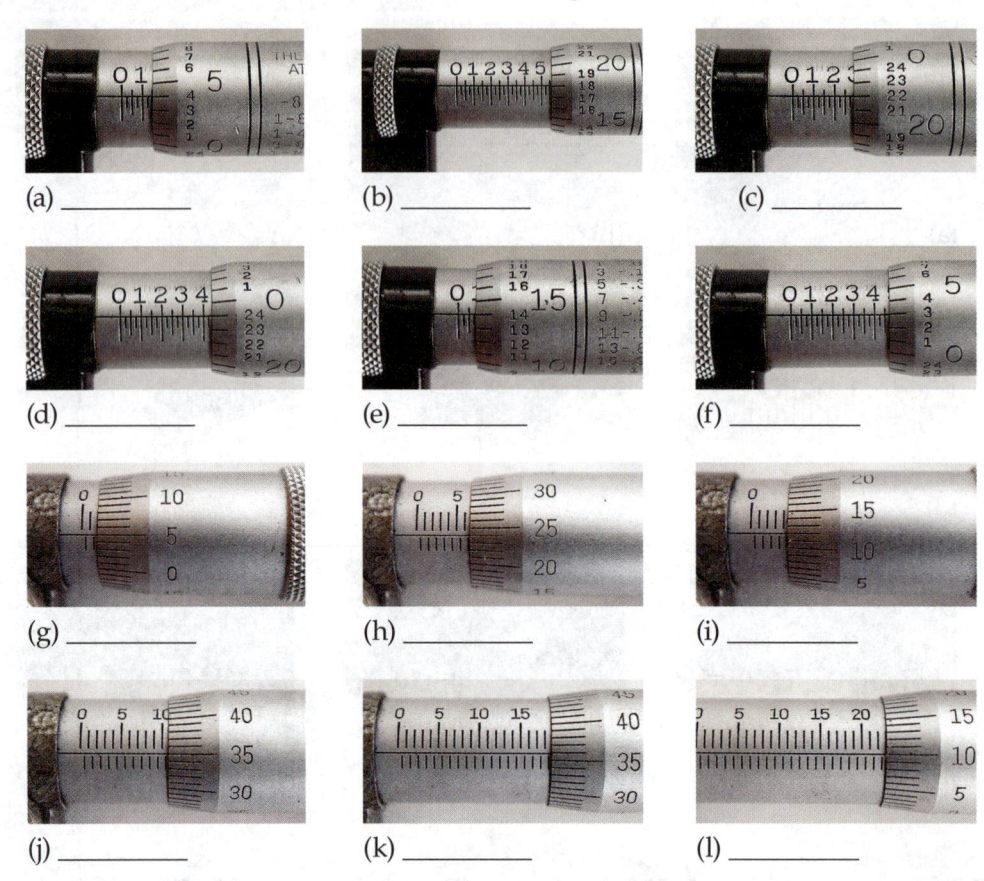

(a) _____   (b) _____   (c) _____

(d) _____   (e) _____   (f) _____

(g) _____   (h) _____   (i) _____

(j) _____   (k) _____   (l) _____

## Measurement Practice Problems 11.4

Record the measurements shown on the following dial indicators and tire gauges.

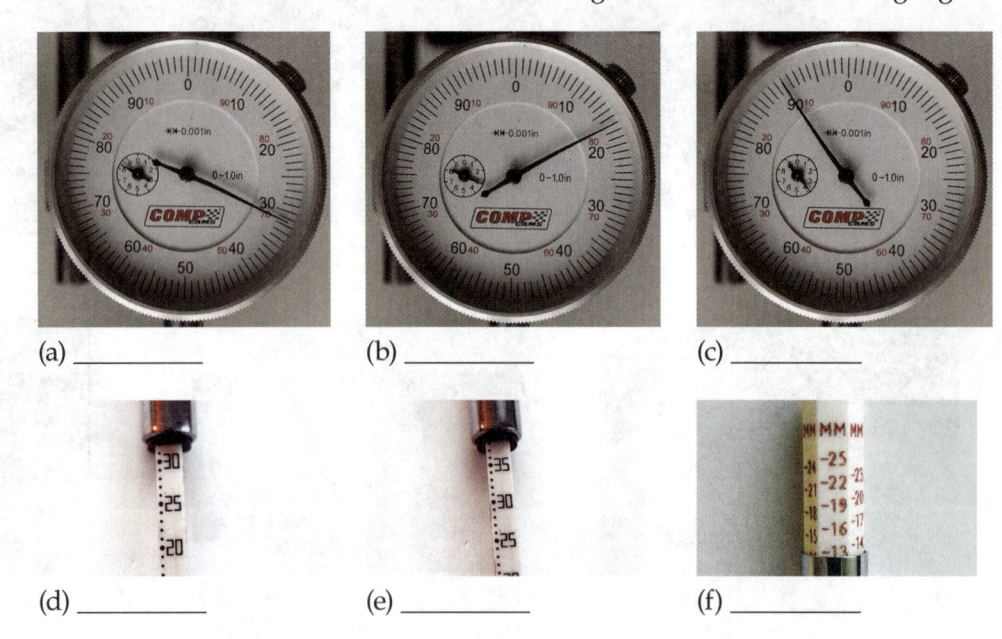

(a) _____   (b) _____   (c) _____

(d) _____   (e) _____   (f) _____

Copyright Goodheart-Willcox Co., Inc. May not be reproduced or posted to a publicly accessible website.

# LESSON 12

# Analyzing Specifications

## OBJECTIVES

*After studying this lesson, you will be able to:*
- Determine and identify specifications from a specification table.
- Compare measured values to specified values.
- Analyze word problems using specification values.

## TECHNICAL TERM

specifications

---

Comparing measured values to specified values is a critical step in automotive maintenance and light repair. From spark plug gap to brake disc thickness to the number of clicks of a parking brake handle, automotive manufacturers have set *specifications* for many different parts and systems. Reading the service information is the first step. Analyzing the data and using the specifications to make a decision about service is the next, critical step to producing quality work.

Most service information is found in an electronic service database, typically accessed through a web-based program. These tables must be carefully analyzed to identify the critical information. Review the following examples.

| Engine — General Specifications ||
|---|---|
| Cylinder Arrangement | Inline 4 |
| Displacement | $cm^3$ (cu in)         1,998 (121.92) |
| Bore and Stroke | mm (in)         86 × 86 (3.39 × 3.39) |
| Valve Arrangement | DOHC |
| Compression Ratio | 9.5:1 |
| Compression Pressure | Unit kPa (kg/$cm^3$, psi)/300 rpms |
|   Standard | 1,226 (12.5, 178) |
|   Minimum | 1,030 (10.5, 149) |
|   Differential | 96 (1.0, 14) |
| Valve Dimensions | Unit mm (inch) |
| Valve Head Diameter | |
|   Intake | 34.0–34.2 (1.339–1.346) |
|   Exhaust | 30.0–30.2 (1.181–1.189) |
| Valve Length | |
|   Intake | 101.19–101.61 (3.9839–4.0004) |
|   Exhaust | 102.11–102.53 (4.0201–4.0366) |
| Valve Stem Diameter | |
|   Intake | 5.965–5.980 (0.2348–0.2354) |
|   Exhaust | 5.945–5.960 (0.2341–0.2346) |

The specification table provides a large amount of information about this engine, and can be used by a technician to determine if measurements are within specification or need to be addressed with service or replacement. Review the following example questions regarding this specification table.

**Example:** Identify the minimum compression pressure.

The minimum compression pressure is 149 psi.

**Example:** The intake valve head measures 34.1 mm. Determine if the intake valve is within specification.

The specification is 34.0 to 34.2, so the 34.1 mm intake valve is within specification.

**Complete analyzing specifications practice problems 12.1, 12.2, and 12.3.**

Name _____ Date _____ Class _____

# Analyzing Specifications
# Practice Problems 12.1

Use the table below to answer problems 12.1 (a) through 12.1 (d).

| A/C Compressor ||| 
|---|---|---|
| Model || Calsonic Kansei V-6 |
| Type || V-6 Variable Displacement |
| Displacement cm³ (cu in) / rev | min | 14.5 (0.885) |
|  | max | 184 (11.228) |
| Cylinder Bore * Stroke mm (in) || 37 (1.46) × [2.3–26.6 (0.091–1.126)] |
| Direction of Rotation || Clockwise (viewed from front) |
| Drive Belt || Poly V |

(a) Identify the minimum cu in displacement of the A/C compressor.

(b) Identify the bore in mm.

(c) Identify the direction of rotation.

(d) Determine if the A/C compressor is single displacement or variable displacement.

Name _____ Date _____ Class _____

## Analyzing Specifications
## Practice Problems 12.2

Use the table below to answer problems 12.2 (a) through 12.2 (e).

| Brake Service Specifications | | |
|---|---|---|
| Front disc thickness (2WD) | Standard | 25.0 mm (0.984 in) |
|  | Minimum | 23.0 mm (0.906 in) |
| Front disc brake pad lining thickness (2WD) | Standard | 12.0 mm (0.472 in) |
|  | Minimum | 1.0 mm (0.039 in) |
| Front disc runout | Maximum | 0.05 mm (0.0020 in) |
| Front disc thickness (4WD) | Standard | 28.0 mm (1.102 in) |
|  | Minimum | 26.0 mm (1.024 in) |
| Front disc brake pad lining thickness (4WD) | Standard | 11.5 mm (0.453 in) |
|  | Minimum | 1.0 mm (0.039 in) |
| Rear brake drum inside diameter | Standard | 254 mm (10.00 in) |
|  | Maximum | 256 mm (10.08 in) |
| Rear drum shoe lining thickness | Standard | 5.0 mm (0.197 in) |
|  | Minimum | 1.0 mm (0.039 in) |

(a) Determine, in mm, the front brake disc minimum thickness for a 4WD.

(b) Determine, in inches, the maximum brake drum diameter.

(c) Determine, in mm, the front brake disc standard thickness for a 2WD.

(d) Calculate, in inches, how much thicker the standard 4WD front brake disc is compared to the standard 2WD front brake disc.

(e) Calculate, in mm, the difference between the standard 4WD front brake pad thickness and the minimum 4WD brake pad thickness.

Name _____  Date _____  Class _____

# Analyzing Specifications
# Practice Problems 12.3

Use the table below to answer problems 12.3 (a) through 12.3 (f).

| Transmission General Specifications ||||||
|---|---|---|---|---|---|
| RPO Codes | 6T71-MH3 (2WD) HM6 (4WD) |||||
| Transaxle Drive | FWD, AWD |||||
| Final Drive Gear Ratio | 3.16:1 |||||
| Pressure Taps | Line Pressure |||||
| Transaxle Fluid Type | DEXRON VI® |||||
| Transaxle Fluid Capacity | 9.0L / 9.5 quarts |||||
| Case Material | Die Cast Aluminum |||||
| Transaxle Net Weight | 104 kg |||||
| Max. Gross Vehicle Weight | 4,000 lb |||||
| Gear | 1st | 2nd | 3rd | 4th | 5th | 6th |
| Gear Ratio | 4.484 | 2.872 | 1.842 | 1.414 | 1.000 | 0.742 |

(a) Identify the final drive gear ratio.

(b) Determine the type of material of the case.

(c) Identify which gear has the gear ratio of 1.842:1.

(d) Identify the fluid capacity in quarts.

(e) Identify the RPO code for the 2WD transaxle.

(f) Determine the type of fluid used in this transaxle.

**Work Space/Notes**

# UNIT 2
# Around the Shop

| | | | |
|---|---|---|---|
| Case Study 1 | Work Uniforms—Addition | Case Study 7 | Hose Length Calculations—Fractions |
| Case Study 2 | Shop Inventory—Subtraction | Case Study 8 | Fluid Volume—Conversion |
| Case Study 3 | Scrap Metal Pricing—Multiplication | Case Study 9 | Workplace Productivity—Graphs and Tables |
| Case Study 4 | Paying for Professional Tools—Division | Case Study 10 | Wage Earnings—Formulas |
| Case Study 5 | Flat-Rate Labor Times—Decimal Arithmetic | Case Study 11 | Shop Equipment—Measurement |
| Case Study 6 | Customer Service Surveys—Greater Than and Less Than | Case Study 12 | Vehicle Identification Number—Analyzing Specifications |

## CAREER PROFILE

**B**ryan Kelly is a former diagnostic technician and currently owns and operates Valley Automotive Repair and Electric in Maple Valley, Washington. As a former diagnostic technician, Bryan used problem solving and mathematical reasoning to diagnose a wide variety of driveability issues and electrical problems. As a shop owner, Bryan uses math every day to calculate workflow and productivity. He also uses ratios and percentages to calculate margins and identify marketing expenses. These math skills helped Bryan learn the business side of automotive service and gave him the problem-solving skill set to manage a successful independent repair shop.

The employees working for Valley Automotive Repair and Electric also use math and arithmetic for a variety of daily tasks. From job estimating and inventory control to conversion between quarts and liters, the shop manager and service writers apply many math calculations throughout the day. Additionally, the technicians are using math to measure parts and compare to specification, analyze scan tool data, and diagnose specific vehicle issues. These math skills add value to Bryan's business because tasks are completed efficiently and accurately.

"Employee training is critical to success," according to Bryan. When the employees are empowered with quality training, they are empowered to make better decisions and produce quality work. When considering hiring a new employee, Bryan looks for a technician who has strong logical reasoning skills and math abilities, as well as the desire to learn new skills.

Bryan Kelly—Owner, Valley Automotive Repair and Electric.

# CASE STUDY 1

# Work Uniforms

## OBJECTIVES
*After studying this case study, you will be able to:*
- Identify the purpose of work uniforms in the automotive service industry.
- Calculate the quantity of uniforms based on job skill scenarios.

## MATH SKILL
- Addition of whole numbers.

Modern automotive dealerships and independent repair facilities strive to present a professional image to their customers. Besides keeping a clean, organized shop area and office, this professional image includes work uniforms for service department employees.

Typically, a workplace uses a uniform company that provides the work shirts and work pants. These uniform companies usually provide laundering services, and may also provide shop towels, entry rugs, and other related items. Use addition of whole numbers to calculate the word problems regarding uniform services.

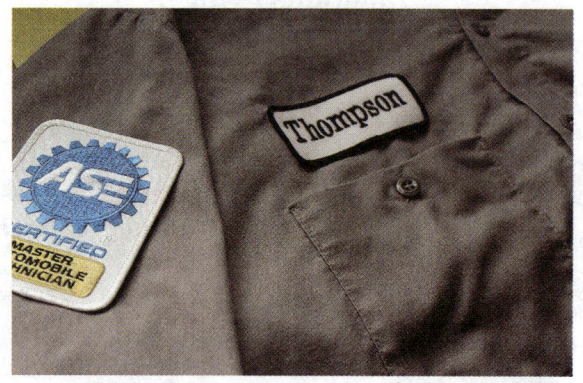

*Goodheart-Willcox Publisher*

Name _____  Date _____  Class _____

# Work Uniforms Job Skill Practice Problems

1.1 A heavy-truck fleet service shop has a uniform contract to receive 136 shirts and 102 pants per week from a uniform company. The fleet service shop hires 3 new employees and needs an additional 24 shirts and 18 pants per week. Calculate the new number of shirts and pants delivered to the heavy-truck fleet service shop each week.

1.2 A new car dealership has a uniform contract to receive 88 shirts and 44 pants per week from a uniform company. The dealership hires 4 new employees, and now needs 44 more shirts and 24 more pants per week delivered. Calculate the new number of shirts and pants delivered to the new car dealership each week.

1.3 A quick-lube oil change shop employs 9 lube technicians and uses a uniform service for these employees. Each week, 27 size small shirts, 36 size large shirts, and 18 size X-large shirts are delivered. Calculate how many total shirts are delivered each week.

1.4 A new car dealership has a uniform contract to receive 164 shirts and 96 pants per week from a uniform company. The dealership hires 3 new employees, and now needs 21 more shirts and 15 more pants per week delivered. Calculate the new number of shirts and pants delivered to the new car dealership each week.

Copyright Goodheart-Willcox Co., Inc. May not be reproduced or posted to a publicly accessible website.

**Name** _____  **Date** _____  **Class** _____

1.5 An independent repair shop has a uniform contract to receive 30 shirts and 30 pants per week from a uniform company. The dealership hires 2 new employees, and now needs 20 more shirts and 20 more pants per week delivered. Calculate the new number of shirts and pants delivered to the independent repair shop each week.

1.6 A tire service shop employs 12 technicians and uses a uniform service for these employees. Each week, 48 size small shirts, 60 size large shirts, and 36 size X-large shirts are delivered. Calculate how many total shirts are delivered each week.

1.7 A new car dealership has a uniform contract to receive 124 shirts and 84 pants per week from a uniform company. The dealership hires 3 new employees, and now needs 33 more shirts and 18 more pants per week delivered. Calculate the new number of shirts and pants delivered to the new car dealership each week.

1.8 A tire service shop employs 9 technicians and uses a uniform service for these employees. Every two weeks, 27 size small shirts, 18 size large shirts, and 36 size X-large shirts are delivered. Calculate how many total shirts are delivered every two weeks.

# CASE STUDY 2

# Shop Inventory

## OBJECTIVES

*After studying this case study, you will be able to:*
- Identify items commonly stocked in an automotive repair shop.
- Calculate inventory based on job skill scenarios.

## MATH SKILL
- Subtraction of whole numbers.

In order for an automotive repair shop to function effectively, many supplies and common parts are kept in stock. This prevents delays and ensures that customer vehicles are getting the service needed in a timely manner. Often, dealership service centers also include a parts department that stock many common parts for the vehicles serviced in that dealership.

Items commonly stocked for technician use include cans of brake clean and penetrating fluid, nitrile gloves, shop towels, and other related items. Commonly stocked items for vehicles include fluids such as engine oil, coolant, transmission fluid, power steering fluid, washer fluid, and gear lube. Other commonly stocked vehicle items include belts, hoses, wiper blades, oil filters, and batteries. Use subtraction of whole numbers to calculate the word problems related to automotive repair inventory.

*Goodheart-Willcox Publisher*

Name _____  Date _____  Class _____

# Shop Inventory Job Skill Practice Problems

2.1 An auto repair shop started the month of May with 35 cans of brake clean spray in stock. There were 6 cans of brake clean spray left at the end of the month. Calculate how many cans must be ordered to refill the stock to 35 cans of brake clean spray.

2.2 An auto repair shop currently has 12 boxes of shop towels in stock. The shop foreman wants to keep 35 boxes of shop towels in stock. Calculate how many boxes need to be ordered.

2.3 A new car dealership parts department started the month of April with 95 quarts of Mercon V Automatic Transmission Fluid (ATF) in stock. During the month of April, 77 quarts of ATF were used. Calculate how many quarts are in stock at the end of the month.

2.4 An auto repair shop keeps 36 car batteries of various sizes in stock. At the end of the month, they had 21 car batteries remaining in stock. Calculate how many car batteries they had to replace this month.

**Name** _____ **Date** _____ **Class** _____

2.5 An auto repair shop started the month of October with 65 gallons of antifreeze in stock. During the month of October, 37 gallons of antifreeze were used. Calculate how many gallons are in stock at the end of the month.

2.6 A new car dealership starts each month with 65 of the two most common oil filters (FL-78 and FL-94) in stock. At the end of the month, there are 13 FL-78 filters and 24 FL-94 filters remaining in stock. Calculate how many of each filter type were used during the month.

2.7 An auto repair shop started the month of May with 90 gallons of antifreeze in stock. During the month of May, 76 gallons of antifreeze were used. Calculate how many gallons are in stock at the end of the month.

2.8 An auto repair shop currently has 19 boxes of shop towels in stock. The shop foreman wants to keep 55 boxes of shop towels in stock. Calculate how many boxes need to be ordered.

# CASE STUDY 3

# Scrap Metal Pricing

## OBJECTIVES
*After studying this case study, you will be able to:*
- Identify types of scrap metal related to automotive service.
- Estimate scrap metal weight based on quantity.
- Calculate value of recycled metal based on scrap metal prices.

## TECHNICAL TERMS
clean metal    dirty metal

## MATH SKILLS
- Multiplication of whole numbers.
- Multiplication of decimal numbers.

Automotive service and repair often generates scrap metal, mostly steel and aluminum. This scrap metal is recycled to be reused, and can be sold to a metal recycler for the going rate at the time. Often, the scrap metal is taken to the metal recycler, weighed, and bought by the recycler.

Scrap metal is considered clean or dirty. *Clean metal* is metal that is not mixed in with any other types of metal. Clean aluminum is 100% aluminum, with no steel or any other material mixed in or added. *Dirty metal* is metal with small amounts of other, cheaper metals mixed in with the higher value metal. Shred steel is the most basic form of scrap metal, and includes nonmetal parts that will be separated later in the process once the steel is "shredded."

*Goodheart-Willcox Publisher*

Estimating the weight of scrap metal allows the value of the scrap metal to be estimated. Use the estimate chart below to determine the total weight of the scrap metal in practice problems 3.1 through 3.4.

| Estimated Weight |||
| --- | --- | --- |
| Item | Pounds | Kilograms |
| Steel Engine Block I4 | 208 | 94 |
| Steel Engine Block V6 | 265 | 119 |
| Steel Engine Block V8 | 320 | 144 |
| Aluminum Engine Block I4 | 38 | 17 |
| Aluminum Cylinder Head | 15 | 7 |
| Steel Front Brake Disc | 7 | 3 |
| Steel Rear Brake Disc | 4 | 2 |

**Name** _____ **Date** _____ **Class** _____

# Scrap Metal Pricing Job Skill Practice Problems

3.1 Randy has 2 steel I4 engine blocks, 2 steel V6 engine blocks, 30 steel front brake discs, and 22 rear brake discs loaded in his truck to haul to the metal recycler. Estimate, in pounds, the total weight of scrap metal loaded in the truck.

3.2 Edgar has 3 steel V8 engine blocks, 18 steel front brake discs, 6 aluminum I4 engine blocks, and 6 aluminum cylinder heads loaded in his truck to haul to the metal recycler. Estimate, in kilograms, the total weight of scrap metal loaded in the truck.

3.3 Ken has 2 steel V6 engine blocks, 43 steel front brake discs, and 27 steel rear brake discs loaded in his truck to haul to the metal recycler. Estimate, in pounds, the total weight of scrap metal loaded in the truck.

3.4 Ty has 8 aluminum cylinder heads, 2 aluminum engine blocks, 14 front brake discs, and 14 rear brake discs loaded in his truck to haul to the metal recycler. Estimate, in kilograms, the total weight of scrap metal loaded in the truck.

Name _____ Date _____ Class _____

The scrap metal price is generally determined based on current supply and demand of the different metals on the market. Price per pound or ton vary daily, and fluctuate greatly based on economic conditions. Refer to the scrap price chart to answer practice problems 3.5 through 3.8.

| Scrap Metal Prices | |
| --- | --- |
| Material | Price |
| Aluminum (clean) | 0.43/lb |
| Aluminum (dirty) | 0.24/lb |
| Steel | 0.08/lb |
| Lead Wheel Weights | 0.28/lb |
| Stainless Steel | 0.32/lb |
| Aluminum Wheels | 0.65/lb |

3.5 Randy hauls 350 pounds of lead wheel weights and 1,643 pounds of steel to the metal recycler. Calculate the total value of this metal.

3.6 Edgar hauls 430 pounds of stainless steel, 680 pounds of dirty aluminum, and 120 pounds of aluminum wheels to the metal recycler. Calculate the total value of this metal.

3.7 Ken hauls 780 pounds of steel, 325 pounds of clean aluminum, and 95 pounds of lead wheel weights to the metal recycler. Calculate the total value of this metal.

3.8 Ty hauls 1,600 pounds of steel, 295 pounds of dirty aluminum, and 26 pounds of aluminum wheels to the metal recycler. Calculate the total value of this metal.

## CASE STUDY 4

# Paying for Professional Tools

### OBJECTIVES
*After studying this case study, you will be able to:*
- Identify the function and purpose of professional tool dealers.
- Calculate tools payment job skill problems.

### MATH SKILL
- Division of whole numbers.

To function as a technician in a repair shop, the correct tools are essential. Professional tools are designed to be high quality, very accurate, easy to use, and extremely durable. A representative from a professional tool company will typically visit each repair shop on the route to sell technicians new tools, demonstrate new products offered, and collect payment for previously bought tools.

*Goodheart-Willcox Publisher*

    A technician is commonly able to purchase tools on a loan basis from a professional tool representative. When the technician has an outstanding balance, the tool representative and the technician work out a payment plan that includes a weekly payment schedule. Use division of whole numbers to calculate the word problems related to paying for professional tools.

Name _____ Date _____ Class _____

# Paying for Professional Tools
# Job Skill Practice Problems

4.1 A technician owes $485 for professional tools purchased last month. If the technician pays back $65 per week, calculate how many weeks until the tools are paid off completely. Round up to the nearest week.

4.2 A technician owes $840 for professional tools purchased last month. The tool representative has asked for the balance to be paid back in 12 weeks. Calculate how much will need to be paid each week in order for the $840 balance to be paid off in 12 weeks.

4.3 A technician owes $278 for professional tools purchased this week. If the technician pays back $35 per week, calculate how many weeks until the tools are paid off completely. Round up to the nearest week.

4.4 A technician owes $318 for professional tools purchased last week, and owes an additional $78 for tools bought this week. Calculate how much the technician will need to pay back each week so the balance is paid off in 9 weeks.

Name _____ Date _____ Class _____

4.5 A technician owes $3,289 for a new toolbox purchased last month. The technician earned a performance bonus of $1,500 and paid all of the bonus toward his toolbox. If he pays $95 per week on the balance of the toolbox, calculate how many weeks until the toolbox is paid off completely. Round up to the nearest week.

4.6 A technician owes $653 for professional tools purchased last month. The tool representative has asked for the balance to be paid back in 9 weeks. Calculate how much will need to be paid each week so the $653 balance is paid off in 9 weeks. Round up to the nearest cent.

4.7 A technician owes $528 for professional tools purchased last week, and owes an additional $98 for tools bought this week. Calculate how much the technician will need to pay back each week so the balance is paid off in 8 weeks.

4.8 A technician owes $678 for professional tools purchased this week. If the technician pays back $65 per week, calculate how many weeks until the tools are paid off completely. Round up to the nearest week.

# CASE STUDY 5

# Flat-Rate Labor Times

## OBJECTIVES

*After studying this case study, you will be able to:*
- Identify the flat-rate labor time of specific tasks using a flat-rate timetable.
- Compute the flat-rate labor time for specific combinations of automotive service.
- Determine the cost estimate and gross pay rate based on the flat-rate system.

## TECHNICAL TERM

flat-rate labor time system

## MATH SKILLS

- Addition of decimal numbers.
- Multiplication of decimal numbers.

The automotive service industry uses a *flat-rate labor time system* to estimate repairs, bill the customer, and pay the technician. This labor time system is based on one-tenth of an hour, which is six minutes.

1 hour = 60 minutes
0.1 hour = (0.1 × 60) = 6 minutes
0.4 hour = (0.4 × 60) = 24 minutes

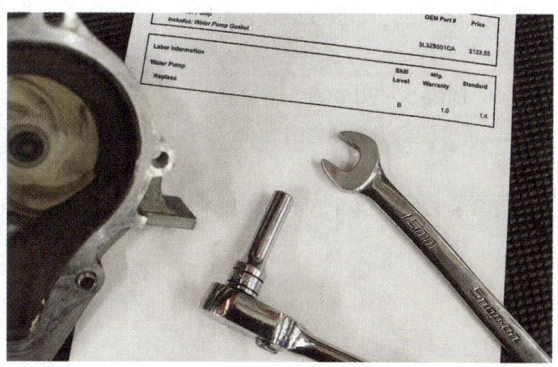

*Goodheart-Willcox Publisher*

| Labor Time | 0.1 | 0.2 | 0.3 | 0.4 | 0.5 | 0.6 | 0.7 | 0.8 | 0.9 | 1.0 |
|---|---|---|---|---|---|---|---|---|---|---|
| Minutes | 6 | 12 | 18 | 24 | 30 | 36 | 42 | 48 | 54 | 60 |

When the service writer is estimating the work for the customer, the flat-rate time is used to calculate how much the labor will cost the customer.

If a repair has a flat-rate labor time of 1.3 hours, and
if the shop has a shop rate of $85.00 per hour, then
the estimate will be 1.3 hours × $85.00 (1.3 × 85 = 110.5).
The estimate presented to the customer will be $110.50 for labor.

If the customer approves the repair, the technician is then given the repair order with the task to perform and the flat-rate labor time for that job. The technician will now get paid 1.3 hours to complete this task, regardless of how much actual time the repair takes.

If the technician earns $25.00/hour as a flat-rate wage, and

the job completed has a flat-rate time of 1.3 hours, then

the technician will earn 1.3 hours × $25.00 (1.3 × 25 = 32.5).

The technician will be paid $32.50 on the paycheck (gross) for completing this task.

**Example:** Use the labor time chart to calculate the flat-rate labor time (standard) to replace the front and rear brake pads and resurface the brake disc at each brake assembly.

| 2008 SUV AWD V6-3.5L | | |
|---|---|---|
| Service Labor Time | Standard | Warranty |
| Brake Pad Replace | | |
| Front | 1.3 | 1.0 |
| Rear | 1.3 | 0.9 |
| To R&R Caliper, Add | | |
| Each | 0.2 | 0.0 |
| To R&R Disc, Add | | |
| One Side | 0.2 | 0.2 |
| Both Sides | 0.4 | 0.4 |
| To Resurface Disc, Add | | |
| Each | 0.4 | 0.4 |
| Bleed Hydraulic System | | |
| Bleed System | 0.5 | 0.4 |

1.3 + 1.3 + 0.4 + 0.4 + 0.4 + 0.4 = 4.2 hours   or   (1.3 × 2) + (0.4 × 4) = 4.2 hours

Name _____ Date _____ Class _____

# Flat-Rate Labor Times
# Job Skill Practice Problems

Use the labor time chart in the example to solve practice problems 5.1 and 5.2.

5.1 Determine the total flat-rate labor time (standard) to replace the front and rear brake pads, R&R both front discs, and resurface both rear discs.

5.2 Determine the total flat-rate labor time (standard) to replace the front brake pads, R&R both front calipers, resurface both front discs, and bleed the hydraulic system.

Use the following labor time chart to solve practice problems 5.3 through 5.10.

| 2010 Midsize Sedan V8-4.6L | | |
|---|---|---|
| Service Labor Time | Standard | Warranty |
| Ignition Coil Replace | | |
| Bank One (one coil) | 0.8 | 0.6 |
| Bank Two (one coil) | 0.3 | 0.2 |
| Each Additional (either bank, up to 6) | 0.2 | 0.2 |
| Compression Check | | |
| Includes R&I Spark Plugs | 1.8 | 0 |
| Throttle Body | | |
| Includes TPS | 0.7 | 0.4 |
| Positive Crankcase Ventilation Valve | | |
| Replace | 0.4 | 0 |
| Exhaust Gas Recirculation Tube | | |
| Front Pipe | 0.3 | 0.2 |
| Rear Pipe | 0.7 | 0.9 |

5.3 Determine the total standard flat-rate labor time to replace one ignition coil from bank one, the positive crankcase ventilation valve (PCV valve), and the exhaust gas recirculation rear pipe.

**Name** _____ **Date** _____ **Class** _____

5.4 If the repair shop has a labor rate of $75.00/hour, determine the estimated labor amount for this work to be performed.

5.5 If the technician performing the work earns $28.50/hour, determine the gross pay for completing these tasks on this vehicle.

5.6 If the technician completed the repairs in 108 minutes, determine if the technician completed the work in less time or in more time than the flat-rate time allowance.

5.7 Determine the warranty flat-rate labor time to replace all four ignition coils on bank one and all four ignition coils on bank two.

5.8 For the labor done in problem 5.7, determine the gross pay for Technician A, who earns $26.75/hour.

5.9 For the labor done in problem 5.7, determine the gross pay for Technician B, who earns $31.25/hour.

5.10 How much more will Technician B earn than Technician A for completing the same work?

Name _____ Date _____ Class _____

Use the following labor time chart to solve practice problems 5.11 through 5.19.

| 2012 Pickup Truck 4WD V6-4.0L | | |
|---|---|---|
| Service Labor Time | Standard | Warranty |
| Control Arm Replace | | |
| UCA, Includes Ball Joint | | |
| One Side | 1.2 | 0.9 |
| Both Sides | 1.5 | 1.1 |
| LCA, Includes Ball Joint | | |
| One Side | 1.2 | 0.9 |
| Both Sides | 1.5 | 1.1 |
| Stabilizer Bar Link Replace | | |
| Rear Suspension | | |
| One Side | 0.4 | 0 |
| Both Sides | 0.6 | 0 |
| Front Suspension | | |
| One Side | 0.4 | 0 |
| Both Sides | 0.6 | 0 |
| Wheel Bearing Replace | | |
| Front Suspension | | |
| One Side | 3.2 | 2.1 |
| Both Sides | 4.4 | 2.8 |
| Rear Axle Bearings | | |
| One Side: R&R Outer Seal | 2.9 | 2.9 |
| Both Sides: R&R Outer Seal | 4.1 | 3.1 |
| Strut/Shock Absorber Replace | | |
| Front Suspension | | |
| One Side | 1.6 | 1.2 |
| Both Sides | 2.4 | 1.5 |
| Rear Suspension | | |
| One Side | 0.6 | 0.5 |
| Both Sides | 0.9 | 0.6 |

5.11 Determine the standard flat-rate labor time to replace both front struts, both sides rear axle bearings, and one side front stabilizer bar link.

5.12 If the repair shop has a labor rate of $85.00/hour, determine the estimated labor amount for this work to be performed.

Name _____ Date _____ Class _____

5.13 If the technician performing the work earns $27.65/hour, determine the gross pay for completing these tasks on this vehicle. Round to the nearest cent.

5.14 If the technician completed the repairs in 385 minutes, determine how many minutes before the flat-rate time allowance the technician completed the repairs.

5.15 Determine the warranty flat-rate labor time to replace both lower control arms and the standard flat-rate time to replace both front wheel bearings.

5.16 If the repair shop has a labor rate of $85.00/hour, determine the estimated labor amount for this work to be performed.

5.17 Determine the gross pay for Technician A, who earns $25.75/hour. Round to the nearest cent.

5.18 Determine the gross pay for Technician B, who earns $29.50/hour.

5.19 How much more will Technician B earn than Technician A for completing the same work?

# CASE STUDY 6

# Customer Service Surveys

## OBJECTIVES
*After studying this case study, you will be able to:*
- Review and analyze customer service survey data.
- Analyze job skill problems related to customer service survey data.

## TECHNICAL TERM
mean value

## MATH SKILLS
- Calculating average (mean) values using whole numbers.
- Calculating greater than and less than problems.

Automotive service technicians are industry professionals working in a high-tech, high-skill industry. Many repair shops and dealerships use customer service surveys to get feedback about the services performed by the automotive technician. These surveys may be taken in written form, electronic form, or even with a follow-up phone call.

In these metrics, the most commonly discussed point is whether or not the vehicle was fixed right the first time. If a vehicle was serviced, but was returned because the issue was not completely repaired, this is known as a "comeback." When a service department is put in the position to deal with a comeback, the profit margins on the repair disappear quickly. As a technician gains experience, the number of comebacks should be reduced to almost zero.

A math concept that may be required to interpret data and determine greater than and less than is calculating the *mean value* of a data set. This concept is commonly referred to as calculating the "average." To calculate the mean, add all of the values and then divide the sum by the quantity of values in the data set. Review the following examples.

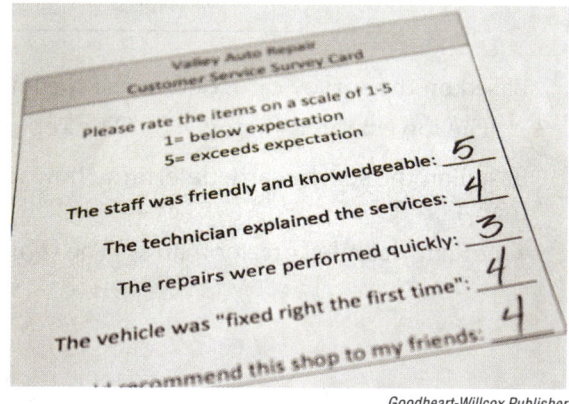

*Goodheart-Willcox Publisher*

**Example:**

Data set: 5, 7, 6, 5, 8, 4, 6

$$5 + 7 + 6 + 5 + 8 + 4 + 6 = 41$$
$$41 \div 7 = 5 \text{ r } 6 \quad \text{or} \quad 5.86 \text{ if rounded}$$

Mean: 5.86

**Example:** Review the customer service survey card and the sample questions.

**Valley Auto Repair**
**Customer Service Survey Card**

Please rate the items on a scale of 1–5

1 = below expectation
5 = exceeds expectation

| | |
|---|---|
| The staff was friendly and knowledgeable: | 4 |
| The technician explained the services: | 4 |
| The repairs were performed quickly: | 3 |
| The vehicle was "fixed right the first time": | 5 |
| I would recommend this shop to my friends: | 4 |

Based on the survey card, determine the lowest rated item.

The lowest rated item is a 3, "The repairs were performed quickly."

Based on the survey card, determine how many items were rated greater than 4.

One item was rated greater than 4, "The vehicle was 'fixed right the first time.'"

Name _____ Date _____ Class _____

## Customer Service Surveys
## Job Skill Practice Problems

Calculate the mean of each data set. If necessary, round to two decimal places.

6.1  4, 7, 9, 3, 4, 2, 9, 7, 8, 5

6.2  12, 14, 16, 18, 12, 13, 16, 19, 16, 15, 17

6.3  240, 360, 198, 402, 378

Analyze the customer service data and solve the job skill problems using greater than, less than, and solving for the mean.

|  | Technician A ||||||
|---|---|---|---|---|---|---|
|  | Survey 1 | Survey 2 | Survey 3 | Survey 4 | Survey 5 | Survey 6 |
| The staff was friendly and knowledgeable: | 5 | 3 | 4 | 4 | 5 | 4 |
| The technician explained the services: | 4 | 2 | 4 | 5 | 5 | 3 |
| The repairs were performed quickly: | 5 | 2 | 4 | 4 | 5 | 3 |
| The vehicle was "fixed right the first time": | 5 | 1 | 4 | 3 | 5 | 3 |
| I would recommend this shop to my friends: | 5 | 2 | 4 | 4 | 5 | 3 |

|  | Technician B ||||||
|---|---|---|---|---|---|---|
|  | Survey 1 | Survey 2 | Survey 3 | Survey 4 | Survey 5 | Survey 6 |
| The staff was friendly and knowledgeable: | 5 | 5 | 5 | 4 | 5 | 5 |
| The technician explained the services: | 3 | 4 | 3 | 4 | 3 | 3 |
| The repairs were performed quickly: | 5 | 5 | 5 | 4 | 5 | 4 |
| The vehicle was "fixed right the first time": | 1 | 3 | 3 | 1 | 1 | 2 |
| I would recommend this shop to my friends: | 4 | 2 | 4 | 4 | 2 | 4 |

6.4  A score of 1 on the "fixed right the first time" item indicates a comeback. Determine which technician had more comebacks.

Name _____ Date _____ Class _____

6.5 Calculate the mean value for Technician B for how well the technician explained the services. Round to two decimal places.

6.6 Calculate the mean value for Technician A for whether the customer would recommend this shop to friends. Round to two decimal places.

6.7 For each technician, calculate the mean for how quickly the services were performed. Round to two decimal places.

6.8 Determine which technician scored better on the survey regarding how quickly the services were performed.

# CASE STUDY 7

# Hose Length Calculations

## OBJECTIVES
*After studying this case study, you will be able to:*
- Identify types of vehicle hoses and lines.
- Calculate hose lengths based on fractional measurements.

## MATH SKILLS
- Add and subtract basic fraction problems.
- Convert mixed numbers and reduce fractions to lowest terms.

---

A variety of rubber hoses and lines are used on a vehicle. These hoses may require replacement once they wear out or start leaking. Also, sometimes lines must be cut apart to be removed if they are old and have become seized to the hose fitting.

Heater hose and vacuum hose are commonly bought by repair shops in large rolls of 25′ or 50′ lengths. Technicians cut off lengths of hose as needed to complete the repair job. Low pressure fuel line may also be repaired in this manner. Typically, low pressure fuel systems that use this type of rubber fuel line are found when restoring classic vehicles with carburetors and low-pressure fuel pumps.

*Goodheart-Willcox Publisher*

**Example:** A technician is replacing a vacuum line from the intake manifold to the exhaust gas recirculation (EGR) valve. The section of vacuum line is 13 5/8″ in length. If this is cut from a new vacuum line roll that is 25′ in length, calculate how many inches of vacuum line remains on the roll.

$$25' \times 12 = 300''$$
$$300'' - 13\ 5/8'' = 286\ 3/8''$$

Name _____  Date _____  Class _____

# Hose Length Calculations
# Job Skill Practice Problems

7.1 A technician is replacing two heater hoses. One heater hose is 32 7/8" in length and one is 29 3/8" in length. Calculate in inches the total amount of heater hose needed to replace these two hoses.

7.2 A technician is replacing three vacuum lines on an engine. The vacuum lines are 15 7/8", 4 1/2", and 9 5/8" in length. There are 30" of vacuum line on the roll. Calculate if there is enough on the roll to replace these three vacuum lines.

7.3 A technician is replacing fuel line on a carbureted engine. The two pieces of fuel line are 9 3/16" and 7 5/8" in length. Calculate in inches the total amount of fuel line needed.

7.4 A technician is replacing a heater hose that is 21 7/8" in length. If there is 48 1/2" on the roll, calculate in inches how much will be left on the roll once the heater hose section is cut off.

Name _____ Date _____ Class _____

7.5 A technician has a section of fuel line that is 26 3/8" long. The vehicle requires two sections of fuel line, each 13 7/8" long. Calculate if the technician's section of fuel line is long enough to fabricate the two sections of fuel line for the vehicle.

7.6 A technician is replacing the vacuum lines on a vacuum-operated blend door heater system. There are four hoses to cut with the following lengths: 5 5/8", 3 1/8", 9 1/2", and 4 1/4". Calculate in inches the total length of vacuum line needed for these four vacuum lines.

7.7 A technician cut three lengths of heater hose from a 10′ roll. The cut lengths are 24 1/4", 29 1/2", and 32 5/8". Calculate in inches the length of hose remaining on the 10′ roll once these three lengths are cut off the roll.

7.8 A technician needs three lengths of low pressure fuel line to repair a carbureted vehicle. The lengths are 4 13/16", 6 5/8", and 9 1/2". Calculate in inches the total length of fuel line needed to fabricate these three lengths.

# CASE STUDY 8

# Fluid Volume

## OBJECTIVES

*After studying this case study, you will be able to:*
- Identify automotive fluid bulk quantities.
- Calculate conversions between fluid amounts and units.
- Analyze job skill problems related to fluid volume conversions.

## MATH SKILL
- Conversion of whole number and decimal values.

---

Automotive service centers that perform a large quantity of fluid services, particularly engine oil changes, stock large volumes of fluids. Often the fluids are kept in 55-gallon drums or larger storage tanks.

The automobile uses a variety of fluids in various quantities, and the required volume specifications may be given in metric or standard volume amounts. Conversion between fluid amounts and volume units may be required to ensure the fluid service is performed correctly. Calculate the fluid volume conversions using the conversion factors provided in the table.

*Goodheart-Willcox Publisher*

| Fluid Volume Conversion Factors |   |           |
|---|---|---|
| 1 gallon | = | 128 ounces |
| 1 gallon | = | 4 quarts |
| 1 gallon | = | 3.78 liters |
| 1 quart  | = | 0.95 liters |
| 1 liter  | = | 0.26 gallons |
| 1 liter  | = | 1000 mL |
| 1 ounce  | = | 27.94 mL |
| 1 liter  | = | 1.06 quarts |

**Example:** An engine requires 6.61 liters of 5W-30 oil. Calculate how many quarts of oil this engine requires.

$$6.61 \times 1.06 = 7.00$$

This engine requires 7 quarts of oil.

Name _____  Date _____  Class _____

# Fluid Volume Job Skill Practice Problems

8.1 Calculate the number of quarts in a 55-gallon drum of oil.

8.2 A technician drains 16 quarts of used oil into a 5-gallon bucket. Calculate how many more quarts could be added to the 5-gallon bucket until it is full.

8.3 An engine requires 11.34 liters of coolant. Calculate how many gallons of coolant this engine requires.

8.4 A technician drains 19 liters of gas from a gas tank. Calculate how many gallons of gas were drained from the gas tank.

8.5 A manual transmission requires 2.1 liters of 80W-90 gear oil. Calculate how many quarts of gear oil are required. Use the conversion for liters to quarts.

**Name** _____ **Date** _____ **Class** _____

8.6 The diesel engine in a pickup truck requires 9.5 liters of 15-W40 engine oil. Calculate how many quarts of oil this engine requires. Use the conversion for liters to quarts.

8.7 A brake system requires 1.9 liters of DOT 3 brake fluid and a clutch system requires 0.9 quarts of DOT 3 brake fluid. Calculate the total amount of DOT brake fluid in quarts required to fill both systems.

8.8 A limited-slip differential requires 8 ounces of a limited-slip additive. Calculate how many liters of the additive are required. Round to 3 decimal places.

# CASE STUDY 9

# Workplace Productivity

## OBJECTIVES

*After studying this case study, you will be able to:*
- Analyze the productivity of a technician and a repair shop.
- Analyze job skill problems related to the productivity graphs of a technician and a repair shop.

## MATH SKILLS
- Analyze data from a table and a graph.
- Solve job skill problems related to data from a table and a graph.

---

The productivity of a repair shop or service department depends on how well the technicians are able to service and repair the vehicles in a timely manner. This repair data and information is often shown on a table and in a graph. Analyzing a graph can help identify areas where productivity can be improved and technicians and service departments can be more effective and profitable.

Analyze the table and graphs, and use the data to answer the job skill problems.

*Goodheart-Willcox Publisher*

**Example:**

### Valley Auto Repair—5-Week Service Report

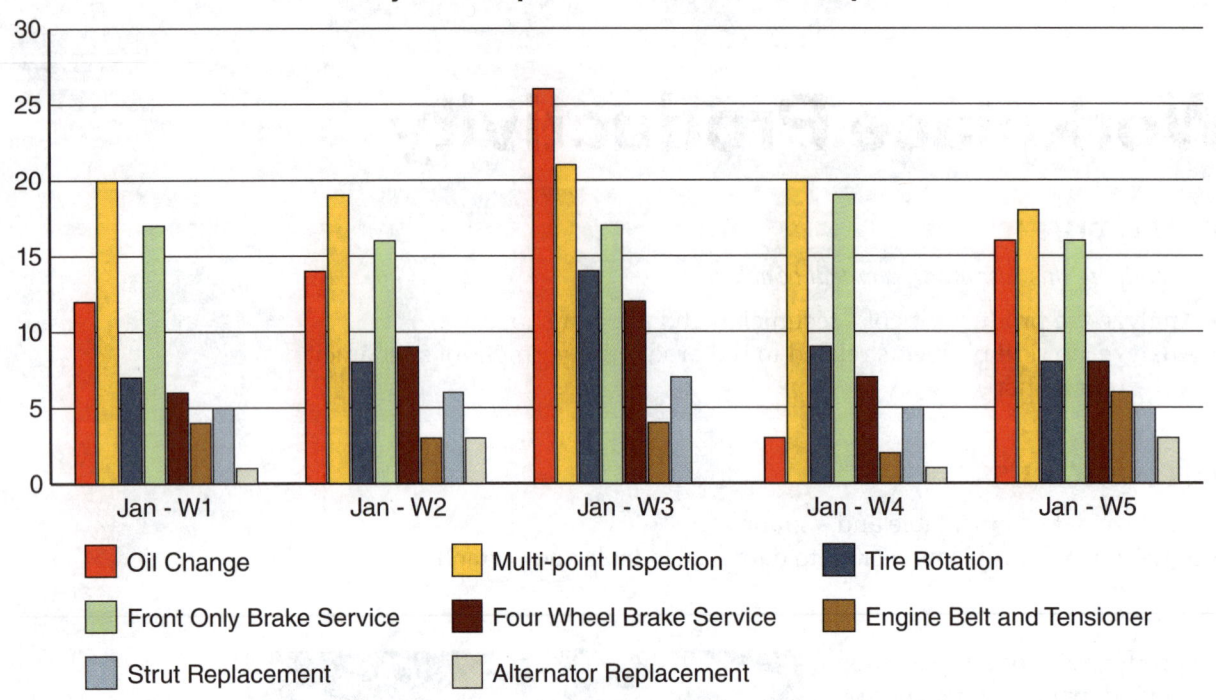

Legend:
- Oil Change
- Multi-point Inspection
- Tire Rotation
- Front Only Brake Service
- Four Wheel Brake Service
- Engine Belt and Tensioner
- Strut Replacement
- Alternator Replacement

Determine which week had the highest number of oil changes.

According to the graph, Week 3 had the most oil changes.

Determine which service procedure is done more often, tire rotation or alternator replacement.

For all 5 weeks, more tire rotations were done than alternator replacements.

Name _____  Date _____  Class _____

# Workplace Productivity
# Job Skill Practice Problems

Use the 5-Week Service Report graph on the previous page to complete practice problems 9.1 through 9.3.

9.1 Determine which week had the most front only brake services.

9.2 Determine which service is more common: tire rotation or strut replacement.

9.3 Determine which week had the fewest engine belt and tensioner services.

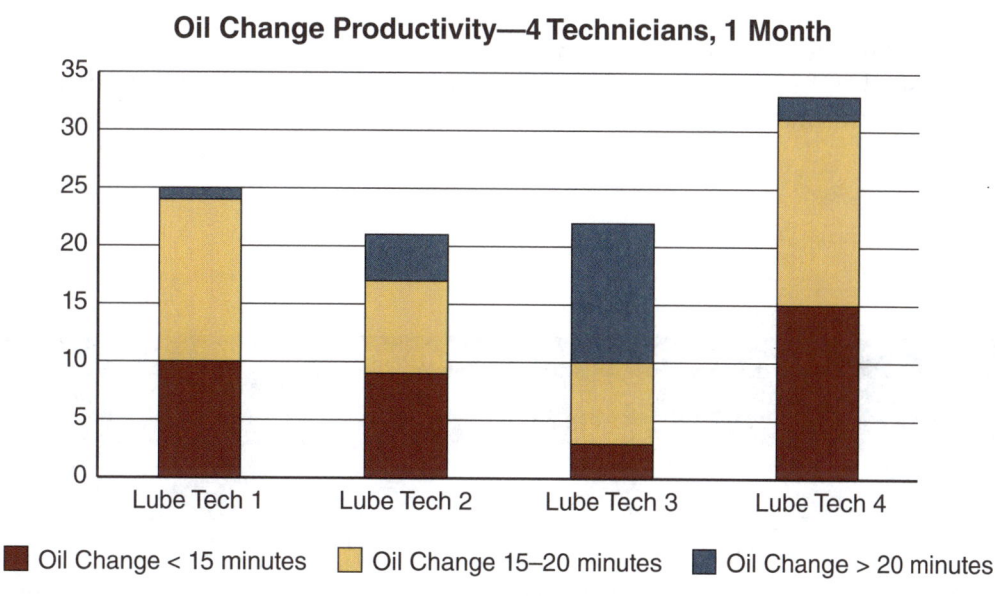

**Oil Change Productivity—4 Technicians, 1 Month**

■ Oil Change < 15 minutes    ☐ Oil Change 15–20 minutes    ■ Oil Change > 20 minutes

The graph shows the performance of 4 technicians and the time they took to complete oil change services during the past month. Brown represents oil changes that were completed in less than 15 minutes, yellow represents oil changes that were completed in 15–20 minutes, and blue indicates oil changes that took longer than 20 minutes. Analyze the graph to complete practice problems 9.4 through 9.8.

9.4 Identify which technician completed the most oil changes in less than 15 minutes.

Name _____ Date _____ Class _____

9.5 Determine which technician had the fewest oil changes that took longer than 20 minutes.

9.6 Calculate how many oil changes for all technicians were performed in less than 15 minutes.

9.7 If the service facility offers a $5 off coupon when an oil change takes longer than 20 minutes, calculate the dollar value of coupons Lube Tech 3 cost the facility this month.

9.8 If the service manager offers a $3 per oil change bonus for each vehicle finished in less than 15 minutes, calculate the total dollar amount of bonuses paid this month.

| Valley Auto Repair—Jobs Completed, May 2017 ||||||
|---|---|---|---|---|---|
|  | Apprentice Technician | Line Tech 1 | Line Tech 2 | Master Technician | Total |
| Tires / Fluids / Filters | 23 | 9 | 3 | 0 | 35 |
| Multi-Point Inspection | 19 | 8 | 7 | 1 | 35 |
| Front Brake Service | 3 | 26 | 2 | 0 | 31 |
| 4-Wheel Brake Service | 2 | 21 | 13 | 0 | 36 |
| Alignment | 2 | 8 | 23 | 4 | 37 |
| Front End Service | 1 | 4 | 14 | 4 | 23 |
| Electrical Diagnosis | 0 | 0 | 1 | 15 | 16 |
| Driveability Diagnosis | 0 | 0 | 2 | 16 | 18 |
| Total: | 50 | 76 | 65 | 40 | 231 |

The table shows the productivity of 4 technicians and the jobs they completed during the month of May 2017. The table also shows the total number of each type of job and the total number of jobs each technician completed. Analyze the table to complete practice problems 9.9 through 9.13.

**Name** _____ **Date** _____ **Class** _____

9.9 Determine which technician is most likely to be assigned a vehicle that requires a 4-wheel brake service.

9.10 Determine which employee completed the most jobs and which employee completed the fewest jobs.

9.11 The master technician is generally assigned the most difficult, most time-consuming jobs to complete. Determine which two jobs the master technician was assigned the most.

9.12 The apprentice technician is generally assigned the easiest, most basic jobs to complete. Determine which two jobs the apprentice technician was assigned the most.

9.13 Calculate the combined total number of front end service jobs and alignment jobs completed by Line Tech 1 and Line Tech 2.

# CASE STUDY 10

# Wage Earnings

## OBJECTIVES

*After studying this case study, you will be able to:*
- Identify formulas related to calculating technician wages and bonuses.
- Calculate gross and net pay using formulas to determine deductions.

## TECHNICAL TERMS

gross pay

net pay

## MATH SKILLS

- Calculate arithmetic operations using formulas.
- Calculate job skill problems following order of operation and using formulas.

The career field related to automotive service and repair has evolved into a high-skill, high-wage opportunity for those willing to learn new vehicle technology and work both intelligently and efficiently. Technicians with accredited training and industry recognized certifications are a valuable asset to an automotive service company, and are paid a respectable wage to maintain, diagnose, and service vehicles.

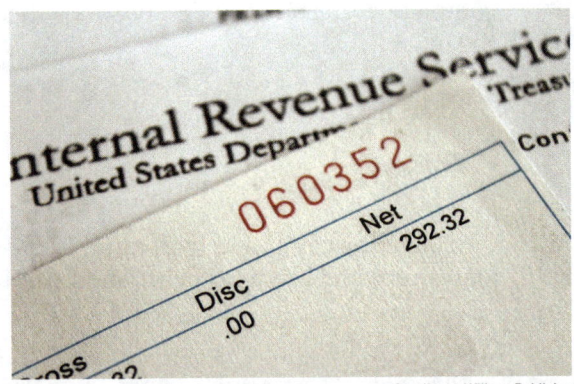

*Goodheart-Willcox Publisher*

An employee in the automotive workplace, like all workplace employees, does not receive in their paycheck all of the money they have earned. Employers withhold some wages for a variety of reasons, including taxes, health insurance, retirement savings, and other options. The amount deducted from a technician's paycheck can be calculated using formulas.

These calculations refer to two common pay-related terms: gross pay and net pay.

*Gross pay*—the total amount of pay received for work, before any deductions are taken out. For example, if an employee earns $10/hour and works a 40-hour week, the total gross pay for that week is $400.

*Net pay*—the total amount of pay on the employee's paycheck, after all required and optional deductions are taken out. This is the actual dollar value of the paycheck, commonly referred to as "take-home" pay.

Review the formula for gross pay.

*gross pay = (total hours worked) × (hourly pay rate) + bonus pay*

**Example:** A lube technician worked 38 hours at a rate of $12.75/hour. The lube technician also received a $25 up-sell bonus for recommending a vehicle for a full brake service job performed by a line technician. Calculate the gross pay using the gross pay formula.

$$\text{gross pay} = (38 \times 12.75) + 25$$
$$\text{gross pay} = \$509.50$$

To calculate net pay, refer to the formula shown. For this example and the practice problems, a total tax withholding rate of 18.5% is used. Actual tax withholding rates vary depending on state of residence, level of income, and other factors.

Review the formula for net pay.

*net pay = gross pay − (gross pay × 0.185) − retirement contributions − health insurance*

**Example:** A technician earned a net pay of $635 in a one-week pay cycle. The technician had 18.5% tax withheld and paid $25 into a retirement account and $89 toward a health insurance premium. Calculate the net pay for this technician.

$$\text{net pay} = \$635 - (\$635 \times 0.185) - \$25 - \$89$$
$$\text{net pay} = \$635 - \$117.48 - \$25 - \$89$$
$$\text{net pay} = \$403.52$$

# Wage Earnings Job Skill Practice Problems

Use the information given to calculate the gross pay in practice problems 10.1 through 10.5.

10.1 A technician worked 40 hours at a rate of $26.50/hour. The technician also received a $50 bonus for earning the highest ratings on customer service surveys for the month. Calculate the gross pay using the gross pay formula.

10.2 An entry-level technician worked 80 hours in two weeks at a rate of $13.25/hour. The technician also received a $20 up-sell bonus for noticing a broken shock absorber mount during a multi-point inspection. Calculate the gross pay using the gross pay formula.

10.3 A technician worked 40 hours at a rate of $21.65/hour and 6 hours of overtime at a rate of $32.48/hour. The technician did not earn any performance bonuses. Calculate the gross pay using the gross pay formula.

10.4 An entry-level technician worked 40 hours at a rate of $16.35/hour. The technician also received a $20 up-sell bonus for noticing a broken ball joint during a multi-point inspection and a $15 up-sell bonus for noticing a leaking differential cover during another multi-point inspection. Calculate the gross pay using the gross pay formula.

10.5 An entry-level technician worked 80 hours in two weeks at a rate of $12.85/hour. The technician did not receive a performance pay bonus during this pay period. Calculate the gross pay using the gross pay formula.

Name _____  Date _____  Class _____

Use the information given to calculate the net pay in practice problems 10.6 through 10.10.

10.6 A technician earned a gross pay of $1,296 in a one-week pay cycle. The technician had 18.5% tax withheld and paid $35 into a retirement account and $79 toward a health insurance premium. Calculate the net pay for this technician.

10.7 A technician earned a gross pay of $945 in a one-week pay cycle. The technician had 18.5% tax withheld and paid $45 into a retirement account and $91 toward a health insurance premium. Calculate the net pay for this technician. Round to the nearest cent.

10.8 An entry-level technician worked 40 hours at a rate of $16.35/hour. The technician also received a $20 up-sell bonus for noticing a broken ball joint during a multi-point inspection. The technician had 18.5% tax withheld and paid $40 into a retirement account and $70 toward a health insurance premium. Calculate the net pay for this technician.

10.9 A line technician worked 40 hours at a rate of $26.75/hour. The technician also received a $20 performance bonus for customer service. The technician had 18.5% tax withheld and paid $65 into a retirement account and $78 toward a health insurance premium. Calculate the net pay for this technician.

10.10 A master technician worked 40 hours at a rate of $28.95/hour. The technician did not earn any performance bonuses. The technician had 18.5% tax withheld and paid $55 into a retirement account and $57 toward a health insurance premium. Calculate the net pay for this technician.

# CASE STUDY 11

# Shop Equipment

## OBJECTIVES

*After studying this case study, you will be able to:*

- Calculate the square footage of major shop equipment and toolboxes.
- Analyze job skill problems related to square footage and area.

## MATH SKILLS

- Rounding up measurements for calculation.
- Calculating square footage and area.

Major automotive repair shop equipment is required to perform most vehicle service and repair, and is found in all repair shops. The most common pieces of equipment are vehicle hoists, toolboxes, tire service machines, parts washers, workbenches, and service carts. When organizing and outfitting a shop space, the area of each item and the square footage of the space must be calculated to ensure there is room for all the items.

*Goodheart-Willcox Publisher*

The first step in calculating the area of the footprint of shop equipment is to round up the measurements to account for the extra space around the equipment. Rounding up requires analyzing the exact measurement and then increasing the measurement to the next whole foot.

**Example:** A toolbox measures 23" deep and 58" wide. Round up the measurements to the nearest foot.

23" is 1 foot 11". Add 1 inch to round up to 24", or 2'.
58" is 4 feet 10". Add 2" to round up to 60", or 5'.
Rounded up, the toolbox is 2' by 5'.

To calculate the area of the shop equipment, multiply the depth by the width. The area indicates the size of the footprint of the equipment or toolbox.

**Example:** Rounded up, a toolbox measures 2' by 7'. Calculate the area of the toolbox.

2' × 7' = 14 square feet

The toolbox has a 14 square-foot area.

Name _____ Date _____ Class _____

# Shop Equipment Job Skill Practice Problems

Round up each measurement to the nearest foot.

11.1 A toolbox measures 22" deep and 92" wide. Round up the measurements to the nearest foot.

11.2 A workbench measures 34" deep and 80" wide. Round up the measurements to the nearest foot.

11.3 A parts washer measures 42" deep and 55" wide. Round up the measurements to the nearest foot.

Calculate the area of the equipment in either square inches or square feet.

11.4 A strut compressor machine on a stand measures 32" wide and 42" deep. Calculate the area of the machine in square inches.

11.5 A two-post hoist requires a minimum of 12' in width and 24' in length for a standard vehicle to fit. Calculate the area, in square footage, taken up by a two-post hoist.

11.6 A tire machine measures 48" wide and 60" deep. Calculate the area of the machine in square feet.

Name _____ Date _____ Class _____

11.7 A shop manager buys three new workbenches for a repair shop. Each workbench top is 32″ deep and 84″ wide. Calculate the total area of new workbench space these workbenches provide, in square inches.

11.8 A shop manager is replacing an old tire balance machine with a brand-new road force balance machine. The old tire balance machine measures 36″ by 48″. The new balance machine measures 50″ by 65″. Calculate the increase in area taken up by the new machine, in square inches.

11.9 A technician has a workbench and a toolbox in his service bay. The workbench measures 30″ deep and 48″ wide and the toolbox measures 29″ deep and 70″ wide. Calculate the total square-foot area of the toolbox and workbench. Round to the nearest tenth foot.

11.10 A shop owner is considering leasing a larger shop and will need the shop to have at least eight service bays. Each service bay will be 30′ deep and 15′ wide. Calculate the minimum total square footage needed in a shop to have eight service bays.

# CASE STUDY 12

# Vehicle Identification Number

## OBJECTIVES

*After studying this case study, you will be able to:*

- Identify the components of a Vehicle Identification Number.
- Analyze job skill problems related to a Vehicle Identification Number.
- Compare vehicle information based on the Vehicle Identification Number.

## TECHNICAL TERM

Vehicle Identification Number (VIN)

## MATH SKILLS

- Analyze data based on an alphanumeric code.
- Analyze and calculate job skill problems based on an alphanumeric code.

Every vehicle built since 1980 has been assigned a unique, 17-digit code known as a ***Vehicle Identification Number (VIN)***. This code is alphanumeric, which means it is made up of letters and numbers, and provides critical information about the vehicle, including a production sequence number. Refer to the table on the next page for a designation breakdown of the 17 digits that make up the VIN.

*Goodheart-Willcox Publisher*

| Vehicle Identification Number [5J6RE4H36AL109643] |||||||
|---|---|---|---|---|---|---|
| World Manufacturer Identifier |||||| Example |
| 1 | 2 | 3 |||| 5J6 |
| Vehicle Attributes ||||||   |
| [Model, Body, Engine, Transmission, Trim Level, Restraint Type] ||||||   |
| 4 | 5 | 6 | 7 | 8 || RE4H3 |
| Check Digit ||||||   |
| 9 |||||| 6 |
| Model Year ||||||   |
| 10 |||||| A |
| Assembly Plant Code ||||||   |
| 11 |||||| L |
| Production Sequence Number ||||||   |
| 12 | 13 | 14 | 15 | 16 | 17 | 109643 |

**Example:** A vehicle's VIN is JTDJW67B3WK012386. Determine which digit is used to identify the model year.

The model year digit is the 10th digit. It is the letter W in this VIN.

Name _____ Date _____ Class _____

# Vehicle Identification Number Job Skill Practice Problems

12.1 A vehicle's VIN is <u>1FMCU0H95DU859385</u>. Determine which digit or digit series is used to identify the vehicle attributes.

12.2 A vehicle's VIN is <u>1G6DM57N030123749</u>. Determine which digit or digit series is used to identify the production sequence number.

12.3 A vehicle's VIN is <u>1C4AC1A50CA017594</u>. Determine which digit or digit series is used to identify the World Manufacturer Identifier.

12.4 A vehicle's VIN is <u>YV1MH1748Y1287695</u>. Determine which digit or digit series is used to identify the assembly plant code.

12.5 A vehicle's VIN is <u>1G3RT37M040133829</u>. Determine which digit or digit series is used to identify the model year.

Digits from the VIN can be compared to a chart to analyze the code and determine specific information about the vehicle. Comparisons of vehicles can also be made by analyzing the VINs. The following table shows some basic VIN data to be used to answer the following VIN-related work problems.

| Common World Manufacturer Identifiers ||||| Model Year Identifier ||||
|---|---|---|---|---|---|---|---|---|
| | | | | Year | Code | Year | Code |
| JF1 | Japan | Fuji Industries | Passenger car | 1996 | T | 2007 | 7 |
| 1B3 | US | Dodge | Passenger car | 1997 | V | 2008 | 8 |
| 1FA | US | Ford | Passenger car | 1998 | W | 2009 | 9 |
| 1GC | US | General Motors | Chevrolet | 1999 | X | 2010 | A |
| 5J6 | US | Honda | Multi-purpose vehicle | 2000 | Y | 2011 | B |
| JN1 | Japan | Nissan | Passenger car | 2001 | 1 | 2012 | C |
| 5N1 | US | Nissan | Multi-purpose vehicle | 2002 | 2 | 2013 | D |
| YV1 | Sweden | Volvo | Passenger car | 2003 | 3 | 2014 | E |
| 1TD | US | Toyota | Passenger car | 2004 | 4 | 2015 | F |
| JTA | Japan | Toyota | Truck | 2005 | 5 | 2016 | G |
| WVG | Germany | Volkswagen | Passenger car | 2006 | 6 | 2017 | H |
| 1VW | US | Volkswagen | Passenger car | | | | |

12.6 A vehicle's VIN is <u>1FACU0H95DU859385</u>. Determine the vehicle manufacturer and country of origin.

12.7 Two vehicles are being compared. One has VIN <u>YV1MH1748Y1287695</u> and the other has VIN <u>YV1MH1748X1589687</u>. Determine which vehicle is older.

12.8 Two vehicles are being compared. One has VIN <u>1C4AC1A50EA017594</u> and the other has VIN <u>1C4AC1A50CA014536</u>. Determine which vehicle is older.

12.9 A vehicle's VIN is <u>WVGCU0H95DU859385</u>. Determine the vehicle manufacturer and country of origin.

12.10 Two vehicles are being compared. One has VIN <u>1FACU0H95DU817564</u> and the other has VIN <u>1FACU0H95DU817943</u>. Determine which vehicle was built first in the production sequence.

# UNIT 3
# Vehicle Maintenance

Case Study 13 **Repair Orders—Addition**
Case Study 14 **Timing Belt Service Intervals—Subtraction**
Case Study 15 **Maintenance Parts—Multiplication**
Case Study 16 **Brake Pad Life—Division**
Case Study 17 **Analyzing Battery Voltage—Decimal Arithmetic**
Case Study 18 **Pressure Sensor Data Analysis—Greater Than and Less Than**
Case Study 19 **Tire Tread Depth—Fractions**
Case Study 20 **Torque Values—Conversion**
Case Study 21 **Coolant Freeze Levels—Graphs and Tables**
Case Study 22 **Torque—Formulas**
Case Study 23 **Tires and Wheels—Measurement**
Case Study 24 **Engine Tune-Up—Analyzing Specifications**

## CAREER PROFILE

Jordan Paster is an entry-level apprentice technician at Scarff Ford in Auburn, Washington. He is enrolled in the Ford ASSET program at a local technical college where he is working toward Ford technician credentials and an associate's degree. As an apprentice, Jordan works under the guidance of mentor technicians as he learns the skills of the automotive service trade.

On the job, Jordan uses math to calculate conversions between quarts and liters, to measure and analyze brakes and tires during full vehicle inspections, and to track his time on each repair order. As a Ford ASSET student, Jordan will continue to apply his high school math skills as he learns about engine performance, electrical systems, and drivelines. He also uses math when modifying and upgrading his personal vehicle, a Porsche 944.

Jordan's goal is to become a driveability diagnostic technician. "I like looking at the engine and thinking, 'This problem is happening,' and then try to figure out why it is happening." As a diagnostic technician, Jordan will use logical and sequential thinking skills to solve driveability issues. A strong math problem-solving background will help Jordan learn to analyze and diagnose vehicle problems.

*Goodheart-Willcox Publisher*

Jordan Paster—Lube Technician/Ford ASSET Student, Scarff Ford.

# CASE STUDY 13

# Repair Orders

## OBJECTIVES

*After studying this case study, you will be able to:*
- Identify the components of a standard automotive repair order.
- Calculate the labor time and parts cost variables of a standard automotive repair order.

## MATH SKILLS
- Addition of whole numbers.
- Analysis of job skill problems related to addition of whole numbers.

When a vehicle is being serviced in any type of repair shop, some form of document is produced to accompany the vehicle and the service being performed. Typically, this document is referred to as a "repair order." The common repair order includes customer and vehicle information, a parts section, a labor section, and an area to show the total cost including parts, labor, taxes, fees, and any other related information.

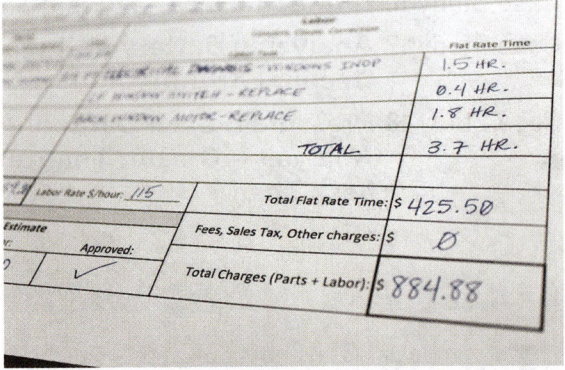

Goodheart-Willcox Publisher

Completing the repair order will require performing basic arithmetic operations, typically addition and multiplication. Review the example section of the repair order showing how to enter parts information.

**Example:**

| Parts/Fees |||
|---|---|---|
| Quantity | Part Number / Description | Cost |
| 1 set | BK358 Brake Pads Front | $37.89 |
| 2 | BK890 Front Brake Disc | $29.40 ea. |
| 2 | MS238 Shock Absorber Rear | $23.59 ea. |
|  |  |  |
|  |  |  |
|  |  |  |
| Used Parts? Discard: _____ Return: _____ | Total Parts Cost: | $143.87 |

The labor section of the repair order will also require performing basic arithmetic operations, typically addition and multiplication. Review the example section of the repair order showing how to enter labor information.

| Labor |||
|---|---|---|
| *Concern, Cause, Correction* |||
| Labor Task || Flat-Rate Time |
| Replace front brake pads || 0.9 hours |
| Replace front brake discs || 0.6 hours |
| Replace rear shocks (both) || 0.7 hours |
|  ||  |
|  ||  |
| Labor Rate/hour: __$90__ | Total Flat-Rate Time: | 2.2 hours |

# Repair Orders Job Skill Practice Problems

For each practice problem, complete all sections of the repair order with the information provided. *All information is fictional and intended for training purposes only.*

| Parts/Fees |||
|---|---|---|
| Quantity | Part Number / Description | Cost |
| | | |
| | | |
| | | |
| | | |
| | | |
| | | |

Used Parts?
Discard: _____
Return: _____

Total Parts Cost: _____

## Labor
*Concern, Cause, Correction*

| Labor Task | Flat-Rate Time |
|---|---|
| | |
| | |
| | |
| | |
| | |

Labor Rate/hour: _____   Total Flat-Rate Time: _____

13.1 **Repair Order #1728:** A 2003 Volvo S60 with a 2.4-liter inline-five engine is in the repair shop for service. The VIN is YV1RH64R731014376, the odometer reading is 98,452 miles, and the license plate is 9TD-GH2. The customer name is Mr. Stafford. His phone number is (313) 123-5559, and he expects to be called as soon as the repairs are finished. The following labor items are to be performed: front brake pad replacement (1.3 hours), front brake disc replacement (0.2 hours each side), and replacement of both front struts (2.4 hours). The new parts needed are ceramic front brake pads (AKB-5864, $58.33), front brake discs (TEK-9871, $34.93 each), and front struts (BST-183-2, $123.59 each). The customer has agreed that the used parts can be discarded, and has signed off on the estimate. The shop labor rate is $105 per hour. The shop is not required to charge sales tax, and the shop charges a $15 environmental impact fee for every repair order, regardless of the work performed. Use the information provided to complete the repair order.

Name _____ Date _____ Class _____

| Parts/Fees |||
|---|---|---|
| Quantity | Part Number / Description | Cost |
|  |  |  |
|  |  |  |
|  |  |  |
|  |  |  |
|  |  |  |
|  |  |  |
| Used Parts?<br>Discard: _____<br>Return: _____ | Total Parts Cost: |  |

**Labor**
*Concern, Cause, Correction*

| Labor Task | Flat-Rate Time |
|---|---|
|  |  |
|  |  |
|  |  |
|  |  |
|  |  |
| Labor Rate/hour: _____ Total Flat-Rate Time: | |

13.2 Repair Order #2398: A 2009 Toyota Corolla with a 1.8 L inline four-cylinder is in the repair shop for service. The VIN is 1NXBU40E99Z193078, the odometer reading is 117,948 miles, and the license plate is 7T4-DF4. The customer name is Mrs. Swift, her phone number is (323) 123-5554, and she expects to be called as soon as the repairs are finished. The following labor items are to be performed: radiator replacement (1.4 hours), upper and lower radiator hose replacement (1.6 hours), and replacement of both rear suspension stabilizer bar end links (0.6 hours). The new parts needed are a radiator (K-983-2, $160.33), upper radiator hose (DY-987, $11.39), lower radiator hose (DY-998, $13.56), and rear stabilizer bar end links (MG-3009, $36.97 each). The customer has agreed that the parts can be discarded, and has signed off on the estimate. The shop labor rate is $95 per hour. The shop is not required to charge sales tax, and the shop charges a $5 coolant disposal fee for this job. Use the information provided to complete the repair order.

Name _____  Date _____  Class _____

| Parts/Fees |||
|---|---|---|
| Quantity | Part Number / Description | Cost |
|  |  |  |
|  |  |  |
|  |  |  |
|  |  |  |
|  |  |  |
|  |  |  |

Used Parts?
Discard: _____
Return: _____

Total Parts Cost: _____

### Labor
*Concern, Cause, Correction*

| Labor Task | Flat-Rate Time |
|---|---|
|  |  |
|  |  |
|  |  |
|  |  |
|  |  |

Labor Rate/hour: _____   Total Flat-Rate Time: _____

13.3 Repair Order #5681: A 2005 Ford F-150 with a 5.4-liter V8 engine is in the repair shop for service. The VIN is 1FTPX14545FB02659, the odometer is 135,989 miles, and the license plate is WNXP-97. The customer's name is Mr. Gates. His phone number is (425) 123-5555, and he is on vacation and does not need to be called when the work is completed. The following labor items are to be performed: an electrical diagnosis to determine the cause of an inoperative power window (1.5 hours), replace the left-front window switch (0.4 hours), and replace a back window motor (1.8 hours). The new parts needed are a window switch (1F-4832, $139.59) and a rear back window motor (1F-88695-1, $319.79). The customer has agreed that the parts can be discarded, and has signed off on the estimate. The shop labor rate is $115 per hour. The shop is not required to charge sales tax, and the shop does not charge any additional fees for this work. Use the information provided to complete the repair order.

# CASE STUDY 14

# Timing Belt Service Intervals

## OBJECTIVES

*After studying this case study, you will be able to:*
- Identify the purpose of a timing belt service interval.
- Calculate the amount of mileage remaining on a timing belt.

## TECHNICAL TERMS

service interval    timing belt

## MATH SKILLS

- Whole number subtraction.
- Solve job skill problems using subtraction.

The *timing belt* connects the crankshaft to the camshaft and is responsible for rotating both shafts in sync with each other. When the camshaft and crankshaft are synchronized, the valves open and close at the correct time, and the engine is able to run properly.

The service issue with timing belts is that after a certain amount of mileage on the belt, the belt may break due to fatigue wear. This becomes an even larger problem if the engine is an interference-fit engine. If a free-wheeling engine breaks a timing belt, the internal engine damage is typically minimal. If the timing belt breaks on an interference-fit engine, the valves and pistons crash into each other, causing bending of the valves and significant damage to the cylinder head.

Manufacturers have established a *service interval* for all engines equipped with a timing belt. This interval indicates the mileage at which the timing belt should be replaced. Running the engine beyond this mileage without replacing the timing belt significantly increases the chance of the belt breaking and causing engine damage.

**Example:** A 3.2 L engine currently has 87,450 miles and the service interval is 90,000 miles. Calculate the number of remaining miles until the timing belt reaches the service interval limit.

$$90{,}000 \text{ miles} - 87{,}450 \text{ miles} = 2{,}550 \text{ miles}$$

This engine has 2,550 miles until the timing belt service interval.

Name _____  Date _____  Class _____

## Timing Belt Service Intervals
## Job Skill Practice Problems

14.1 A 1.8 L DOHC engine currently has 94,248 miles and the service interval is 105,000 miles. Calculate the number of remaining miles until the timing belt reaches the service interval limit.

14.2 A 1.9 L engine currently has 63,567 miles and the service interval is 105,000 miles. Calculate the number of remaining miles until the timing belt reaches the service interval limit.

14.3 A 4.0 L engine currently has 54,038 miles and the service interval is 102,000 miles. Calculate the number of remaining miles until the timing belt reaches the service interval limit.

14.4 A 1.6 L engine currently has 48,932 miles and the service interval is 60,000 miles. Calculate the number of remaining miles until the timing belt reaches the service interval limit.

14.5 A 1.8 L engine currently has 74,331 miles and the service interval is 52,000 miles. Calculate the number of miles driven beyond the service interval.

**Name** _____ **Date** _____ **Class** _____

14.6 A 1.6 L engine currently has 279,357 miles and the service interval is every 90,000 miles. If the timing belt was replaced at exactly 270,000 miles, calculate the number of remaining miles until the timing belt reaches the next service interval.

14.7 A 1.6 L engine currently has 59,208 miles and the service interval is 60,000 miles. Calculate the number of remaining miles until the timing belt reaches the service interval limit.

14.8 A 2.0 L SOHC engine currently has 79,338 miles and the service interval is 120,000 miles. Calculate the number of remaining miles until the timing belt reaches the service interval limit.

14.9 A 3.3 L engine currently has 34,987 miles and the service interval is 105,000 miles. Calculate the number of remaining miles until the timing belt reaches the service interval limit.

14.10 A 4.7 L engine currently has 41,317 miles and the service interval is 60,000 miles. Calculate the number of remaining miles until the timing belt reaches the service interval limit.

# CASE STUDY 15

# Maintenance Parts

## OBJECTIVES

*After studying this case study, you will be able to:*
- Identify common maintenance items that require multiple quantities.
- Calculate price and quantities needed for multiple parts and vehicles.

## MATH SKILLS
- Multiplication of whole and decimal numbers.
- Analyze and solve word problems related to multiplication.

Vehicle maintenance and light repair often include changing many common parts, such as filters, spark plugs, belts, hoses, tires, light bulbs, and wiper blades. Some of these items, such as spark plugs, require more than one part when service is being performed. Calculating price and parts needed when performing vehicle maintenance requires multiplication.

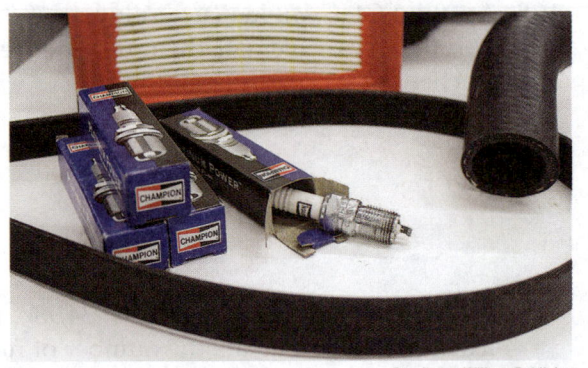

*Goodheart-Willcox Publisher*

**Example:** A dealership technician is changing the spark plugs on four identical vehicles that are equipped with gasoline-powered V6 engines. Calculate the number of spark plugs needed to complete all four vehicles.

$$4 \times 6 = 24$$

24 spark plugs are needed to complete the vehicles.

## Maintenance Parts Job Skill Practice Problems

15.1 A service writer is preparing an estimate for a spark plug service on a vehicle with a V8 engine. The spark plugs cost $6.75 each. Calculate the cost of the spark plugs needed for this engine.

15.2 A vehicle uses six identical light bulbs for the rear brake lights and rear turn signal lights. Although only one bulb is burned out, the customer wants all six bulbs replaced. If the bulbs cost $1.59 each, calculate the price to replace the bulbs.

15.3 A fleet service technician is replacing the wiper blades on 13 identical vehicles. Each vehicle requires two 19-inch wiper blades. Calculate the total number of wiper blades needed to service all of the vehicles.

15.4 A service writer is preparing an estimate for a spark plug service on a vehicle with a V6 engine. The spark plugs cost $13.00 each. Calculate the cost of the spark plugs needed for this engine.

15.5 A service writer is preparing an estimate for a set of five tires (full-size spare). Brand G tires cost $67 each and Brand Y tires cost $73 each. Calculate the total price for each brand of tires.

15.6 A fleet service manager is ordering six identical serpentine belts for a fleet of Police Interceptor vehicles. The price is $29.50 per belt. Calculate the total cost for the six belts.

15.7 A vehicle requires four H7 headlight bulbs. The price of these bulbs is $8.59 per bulb. Calculate the price to replace all four headlight bulbs.

15.8 A technician is considering the potential cost savings of buying oil filters in bulk for his own car. The filters normally cost $5.79 each. A case of 12 oil filters costs $65.00. Determine if it costs less to purchase the case of filters or to buy the 12 filters individually.

15.9 A fleet manager is ordering new sets of tires for a fleet of work trucks. There are six Chevy trucks in the fleet, and they use P265/70R16 tires that cost $71 each. There are four Ford trucks in the fleet, and they use P275/70R15 tires that cost $83 each. Calculate the total cost of replacing all four tires on all of the trucks in the fleet.

15.10 A customer wants to upgrade the four H9 headlight bulbs to high performance xenon ultra-white bulbs. The price of these bulbs is $14.99 per bulb. Calculate the price to upgrade all four headlight bulbs.

# CASE STUDY 16

# Brake Pad Life

## OBJECTIVES

*After studying this case study, you will be able to:*
- Identify brake pad current and new measurements.
- Calculate remaining brake pad life based on mileage and wear.

## MATH SKILLS
- Division of whole numbers.
- Analyze and solve word problems using division.

As brake pads are applied, the brake pad material is slowly worn away from the pad surface and becomes brake dust. During a brake inspection, the remaining thickness of the brake pads is measured, and documented on the repair order. Brake inspections are performed to determine if the brakes require service. If the brakes do not require service, the remaining pad measurement can be used to calculate the remaining life of the brake pads.

*Goodheart-Willcox Publisher*

To calculate the remaining life of the brake pads, the current vehicle mileage and the mileage when the brake pads were installed are required. Also, the nominal, or new, thickness of the brake pads is needed as well as the current thickness of the brake pads. With these four points of information, the estimated remaining brake pad life can be calculated. This is considered to be only an estimate, based on the performance of the vehicle up to this point.

**Example:** The brakes of a 2012 sedan are being inspected. The front brake pads are the original, factory-installed brake pads and were 12 mm thick new. With 37,856 miles on the vehicle, the front brake pads measure 6 mm thick. The minimum allowable brake pad thickness is 2 mm. Calculate the estimated remaining brake pad life on this vehicle.

$$12 \text{ mm} - 6 \text{ mm} = 6 \text{ mm}$$

The brake pads have worn a total of 6 mm in 37,856 miles.

$$37,856 \text{ miles} \div 6 \text{ mm} = 6,309 \text{ miles per millimeter of wear}$$

$$6 \text{ mm} - 2 \text{ mm} = 4 \text{ mm}$$

4 mm of remaining brake pad wear

$$6,309 \text{ miles} \times 4 \text{ mm} = 25,236 \text{ miles}$$

25,236 estimated remaining miles on these brake pads

Name _____ Date _____ Class _____

# Brake Pad Life Job Skill Practice Problems

16.1 The brakes of a 2013 SUV are being inspected. The front brake pads are the original, factory-installed brake pads and were 11 mm thick new. With 45,126 miles on the vehicle, the front brake pads measure 5 mm thick. The minimum allowable brake pad thickness is 2 mm. Calculate the estimated remaining brake pad life on this vehicle.

16.2 The brakes of a 2015 luxury sedan are being inspected. The front brake pads are the original, factory-installed brake pads and were 12 mm thick new. With 21,029 miles on the vehicle, the front brake pads measure 9 mm thick. The minimum allowable brake pad thickness is 2 mm. Calculate the estimated remaining brake pad life on this vehicle.

16.3 The brakes of a 2009 compact car are being inspected. The front brake pads are the original, factory-installed brake pads and were 10 mm thick new. With 65,126 miles on the vehicle, the front brake pads measure 3 mm thick. The minimum allowable brake pad thickness is 2 mm. Calculate the estimated remaining brake pad life on this vehicle.

16.4 The brakes of a 2010 SUV are being inspected. The rear brake pads are the original, factory-installed brake pads and were 7 mm thick new. With 65,126 miles on the vehicle, the rear brake pads measure 3 mm thick. The minimum allowable brake pad thickness is 2 mm. Calculate the estimated remaining brake pad life on this vehicle.

Name _____  Date _____  Class _____

16.5 The brakes of a 2011 pickup truck are being inspected. The front brake pads are the original, factory-installed brake pads and were 12 mm thick new. The rear brake pads are the original, factory-installed brake pads and were 7 mm thick new. With 55,106 miles on the vehicle, the front brake pads measure 5 mm thick and the rear brake pads measure 4 mm thick. The minimum allowable brake pad thickness is 2 mm. Calculate the estimated remaining front and rear brake pad life and determine which set of brakes will reach the 2 mm limit first.

16.6 The brakes of a 2010 pickup truck are being inspected. The front brake pads are the original, factory-installed brake pads and were 12 mm thick new. With 65,027 miles on the vehicle, the front brake pads measure 3 mm thick. The minimum allowable brake pad thickness is 2 mm. Calculate the estimated remaining brake pad life on this vehicle.

16.7 The brakes of a 2009 compact car are being inspected. The front brake pads are the original, factory-installed brake pads and were 11 mm thick new. With 40,391 miles on the vehicle, the front brake pads measure 4 mm thick. The minimum allowable brake pad thickness is 2 mm. Calculate the estimated remaining brake pad life on this vehicle.

16.8 The brakes of a 2015 SUV are being inspected. The front brake pads are the original, factory-installed brake pads and were 12 mm thick new. With 15,424 miles on the vehicle, the front brake pads measure 5 mm thick. The minimum allowable brake pad thickness is 2 mm. Calculate the estimated remaining brake pad life on this vehicle.

# CASE STUDY 17

# Analyzing Battery Voltage

## OBJECTIVES

*After studying this case study, you will be able to:*
- Identify battery voltage values during different stages of battery use.
- Analyze and compare battery voltages.

## TECHNICAL TERMS

charging battery
cranking battery
stabilized battery
surface charge

## MATH SKILLS

- Calculate decimal arithmetic operations.
- Analyze and solve job skill problems with decimal number arithmetic.

The modern automotive battery is a maintenance-free, lead-acid, wet cell battery that produces a significant current capable of cranking an engine during start-up. The automotive battery generally has four stages of voltage in the battery cycle. These stages are:

*Stabilized Battery*—The stabilized battery is the neutral state of the battery, and the voltage should read 12.6 volts. This stage indicates the vehicle is shut down, powered down, and in "sleep" mode. The amperage draw should be less than 0.035 amps.

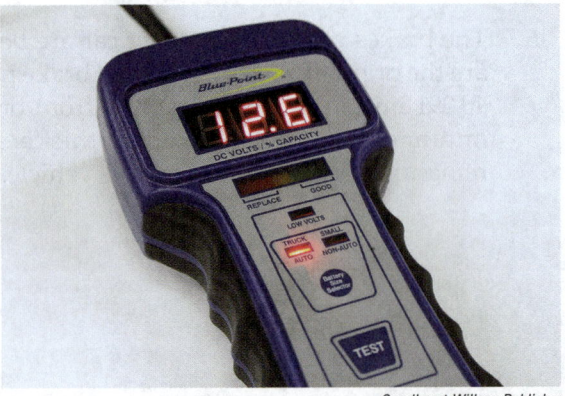

*Goodheart-Willcox Publisher*

*Cranking Battery*—The cranking battery is the "work" stage of the battery and voltage is at its lowest measured value. The minimum voltage for this stage is 9.6 volts, although the voltage is typically around 10 or 11 volts. The battery voltage is low because the battery is delivering 200 to 400 amps or more to the starter motor to crank the engine.

*Charging Battery*—The charging battery stage is the "recovery" stage of the battery and voltage should be around 13.6 to 14.6 volts. Now that the engine is running, the alternator is recharging the battery and creating voltage higher than 12.6 volts. Some modern charging systems vary alternator output voltage depending on demand, and voltage may be lower than 13.6 under certain conditions.

*Surface Charge*—The surface charge stage is directly after the running engine is shut off. At first, the battery voltage will measure near charging voltage, but will slowly drop down to 12.6 volts. This drop takes time, and testing during this time may indicate false readings. The surface charge can be removed from the battery by turning on the headlights and high-beam lights for 15 seconds or so, depending on the vehicle.

Use the provided battery voltage information to answer the word problems regarding analyzing battery voltage.

**Example:** A vehicle battery voltage is being measured with the engine running. The battery voltage measures 13.8 volts. Calculate how much higher the charging system voltage is above the normal stabilized battery voltage of 12.6 volts.

$$13.8 \text{ volts} - 12.6 \text{ volts} = 1.2 \text{ volts}$$

This battery is charging 1.2 volts above normal stabilized voltage.

# Analyzing Battery Voltage
## Job Skill Practice Problems

**17.1** A 2003 sedan is being diagnosed for electrical problems. The technician first checks the battery and measures 11.9 volts on a stabilized battery. Calculate how many volts below normal stabilized voltage this battery measures.

**17.2** A 2007 pickup truck is being diagnosed for starting system problems. The technician measures 9.1 volts using a digital multimeter at the battery terminals during cranking. Calculate how far below the normal cranking threshold this battery voltage is during cranking.

**17.3** A lead-acid, maintenance-free automotive battery measures 12.6 volts and is made up of 6 cells. Calculate the amount of voltage per cell.

**17.4** A 2014 compact car is being tested for charging system operation. The battery voltage measures 13.9 volts using a digital multimeter when the engine is running. Calculate how much higher the charging system voltage is above the stabilized battery voltage.

**Name** _____  **Date** _____  **Class** _____

17.5 A 2009 sedan is being diagnosed for a key-off amperage draw. After sitting overnight, the battery voltage reads 12.6 volts when measured with a digital multimeter. Calculate how much the battery voltage dropped from the stabilized battery voltage value.

17.6 A 2013 pickup truck is being diagnosed for a charging system issue. The battery voltage measures 12.3 volts when the engine is running at 2,000 rpm. The charging system voltage specification is 14.6 volts at 2,000 rpm. Calculate how far below the charging system voltage specification this battery measures.

17.7 A 2009 sedan is being diagnosed for starting system problems. The technician measures 8.3 volts using a digital multimeter at the battery terminals during cranking. Calculate how far below the normal cranking threshold this battery voltage is during cranking.

17.8 A 2016 luxury sedan is being diagnosed for a charging system issue. The battery voltage measures 12.1 volts when the engine is running at 2,000 rpm. The charging system voltage specification is 14.6 volts at 2,000 rpm. Calculate how far below the charging system voltage specification this battery measures.

# CASE STUDY 18

# Pressure Sensor Data Analysis

## OBJECTIVES

*After studying this case study, you will be able to:*
- Identify engine oil and fuel pressure sensor parameters.
- Analyze pressure sensor data and readings.

## MATH SKILLS
- Identify greater than and less than values.
- Analyze job skill problems related to greater than and less than values.

Correct engine oil pressure and fuel pressure are critical to engine operation, and can be affected by vehicle maintenance tasks. Engine oil pressure is developed through the volume of oil pumped through the mechanical engine oil pump. In modern port and direct injection systems, fuel is pumped through an electric fuel pump to the engine. Both of these fluids have specified pressure values and can be measured and compared with those values to determine if they are within specification.

*Goodheart-Willcox Publisher*

Factors affecting low oil pressure include low oil level, obstructed oil pickup tube, and worn internal engine tolerances. Factors affecting low fuel pressure include a defective fuel pump, clogged fuel filter, and an inoperative fuel pressure regulator.

Analyze the data and pressure values to determine if the fluid pressures are within specification.

**Example:** A 2.3 L four-cylinder engine is being tested for adequate oil pressure. An oil pressure gauge is connected to the oil pressure sensor and the engine is started. The oil pressure specification is 45±3 psi, with the engine at operating temperature and at 1,500 rpm. When the engine is at operating temperature and the rpm at 1,500, the oil pressure gauge reads 39 psi. Determine if the oil pressure is within specification.

$$39 \text{ psi} < 45 \pm 3 \text{ psi}$$

The oil pressure is below specification.

Name _____ Date _____ Class _____

# Pressure Sensor Data Analysis
# Job Skill Practice Problems

18.1  A 4.0 L inline six-cylinder engine has a fuel pressure specification of 55±5 psi. This vehicle is being diagnosed for a low power on acceleration concern. When accessed through the scan tool live data, the fuel pressure reading is 58 psi. Determine if the fuel pressure is within specification.

18.2  A 1.9 L four-cylinder engine is being tested for adequate oil pressure. An oil pressure gauge is connected to the oil pressure sensor and the engine is started. The oil pressure specification is 30±4 psi, with the engine at operating temperature and at 1,500 rpm. When the engine is at operating temperature and the rpm at 1,500, the oil pressure gauge reads 21 psi. Determine if the oil pressure is within specification.

18.3  A 4.6 L eight-cylinder engine is being tested for a no-start condition. The fuel pressure specification is 45–65 psi. With a fuel pressure gauge connected to the service port on the fuel rail, the fuel pressure value is around 22 psi. Determine if the fuel pressure is within specification.

18.4  A 3.5 L V6 engine has a fuel pressure specification of 39±5 psi. This vehicle is being diagnosed for a rough idle concern. When accessed through the scan tool live data, the fuel pressure reading is 36 psi. Determine if the fuel pressure is within specification.

Name _____ Date _____ Class _____

18.5 A 1.6 L four-cylinder engine is being tested for adequate oil pressure. An oil pressure gauge is connected to the oil pressure sensor and the engine is started. The oil pressure specification is 60±7 psi, with the engine at operating temperature and at 1,500 rpm. When the engine is at operating temperature and the rpm at 1,500, the oil pressure gauge reads 51 psi. Determine if the oil pressure is within specification.

18.6 A 4.5 L eight-cylinder engine is being tested for a no-start condition. The fuel pressure specification is 52–68 psi. With a fuel pressure gauge connected to the service port on the fuel rail, the fuel pressure value is around 29 psi. A new fuel filter is installed and the fuel pressure value, when tested, reads 55 psi. Determine if the fuel pressure is within specification following the fuel filter service.

18.7 A 5.7 L V8 engine has a fuel pressure specification of 45±5 psi. This vehicle is being diagnosed for a low power on acceleration concern. When accessed through the scan tool live data, the fuel pressure reading is 38 psi. Determine if the fuel pressure is within specification.

18.8 A 5.0 L eight-cylinder engine is being tested for a no-start condition. The fuel pressure specification is 61±5 psi. With a fuel pressure gauge connected to the service port on the fuel rail, the fuel pressure value is around 58 psi. Determine if the fuel pressure is within specification.

# CASE STUDY 19

# Tire Tread Depth

### OBJECTIVES
*After studying this case study, you will be able to:*
- Identify tire tread depth fraction measurement values.
- Compare tire tread depth measurement values to specification.

### TECHNICAL TERM
tire tread

### MATH SKILLS
- Add and subtract fractions.
- Analyze and solve job skill problems using fractions.

The *tire tread* is the patterned section around the outside of the tire that contacts the road. As the vehicle is driven, the tread rubber slowly wears away, and the tread depth becomes less deep. This wear will occur faster if tire rotations are ignored, or as a result of aggressive driving. Worn suspension parts also cause alignment angle issues and lead to uneven tire wear. An important part of vehicle maintenance is measuring and recording the tire tread depth using a tire tread depth gauge.

*Goodheart-Willcox Publisher*

A tire tread depth gauge measures depth in thirty-seconds of an inch. When measuring tire tread depth, the reading is always a fraction with 32 as the denominator. This applies even if the tread depth is an even number, such as 8/32″. Although the fraction 8/32 could be reduced to 1/4, it remains written as 8/32.

The US Department of Transportation requires a minimum 2/32″ (4/32″ for commercial vehicles and heavy trucks) when measured in a major tread groove. The tread depth of brand new tires typically ranges from 11/32″ to 16/32″; this information can usually be found on the tire manufacturer's website or other tire suppliers' websites.

**Example:** A pickup truck tire tread depth is being measured. The left front tire measures 5/32″ tread depth. Calculate the remaining tire tread.

5/32″ − 2/32″ = 3/32″

The tire has 3/32″ tire tread depth remaining.

If the number of miles that a tire has been driven on since it was brand new is known, the estimated amount of remaining tire tread life can be calculated. (This is an estimate, and there are many factors that could change the tire wear as the vehicle is driven.)

**Example:** A technician working for a major tire retail chain is estimating for a customer the amount of remaining tire tread life on a pickup truck. The tire tread depth is measured and all four tires have 5/32″ tire tread remaining. The tire tread when the tires were brand new was 14/32″. The tires were installed 50,400 miles ago at the same shop. Calculate the estimated remaining mileage on the tires until they reach the minimum allowable tread depth.

14/32″ − 5/32″ = 9/32″

The tires have worn 9/32″ so far.

50,400 miles ÷ 9 = 5,600 miles

The tires have worn approximately 1/32″ per 5,600 miles of tread wear.

5/32″ − 2/32″ = 3/32″

3/32″ tire tread depth remaining

3 × 5,600 miles = 16,800 miles

16,800 miles estimated tire tread life remaining on the tires

**Name** _____ **Date** _____ **Class** _____

## Tire Tread Depth Job Skill Practice Problems

19.1 A compact car tire tread depth is being measured. The right rear tire measures 6/32″ tread depth. Calculate the remaining tire tread of the tire.

19.2 An SUV tire tread depth is being measured. The left front tire measures 5/32″ tread depth. When the tire was brand new, the tread depth was 12/32″. Calculate the amount of tire tread depth wear.

19.3 A luxury sedan tire tread depth is being measured. The left front tire measures 8/32″ tread depth. The right front tire measures 7/32″ tread depth. The tires were 11/32″ tread depth brand new. Calculate which tire has worn more.

19.4 A hybrid car tire tread depth is being measured. The left rear tire measures 9/32″ tread depth. Calculate the remaining tire tread of the tire.

19.5 An SUV tire tread depth is being measured. The right front tire measures 3/32″ tread depth. When the tire was brand new, the tread depth was 12/32″. Calculate the amount of tire tread depth wear.

Copyright Goodheart-Willcox Co., Inc. May not be reproduced or posted to a publicly accessible website.

19.6 A technician working for a major tire retail chain is estimating for a customer the amount of remaining tire tread life on a compact car. The tire tread depth is measured and all four tires have 4/32" tire tread remaining. The tire tread when the tires were brand new was 11/32". The tires were installed 44,100 miles ago at the same shop. Calculate the estimated remaining mileage on the tires until they reach the minimum allowable tread depth.

19.7 A dealership technician performing a used-car inspection is estimating the amount of remaining tire tread life on a midsize SUV. The tire tread depth is measured and all four tires have 11/32" tire tread remaining. The tire tread when the tires were brand new was 15/32". The tires were installed 19,000 miles ago at the same dealership. Calculate the estimated remaining mileage on the tires until they reach the minimum allowable tread depth.

19.8 A fleet service technician working for a municipal fleet service garage is estimating the amount of remaining tire tread life of a work truck. The tire tread depth is measured and all four tires have 5/32" tire tread remaining. The tire tread when the tires were brand new was 14/32". The tires were installed 61,200 miles ago at the same fleet service shop. Calculate the estimated remaining mileage on the tires until they reach the minimum allowable tread depth.

# CASE STUDY 20

# Torque Values

## OBJECTIVES

*After studying this case study, you will be able to:*
- Identify torque value scales, both metric and standard.
- Convert torque value within standard value scales and between metric and standard.

## TECHNICAL TERM

torque value

## MATH SKILLS

- Convert values between torque value scales.
- Analyze job skill problems related to torque values and conversion factors.

---

All fasteners on the vehicle have been assigned a torque value by the vehicle manufacturer. The *torque value* is the level of rotational force used to tighten a bolt or nut with a torque instrument, commonly a torque wrench. All too often, entry-level technicians and "do-it-yourselfers" will ignore torque value specifications. This can damage threads or bolts if fasteners are too tight and cause safety issues if fasteners are too loose. Careful use of a torque wrench and attention to torque values will ensure that the work is performed according to manufacturer's procedures and recommendations.

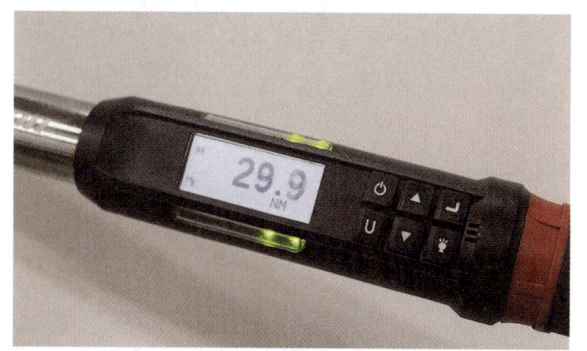

*Goodheart-Willcox Publisher*

The three most common torque value scales listed in automotive service manuals are inch-pounds, foot-pounds, and Newton-meters. Refer to the table for the conversion factors between these torque value scales.

Copyright Goodheart-Willcox Co., Inc. May not be reproduced or posted to a publicly accessible website.

143

| Torque Value Conversion Factors | | |
|---|---|---|
| 1 inch-pound | = | 0.083 foot-pound |
| 1 inch-pound | = | 0.113 Newton-meter |
| 1 foot-pound | = | 12 inch-pounds |
| 1 foot-pound | = | 1.35 Newton-meters |
| 1 Newton-meter | = | 0.737 foot-pound |
| 1 Newton-meter | = | 8.85 inch-pounds |

**Example:** After replacing the drain plug washer on an oil pan drain bolt, the technician determines the torque value of the bolt to be 13 foot-pounds. Convert the value into Newton-meters.

$$13 \times 1.35 = 17.55$$

The torque value in Newton-meters is 17.55 N·m.

Name _____ Date _____ Class _____

# Torque Values Job Skill Practice Problems

Use the Torque Value Conversion Factors table on the previous page to complete practice problems 20.1 through 20.8.

20.1 An engine valve cover bolt torque value is 39 inch-pounds. Convert this value to foot-pounds.

20.2 The torque value of a water pump bolt is 41 Newton-meters. The water pump bolts were tightened to 34 foot-pounds. Determine if the bolts were under-tightened or overtightened.

20.3 An engine has a spark plug torque value of 34 foot-pounds. Convert the spark plug torque value into inch-pounds.

20.4 A cylinder head bolt torque value is 98 foot-pounds. Convert this torque value into Newton-meters.

**Name** _____  **Date** _____  **Class** _____

20.5 A plastic intake manifold has a critical torque value of 18 Newton-meters. The intake manifold bolts were tightened to 175 inch-pounds. Determine if the bolts were undertightened or overtightened.

20.6 A thermostat housing has a torque value specification of 150 inch-pounds. Convert this torque value into foot-pounds.

20.7 An engine has a throttle body bolt torque value of 192 inch-pounds. Convert this torque value into Newton-meters.

20.8 An engine has a timing chain cover bolt torque value of 21±3 foot-pounds. Convert this torque value range into inch-pounds.

# CASE STUDY 21

# Coolant Freeze Levels

## OBJECTIVES
*After studying this case study, you will be able to:*
- Identify coolant freeze level protection levels.
- Analyze freeze level chart and determine water and coolant percentages.

## TECHNICAL TERM
refractometer

## MATH SKILLS
- Identify data from charts and tables.
- Analyze job skill problems related to data from charts and tables.

---

The engine coolant mixture circulating in the cooling system is a mixture of antifreeze and demineralized water. The antifreeze is most likely ethylene-glycol based, not propylene-glycol. The freezing point of the fluid will depend on the concentration of antifreeze in the water. The optimal and recommended mixture is 50% antifreeze and 50% water. The 50-50 mixture of ethylene-glycol and water provides a freezing point of –34°F.

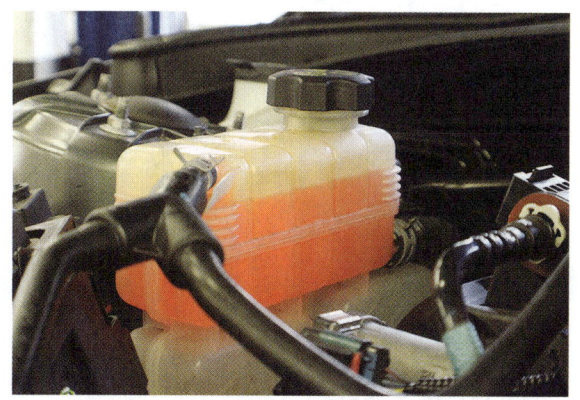

*Goodheart-Willcox Publisher*

The coolant freeze level is measured using a *refractometer*. The internal lens of the refractometer has a scale that indicates the concentration of ethylene-glycol mixed with the water. A multi-point inspection often includes checking the freeze level protection of the coolant as a test to determine if a coolant system flush is necessary.

Review the following chart and example to understand how to determine coolant mixtures. Note that the *x*-axis values change from a positive temperature to a negative temperature as coolant is added to the mixture.

**Ethylene-Glycol Water Freeze Level Chart**

*(Bar chart: Percent Ethylene-Glycol vs. Freeze Level of Coolant Mixture)*

| Freeze Level | % Ethylene-Glycol |
|---|---|
| 32°F | 0% |
| 25°F | 10% |
| 20°F | 16% |
| 15°F | 21% |
| 10°F | 25% |
| 5°F | 29% |
| 0°F | 33% |
| –5°F | 36% |
| –10°F | 39% |
| –20°F | 44% |
| –30°F | 48% |
| –34°F | 50% |
| –40°F | 52% |
| –50°F | 56% |

**Example:** A cooling system freeze level is tested using a refractometer. The refractometer scale reads –27°F. Determine the concentration level of antifreeze in the coolant mixture.

–27°F is approximately 47% ethylene-glycol on the chart.

The mixture is 47% ethylene-glycol and 53% water.

Name _____ Date _____ Class _____

# Coolant Freeze Levels Job Skill Practice Problems

Use the chart on the previous page to complete practice problems 21.1 through 21.6.

21.1 A cooling system freeze level is tested using a refractometer. The refractometer scale reads –5°F. Determine the concentration level of antifreeze in the coolant mixture.

21.2 A cooling system freeze level is tested using a refractometer. The refractometer scale reads –40°F. Determine the concentration level of antifreeze in the coolant mixture.

21.3 A cooling system freeze level is tested using a refractometer. The refractometer scale reads 10°F. Determine the concentration level of antifreeze in the coolant mixture.

21.4 A technician replaced a leaking radiator hose and is preparing a coolant mixture to refill the system. If the technician mixes 1 quart of ethylene-glycol and 3 quarts of water, determine the freeze level of the mixture.

21.5 A technician is performing a complete coolant flush on a vehicle. The flush machine holds 7 gallons. Calculate how much water and how much ethylene-glycol antifreeze should be added to the 7-gallon tank to achieve a 50-50 mixture.

21.6 A technician has replaced a radiator and refills the system with 1 gallon of ethylene-glycol antifreeze and 2 gallons of demineralized water. Calculate the expected freeze level of this coolant mixture.

Use the following refractometer reading to complete practice problems 21.7 and 21.8.

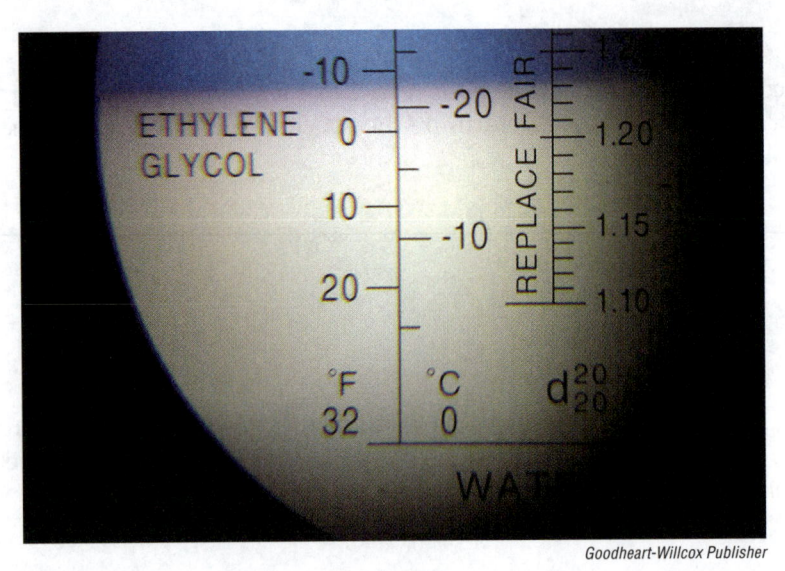

Goodheart-Willcox Publisher

21.7 A technician is using a refractometer to measure the concentration of ethylene-glycol. Use the refractometer shown to determine the freeze level in °F.

21.8 A technician is using a refractometer to measure the concentration of ethylene-glycol. Use the refractometer shown to determine the freeze level in °C.

# CASE STUDY 22

# Torque

## OBJECTIVES
*After studying this case study, you will be able to:*
- Identify the components of the formula for torque.
- Calculate torque values based on the formula.

## TECHNICAL TERM
torque

## MATH SKILLS
- Calculate values based on a formula.
- Analyze job skill problems related to the torque formula.

***

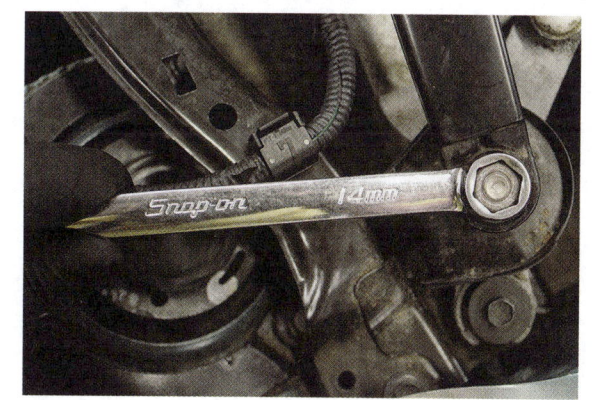

*Torque* is the measurement of rotational force. The simplest example of torque is placing a wrench on a bolt head and pulling on the wrench in order to rotate the bolt. If enough force is exerted on the wrench, the bolt will rotate. The rotation is measured as *torque*.

The formula for torque is:

$$\tau = \text{force} \times \text{length}$$

*Goodheart-Willcox Publisher*

The force value is the amount of force, typically indicated as pound or Newton, applied to a pivot arm, such as a wrench.

The length value is the length of the pivot arm, from the point of rotation to the point where the force is applied. This value is typically indicated as inches, feet, or meters.

**Example:** If a wrench is 2 feet long and 25 pounds of force are applied to the end of the wrench, calculate the amount of torque at the other end of the wrench.

$$2 \text{ ft} \times 25 \text{ lb} = 50 \text{ ft lb}$$

The torque is 50 foot-pounds.

The formula for torque can be rewritten if a different part of the equation is the unknown. For example, if the force value is the unknown, the formula can be rewritten as:

$$\text{force} = \frac{\tau}{\text{length}}$$

**Example:** The torque applied by the torque wrench is 50 ft lb. The length of the torque wrench is 2′. Calculate the amount of force needed to apply 50 ft lb.

$$50 \text{ ft lb} \times 2 \text{ ft} = 25 \text{ lb}$$

25 pounds of force is needed.

The formula for torque can also be rewritten if another, different part of the equation is the unknown. For example, if the length value is the unknown, the formula can be rewritten as:

$$length = \frac{\tau}{force}$$

**Example:** The torque applied by the torque wrench is 50 ft lb. The force applied to the torque wrench is 25 pounds. Calculate the length needed to apply 50 ft lb.

$$50 \text{ ft lb} \times 25 \text{ lb} = 2 \text{ ft}$$

2 feet of length is needed.

**Name** _____ **Date** _____ **Class** _____

## Torque Job Skill Practice Problems

22.1 A breaker bar with a socket is 0.6 meters (60 cm) long and 65 Newtons of force are applied to the end of the breaker bar. Calculate the amount of torque at the other end of the breaker bar.

22.2 A wrench is 9″ long and 30 pounds of force are applied to the end of the wrench. Calculate the amount of torque at the other end of the wrench.

22.3 A ratchet with a socket is 3′ long and 60 pounds of force are applied to the end of the ratchet. Calculate the amount of torque at the other end of the ratchet.

22.4 The torque needed to loosen a bolt is 130 Newton-meters. The length of a torque wrench is 0.8 meters (80 cm). Calculate the amount of force required to loosen this bolt.

22.5 The torque needed to loosen a bolt is 75 foot-pounds. The length of a torque wrench is 3 feet. Calculate the amount of force required to loosen this bolt.

22.6 The torque needed to loosen a bolt is 340 inch-pounds. The length of a torque wrench is 24″. Calculate the amount of force required to loosen this bolt. Round the answer to the nearest tenth pound.

22.7 The torque applied by the torque wrench is 135 ft lb. The force applied to the torque wrench is 45 pounds. Calculate the length needed to apply 135 ft lb.

22.8 The torque applied by the torque wrench is 200 N·m. The force applied to the torque wrench is 160 Newtons. Calculate the length needed to apply 200 N·m.

22.9 The torque applied by the torque wrench is 175 in lb. The force applied to the torque wrench is 25 pounds. Calculate the length needed to apply 175 in lb.

# CASE STUDY 23

# Tires and Wheels

## OBJECTIVES

*After studying this case study, you will be able to:*

- Identify tire and wheel measurement procedures.
- Analyze tire and wheel measurement tools.

## TECHNICAL TERM

lug spacing gauge

## MATH SKILL

- Perform an accurate reading of a measurement tool.

---

Tires and wheels are very common maintenance items and often require measurements for a variety of purposes. Tires are measured for tread depth and for inflation pressure. Wheels are measured to determine wheel lug spacing size and for wheel width. Specific tools are used for these measurements. Review the tool pictures below.

Lug Spacing Gauge

Tape Measure

*Goodheart-Willcox Publisher*

**156** Math for Automotive Technicians

Tread Depth Gauge

Tire Pressure Gauge

*Goodheart-Willcox Publisher*

The *lug spacing gauge* is designed to identify the exact size of lug nut spacing. This information is required when replacing stock wheels with custom wheels. The gauge is placed into the wheel holes or on the wheel studs and the scale indicates the measurement value.

Review the following examples.

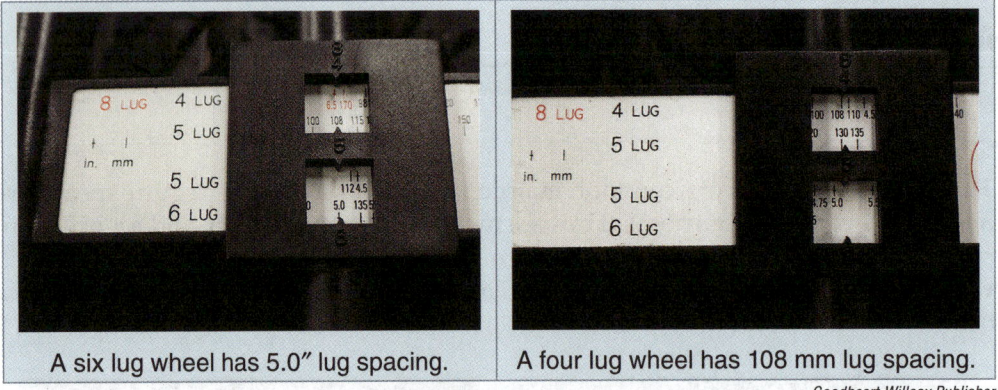

A six lug wheel has 5.0" lug spacing.

A four lug wheel has 108 mm lug spacing.

*Goodheart-Willcox Publisher*

A tape measure is used to measure the width of a wheel, from bead seat to bead seat. This measurement is required if wider or narrower wheels are being considered, for performance or aesthetic purposes. The tape measure is read to the closest 1/16".

Review the following examples.

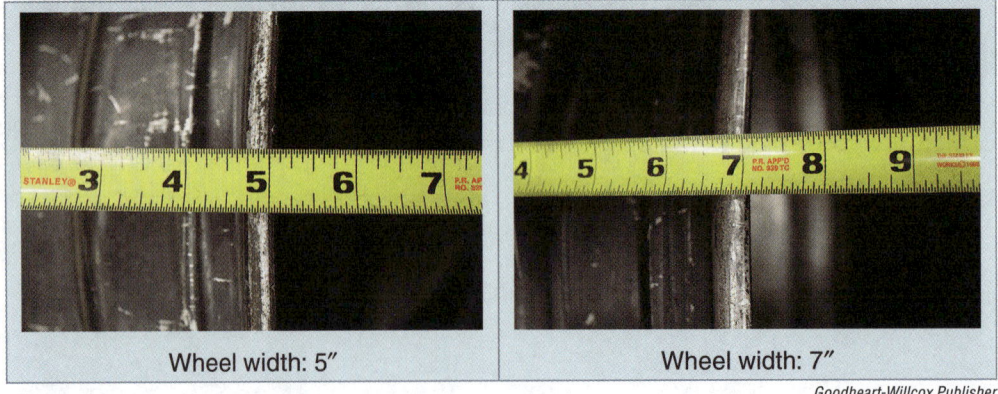

Wheel width: 5"

Wheel width: 7"

*Goodheart-Willcox Publisher*

A tire tread depth gauge is used to determine the exact measurement of the remaining tire tread. A tread depth gauge tip is pressed down into the tread section and then the scale is read. The gauge typically includes a metric scale and an inch scale.

Review the following examples.

| The inch tread depth gauge reads 10/32″. | The metric tread depth gauge reads 9 mm. |
|---|---|

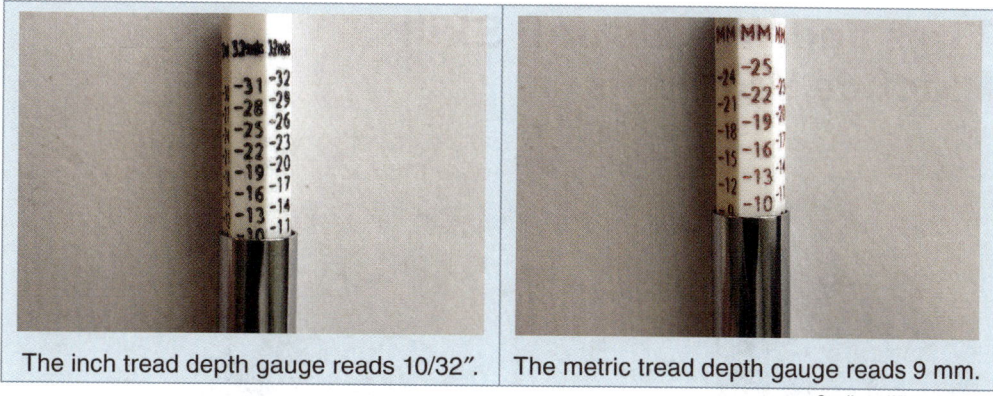

Goodheart-Willcox Publisher

A tire pressure gauge is used to determine the exact amount of air pressure inside the tire. A tire pressure gauge is pushed against a valve stem core with the cap removed, and the pressure inside the tire forces a slider inside the gauge out. The slider contains a scale that indicates the tire pressure value.

Review the following examples.

| The tire pressure gauge reads 29 psi. | The tire pressure gauge reads 31 psi. |
|---|---|

Goodheart-Willcox Publisher

## Tires and Wheels Job Skill Practice Problems

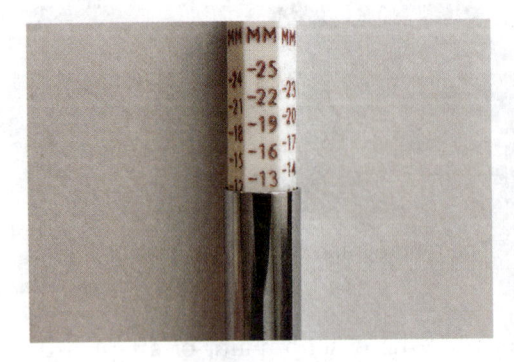

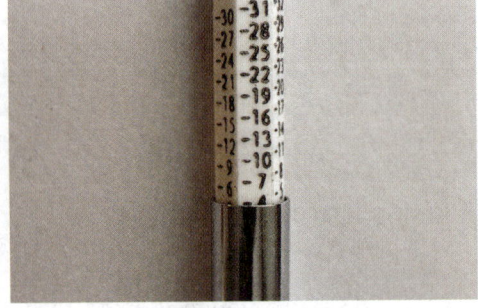

23.1 Tread depth: _____

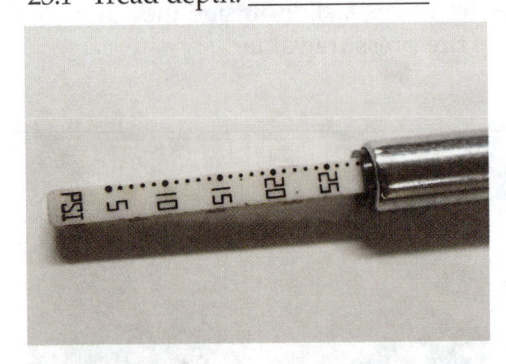

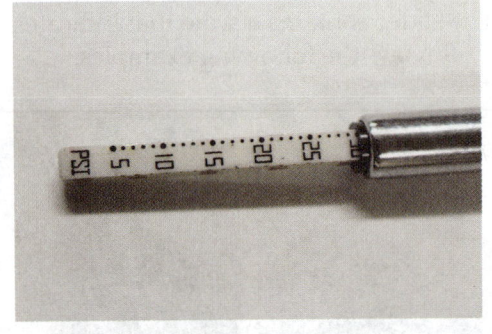

23.2 Tread depth: _____

23.3 Tire pressure: _____

23.4 Tire pressure: _____

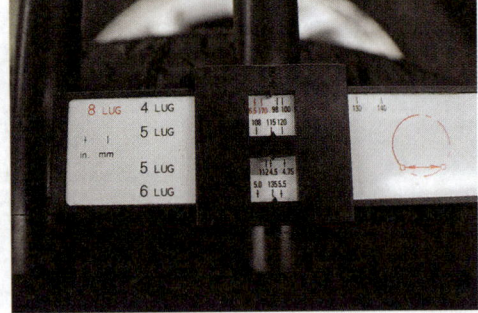

23.5 Wheel width: _____

23.6 5 lug metric lug spacing: _____

# CASE STUDY 24

# Engine Tune-Up

## OBJECTIVES

*After studying this case study, you will be able to:*
- Identify common tests performed as part of a tune-up check.
- Interpret and analyze measurements and specifications related to tune-ups.

## MATH SKILLS
- Calculate basic arithmetic operations.
- Solve job skill problems related to analyzing specifications.

At one time, an engine tune-up was an often-performed service item that required manually adjusting many mechanical engine control systems. This concept of a tune-up is now extinct, since carburetors have been replaced with port and direct injection, and distributors and points have been replaced with coil-on-plug, computer-controlled ignition systems. Although the engine control systems have evolved from mechanical controls to electronic controls, there are still a few tests that can be considered tune-up checks. These tests are fuel pressure testing, spark plug gap measurement, idle speed verification, and valve clearance measurement, if adjustable.

*Goodheart-Willcox Publisher*

Refer to the table on the next page for tune-up specifications to understand how to solve the example. *These are fictional specifications. Use manufacturer service information for specific vehicle applications. Keep in mind that manufacturers may not provide information for some specifications.*

## Engine Tune-Up Specifications

| Engine | Fuel Pressure Specification | Spark Plug Gap | Valve Clearance | Idle Speed |
|---|---|---|---|---|
| I4 1.6 L | 53–60 psi | 1.0–1.1 mm | Nonadjustable | 600±50 rpm |
| I4 2.4 L | 47–54 psi | 1.0 mm | intake: 0.21–0.25 mm exhaust: 0.25–0.29 mm | 700±50 rpm |
| I4 2.5 L | engine running: 55–58 psi | 1.25–1.35 mm | intake: 0.22–0.28 mm exhaust: 0.27–0.33 mm | 650±100 rpm |
| V6 3.6 L | 40–65 psi | 1.1 mm (0.043 in) | Nonadjustable | 640–800 rpm |
| V6 3.9 L | 56–62 psi (ignition on, engine off) | 1.02 mm (0.040 in) | 0.024–0.064 mm | No information provided |
| V8 6.2 L | 50–60 psi Does not decrease more than 5 psi in 1 minute | 1.02 mm (0.040 in) | Nonadjustable | No load, P/N 650±100 |

**Example:** A compact car with an I4, 2.4-liter engine is being tested as part of a tune-up service. The fuel pressure gauge reads 38 psi. Calculate how far below the minimum specification the fuel pressure gauge indicates.

The fuel pressure range is 47–54 psi.

47 psi – 38 psi = 9 psi

The fuel pressure is 9 psi below specification.

Name _____  Date _____  Class _____

# Engine Tune-Up Job Skill Practice Problems

Use the Engine Tune-Up Specifications table on the previous page to complete practice problems 24.1 through 24.8.

24.1 A midsize SUV with a V6, 3.9 L engine is being tested as part of a tune-up service. The cylinder 1 valve clearance is measured at 0.054 mm. Determine if this measurement is within specification.

24.2 A muscle car with a V8, 6.2 L engine is being tested as part of a tune-up service. The engine idle speed is measured using a scan tool. The scan tool reads 780 rpm with no engine load and the transmission in neutral. Calculate how far out of specification the idle speed is reading.

24.3 A compact car with an I4, 1.6 L engine is being tested as part of a tune-up service. The spark plug being inspected measures 1.3 mm. Determine if the gap is larger or smaller than specification.

24.4 A sedan with a V6, 3.6 L engine is being tested as part of a tune-up service. The fuel pressure measures at 46 psi and the engine idle speed measures around 605 rpm. Determine if either value is out of specification and, if applicable, calculate the adjustment needed to repair or correct the condition.

**Name** _____ **Date** _____ **Class** _____

24.5 A technician is measuring the valve clearance on cylinder 1 of an I4, 2.5 L engine. The exhaust valve clearance measures 0.31 mm and the intake valve clearance measures 0.30 mm. Calculate if either value is out of specification and calculate the adjustment needed to repair or correct the condition.

24.6 A technician is testing fuel pressure on a pickup truck with a V8, 6.2 L engine. The fuel pressure reads 58 psi at engine start-up and drops to 51 psi after one minute. Determine if this fuel pressure reading is within specification.

24.7 A technician is reviewing scan tool live data on a minivan equipped with a V6, 3.9 L engine. The PID (parameter ID) for idle speed indicates between 735 and 760 rpm. Determine if this idle speed is within specification.

24.8 A technician is measuring the valve clearance on cylinder 3 of an I4, 2.4 L engine. The exhaust valve clearance measures 0.24 mm and the intake valve clearance measures 0.19 mm. Calculate if either value is out of specification and calculate the adjustment needed to repair or correct the condition.

# UNIT 4
# Chassis

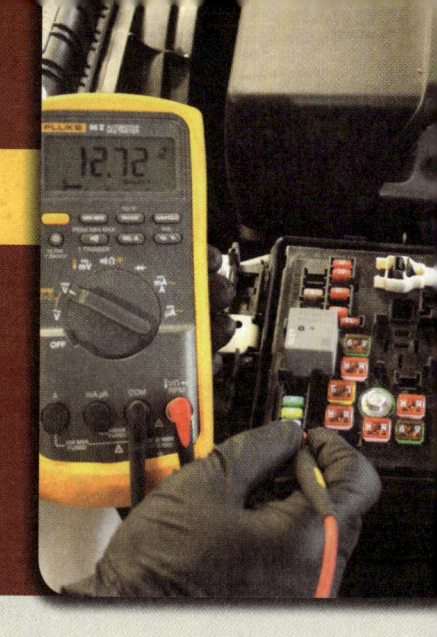

Case Study 25 **Unsprung Weight—Addition**
Case Study 26 **Service Intervals—Subtraction**
Case Study 27 **Tire Size Aspect Ratio—Multiplication**
Case Study 28 **Stopping Distance Factors—Division**
Case Study 29 **Alignment Angles—Decimal Arithmetic**
Case Study 30 **Analyzing Tires—Greater Than and Less Than**
Case Study 31 **Ride Height Measurements—Fractions**
Case Study 32 **Linear Measurement—Conversion**
Case Study 33 **Brake Fluid Testing—Graphs and Tables**
Case Study 34 **Tire Diameter—Formulas**
Case Study 35 **Disc Brake Micrometer—Measurement**
Case Study 36 **Brake System—Analyzing Specifications**

## CAREER PROFILE

As a sales and service technician, Kirk Tobel is responsible for working with customers to help service and maintain the tires, chassis components, and electrical systems of their vehicles. In addition to new tires, this regional chain store services brakes, batteries, steering and suspension systems, and alignments, and fits custom tire and wheel packages.

Kirk started his automotive career in high school, in his hometown of Enumclaw, Washington. In addition to taking auto shop classes in high school, Kirk worked in the service garage of a local gas station. His passion for cars and his strong interest in how things work has led him to "a great career in the automotive industry." On the job, Kirk uses math every day to measure brake rotors, drums, pads, and shoes. In addition to brakes, math is used to measure tires for wear and to calculate custom tire and wheel packages.

As a leader in the shop, Kirk often mentors entry-level technicians. "Being an organized worker and having strong communication skills are very important for new technicians," Kirk explained. As a mentor, Kirk believes that a strong foundation of basic math skills and the aptitude for logical thinking skills are important to becoming a successful technician in the automotive service industry.

*Goodheart-Willcox Publisher*

Kirk Tobel—Sales and Service Technician, Les Schwab Tire Centers.

# CASE STUDY 25

# Unsprung Weight

## OBJECTIVES

*After studying this case study, you will be able to:*
- Identify parts considered unsprung weight and parts considered sprung weight.
- Calculate the total unsprung weight value.

## TECHNICAL TERMS

suspension springs     unsprung weight

## MATH SKILL
- Addition of whole numbers.

The *suspension springs*, whether they are coil, leaf, torsion bar, or air springs, support the weight of most of the vehicle. There are a few parts that are not supported by the suspension springs, and those parts are considered *unsprung weight*. These parts are *below* the springs, parts like the wheels, tires, hubs, lower control arms, knuckles, shock absorbers, and axles. The sprung weight parts are the rest of the vehicle that is supported by the springs, such as the engine, body, fuel tank, and interior.

*Goodheart-Willcox Publisher*

The greater the weight of the unsprung weight parts, the more of an effect they have on the handling characteristics of the suspension system. The most common changes to unsprung weight are changing the tires and wheels to heavier or lighter replacements.

**Example:** Using the parts table, calculate the total weight of the unsprung weight parts on the 2015 sports car. Some of the parts listed are not included in the unsprung weight, so do not include them in the addition problem.

| 2015 Sports Car | |
|---|---|
| Parts | Weight |
| Tires | 98 pounds |
| Wheels | 85 pounds |
| Brakes (front) | 18 pounds |
| Brakes (rear) | 13 pounds |
| Shock Absorbers | 6 pounds |
| Fuel Tank (full) | 88 pounds |
| Rear Axle | 170 pounds |
| Control Arms | 12 pounds |

98 lb + 85 lb + 18 lb + 13 lb + 6 lb + 170 lb + 12 lb = 402 lb

Unsprung weight = 402 lb

# Unsprung Weight
## Job Skill Practice Problems

25.1 Calculate the total weight of the unsprung weight parts on the 2014 midsize sedan. Some of the parts listed are not included in the unsprung weight, so do not include them in the addition problem.

| 2014 Midsize Sedan ||
| --- | --- |
| Parts | Weight |
| Tires | 82 pounds |
| Wheels | 79 pounds |
| Brakes (front) | 17 pounds |
| Brakes (rear) | 10 pounds |
| Struts | 6 pounds |
| Radiator | 9 pounds |
| Spare Tire | 17 pounds |
| Control Arms | 12 pounds |

25.2 Calculate the total weight of the unsprung weight parts on the 2017 sport-utility vehicle. Some of the parts listed are not included in the unsprung weight, so do not include them in the addition problem.

| 2017 Sport-Utility Vehicle ||
| --- | --- |
| Parts | Weight |
| Tires | 38 kg |
| Wheels | 36 kg |
| Brakes (front) | 8 kg |
| Brakes (rear) | 5 kg |
| Struts | 3 kg |
| Front Axle | 68 kg |
| Rear Axle | 71 kg |
| Spare Tire | 7 kg |

Name _____ Date _____ Class _____

25.3 Calculate the total weight of the unsprung weight parts on the 2013 compact car. Some of the parts listed are not included in the unsprung weight, so do not include them in the addition problem.

| 2013 Compact Car ||
|---|---|
| Parts | Weight |
| Tires | 64 pounds |
| Wheels | 77 pounds |
| Brakes (front) | 11 pounds |
| Brakes (rear) | 8 pounds |
| Struts | 6 pounds |
| Engine | 550 pounds |
| Hubs/Wheel Bearing | 19 pounds |
| Control Arms | 12 pounds |

25.4 Calculate the total weight of the unsprung weight parts on the 2016 midsize luxury car. Some of the parts listed are not included in the unsprung weight, so do not include them in the addition problem.

| 2016 Midsize Luxury Car ||
|---|---|
| Parts | Weight |
| Tires | 39 kg |
| Wheels | 31 kg |
| Brakes (front) | 9 kg |
| Brakes (rear) | 6 kg |
| Struts | 5 kg |
| Control Arms | 21 kg |
| Rear Suspension Arms | 19 kg |
| Wheel Bearings | 7 kg |

**Name** _____  **Date** _____  **Class** _____

25.5 Calculate the total weight of the unsprung weight parts on the 2015 hybrid compact car. Some of the parts listed are not included in the unsprung weight, so do not include them in the addition problem.

| 2015 Hybrid Compact Car ||
| Parts | Weight |
|---|---|
| Tires | 41 kg |
| Wheels | 32 kg |
| Brakes (front) | 8 kg |
| Brakes (rear) | 5 kg |
| Struts | 7 kg |
| Control Arms | 23 kg |
| Rear Suspension Arms | 18 kg |
| Wheel Bearings | 7 kg |
| Fuel Tank (full) | 40 kg |

# CASE STUDY 26

# Service Intervals

## OBJECTIVES
*After studying this case study, you will be able to:*
- Determine the correct service interval and service item.
- Calculate the mileage until the next service interval.

## MATH SKILL
- Subtraction of whole numbers.

Vehicle manufacturers have developed a service schedule for routine maintenance. This service information is located on a service table, and is based on mileage. Use the fictional service information table to determine how many miles until the next service item is required.

*Goodheart-Willcox Publisher*

| Service Interval Table (miles) | | | | | | | |
|---|---|---|---|---|---|---|---|
| | 15,000 | 30,000 | 45,000 | 60,000 | 75,000 | 90,000 | 105,000 |
| **Inspect Brakes** | x | | x | | x | | x |
| **Inspect Suspension** | x | | x | | x | | x |
| **Rotate Tires** | x | x | x | x | x | x | x |
| **Inspect Drive Belt** | x | x | x | x | x | x | x |
| **Inspect Power Steering Fluid** | | | | x | | | |
| **Replace Power Steering Fluid** | | | | | | x | |
| **Replace Differential Fluid** | | | x | | | x | |
| **Replace Transfer Case Fluid** | | | x | | | x | |
| **Replace Transmission Fluid (M)** | | | x | | | x | |

**Example:** Vehicle A has 43,987 miles on the odometer. Calculate the number of miles until the differential fluid needs to be replaced.

45,000 miles – 43,987 miles = 1,013 miles

1,013 miles

# Service Intervals Job Skill Practice Problems

Use the Service Interval Table to complete practice problems 26.1 through 26.8.

26.1 Vehicle B has 62,989 miles on the odometer. Calculate the number of miles until the power steering fluid needs to be replaced.

26.2 Vehicle C has 22,459 miles on the odometer. Calculate the number of miles until the next tire rotation.

26.3 Vehicle D has 97,009 miles on the odometer. Calculate the number of miles until the next brake inspection.

26.4 Vehicle E has 72,312 miles on the odometer. Calculate the number of miles until the next transfer case fluid service.

**Name** _____  **Date** _____  **Class** _____

26.5 Vehicle F has 12,459 miles on the odometer. Calculate the number of miles until the suspension needs to be inspected.

26.6 Vehicle G has 52,775 miles on the odometer. Calculate the number of miles until the drive belt needs to be inspected.

26.7 Vehicle H has 102,449 miles on the odometer. Calculate the number of miles until the next tire rotation.

26.8 Vehicle J has 6,779 miles on the odometer. Calculate the number of miles until the power steering fluid needs to be inspected.

# CASE STUDY 27

# Tire Size Aspect Ratio

## OBJECTIVES
*After studying this case study, you will be able to:*
- Identify the aspect ratio of the tire size.
- Calculate the height of the tire using the aspect ratio.

## TECHNICAL TERM
aspect ratio

## MATH SKILL
- Multiplication of whole numbers and decimal numbers.

The *aspect ratio* indicates the height of the tire sidewall based on a percentage of the tire width. The tire width and aspect ratio are indicated in the tire size information. See the table for tire size information.

*Goodheart-Willcox Publisher*

| P215/65R15 |||||
|---|---|---|---|---|
| P | 215 mm | /65% | R | 15" |
| Passenger | Width | Aspect Ratio | Radial | Wheel Diameter |

**Example:** To calculate the height of the tire sidewall of a P215/65R15 tire, multiply the tire width (215 mm) by the aspect ratio (65). When calculating a percentage, 65% is equal to 0.65.

$$215 \text{ mm} \times 0.65 \text{ mm} = 139.75 \text{ mm}$$

The sidewall height is 139.75 mm.

Name _____  Date _____  Class _____

# Tire Size Aspect Ratio Job Skill Practice Problems

27.1  Calculate the height of the tire sidewall of a 225/45R17 tire.




27.2  Calculate the height of the tire sidewall of a 235/65R18 tire.




27.3  Calculate the height of the tire sidewall of a 205/65R14 tire.




27.4  Calculate the height of the tire sidewall of a 245/55R16 tire.




27.5  Calculate the height of the tire sidewall of a 295/45R18 tire.

**Name** _____  **Date** _____  **Class** _____

27.6  Calculate the height of the tire sidewall of a 265/75R15 tire.




27.7  Calculate the height of the tire sidewall of a 235/55R15 tire.




27.8  Calculate the height of the tire sidewall of a 195/65R14 tire.




27.9  Calculate the height of the tire sidewall of a 285/75R16 tire.




27.10  Calculate the height of the tire sidewall of a 235/55R17 tire.

# CASE STUDY 28

# Stopping Distance Factors

## OBJECTIVES

*After studying this case study, you will be able to:*
- Identify factors affecting stopping distance.
- Determine how worn tires and brake pads affect stopping distance.

## MATH SKILL
- Division of whole numbers.

There are a variety of factors that affect stopping distance. These factors include tire tread wear, brake pad wear, and shock or strut wear. As these critical chassis components wear, they increase stopping distance and can decrease handling capabilities in a panic situation. As a service technician, recognizing these factors can help you make decisions to ensure a customer's car is safe to drive in all conditions.

Goodheart-Willcox Publisher

**Example:** A car with 11/32" tire tread depth is able to stop from 60 mph in 189 feet in 2 seconds. The same vehicle with consistent road conditions and speed, but with 3/32" tire tread depth, is able to stop from 60 mph in 386 feet in 3 seconds. Calculate the stopping distance rates in feet per second. Round to the nearest tenth.

$$189 \text{ feet} \div 2 \text{ seconds} = 94.5 \text{ ft/s}$$
$$386 \text{ feet} \div 3 \text{ seconds} = 128.7 \text{ ft/s}$$

The lower stopping rate (94.5 ft/s) indicates a better ability to stop.

Name _____ Date _____ Class _____

## Stopping Distance Factors
## Job Skill Practice Problems

In the following practice problems, round to the nearest tenth when necessary.

28.1 A car with 11 mm brake pads is able to stop from 70 mph in 229′ in 3 seconds. The same vehicle with consistent road conditions and speed, but with 2 mm brake pads, is able to stop from 70 mph in 487′ in 5 seconds. Calculate the stopping distance rates in feet per second.

28.2 A light truck with new shock absorbers is able to stop from 65 mph in 365′ in 3 seconds. The same vehicle with consistent road conditions and speed, but with worn shock absorbers, is able to stop from 65 mph in 412′ in 4 seconds. Calculate the stopping distance rates in feet per second.

28.3 A light truck pulling a loaded trailer with 12/32″ tire tread depth is able to stop from 70 mph in 360′ in 3 seconds. The same vehicle with consistent road conditions and speed, but with 2/32″ tire tread depth, is able to stop from 70 mph in 568′ in 6 seconds. Calculate the stopping distance rates in feet per second.

Name _____ Date _____ Class _____

28.4 A sport-utility vehicle with 12 mm brake pads is able to stop from 60 mph in 305′ in 3 seconds. The same vehicle with consistent road conditions and speed, but with 2 mm brake pads, is able to stop from 60 mph in 537′ in 6 seconds. Calculate the stopping distance rates in feet per second.

28.5 A light truck with new shock absorbers is able to stop from 65 mph in 327′ in 3 seconds. The same vehicle with consistent road conditions and speed, but with worn shock absorbers, is able to stop from 65 mph in 404′ in 4 seconds. Calculate the stopping distance rates in feet per second.

28.6 A sports car with new tires is able to stop from 70 mph in 309′ in 2 seconds. The same vehicle with consistent road conditions and speed, but with worn tires, is able to stop from 70 mph in 408′ in 5 seconds. Calculate the stopping distance rates in feet per second.

# CASE STUDY 29

# Alignment Angles

## OBJECTIVES

*After studying this case study, you will be able to:*
- Identify alignment angle measurements for common alignment angles.
- Calculate the alignment angle ranges.
- Calculate cross-camber and cross-caster.

## TECHNICAL TERMS

cross-camber   cross-caster

## MATH SKILLS

- Addition and subtraction of decimal numbers.
- Compare decimal numbers to determine greater than and less than.

The most commonly measured and adjusted alignment angles include camber, caster, and toe. An alignment is performed using an alignment machine and a computerized program to assist with adjustments. Most alignment angle specifications are written as a plus or minus range specification.

Camber specification: 1.2°±0.3°

This specification indicates that the perfect value is 1.2° but the range of acceptable values is from 0.9° to 1.5°.

*Goodheart-Willcox Publisher*

The terms *cross-camber* and *cross-caster* refer to the difference between the camber angle or caster angle from one side to another.
- If the cross value is zero, the two measurements are identical and there will not be an effect on handling characteristics.
- If the cross value is out of specification, there will be an effect on handling characteristics.

The table below shows measurements of a vehicle's camber and caster angles.

| Alignment Measurements | | |
|---|---|---|
| Front Wheels | Left | Right |
| Camber | 1.3° | 0.5° |
| Caster | 5.4° | 5.4° |

To find the cross-camber, find the difference between the left and right camber angles.

$$1.3° - 0.5° = 0.8°$$
$$\text{Cross-camber} = 0.8°$$

To find the cross-caster, find the difference between the left and right caster angles.

$$5.4° - 5.4° = 0°$$
$$\text{Cross-caster} = 0°$$

**Example:** Determine the minimum and maximum values of the alignment angle shown.

Camber: 0.5°±0.3°

$$0.5° + 0.3° = 0.8° \text{ maximum}$$
$$0.5° - 0.3° = 0.2° \text{ minimum}$$

**Example:** Use the alignment angle range to determine if the current measurement is within specification or out of specification.

Caster specification: 5.10°±0.50°
Current measurement: 4.52°

$$5.10° - 0.50° = 4.60°$$
$$4.60° > 4.52°$$

The measurement is out of specification.

**Example:** Calculate the cross-caster value based on the left and right caster values. Determine if the cross-caster is within specification.

Left caster value: 4.3°
Right caster value: 3.9°
Specification: 0.0°±0.1°

$$4.3° - 3.9° = 0.4°$$
$$0.4° > 0.1°$$

The cross-caster is out of specification.

# Alignment Angles Job Skill Practice Problems

29.1 Determine the minimum and maximum values of the camber angle 1.2°±0.3°.

29.2 Determine the minimum and maximum values of the caster angle 4.5°±0.6°.

29.3 Determine the minimum and maximum values of the camber angle 0.8°±0.4°.

29.4 Determine the minimum and maximum values of the caster angle 5.2°±0.5°.

29.5 Determine if 3.87° of caster is within the specification range of 4.25°±0.75°.

29.6 Determine if 1.02° of camber is within the specification range of 0.25°±0.75°.

29.7 Determine if 6.12° of caster is within the specification range of 5.75°±0.25°.

**Name** _____ **Date** _____ **Class** _____

29.8 Determine if 0.89° of camber is within the specification range of 0.25°±0.75°.

29.9 Calculate the cross-camber value and determine if the cross-camber is within specification.
    Left camber value: 1.2°
    Right camber value: 0.9°
    Specification: 0.0°±0.2°

29.10 Calculate the cross-camber value and determine if the cross-camber is within specification.
    Left camber value: 0.3°
    Right camber value: 0.2°
    Specification: 0.0°±0.2°

29.11 Calculate the cross-caster value and determine if the cross-caster is within specification.
    Left camber value: 3.2°
    Right camber value: 3.9°
    Specification: 0.0°±0.5°

29.12 Calculate the cross-caster value and determine if the cross-caster is within specification.
    Left camber value: 7.1°
    Right camber value: 6.9°
    Specification: 0.0°±0.3°

# CASE STUDY 30

# Analyzing Tires

## OBJECTIVES
*After studying this case study, you will be able to:*
- Identify and compare UTQG tire ratings.
- Compare UTQG tire ratings to identify higher and lower quality tires.

## TECHNICAL TERM
Uniform Tire Quality Grading (UTQG) system

## MATH SKILLS
- Identify greater than and less than values.
- Analyze greater than and less than values.

The **Uniform Tire Quality Grading (UTQG) system** rates tires on temperature, treadwear, and traction. These ratings can be used to identify tire quality and help the tire consumer compare the differences between two otherwise similar tires. The UTQG ratings are part of the tire sidewall information. The temperature rating indicates how well a tire handles heat at high speeds. The scale from best to worst is A, B, and C. The traction rating indicates how well the tire stops on wet pavement. The scale from best to worst is AA, A, B, and C. The treadwear rating indicates the durability of the tire's tread. A higher number means longer tread life.

Review the table describing the UTQG ratings and the UTQG ranges for each category. Refer to this table as a reference when answering the job skill problems.

*Goodheart-Willcox Publisher*

| UTQG Ratings |||
|---|---|---|
| Temperature | Traction | Treadwear |
| A | AA | 800 |
| B | A | 600 |
| C | B | 400 |
|   | C | 200 |

**Example:** A customer has a budget of $350 for a set of new tires, and wants to purchase tires with the highest overall UTQG rating. Compare the four tires in the table to determine the best tire option within the customer's budget.

| Tire | Size | Price | Temperature | Traction | Treadwear |
|---|---|---|---|---|---|
| Tire A | P195/65R14 | $65/tire | B | B | 430 |
| Tire B | P195/65R14 | $89/tire | B | AA | 600 |
| Tire C | P195/65R14 | $78/tire | C | B | 500 |
| Tire D | P195/65R14 | $81/tire | A | A | 500 |

Tire B is the only tire not within the budget: $89 × 4 = $356.

$356 > $350

Tire D has the highest temperature and traction ratings. A is better than B or C.

Tire D and Tire C have equal treadwear ratings.

Tire D has the best overall UTQG rating and is within the budget at $324.

**Name** _____  **Date** _____  **Class** _____

## Analyzing Tires Job Skill Practice Problems

A customer has a budget of $400 for a set of four new tires, and wants to purchase tires with the highest overall UTQG rating. Compare the five tires in the table to answer the customer's questions about the tires in practice problems 30.1 through 30.5.

| Tire | Size | Price | Temperature | Traction | Treadwear |
|------|------|-------|-------------|----------|-----------|
| Tire A | P265/45R17 | $85/tire | B | B | 400 |
| Tire B | P265/45R17 | $89/tire | B | AA | 430 |
| Tire C | P265/45R17 | $99/tire | C | A | 520 |
| Tire D | P265/45R17 | $95/tire | A | B | 500 |
| Tire E | P265/45R17 | $103/tire | A | A | 650 |

30.1 Which tires are within the budget?

30.2 Which tire has the best treadwear rating?

30.3 Which tire has a B or an A temperature rating and the highest traction rating?

30.4 Which tires have a treadwear rating of < 490?

30.5 Which tire is within budget and has the highest traction rating?

Name _____ Date _____ Class _____

A customer has a budget of $350 for a set of four new tires, and wants to purchase tires with the highest overall UTQG rating. Compare the five tires in the table to answer the customer's questions about the tires in practice problems 30.6 through 30.10.

| Tire | Size | Price | Temperature | Traction | Treadwear |
|---|---|---|---|---|---|
| Tire A | P205/75R15 | $59/tire | B | B | 380 |
| Tire B | P205/75R15 | $69/tire | B | AA | 400 |
| Tire C | P205/75R15 | $75/tire | B | A | 650 |
| Tire D | P205/75R15 | $65/tire | A | B | 550 |
| Tire E | P205/75R15 | $73/tire | C | A | 550 |

30.6 Which tires are > $66?

30.7 Which tires have a treadwear rating of > 500?

30.8 Which tires have a B or an A temperature rating and an A or AA traction rating?

30.9 Which tire has a higher treadwear rating, tire C or tire E?

30.10 If traction is most important to the customer, which tire should be recommended?

**Name** _____  **Date** _____  **Class** _____

A customer has a budget of $900 for a set of new rear tires, and wants to purchase tires with the highest overall UTQG rating. Compare the five tires in the table to answer the customer's questions about the tires in practice problems 30.11 through 30.15.

| Tire | Size | Price | Temperature | Traction | Treadwear |
|---|---|---|---|---|---|
| Tire A | 325/30ZR19 | $415/tire | A | AA | 320 |
| Tire B | 325/30ZR19 | $270/tire | A | AA | 300 |
| Tire C | 325/30ZR19 | $431/tire | A | AA | 340 |
| Tire D | 325/30ZR19 | $418/tire | A | AA | 220 |
| Tire E | 325/30ZR19 | $578/tire | A | AA | 220 |

30.11 Which tire has a better treadwear rating, Tire B or Tire D?

30.12 Which tires are within the $900 budget?

30.13 Which tires cost at least $800 total and have a treadwear rating of > 290?

30.14 Which tires have a total price of < $832?

30.15 Which tire is within budget and has the highest overall UTQG rating?

# CASE STUDY 31

# Ride Height Measurements

## OBJECTIVES

*After studying this case study, you will be able to:*
- Identify ride height measurement values.
- Compare ride height measurements between left and right sides of the vehicle.
- Compare ride height measurements to manufacturer specifications.

## TECHNICAL TERM

ride height

## MATH SKILLS

- Add and subtract common tape measure fractions.
- Compare tape measure fractions to specifications.

The *ride height* is the position of the vehicle body relative to the wheel and compared to the ground. Ride height typically determines the amount of body to ground clearance and fender clearance to the tire. Often a vehicle ride height can be modified to lower the vehicle closer to the ground for appearance or raise the vehicle to accommodate larger tires.

A common procedure for measuring ride height is to measure from the top of the wheel-well arc on the fender to the ground. This measurement should be almost the same on both sides, but may not be the same front to back. A measurement of greater than 1/4" from side to side indicates there may be an issue with the suspension.

*Goodheart-Willcox Publisher*

**Example:** A technician measures the ride height of a 2001 midsize sedan and records the measurements as shown:

Left front: 31 5/8"            Left rear: 33 5/16"
Right front: 31 3/8"           Right rear: 33 5/8"

Determine the side-to-side variance of these ride height measurements.

Front:   31 5/8" − 31 3/8" = 2/8" = 1/4"
Rear:    33 5/16" − 33 5/8" = 33 5/16" − 33 10/16" = −5/16"

The front ride height difference is 1/4", the maximum allowable variance.

The rear ride height difference is 5/16", slightly above the maximum allowable variance of 1/4".

Name _____  Date _____  Class _____

# Ride Height Measurements
# Job Skill Practice Problems

31.1  A technician measures the ride height of a 2009 4X4 pickup truck and records the measurements as shown:
   Left front: 38 5/8"
   Right front: 38 1/4"
   Left rear: 39 1/8"
   Right rear: 39 1/4"
Determine the side-to-side variance of these ride height measurements.

31.2  A technician measures the ride height of a 2013 large sport-utility vehicle and records the measurements as shown:
   Left front: 35 5/8"
   Right front: 36 1/8"
   Left rear: 37 3/8"
   Right rear: 37 1/4"
Determine the side-to-side variance of these ride height measurements.

31.3  A technician measures the ride height of a 2011 minivan and records the measurements as shown:
   Left front: 32 13/16"
   Right front: 32 7/8"
   Left rear: 32 7/8"
   Right rear: 33 1/16"
Determine the side-to-side variance of these ride height measurements.

Name _____ Date _____ Class _____

31.4 A set of lowering springs is being installed on a 2009 compact sedan. The lowering springs are designed to lower the front ride height 2 1/2" and the rear ride height 2 3/4". Calculate the new ride height if the current ride height measures as shown:
   Left front: 30 5/16"
   Right front: 30 5/8"
   Left rear: 31 7/8"
   Right rear: 31 11/16"

31.5 A suspension lift kit is being installed on a 2003 full-size pickup truck to accommodate larger tires and wheels. The lift kit is designed to raise the front ride height 4 7/8" and the rear ride height 5 1/8". Calculate the new ride height if the current ride height measures as shown:
   Left front: 37 5/8"
   Right front: 37 5/8"
   Left rear: 38 1/8"
   Right rear: 38 3/16"

31.6 A 1972 pickup truck is equipped with custom air spring suspension. When the air springs are fully inflated and raised up, the front ride height is 33 1/2" and the rear ride height is 35 1/8". When the air springs are fully deflated and the truck is as low as possible, the front ride height is 26 3/8" and the rear ride height is 28 5/8". Calculate the range of travel for the front and rear springs.

# CASE STUDY 32

# Linear Measurement

## OBJECTIVES

*After studying this case study, you will be able to:*
- Convert disc brake measurements between standard and metric.
- Convert drum brake measurements between standard and metric.

## MATH SKILLS
- Apply conversion factors to linear measurements.
- Multiplication of whole and decimal numbers.

Measuring disc and drum brakes is critical to determining whether the disc or drum can be machined or should be replaced. When measuring brake parts, it is possible that the measurement tool and the specification might be in different measurement scales (standard or metric). To resolve this and calculate the measurement in another scale, a conversion factor is required. Use the table below to determine the conversion factors required for linear brake measurement conversions.

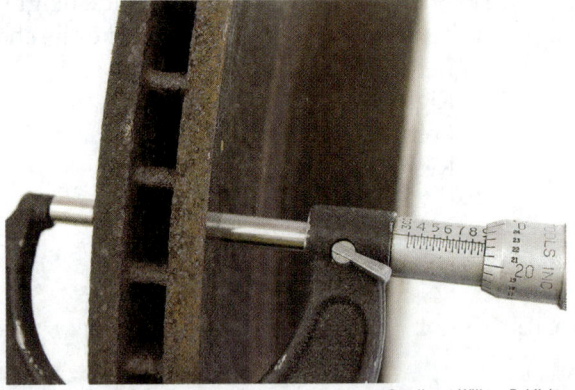

*Goodheart-Willcox Publisher*

| Standard | | Metric |
|---|---|---|
| 1" | = | 25.4 mm |
| 1" | = | 2.54 cm |
| 1' | = | 304.8 mm |
| 1' | = | 30.48 cm |
| 3.28' | = | 1 meter |
| 0.393" | = | 1 cm |
| 0.0393" | = | 1 mm |

**Example:** A brake disc is measured to be 1.050". The discard specification is given in millimeters. The conversion factor for inches to millimeters is 1" = 25.4 mm. Determine the thickness of the brake disc in millimeters.

$$1.050 \times 25.4 = 26.67$$

So, 1.050" is equal to 26.67 millimeters.

**Example:** A brake drum is measured to be 280.01 mm in diameter. The maximum diameter is given in inches. The conversion factor for inches to millimeters is 25.4 mm = 1″.

$$280.01 \div 25.4 = 11.024$$
So, 280.01 millimeters is equal to 11.024″.

Name _____ Date _____ Class _____

## Linear Measurement Job Skill Practice Problems

Use the conversion table to complete practice problems 32.1 through 32.12.

32.1  A brake disc is measured to be 0.987″. Determine the thickness of this brake disc in millimeters.

32.2  A brake disc is measured to be 25.46 mm. Determine the thickness of this brake disc in inches.

32.3  A brake disc is measured to be 1.037″. Determine the thickness of this brake disc in millimeters.

32.4  A brake disc is measured to be 22.67 mm. Determine the thickness of this brake disc in inches.

32.5  A brake disc is measured to be 0.879″. Determine the thickness of this brake disc in millimeters.

**Name** _____ **Date** _____ **Class** _____

32.6 A brake disc is measured to be 23.06 mm. Determine the thickness of this brake disc in inches.

32.7 A brake drum is measured to be 10.977″. Determine the thickness of this brake drum in millimeters.

32.8 A brake drum is measured to be 223.89 mm. Determine the thickness of this brake drum in inches.

32.9 A brake drum is measured to be 10.545″. Determine the thickness of this brake drum in millimeters.

32.10 A brake drum is measured to be 290.16 mm. Determine the thickness of this brake drum in inches.

32.11 A brake drum is measured to be 10.379″. Determine the thickness of this brake drum in millimeters.

32.12 A brake drum is measured to be 289.56 mm. Determine the thickness of this brake drum in inches.

# CASE STUDY 33

# Brake Fluid Testing

## OBJECTIVES

*After studying this case study, you will be able to:*
- Identify brake fluid testing results.
- Compare the brake fluid test results of multiple vehicles.

## MATH SKILLS

- Interpret data from a table and from a graph.
- Plot data on a graph.

Brake fluid has a service life and must be tested to determine if the fluid needs to be flushed and replaced. Simply looking at the color of the brake fluid is not a sufficient test procedure. Brake fluid must be tested for copper content and moisture content caused by contamination and breakdown of brake fluid additives and corrosion inhibitors.

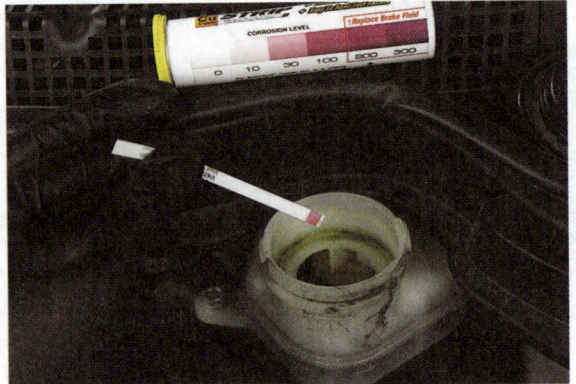

*Goodheart-Willcox Publisher*

**Example:** Technician A is responsible for performing a maintenance inspection on all of the used vehicles purchased for resale in the used vehicle department. The inspection includes testing brake fluid to determine the condition of the brake fluid and if a brake fluid flush is required before the vehicle can be resold. Use the table and graph to answer the questions.

|       | Moisture Test | Copper Test |
|-------|---------------|-------------|
| Car 1 | 2%            | 60 ppm      |
| Car 2 | 2%            | 55 ppm      |
| Car 3 | > 4%          | 230 ppm     |
| Car 4 | > 4%          | 340 ppm     |
| Car 5 | 1%            | 30 ppm      |
| Car 6 | 1%            | 65 ppm      |
| Car 7 | 2%            | 55 ppm      |
| Car 8 | 2%            | 85 ppm      |

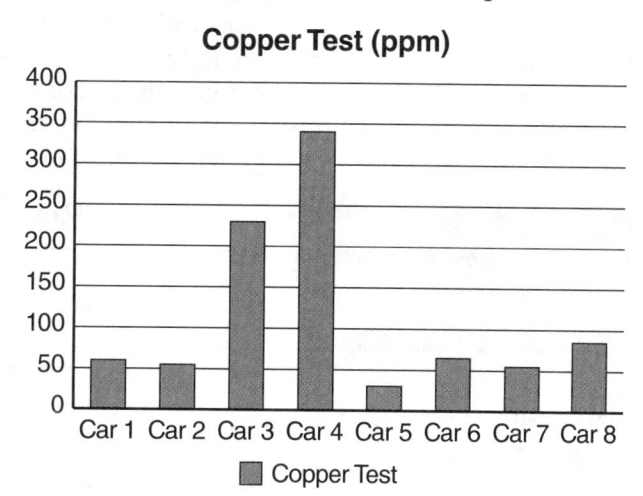

How many cars are above 50 ppm?

> 7 cars are above 50 ppm.

Which car has the lowest copper content?

> Car 5 has the lowest copper content at 30 ppm.

How many cars are above 200 ppm?

> 2 cars are above 200 ppm.

Name _____ Date _____ Class _____

## Brake Fluid Testing Job Skill Practice Problems

Technician B is responsible for performing a maintenance inspection on all of the used vehicles purchased for resale in the used vehicle department. The inspection includes testing brake fluid to determine the condition of the brake fluid, and to determine if a brake fluid flush is required before the vehicle can be resold. Use the following table and graph to complete practice problems 33.1 through 33.4.

|       | Copper Test | Moisture Test |
|-------|-------------|---------------|
| Car 1 | 30 ppm      | 1%            |
| Car 2 | 40 ppm      | 2%            |
| Car 3 | 55 ppm      | 1%            |
| Car 4 | 120 ppm     | 1%            |
| Car 5 | 35 ppm      | 1%            |
| Car 6 | 230 ppm     | 4%            |
| Car 7 | 250 ppm     | 3%            |
| Car 8 | 40 ppm      | 4%            |

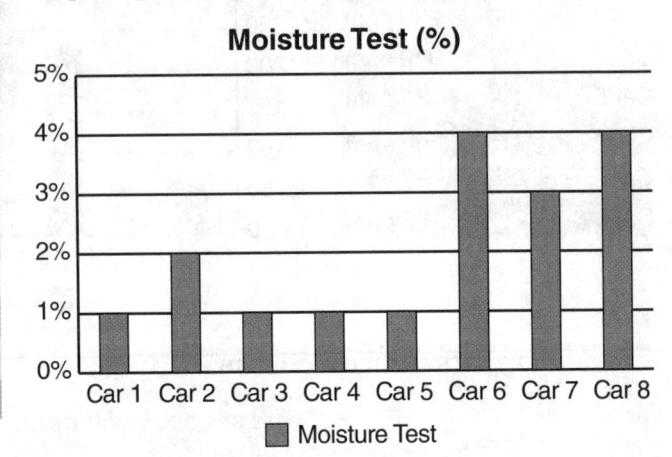

33.1 If brake fluid with 3% or greater moisture is recommended for service, how many vehicles require a brake fluid flush?

33.2 How many vehicles tested at 1% moisture?

33.3 Which vehicles have greater than 100 ppm of copper content in the brake fluid?

33.4 Which vehicles have 1% moisture and less than 40 ppm of copper?

Name _____ Date _____ Class _____

Technician C is responsible for performing a maintenance inspection on all of the municipal service vehicles managed by the public works department. The inspection includes testing the condition of the brake fluid to determine if a brake fluid flush is required before the vehicle can return to service. Use the following table and graph to complete practice problems 33.5 through 33.8.

|  | Copper Test | Moisture Test |
|---|---|---|
| Car 1 | 240 ppm | 2% |
| Car 2 | 30 ppm | 1% |
| Car 3 | 40 ppm | 4% |
| Car 4 | 105 ppm | 1% |
| Car 5 | 55 ppm | 1% |
| Car 6 | 35 ppm | 1% |
| Car 7 | 210 ppm | 4% |
| Car 8 | 45 ppm | 2% |

**Copper Test (ppm)**

Car 1  Car 2  Car 3  Car 4  Car 5  Car 6  Car 7  Car 8
☐ Copper Test

33.5 Use the data in the table to create a bar graph showing the copper test results of cars 1 through 8.

33.6 Which cars have a copper content higher than 100 ppm?

33.7 How many cars have a copper content less than 50 ppm?

33.8 If brake fluid service is required for greater than 200 ppm and greater than or equal to 4% moisture, which cars require service?

Technician D is responsible for performing a maintenance inspection on all of the police vehicles managed by a local police department. The inspection includes testing the condition of the brake fluid to determine if a brake fluid flush is required before the vehicle can return to service. Use the following table and graph to complete practice problems 33.9 through 33.13.

|        | Copper Test | Moisture Test |
|--------|-------------|---------------|
| Car 1  | 45 ppm      | 2%            |
| Car 2  | 130 ppm     | 3%            |
| Car 3  | 230 ppm     | 3%            |
| Car 4  | 85 ppm      | 4%            |
| Car 5  | 25 ppm      | 2%            |
| Car 6  | 65 ppm      | 1%            |
| Car 7  | 30 ppm      | 1%            |
| Car 8  | 245 ppm     | 3%            |
| Car 9  | 85 ppm      | 1%            |
| Car 10 | 90 ppm      | 1%            |

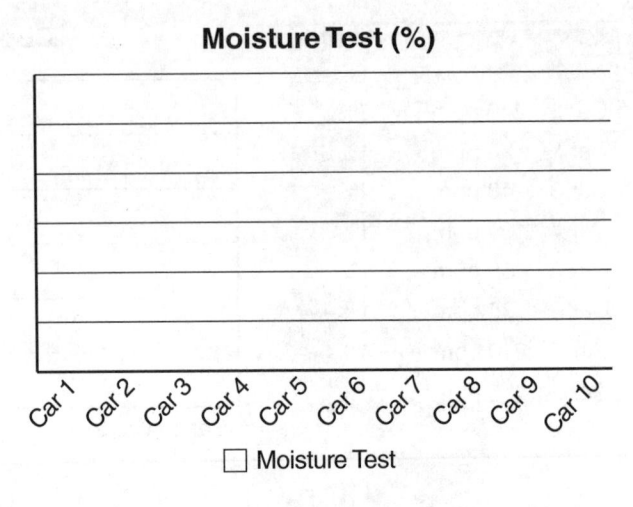

**Moisture Test (%)**

☐ Moisture Test

33.9 Use the data in the table to create a bar graph showing the moisture percentage for each car.

33.10 Which cars have a copper content greater than 100 ppm?

33.11 Which car has the highest copper content but only 1% moisture?

33.12 If brake fluid service is required for greater than 200 ppm and greater than or equal to 4% moisture, which cars require service?

33.13 If the brake fluid service requirement is changed to require fluid service for a vehicle with greater than 100 ppm or greater than 3% moisture, which cars require service?

# CASE STUDY 34

# Tire Diameter

## OBJECTIVES

*After studying this case study, you will be able to:*
- Calculate tire diameter using the formula.
- Calculate the change in tire diameter based on new tire sizes.
- Calculate total driveline ratio based on tire size changes.

## MATH SKILLS
- Solve job skill problems using a formula.
- Solve for a value using a formula to calculate changes.

Although vehicles are equipped with a stock tire size, it is common for a vehicle to have tires that are a different size from stock. When the tire size is changed from stock, the tire diameter may change. Use the given formulas to calculate how the change of tire size affects tire diameter size and the total driveline ratio.

*Goodheart-Willcox Publisher*

*Tire size formula:*

$$\text{tire diameter} = \frac{\text{section width} \times \text{aspect ratio}}{1{,}270} + \text{wheel diameter}$$

*Driveline formula:*

$$\text{new total driveline ratio} = \frac{\text{old tire diameter}}{\text{new tire diameter}} \times \text{differential gear ratio}$$

**Example:** The owner of a 2WD pickup truck is planning to install larger tires and wheels to improve ground clearance. The stock tires are P225/70R15 and the new tires are P235/75R16. Use the tire size formula to determine the stock tire diameter and the new tire diameter, and then calculate the change in tire diameter.

Stock tire diameter = [(225 × 70) ÷ 1,270] + 15
Stock tire diameter = 27.4″
New tire diameter = [(235 × 75) ÷ 1,270] + 16
New tire diameter = 29.9″
Change in tire diameter = new diameter − stock diameter
Change in tire diameter = 29.9 − 27.4
Change in tire diameter = 2.5″

Copyright Goodheart-Willcox Co., Inc. May not be reproduced or posted to a publicly accessible website.

**Example:** When different size tires and wheels are installed, the total driveline ratio is altered because the tire diameter changes. The driveline ratio is based on the differential gear ratio and the diameter of the rear tires. The owner of a base model sedan has decided to install performance wheels and tires. The stock tires are P245/55R18 and the performance tires are P285/35R20. The final drive differential ratio of the vehicle is 3.70:1. Use the driveline formula to calculate the new total driveline ratio at the tires.

$$\text{Stock LS tire diameter} = [(245 \times 55) \div 1{,}270] + 18$$
$$\text{Stock LS tire diameter} = 28.6''$$
$$\text{New SS tire diameter} = [(285 \times 35) \div 1{,}270] + 20$$
$$\text{New SS tire diameter} = 27.9''$$
$$\text{New total driveline ratio} = (28.6 \div 27.9) \times 3.70$$
$$\text{New total driveline ratio} = 3.79:1$$

The total driveline ratio at the tires changed from 3.70:1 to 3.79:1 when the tire size was changed.

Name _____  Date _____  Class _____

# Tire Diameter Job Skill Practice Problems

34.1 The owner of a 4×4 pickup truck is planning to install larger tires and wheels to improve ground clearance. The stock tires are P265/70R17 and the new tires are P285/70R18. Use the tire size formula to determine the stock tire diameter and the new tire diameter, and then calculate the change in tire diameter.

*Solve:*

Stock tire diameter = _____

New tire diameter = _____

Change in tire diameter = new diameter – stock diameter

Change in tire diameter = _____

34.2 The owner of a sedan is planning to install stock tires and wheels and remove the larger tires and wheels on the vehicle. The stock tires are P225/60R18 and the current tires are P245/35R20. Use the tire size formula to determine the stock tire diameter and the current tire diameter, and then calculate the change in tire diameter.

*Solve:*

Stock tire diameter = _____

Current tire diameter = _____

Change in tire diameter = stock diameter – current diameter

Change in tire diameter = _____

34.3 The owner of a luxury sedan is planning to install different tires and wheels and remove the stock tires and wheels on the vehicle. The stock tires are P235/65R18 and the new tires are P235/35R20. Use the tire size formula to determine the stock tire diameter and the new tire diameter, and then calculate the change in tire diameter.

*Solve:*

Stock tire diameter = _____

New tire diameter = _____

Change in tire diameter = stock diameter – new diameter

Change in tire diameter = _____

34.4 The owner of a large SUV is changing tire sizes from P265/65R18 to 275/55R20. This vehicle has a final drive differential ratio of 3.08:1. Calculate the change of total drive ratio at the tires when the new tires are installed.
*Solve:*

Original tire diameter = _____

New tire diameter = _____

New total driveline ratio = _____

The total driveline ratio at the tires changed from 3.08:1 to _____ when the tire size was changed.

34.5 The owner of a pickup truck is changing tire sizes from P245/75R16 to 265/65R17. The vehicle has a final drive differential ratio of 3.91:1. Calculate the change of total drive ratio at the tires when the new tires are installed.
*Solve:*

Original tire diameter = _____

New tire diameter = _____

New total driveline ratio = _____

The total driveline ratio at the tires changed from 3.91:1 to _____ when the tire size was changed.

34.6 The owner of a RWD modern muscle car is changing tire sizes from P255/70R17 to 275/45R18. The vehicle has a final drive differential ratio of 4.11:1. Calculate the change of total drive ratio at the tires when the new tires are installed.
*Solve:*

Original tire diameter = _____

New tire diameter = _____

New total driveline ratio = _____

The total driveline ratio at the tires changed from 4.11:1 to _____ when the tire size was changed.

# CASE STUDY 35

# Disc Brake Micrometer

## OBJECTIVES

*After studying this case study, you will be able to:*
- Analyze a disc brake inch micrometer.
- Identify measurement values using a disc brake inch micrometer.

## MATH SKILLS
- Interpret values on a specialty measurement tool.
- Addition of decimal numbers.

A brake disc must be measured for thickness using a micrometer. This measurement is performed to determine if the brake disc is worn beyond minimum thickness and to determine if the brake disc has thickness variation. A unique brake micrometer is a specialty tool designed to measure from 0.300″ to 1.300″. This range covers almost all brake discs in production, and is read in the same manner as a 0″ to 1″ micrometer. Review the following examples.

*Goodheart-Willcox Publisher*

**Example:** Read the micrometers shown to determine the brake disc thickness.

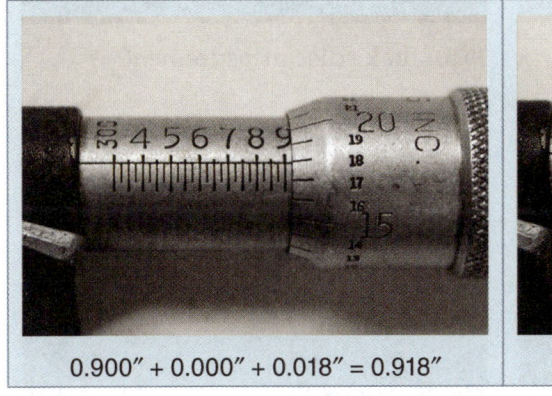

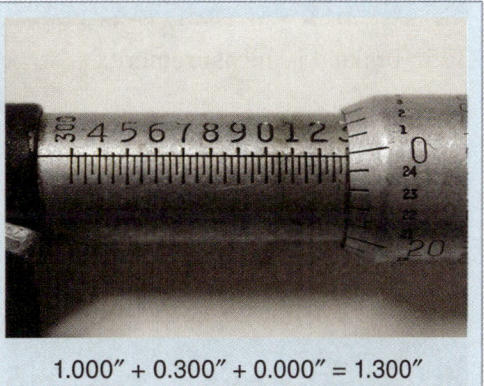

0.900″ + 0.000″ + 0.018″ = 0.918″    1.000″ + 0.300″ + 0.000″ = 1.300″

*Goodheart-Willcox Publisher*

Name _____ Date _____ Class _____

# Disc Brake Micrometer Job Skill Practice Problems

Read the micrometers shown to determine the brake disc thickness to complete practice problems 35.1 through 35.8.

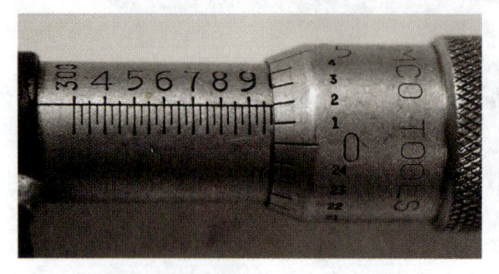

35.1. Brake disc measurement: _____

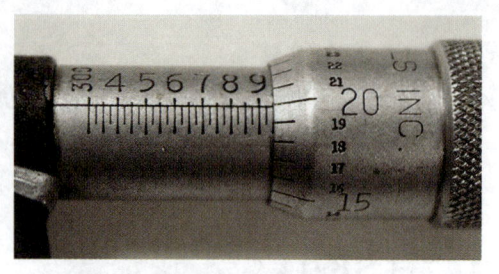

35.2. Brake disc measurement: _____

35.3. Brake disc measurement: _____

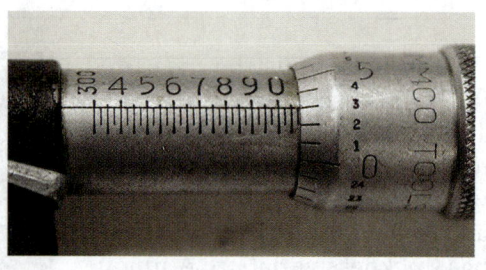

35.4. Brake disc measurement: _____

35.5. Brake disc measurement: _____

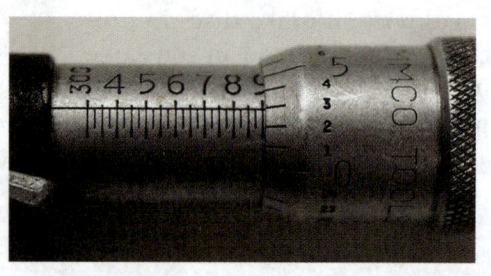

35.6. Brake disc measurement: _____

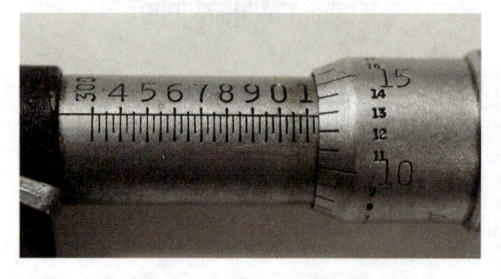

35.7. Brake disc measurement: _____

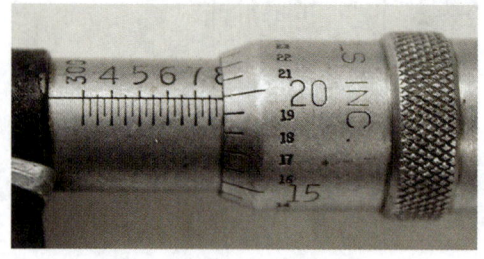

35.8. Brake disc measurement: _____

# CASE STUDY 36

# Brake System

## OBJECTIVES

*After studying this case study, you will be able to:*
- Identify and interpret brake system specifications.
- Compare brake system measurements to specification.

## MATH SKILLS
- Compare values to specifications.
- Addition and subtraction of decimal numbers.

As the brake system functions, the brake disc and brake drum slowly wear. These parts must be measured and compared to specification to determine if they can be machined or if they need to be replaced. The nominal thickness is the starting value and the service limit or discard thickness is the size that would require replacement.

*Goodheart-Willcox Publisher*

**Example:** Use the brake system specification table to answer the questions about this vehicle.

| Item | Measurement | Qualification | Nominal | Service Limit |
|---|---|---|---|---|
| Brake Disc | Thickness | Front (except SS) | 0.827" | 0.758" |
| | | Front SS | 0.984" | 0.906" |
| | | Rear | 0.354" | 0.315" |
| | Runout | | | 0.0016" |
| Brake Pad | Thickness | Front (except SS) | 0.394" | 0.063" |
| | | Front SS | 0.433" | 0.063" |
| | | Rear | 0.345" | 0.063" |
| Brake Drum | Drum I.D. | | 7.870" | 7.905" |
| | Shoe Lining | | 0.157" | 0.076" |

A front brake disc on an SS model car measures 0.921". Is this disc within the service limit?

The specification is 0.906", so 0.921" > 0.906".

Yes, the disc is within specification and does not require service.

A front disc brake pad on a non-SS model car measures 0.057". Is this pad within the service limit?

The specification is 0.063", so 0.057" < 0.063".

No, the brake pad is worn beyond specification and requires replacement.

Name _____  Date _____  Class _____

# Brake System Job Skill Practice Problems

Use the following brake system specification table to complete practice problems 36.1 through 36.6.

| Item | Measurement | Qualification | Nominal | Service Limit |
|---|---|---|---|---|
| Brake Disc | Thickness | Front (except GT) | 0.957" | 0.818" |
|  |  | Front GT | 1.034" | 0.896" |
|  |  | Rear | 0.334" | 0.305" |
|  | Runout |  |  | 0.0015" |
| Brake Pad | Thickness | Front (except GT) | 0.433" | 0.063" |
|  |  | Front GT | 0.433" | 0.063" |
|  |  | Rear | 0.365" | 0.063" |
| Brake Drum | Drum I.D. |  | 9.570" | 9.730" |
|  | Shoe Lining |  | 0.187" | 0.076" |

36.1 The front brake disc of a GT model measures 1.009". Is this disc within the service limit?

36.2 The front brake disc of a GT model measures 0.980". How much has it worn from the nominal thickness?

36.3 The rear brake disc measures 0.309". Is this disc within the service limit?

36.4 The brake drum measures 9.645". How much more can the drum wear before it reaches the service limit?

36.5 The left front brake disc runout measures 0.0018" and the right front brake disc runout measures 0.0020". Is either disc beyond the service limit?

36.6 The front brake disc of a non-GT model measures 0.806". Is this disc within the service limit?

Copyright Goodheart-Willcox Co., Inc. May not be reproduced or posted to a publicly accessible website.

Use the following brake system specification table to complete practice problems 36.7 through 36.12.

| Item | Measurement | Qualification | Nominal | Service Limit |
|---|---|---|---|---|
| **AWD** | | | | |
| Brake Disc | Thickness | Front | 1.106" | 1.024" |
| | | Rear | 0.437" | 0.354" |
| | Runout | | | 0.0015" |
| Brake Pad | Thickness | Front | 0.480" | 0.063" |
| | | Rear | 0.402" | 0.063" |
| **FWD** | | | | |
| Brake Disc | Thickness | Front | 1.015" | 0.989" |
| | | Rear | 0.407" | 0.334" |
| | Runout | | | 0.0015" |
| Brake Pad | Thickness | Front | 0.480" | 0.063" |
| | | Rear | 0.402" | 0.063" |

36.7 The front brake disc of an AWD model measures 1.089". How far has it worn from the nominal thickness?

36.8 The rear brake pad of a FWD model measures 0.238". How far has it worn from the nominal thickness?

36.9 The front brake disc of an AWD model measures 0.0009" of runout. Is this disc within the service limit?

36.10 The rear brake disc of a FWD model measures 0.298". How far past the service limit has the disc worn?

36.11 The front brake disc of an AWD model measures 1.016". How far has this disc worn from the nominal thickness?

36.12 The rear brake pad of a FWD model measures 0.138". How much more pad material can wear until the pad reaches the service limit?

# UNIT 5
# Engine Mechanical

Case Study 37 **Valve Overlap and Duration—Addition**
Case Study 38 **Camshaft Lobe—Subtraction**
Case Study 39 **Rocker Arm Ratio—Multiplication**
Case Study 40 **Compression Ratio—Division**
Case Study 41 **Engine Block Calculations—Decimal Arithmetic**
Case Study 42 **Piston Bore Clearance—Greater Than and Less Than**
Case Study 43 **Engine Parts—Fractions**
Case Study 44 **Engine Size—Conversion**
Case Study 45 **Cooling System—Graphs and Tables**
Case Study 46 **Engine Power and Efficiency—Formulas**
Case Study 47 **Cam and Crank Journal—Measurement**
Case Study 48 **Cylinder Bore—Analyzing Specifications**

## CAREER PROFILE

Sinh Bui works as an engine builder and engine machinist at Action Machine in Seattle, Washington. After working the "cleaning tank" for six months, he has spent three years specializing in cylinder heads and five years specializing in engine blocks. Sinh started using metalworking machines in high school, where his shop class teacher allowed him to rebuild old machines and use them to shape and turn metal. He was also spending much of his free time during high school doing engine swaps with his friends and their cars.

According to Sinh, "Measurement as a machinist is more of a feel—it takes practice, repetitiveness, to really learn to measure accurately." In addition to the steady requirement of measurement, Sinh uses math to calculate a variety of engine dimensions, including stroke, cylinder bore, crank journals, and connecting rods. The machines used in a machine shop are capable of incredible tasks, but the accuracy of the machinist in setting up the machine determines the outcome.

As an experienced machinist, Sinh helps mentor apprentice machinists in the shop. His advice to entry-level technicians: "Be ready to work—it's a lot of work and a lot of hours, it's not movie magic." Sinh's analytical skills help him solve complex engine mapping and machining work. The thought process for this type of work requires working backward to solve a problem. With many, many hours of on-the-job experience, Sinh has gone from "a pretty good wrench" to a highly skilled engine machinist.

Sinh Bui—Engine Builder and Machinist, Action Machine.

# CASE STUDY 37

# Valve Overlap and Duration

## OBJECTIVES

*After studying this case study, you will be able to:*
- Identify the purpose of valve overlap.
- Calculate and analyze intake and exhaust valve angles in relation to valve overlap.

## TECHNICAL TERMS

bottom dead center  
exhaust duration  
intake duration  
top dead center  
valve overlap

## MATH SKILLS
- Addition of whole numbers.
- Analyze angle values based on degrees of a circle.

---

In a four-stroke engine, a complete operating cycle takes place every two crankshaft revolutions (720° of crankshaft rotation). One piston stroke occurs during every 180° of crankshaft rotation. A piston stroke is the movement of the piston in the cylinder from one end of its travel to the other. *Top dead center* is the uppermost point, or top, of piston travel in the cylinder. *Bottom dead center* is the lowest point of piston travel in the cylinder. As the internal engine parts move through the cycle, the piston alternates between top dead center and bottom dead center.

*Goodheart-Willcox Publisher*

The camshaft is the engine component that opens and closes the intake and exhaust valves at the correct times in the engine operating cycle. There are three values that can be identified from camshaft specifications: valve overlap, intake duration, and exhaust duration.

*Valve overlap* is a period during the engine operating cycle when a cylinder's intake and exhaust valves are open at the same time.

*Intake duration* is the total number of degrees from when the intake valve opens to when it closes.

*Exhaust duration* is the total number of degrees from when the exhaust valve opens to when it closes.

The camshaft opens and closes the valves a certain number of degrees from the top dead center position and from the bottom dead center position. These measurements are the starting point when calculating valve overlap.

Review the following diagram. Note that the exhaust valve is open during the end of the power stroke, and the intake valve is open at the beginning of the compression stroke. Both valves are open as the engine transitions from exhaust stroke back to intake stroke. Note that valve overlap occurs only at top dead center (TDC). At bottom dead center (BDC), the valves are open on different revolutions of the cycle.

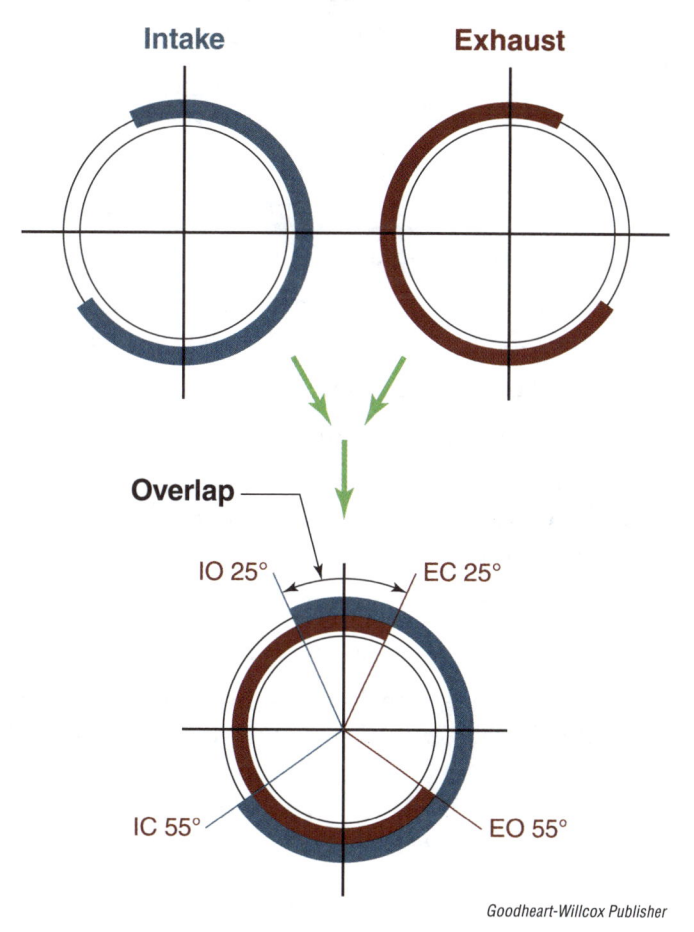

*Goodheart-Willcox Publisher*

The number of degrees before top dead center (BTDC), after top dead center (ATDC), before bottom dead center (BBDC), and after bottom dead center (ABDC) that a valve opens or closes is used to calculate valve overlap and valve duration.

**Example:**

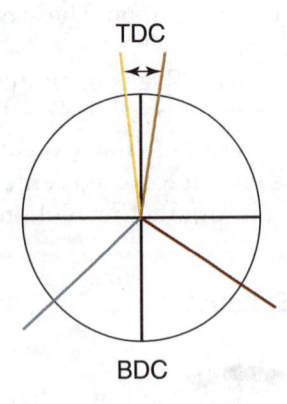

| | Valve Action | Timing |
|---|---|---|
| | Intake Opens | 7° BTDC |
| | Intake Closes | 48° ABDC |
| | Exhaust Opens | 57° BBDC |
| | Exhaust Closes | 9° ATDC |

$$\text{Valve overlap} = {}^\circ\text{BTDC that intake valve opens} + {}^\circ\text{ATDC that exhaust valve closes}$$

Valve overlap = 7° + 9° = 16°

$$\text{Intake valve duration} = {}^\circ\text{BTDC that intake opens} + \text{intake stroke (TDC to BDC} = 180°) + {}^\circ\text{ABDC that intake valve closes}$$

Intake valve duration = 7° + 180° + 48°

Intake valve duration = 235°

$$\text{Exhaust valve duration} = {}^\circ\text{BBDC that exhaust valve opens} + \text{exhaust stroke (TDC to BDC} = 180°) + {}^\circ\text{ATDC that exhaust valve closes}$$

Exhaust valve duration = 57° + 180° + 9°

Exhaust valve duration = 246°

Based on the calculations, this camshaft has 16° of valve overlap. The intake valve duration is 235°, and the exhaust valve duration is 246°.

Name _____  Date _____  Class _____

# Valve Overlap and Duration
## Job Skill Practice Problems

37.1 Calculate the valve overlap, intake valve duration, and exhaust valve duration for the camshaft specified. Draw the open and close lines for each valve in the circle diagram.

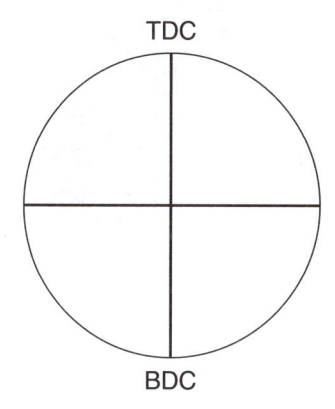

| Valve Action | Timing |
|---|---|
| Intake Opens | 39° BTDC |
| Intake Closes | 71° ABDC |
| Exhaust Opens | 79° BBDC |
| Exhaust Closes | 31° ATDC |

37.2 Calculate the valve overlap, intake valve duration, and exhaust valve duration for the camshaft specified. Draw the open and close lines for each valve in the circle diagram.

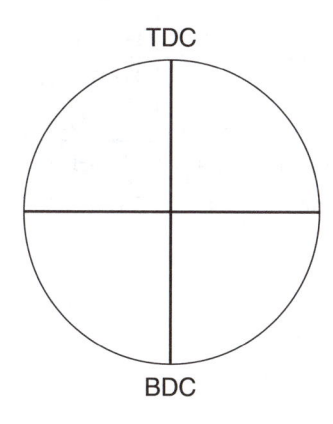

| Valve Action | Timing |
|---|---|
| Intake Opens | 21° BTDC |
| Intake Closes | 67° ABDC |
| Exhaust Opens | 69° BBDC |
| Exhaust Closes | 23° ATDC |

**Name** _____ **Date** _____ **Class** _____

37.3 Calculate the valve overlap, intake valve duration, and exhaust valve duration for the camshaft specified. Draw the open and close lines for each valve in the circle diagram.

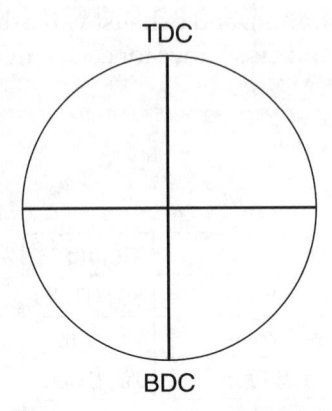

TDC

BDC

| | Valve Action | Timing |
|---|---|---|
| | Intake Opens | 31° BTDC |
| | Intake Closes | 67° ABDC |
| | Exhaust Opens | 67° BBDC |
| | Exhaust Closes | 31° ATDC |

37.4 Calculate the valve overlap, intake valve duration, and exhaust valve duration for the camshaft specified. Draw the open and close lines for each valve in the circle diagram.

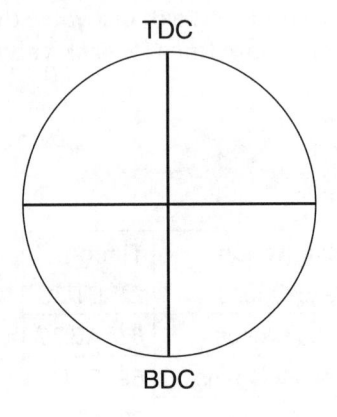

TDC

BDC

| | Valve Action | Timing |
|---|---|---|
| | Intake Opens | 41° BTDC |
| | Intake Closes | 73° ABDC |
| | Exhaust Opens | 81° BBDC |
| | Exhaust Closes | 33° ATDC |

# CASE STUDY 38

# Camshaft Lobe

## OBJECTIVES
*After studying this case study, you will be able to:*
- Identify the camshaft lobe and base circle.
- Determine the camshaft lobe lift value.

## MATH SKILLS
- Subtraction of whole numbers.
- Subtraction of decimal numbers.

---

The camshaft lobe is designed to activate the valvetrain and push open the intake and exhaust valves during engine operation. The camshaft consists of a lobe and a base circle. The lobe is the pointed part that forces the valve open. The base circle is the round part that allows the valve to remain closed. A micrometer is used to measure the lobe and the base circle.

*Goodheart-Willcox Publisher*

**Example:** A camshaft lobe measures 29.00 mm and the base circle measures 23.00 mm. Calculate the camshaft lobe lift.

$$29.00 \text{ mm} - 22.00 \text{ mm} = 7.00 \text{ mm}$$

The camshaft lobe has 7.00 mm of lobe lift.

Name _____  Date _____  Class _____

# Camshaft Lobe Job Skill Practice Problems

38.1 A camshaft has four intake lobes and the base circle for all lobes measures 2.358″. The intake lobes measure 2.708″ for cylinder one, 2.709″ for cylinder two, 2.707″ for cylinder three, and 2.710″ for cylinder four. Calculate the camshaft lobe lift for each cylinder.

38.2 A camshaft has intake and exhaust lobes for all eight cylinders. For cylinder one, the intake lobe lift is calculated to be 0.403″ and the exhaust lobe lift is calculated to be 0.391″. Calculate the difference between the intake lobe lift and the exhaust lobe lift.

38.3 A camshaft lobe measures 31.54 mm and the base circle measures 26.89 mm. Calculate the camshaft lobe lift.

38.4 A camshaft has four exhaust lobes and the base circle for all lobes measures 1.980″. The exhaust lobes measure 2.304″ for cylinder one, 2.305″ for cylinder two, 2.307″ for cylinder three, and 2.306″ for cylinder four. Calculate the camshaft lobe lift for each cylinder.

Name _____ Date _____ Class _____

38.5 A camshaft lobe measures 2.454" and the base circle measures 1.890". Calculate the camshaft lobe lift.

38.6 A camshaft has two sets of intake lobes, one for primary operation and one for high performance operation. The primary lobes have a camshaft lobe lift of 32.791 mm. The secondary lobes have a camshaft lobe lift of 35.354 mm. Calculate the difference between the primary lobes and the secondary lobes.

38.7 A stock camshaft has an intake lobe lift of 0.283" and an exhaust lobe lift of 0.283". A high performance camshaft has an intake lobe lift of 0.333" and an exhaust lobe lift of 0.334". Calculate the increase in intake and exhaust lobe lift with the performance camshaft.

38.8 A camshaft intake lobe measures 2.356" and the exhaust lobe measures 2.349". The base circle measures 1.950". Calculate the camshaft lobe lift for intake and exhaust.

# CASE STUDY 39

# Rocker Arm Ratio

## OBJECTIVES

*After studying this case study, you will be able to:*
- Determine the function of the rocker arm ratio.
- Calculate the effect of the rocker arm ratio on the overall valve lift.

## TECHNICAL TERM

rocker arm ratio

## MATH SKILLS

- Multiplication of whole and decimal numbers.
- Analyze ratio values in relation to job skill problems.

The rocker arm transmits motion from the camshaft lobe to the engine valve. The rocker arm typically has a pivot point in the center, and one side of the pivot connects to the camshaft side of the valvetrain and the other connects to the valve side. The rocker arm dimensions are different on each side of the pivot point, creating a different output compared to the input. This difference is the rocker arm ratio.

*Goodheart-Willcox Publisher*

The *rocker arm ratio* is a multiplier of the camshaft lobe and increases the total valve movement in the cylinder head. To find the rocker arm ratio, divide the distance to the center point on the valve side by the distance to the center point on the camshaft side. The effect of the ratio on the movement of the valve can then be calculated.

Rocker ratio = Y/X

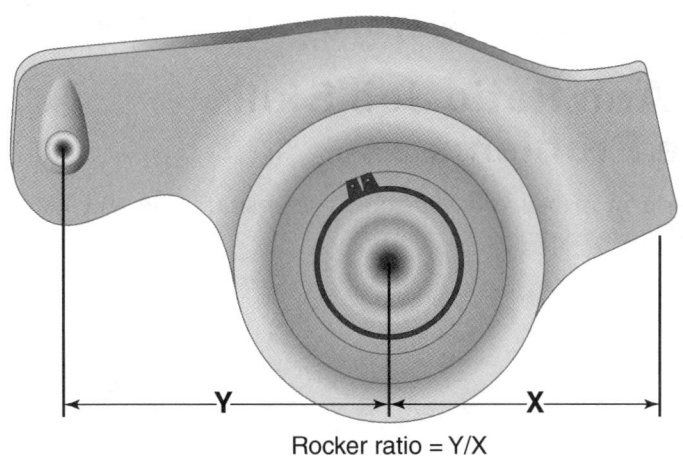

*Goodheart-Willcox Publisher*

NOTE: Some engine valvetrain configurations require a valve lash value. The valve lash value is the measurement of the small gap between the rocker arm and the valve. In this case study, the valve lash value is zero and will not affect calculations in the practice problems.

Review the following examples.

**Example:** If the rocker arm is 0.750″ to the center point on the camshaft side and 1.250″ to the center point on the valve side, calculate the rocker arm ratio. Round to the nearest hundredth.

$$1.250″ \div 0.750″ = 1.67$$
$$1.67:1.0$$
$$1.67:1 \text{ rocker arm ratio}$$

**Example:** If the rocker arm ratio is 1.67:1, calculate the total valve movement if the camshaft lobe lift is 0.290″ and has zero valve lash. Round to the nearest hundredth.

$$0.290″ \times 1.67$$
$$0.290″ \times 1.67 = 0.48″$$
$$\text{Total valve movement} = 0.48″$$

Name _____  Date _____  Class _____

## Rocker Arm Ratio Job Skill Practice Problems

39.1 A rocker arm measures 0.900" on the camshaft side and 1.667" on the valve side. Calculate the rocker arm ratio.

39.2 A rocker arm measures 0.950" on the camshaft side and 1.685" on the valve side. Calculate the rocker arm ratio.

39.3 A rocker arm measures 0.985" on the camshaft side and 1.6752" on the valve side. Calculate the rocker arm ratio.

39.4 A V8 engine has a rocker arm ratio of 1.73:1 and a camshaft with an intake valve lift of 0.405". Calculate the total valve movement with zero valve lash.

Name _____ Date _____ Class _____

39.5 A V8 engine has a rocker arm ratio of 1.65:1 and a camshaft with an intake valve lift of 0.365". Calculate the total valve movement with zero valve lash.

39.6 A V6 engine has a rocker arm ratio of 1.5:1. The camshaft intake lobe value is 0.289" and the exhaust lobe lift is 0.291". Calculate the total valve movement for intake and exhaust valve with zero valve lash.

39.7 A V8 engine has stock rocker arms with a 1.5:1 ratio. The intake and exhaust camshaft lobe lift is 0.305" on the stock camshaft. A performance camshaft has intake lobe lift of 0.343" and exhaust lobe lift of 0.349". Calculate the total valve movement increase with the performance camshaft compared to the stock camshaft with zero valve lash.

39.8 A V8 engine has a performance camshaft with 0.361" lobe lift on intake and exhaust. The stock rocker arms are 1.5:1 ratio. Calculate the change in total valve movement with 1.6:1 ratio rocker arms.

# CASE STUDY 40

# Compression Ratio

## OBJECTIVES
*After studying this case study, you will be able to:*
- Identify piston displacement volume and combustion chamber volume.
- Calculate the compression ratio of an engine cylinder.

## TECHNICAL TERMS
combustion chamber volume
piston displacement

## MATH SKILLS
- Whole number and decimal division.
- Solve for an unknown variable.

The compression ratio is a comparison of the volume of the cylinder with the piston at the bottom of the stroke (bottom dead center, BDC) to the volume of the cylinder with the piston at the top of the stroke (top dead center, TDC). In a gasoline, spark ignition engine, raising the compression ratio generally means an increase in power. However, if the compression ratio is raised too high, the engine will have issues with detonation, which is combustion occurring too soon in the process.

*Goodheart-Willcox Publisher*

Two values are needed to calculate the compression ratio: piston displacement and combustion chamber volume.

**Piston displacement** is the volume of air the piston displaces during the stroke from BDC to TDC. This value is the total engine displacement divided by the number of cylinders.

**Combustion chamber volume** is the volume in the cylinder head and the thickness of the cylinder head gasket when the piston is at TDC.

To calculate the compression ratio, use the formula:

$$\text{compression ratio} = \frac{\text{piston displacement} + \text{combustion volume}}{\text{combustion volume}}$$

If the total displacement of the engine is known, find the displacement for each cylinder by dividing the total displacement by the number of cylinders.

**Example:** A V8 engine has 280 cubic inches of displacement. The combustion chamber volume is approximately 3.97 cubic inches. Calculate the compression ratio of this engine.

280 cubic inches ÷ 8 cylinders = 35 cubic inches per cylinder

$$\frac{35 \text{ cubic inches} + 3.97 \text{ cubic inches}}{3.97 \text{ cubic inches}} = 9.82$$

9.82:1 compression ratio

Name _____ Date _____ Class _____

## Compression Ratio Job Skill Practice Problems

*Practice problem values are fictional; specific engine sizes are affected by many different variables.*

40.1 A V6 engine has 211 cubic inches of displacement. The combustion chamber volume is approximately 3.77 cubic inches. Calculate the compression ratio of this engine.

40.2 A V6 engine has 217 cubic inches of displacement. The combustion chamber volume is approximately 3.47 cubic inches. Calculate the compression ratio of this engine.

40.3 A V8 engine has 370 cubic inches of displacement. The combustion chamber volume is approximately 4.97 cubic inches. Calculate the compression ratio of this engine.

**Name** _____ **Date** _____ **Class** _____

40.4 A V8 engine has 330 cubic inches of displacement. The combustion chamber volume is approximately 4.68 cubic inches. Calculate the compression ratio of this engine.

40.5 An inline 4-cylinder engine has 134 cubic inches of displacement. The combustion chamber volume is approximately 3.72 cubic inches. Calculate the compression ratio of this engine.

40.6 An inline 5-cylinder engine has 223 cubic inches of displacement. The combustion chamber volume is approximately 4.79 cubic inches. Calculate the compression ratio of this engine.

# CASE STUDY 41

# Engine Block Calculations

## OBJECTIVES

*After studying this case study, you will be able to:*
- Identify engine block size values and calculations.
- Calculate engine displacement.
- Calculate changes to engine displacement with changes to bore and stroke.

## TECHNICAL TERMS

bore                  stroke

## MATH SKILLS

- Perform decimal arithmetic operations.
- Compare and analyze numerical values.

---

The engine block is machined and constructed to extremely high levels of precision and tolerance. The pistons must fit perfectly into the cylinders and the block must hold the crankshaft and cylinder heads perfectly. To determine the volume of the engine, two specific engine values must be known.

*Bore*—The engine bore is the diameter of the cylinder, machined into the block.

*Stroke*—The engine stroke is the distance the piston travels within the cylinder, from top dead center (TDC) to bottom dead center (BDC).

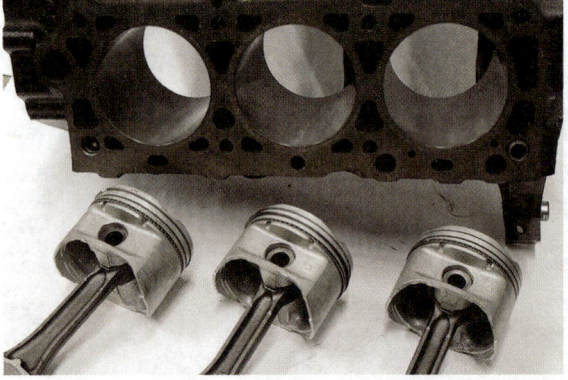

*Goodheart-Willcox Publisher*

Calculating the engine size, or displacement, requires calculations using the bore and stroke values. High performance applications can alter the engine displacement by changing the bore value, the stroke value, or both. The bore is changed by machining the engine block to a larger bore diameter, and the stroke is changed by installing a crankshaft with a different throw length. Review the following examples.

**Example:** A V8 engine has a bore of 3.629" and a stroke of 3.649". Use the formula to calculate the engine displacement.

*Engine displacement = bore × bore × 0.7854 × stroke × # of cylinders*

Engine displacement = 3.629" × 3.629" × 0.7854 × 3.649" × 8

Engine displacement = 301.9 cubic inches

**Example:** A V8 engine has a bore of 3.780″ and a stroke of 3.270″. The engine requires a rebuild, including machining the engine bore 0.030″ oversized. Calculate the increase in engine displacement from stock size to rebuilt size.

Stock engine displacement = 3.780″ × 3.780″ × 0.7854 × 3.270″ × 8

Stock engine displacement = 293.6 cubic inches

Rebuilt bore = 3.780″ + 0.030″ = 3.810″

Rebuilt engine displacement = 3.810″ × 3.810″ × 0.7854 × 3.270″ × 8

Rebuilt engine displacement = 298.2 cubic inches

$\dfrac{\text{Rebuilt}}{\text{displacement increase}}$ = 298.2 cubic inches − 293.6 cubic inches = 4.6 cubic inches

# Engine Block Calculations
## Job Skill Practice Problems

41.1 A V6 engine has a bore of 3.7000" and a stroke of 3.7836". Calculate the engine displacement. Round to the nearest tenth.

41.2 An inline 4-cylinder engine has a bore of 3.445" and a stroke of 3.976". Calculate the engine displacement. Round to the nearest tenth.

41.3 An inline 5-cylinder engine has a bore of 3.7600" and a stroke of 4.020". Calculate the engine displacement. Round to the nearest tenth.

41.4 An inline 3-cylinder engine has a bore of 2.8346" and a stroke of 3.2239". Calculate the engine displacement. Round to the nearest tenth.

Name _____ Date _____ Class _____

41.5 A V8 engine has a bore of 3.897" and a stroke of 6.622". The engine is being rebuilt by an engine machine shop, including machining the engine bore 0.060" larger. Calculate the new engine displacement with the larger bore size. Round to the nearest tenth.

41.6 A V8 engine has a bore of 4.000" and a stroke of 3.480". The engine is being rebuilt, including a new crankshaft with a longer throw, changing the stroke to 3.750". Calculate the increase in displacement from stock to performance. Round to the nearest tenth.

41.7 A V8 engine has a bore of 4.250" and a stroke of 4.000". The engine is being rebuilt, including machining the bore 0.060" larger and a new crankshaft with a longer throw, changing the stroke to 4.250". Calculate the engine displacement after the rebuild. Round to the nearest tenth.

41.8 An inline 6-cylinder engine has a bore of 3.390" and a stroke of 3.390". The engine is being rebuilt with a stroker kit, increasing the stroke to 3.7795". Calculate the increase in displacement from stock to performance. Round to the nearest tenth.

# CASE STUDY 42

# Piston Bore Clearance

## OBJECTIVES
*After studying this case study, you will be able to:*
- Identify piston and cylinder bore size specifications.
- Calculate and analyze piston to bore clearance.

## TECHNICAL TERM
clearance

## MATH SKILLS
- Analyze numerical values to determine greater than or less than.
- Solve job skill problems using greater than and less than calculations.

The piston and cylinder bore are designed and machined to extremely precise size tolerances in order to accurately fit together. The very small space between the cylinder bore and the piston is known as *clearance*. This clearance space has a specific range of tolerance. If it is too small, the piston will be too tight in the bore; if it is too large, the piston will move around too much in the bore, the parts will wear, and additional engine wear will occur.

*Goodheart-Willcox Publisher*

To determine if the cylinder bore clearance is within the acceptable range, the measurements of the piston and the cylinder bore must be known.

**Example:** An engine has a piston bore clearance specification range of 0.0003″ to 0.0010″. The piston measures 3.9994″ and the cylinder bore measures 4.0001″. Calculate the piston bore clearance and determine if the value is greater than or less than the specification.

$$4.0001″ - 3.9994″ = 0.0007″$$
$$0.0003″ < \mathbf{0.0007″} < 0.0010″$$

The cylinder bore clearance is within the specification range.

Name _____  Date _____  Class _____

# Piston Bore Clearance Job Skill Practice Problems

42.1 A V6 engine has a piston bore clearance range of 0.00140″ to 0.00354″. The piston diameters and cylinder bore measurements are shown below. Calculate the piston bore clearance for each cylinder and determine if the clearance is within the specification range.

| Cylinder | Bore (in) | Piston (in) | Clearance |
|---|---|---|---|
| #1 | 3.7011 | 3.6996 | _____ |
| #2 | 3.7012 | 3.6997 | _____ |
| #3 | 3.7010 | 3.6998 | _____ |
| #4 | 3.7011 | 3.6999 | _____ |
| #5 | 3.7011 | 3.6995 | _____ |
| #6 | 3.7013 | 3.6998 | _____ |

42.2 A V8 engine has a piston bore clearance range of 0.0006″ to 0.0014″. The piston diameters and cylinder bore measurements are shown below. Calculate the piston bore clearance for each cylinder and determine if the clearance is within the specification range.

| Cylinder | Bore (in) | Piston (in) | Clearance |
|---|---|---|---|
| #1 | 4.0657 | 4.0648 | _____ |
| #2 | 4.0656 | 4.0649 | _____ |
| #3 | 4.0658 | 4.0647 | _____ |
| #4 | 4.0655 | 4.0648 | _____ |
| #5 | 4.0659 | 4.0649 | _____ |
| #6 | 4.0658 | 4.0646 | _____ |
| #7 | 4.0657 | 4.0647 | _____ |
| #8 | 4.0658 | 4.0648 | _____ |

42.3 An inline 4-cylinder engine has a piston bore clearance range of 0.00059″ to 0.00157″. The piston diameters and cylinder bore measurements are shown below. Calculate the piston bore clearance for each cylinder and determine if the clearance is within the specification range.

| Cylinder | Bore (in) | Piston (in) | Clearance |
|---|---|---|---|
| #1 | 3.50402 | 3.50299 | _____ |
| #2 | 3.50399 | 3.50298 | _____ |
| #3 | 3.50395 | 3.50296 | _____ |
| #4 | 3.50390 | 3.50298 | _____ |

42.4 A VR6 engine has a piston bore clearance range of 0.055 mm to 0.075 mm. The piston diameters and cylinder bore measurements are shown below. Calculate the piston bore clearance for each cylinder and determine if the clearance is within the specification range.

| Cylinder | Bore (mm) | Piston (mm) | Clearance |
|---|---|---|---|
| #1 | 89.011 | 88.945 | _____ |
| #2 | 89.013 | 88.944 | _____ |
| #3 | 89.017 | 88.945 | _____ |
| #4 | 89.010 | 88.946 | _____ |
| #5 | 89.029 | 88.948 | _____ |
| #6 | 89.014 | 88.947 | _____ |

# CASE STUDY 43

# Engine Parts

## OBJECTIVES
*After studying this case study, you will be able to:*
- Identify the need for precision values regarding engine dimensions.
- Identify the fraction decimal equivalencies of engine parts.

## MATH SKILLS
- Identify fraction decimal equivalencies.
- Round a decimal value to the closest fractional value.

The high precision and small tolerance limits of engine parts require measurement tools that are equally precise. Using a fractional ruler or tape measure is not accurate enough for precision measurement, but can be used for the purpose of estimating under certain circumstances.

All fractions have a decimal equivalency, that is, a decimal number equal to the fraction. If a ruler is divided into sixteenths of an inch, each sixteenth is equal to 0.0625″.

*Goodheart-Willcox Publisher*

A working knowledge of these fraction decimal equivalencies will become second nature to a practiced engine builder or machinist. Review the table and the example.

| Fraction | Decimal | Fraction | Decimal |
|---|---|---|---|
| 1/16 | 0.0625 | 9/16 | 0.5625 |
| 1/8 | 0.1250 | 5/8 | 0.6250 |
| 3/16 | 0.1875 | 11/16 | 0.6875 |
| 1/4 | 0.2500 | 3/4 | 0.7500 |
| 5/16 | 0.3125 | 13/16 | 0.8125 |
| 3/8 | 0.3750 | 7/8 | 0.8750 |
| 7/16 | 0.4375 | 15/16 | 0.9375 |
| 1/2 | 0.5000 | 1 | 1.0000 |

**Example:** A wrist pin measures 0.4375″ in diameter. Determine the fractional equivalent of the wrist pin diameter measurement.

$$0.4375″ = 7/16″$$

The fractional equivalent of the wrist pin is 7/16″.

# Engine Parts Job Skill Practice Problems

43.1  A main bearing cap bolt is 3 13/16" long. Determine the decimal equivalent of the main bearing cap bolt.

43.2  A valve spring is 1.9375" tall when measured at free height (uninstalled). Determine the fractional equivalent of the valve spring.

43.3  A block core (freeze) plug is 1 7/8" diameter. Determine the decimal equivalent of the block core (freeze) plug.

43.4  A rear main seal is 2.250" in diameter. Determine the fractional equivalent of the rear main seal.

43.5  An exhaust valve head measures 1 3/8" in diameter. Determine the decimal equivalent of the exhaust valve head.

Name _____ Date _____ Class _____

43.6 An intake valve head measures 1.8100″. Determine the fractional equivalent and round the decimal to the nearest sixteenth of an inch.

43.7 An exhaust manifold stud measures 1.0710″. Determine the fractional equivalent and round the decimal to the nearest sixteenth of an inch.

43.8 A wrist pin measures 0.5590″. Determine the fractional equivalent and round the decimal to the nearest sixteenth of an inch.

43.9 A crankshaft main journal measures 2.4560″. Determine the fractional equivalent and round the decimal to the nearest sixteenth of an inch.

43.10 A valve stem measures 0.3748″. Determine the fractional equivalent and round the decimal to the nearest sixteenth of an inch.

# CASE STUDY 44

# Engine Size

## OBJECTIVES

*After studying this case study, you will be able to:*
- Identify common engine size designations.
- Convert engine size unit values.

## MATH SKILLS
- Convert values using a conversion factor.
- Multiply and divide whole and decimal numbers.

The size of an engine is based on the amount of volume the cylinders displace as they move in the cylinders. This value is typically designated in one of three units: cubic inches (CID), liters, or cubic centimeters. Converting between these units requires using a conversion factor.

Refer to the conversion factor table and the following examples.

*Goodheart-Willcox Publisher*

| Engine Conversion Factors | | |
|---|---|---|
| 1 cubic inch | = | 0.0163 liters |
| 1 liter | = | 61.024 cubic inches |
| 1 liter | = | 1000 cubic centimeters |
| 1 cubic inch | = | 16.3 cubic centimeters |

**Example:** A V8 engine has a displacement of 350 cubic inches. Calculate the engine size in liters.

$$350 \text{ cubic inches} \times 0.0163 \text{ liters} = 5.71 \text{ liters}$$
$$350 \text{ CID} = 5.7 \text{ liters}$$

**Example:** An inline 6-cylinder engine has a displacement of 250 cubic inches. Calculate the size of one cylinder in liters.

$$250 \text{ cubic inches} \div 6 = 41.67 \text{ cubic inches}$$
$$41.67 \text{ cubic inches} \times 0.0163 \text{ liters} = 0.68 \text{ liters}$$

One cylinder of a 250 CID inline 6-cylinder engine is 0.68 liters.

Name _____  Date _____  Class _____

# Engine Size Job Skill Practice Problems

44.1  A V8 engine has a displacement of 454 cubic inches. Calculate the engine size in liters. Round to the nearest tenth.

44.2  An inline 4-cylinder engine has a displacement of 2.2 liters. Calculate the engine size in cubic inches. Round to the nearest tenth.

44.3  An inline 5-cylinder engine has a displacement of 2.5 liters. Calculate the engine size in cubic centimeters. Round to the nearest tenth.

44.4  Two V8 engines are being compared. One has a displacement of 4.6 liters and the other has a displacement of 289 cubic inches. Determine which engine has a larger *total* volume.

44.5  Two inline engines are being compared. One has a displacement of a 4.0 liter inline 6-cylinder and the other has a displacement of a 116 cubic inch inline 4-cylinder. Determine which engine has a smaller volume *per cylinder*.

44.6 Two V6 engines are being compared. One has a displacement of 3500 cubic centimeters and the other has a displacement of 213.5 cubic inches. Determine which engine has a smaller *total* volume.

44.7 A car has two engine options, a 140 cubic inch displacement inline 4-cylinder and a 5.0 liter displacement V8. Determine which engine has a larger volume *per cylinder*.

44.8 Two pickup trucks are being compared. One truck has a 6700 cubic centimeter displacement V8 diesel engine. The other has a 408.8 cubic inch displacement inline 6-cylinder engine. Calculate which engine has a larger *total* volume.

44.9 Two hybrid vehicles are being compared. One hybrid has a 1000 cubic centimeter displacement inline 3-cylinder engine. The other hybrid has a 122 cubic inch displacement inline 4-cylinder engine. Determine which engine has a smaller *total* displacement volume.

44.10 The 2013 model year of a muscle car has a V8 engine with a displacement volume of 7000 cubic centimeters. The 2003 model year of the same muscle car has a V8 engine with a displacement volume of 350 cubic inches. Calculate how many more *liters per cylinder* the 2013 V8 engine has compared to the 2003 V8 engine.

# CASE STUDY 45

# Cooling System

## OBJECTIVES

*After studying this case study, you will be able to:*
- Identify cooling system temperature changes over time.
- Calculate thermostat-related diagnostic problems.

## MATH SKILLS
- Analyze changes in data over time.
- Analyze data in graph and table formats.

---

The engine cooling system is designed to maintain proper engine operating temperature during all engine operation conditions. From engine start-up to highway driving, the cooling system temperature rises and levels off in a properly operating system. By graphing the temperature, a technician can analyze the operation of the system. Most scan tools show engine temperature in graph form that can be analyzed for operation of the system as well.

*Goodheart-Willcox Publisher*

**Example:** Review the engine speed and engine temperature data in the table and graph.

| Time Elapsed | Start-up | 1 min | 2 min | 3 min | 4 min | 5 min | 6 min |
|---|---|---|---|---|---|---|---|
| Engine Speed | 1,130 rpm | 980 rpm | 770 rpm | 780 rpm | 775 rpm | 770 rpm | 775 rpm |
| Engine Coolant Temperature | 61°F | 111°F | 149°F | 191°F | 185°F | 186°F | 185°F |

**Engine Cooling System Graph**

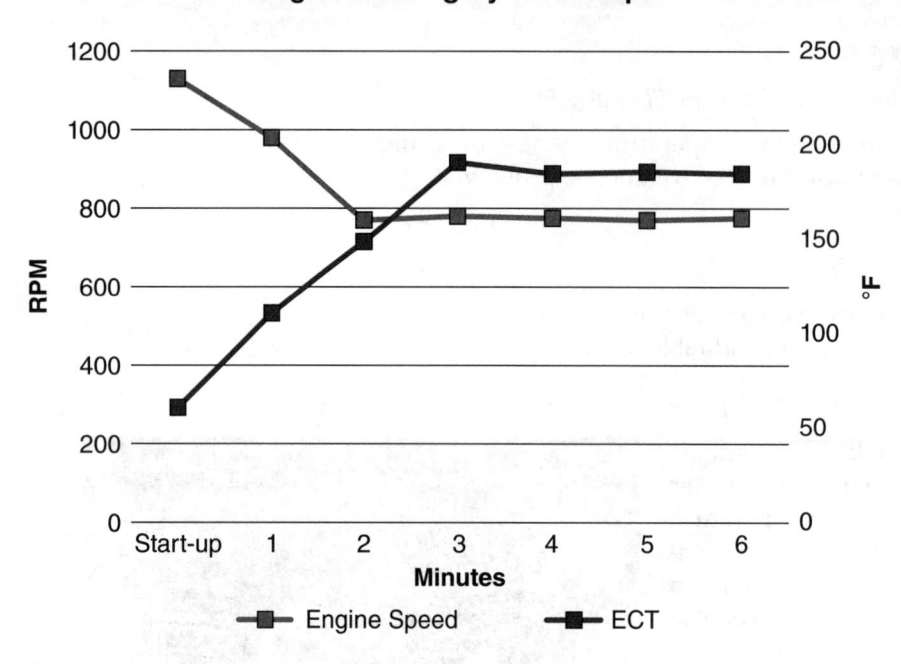

Determine at what time the thermostat opened.

> The thermostat opened at the 3-minute mark, at the max temperature of 191°F.

Determine the normal operating temperature value.

> The normal temperature value is around 185°F.

Name _____  Date _____  Class _____

# Cooling System Job Skill Practice Problems

Refer to the following table to complete practice problems 45.1 through 45.4.

| Engine #1* | | | | | | | |
|---|---|---|---|---|---|---|---|
| Time Elapsed | Start-up | 1 min | 2 min | 3 min | 4 min | 5 min | 6 min |
| Engine Speed | 1,078 rpm | 930 rpm | 730 rpm | 730 rpm | 735 rpm | 735 rpm | 734 rpm |
| Engine Coolant Temperature | 61°F | 111°F | 149°F | 141°F | 145°F | 146°F | 145°F |
| **Engine #2*** | | | | | | | |
| Time Elapsed | Start-up | 1 min | 2 min | 3 min | 4 min | 5 min | 6 min |
| Engine Speed | 1,120 rpm | 970 rpm | 770 rpm | 780 rpm | 775 rpm | 770 rpm | 775 rpm |
| Engine Coolant Temperature | 81°F | 118°F | 159°F | 205°F | 197°F | 196°F | 197°F |

*The engines are identical engines in separate vehicles, operating under identical conditions.

45.1 Calculate the change in engine temperature for engine #1 from the 3-minute mark to the 6-minute mark.

45.2 Calculate the change in engine temperature for engine #2 from the 3-minute mark to the 4-minute mark.

45.3 Analyze the data to determine which engine has a stuck open thermostat.

45.4 Determine the normal operating temperature of engine #2.

Refer to the following graphs to complete practice problems 45.5 through 45.8.

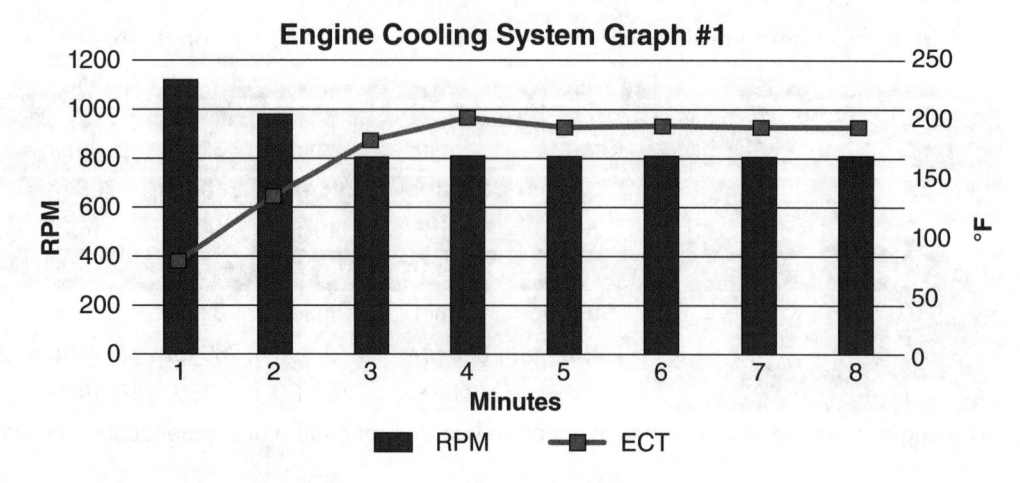

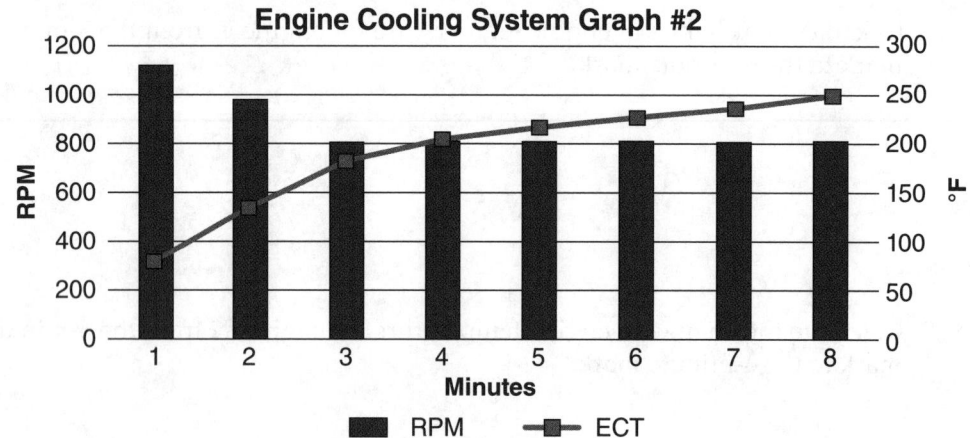

**Engine Cooling System Graph #1**

**Engine Cooling System Graph #2**

45.5 Determine the engine coolant temperature for each engine at the 4-minute mark.

45.6 Determine the engine operating temperature of the engine in graph #1.

45.7 Calculate the change in engine temperature from the 4-minute mark to the 8-minute mark for engine #2.

Name _____  Date _____  Class _____

45.8 Analyze the data in both graphs. Determine which engine is operating normally and which engine is operating with a cooling system problem (overheating).




Refer to the following table and graph to complete practice problem 45.9.

| Time Elapsed | Start-up | 1 min | 2 min | 3 min | 4 min | 5 min | 6 min |
|---|---|---|---|---|---|---|---|
| Engine Speed | 1,008 rpm | 850 rpm | 850 rpm | 852 rpm | 851 rpm | 850 rpm | 851 rpm |
| Engine Coolant Temperature | 140°F | 191°F | 199°F | 198°F | 185°F | 199°F | 185°F |

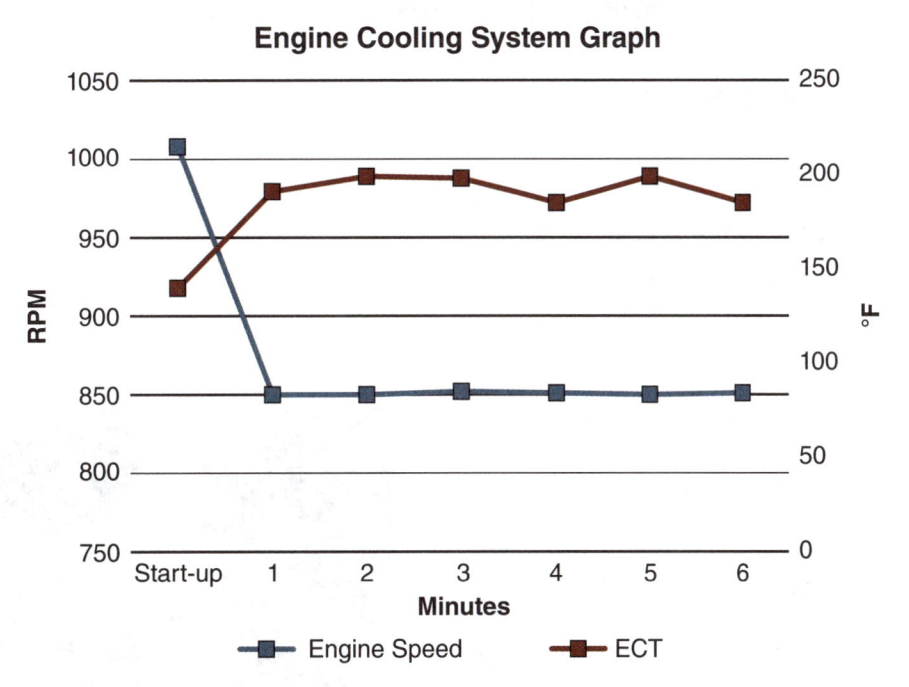

**Engine Cooling System Graph**

45.9 This engine is equipped with a 195°F thermostat. Analyze the graph and determine if the engine temperature exceeds the thermostat maximum by more than 5°F.

# CASE STUDY 46

# Engine Power and Efficiency

## OBJECTIVES

*After studying this case study, you will be able to:*
- Calculate the horsepower and volumetric efficiency of an engine.
- Calculate changes in horsepower and volumetric efficiency.

## TECHNICAL TERMS

horsepower

volumetric efficiency (VE)

## MATH SKILLS

- Solve problems using a formula.
- Solve for values based on formula calculations.

The internal combustion engine is an air pump designed to produce power. The more air the engine is able to flow, the more power it is able to produce during combustion. A formula can be used to calculate both horsepower and volumetric efficiency of an engine.

*Horsepower* is a calculation of the rate of work produced. Two variables are needed in order to calculate horsepower: engine speed (rpm) and torque.

*Goodheart-Willcox Publisher*

$$horsepower = \frac{rpm \times torque}{5,252}$$

**Example:** A 4.6 L engine is being measured for power output. At 4,000 rpm, the torque value of the engine is 235 foot-pounds. Calculate the horsepower produced at this engine speed.

$$horsepower = \frac{4,000 \text{ rpm} \times 235 \text{ foot-pounds}}{5,252}$$

$$horsepower = \frac{940,000}{5,252}$$

$$horsepower = 179.0$$

*Volumetric efficiency (VE)* is the calculated value of airflow efficiency of an engine. As the internal parts of the engine move and rotate, they are pumping air into and out of the cylinder. The VE is a ratio of the total possible volume of air compared to the actual volume of air flowing through an engine. This is expressed as a percentage.

Factors that promote VE are related to improving airflow. Examples include forced induction (turbocharging or supercharging), performance camshafts, cylinder heads designed with multiple intake and exhaust valves, and improved flow intake and exhaust manifold systems. Certain high-performance engine modifications can achieve a volumetric efficiency greater than a 1:1 ratio.

$$volumetric\ efficiency\ (VE) = \frac{actual\ airflow\ volume}{possible\ airflow\ volume}$$

**Example:** A 4.6 L engine is being measured for volumetric efficiency. The possible airflow volume is 600 cubic centimeters. The actual airflow volume is 570 cubic centimeters. Calculate the volumetric efficiency.

$$volumetric\ efficiency\ (VE) = \frac{570\ cubic\ centimeters}{600\ cubic\ centimeters}$$

$$volumetric\ efficiency\ (VE) = 0.95\ or\ 95\%$$

Name _____ Date _____ Class _____

# Engine Power and Efficiency
# Job Skill Practice Problems

46.1 A 2.2 L engine is being measured for power output. At 4,500 rpm, the torque value is 185 foot-pounds. Calculate the horsepower produced at this engine speed. Round to the nearest tenth.

46.2 A 5.0 L engine is being measured for power output. At 4,250 rpm, the torque value is 390 foot-pounds. Calculate the horsepower produced at this engine speed. Round to the nearest tenth.

46.3 A 6.7 L diesel engine is being measured for power output. At 1,500 rpm, the torque value is 660 foot-pounds. Calculate the horsepower produced at this engine speed. Round to the nearest tenth.

46.4 A 2.4 L engine is being measured for volumetric efficiency. The possible airflow volume is 300 cubic centimeters. The actual airflow volume is 275 cubic centimeters. Calculate the volumetric efficiency.

46.5 A 4.0 L engine is being measured for volumetric efficiency. The possible airflow volume is 500 cubic centimeters. The actual airflow volume is 480 cubic centimeters. Calculate the volumetric efficiency.

Name _____ Date _____ Class _____

46.6 A 3.5 L engine is being measured for power output. At 3,000 rpm, the torque value is 120 foot-pounds. At 5,000 rpm, the torque value is 185 foot-pounds. Calculate the change in horsepower from 3,000 rpm to 5,000 rpm. Round to the nearest tenth.

46.7 A 5.7 L engine is being tested for power output gains. During the baseline test, at 5,000 rpm the torque value is 290 foot-pounds. With a high-performance camshaft and high-flow intake manifold installed, the torque value at 5,000 rpm increases to 365 foot-pounds. Calculate the horsepower output gain produced by these engine improvements. Round to the nearest tenth.

46.8 A 3.0 L turbocharged engine is being tested for power output gains. During the baseline test, at 5,600 rpm the torque value is 235 foot-pounds. With new high-performance camshafts installed, the torque value at 5,600 rpm is 370 foot-pounds. Calculate the horsepower output gain produced by these engine improvements. Round to the nearest tenth.

46.9 A 5.7 L engine is being modified for volumetric efficiency. The possible airflow volume is 750 cubic centimeters. The baseline actual airflow volume is 680 cubic centimeters. With high-flow exhaust headers and exhaust system and a cylinder head valve job, the improved actual airflow is 725 cubic centimeters. Calculate the change in volumetric efficiency with the engine improvements.

46.10 A 2.4 L engine is being upgraded from naturally aspirated (NA) to forced induction by adding a complete turbocharger kit. The possible airflow volume is 600 cubic centimeters. The baseline (NA) actual airflow volume is 540 cubic centimeters. With the turbocharger installed, the actual airflow volume is 635 cubic centimeters. Calculate the change in volumetric efficiency with the engine improvements.

# CASE STUDY 47

# Cam and Crank Journal

## OBJECTIVES

*After studying this case study, you will be able to:*
- Identify the procedure for measuring out-of-round and taper.
- Measure crankshaft and camshaft journals using a metric micrometer.

## TECHNICAL TERMS

out-of-round      taper

## MATH SKILLS

- Use a metric micrometer to measure crankshaft and camshaft journals.
- Compare measurements to specification.

Crankshaft and camshaft journals are the precision machined surfaces of the shaft that are used to connect the block and connecting rods. During an engine overhaul, accurate measurements of these journals are necessary to determine if and how parts will be refinished or replaced.

All journals are measured in four places to identify taper and out-of-round of the journals. The X-Y measurements indicate *out-of-round* and the A-B measurements indicate *taper*.

*Goodheart-Willcox Publisher*

**Out-of-round**   X – Y
**Taper**          A – B

*Goodheart-Willcox Publisher*

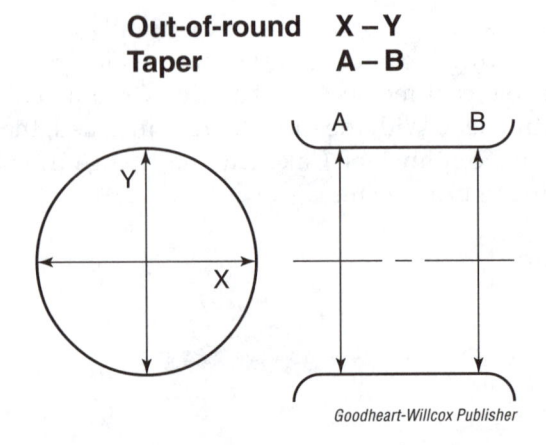

**Example:** The micrometers shown are the crankshaft main journal X and Y measurements. Read the micrometers and calculate the out-of-round value of this journal.

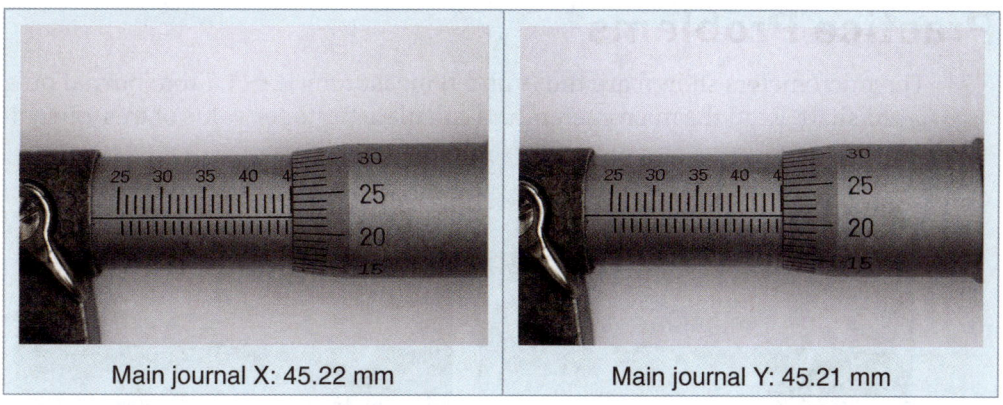

Main journal X: 45.22 mm

Main journal Y: 45.21 mm

*Goodheart-Willcox Publisher*

45.22 mm − 45.21 mm = 0.01 mm
The out-of-round value is 0.01 mm.

# Cam and Crank Journal Job Skill Practice Problems

**47.1** The micrometers shown are the A and B measurements of a rod journal on a crankshaft. Read the micrometers and calculate the taper value of this journal.

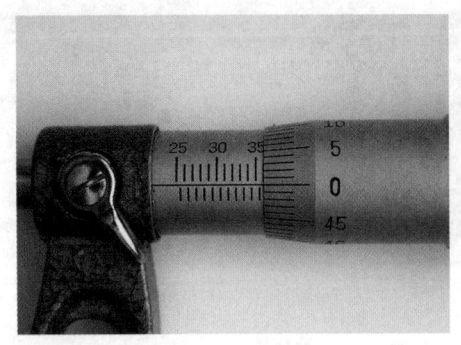

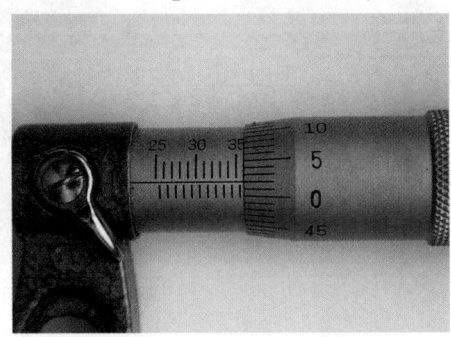

Rod journal A: _____    Rod journal B: _____

**47.2** The micrometers shown are the X and Y measurements of a camshaft main journal. Read the micrometers and calculate the out-of-round value.

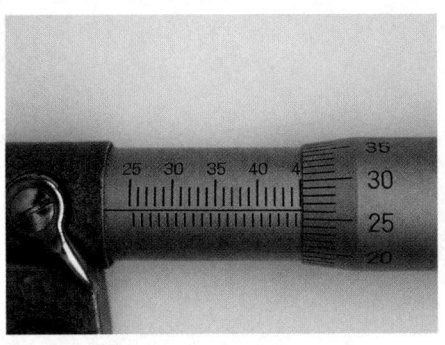

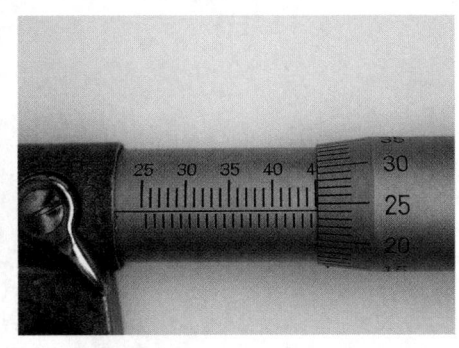

Main journal X: _____    Main journal Y: _____

**47.3** The micrometers shown are the X and Y measurements of a crankshaft main journal. Read the micrometers and calculate the out-of-round value.

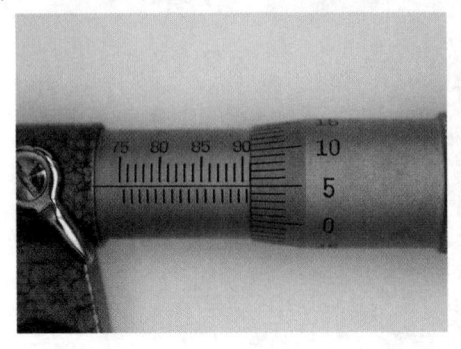

Main journal X: _____    Main journal Y: _____

Name _____ Date _____ Class _____

47.4 The micrometers shown are the A and B measurements of a crankshaft main journal. Read the micrometers and calculate the taper value. If the taper limit value is 0.03 mm, determine if this journal is within specification.

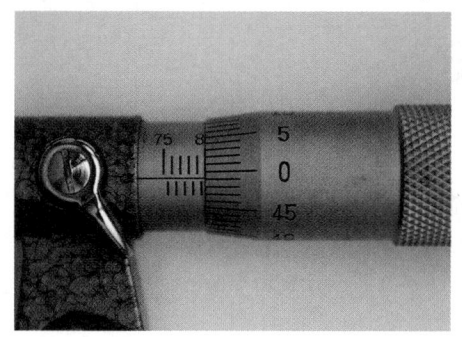

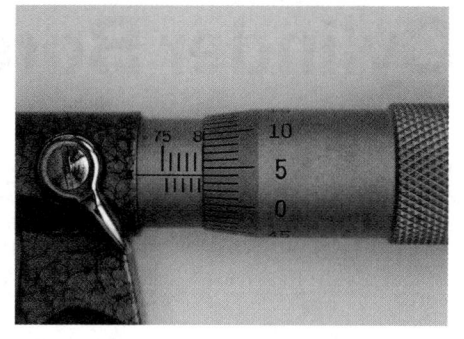

Main journal A: _____    Main journal B: _____

47.5 The micrometers shown are the X and Y measurements of a crankshaft rod journal. Read the micrometers and calculate the out-of-round value. If the out-of-round limit value is 0.02 mm, determine if this journal is within specification.

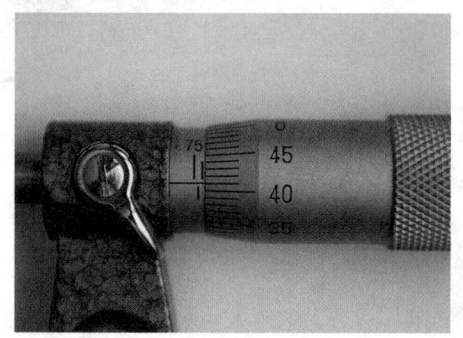

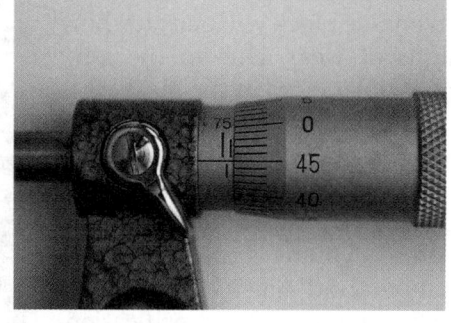

Rod journal X: _____    Rod journal Y: _____

# CASE STUDY 48

# Cylinder Bore

## OBJECTIVES

*After studying this case study, you will be able to:*
- Identify cylinder bore taper and out-of-round measurements.
- Calculate taper and out-of-round values of a cylinder bore.

## MATH SKILLS

- Analyze specifications and compare measured values to specification values.
- Analyze Job Skill problems by comparing measured values to specification.

Over time, the cylinder walls of an engine block will start to show signs of wear. Due to the very small tolerances in the block, this wear can lead to excessive blow-by gases, low compression, and lowered power and economy. During a major engine teardown, cylinder bore taper and out-of-round must be measured and compared to specification. These values will be used by the engine machine shop when they recondition the block. If the measured value equals the specification value, the value is at the limit and considered out of specification.

*Goodheart-Willcox Publisher*

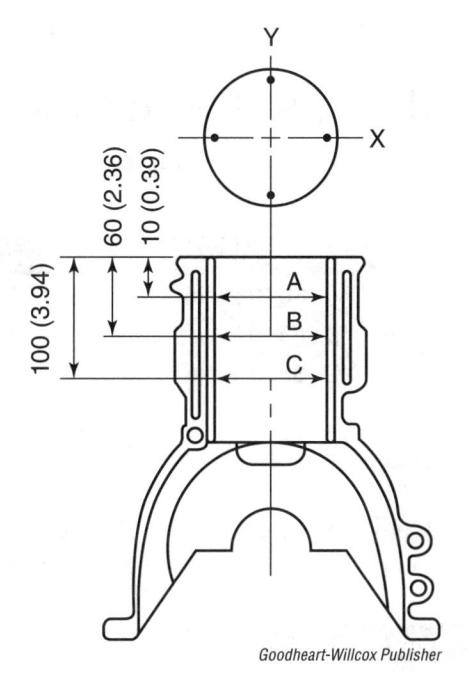

The *x*-axis and the *y*-axis refer to side-to-side and front-to-back distances within the cylinder bore. The A, B, and C values refer to the distances from the top of the bore being measured.

To measure taper: To measure and identify taper of the cylinder wall, compare the XA, XB, and XC measurements. Subtract the smallest value from the largest value to calculate the taper amount.

To measure out-of-round: To measure and identify out-of-round of the cylinder wall, compare the XA and YA measurements. The X and Y values will be the same if the cylinder is round, and will differ if the cylinder has an out-of-round condition. Subtract the values to calculate the out-of-round amount.

**Example:** An engine cylinder bore is being measured for out-of-round. The XA value is 3.4996″ and the YA value is 3.4992″. The tolerance specification value for this measurement is 0.0005″. Determine if the cylinder bore is within specification.

$$3.4996″ - 3.4992″ = 0.0004″$$
$$0.0004″ < 0.0005″$$

The out-of-round is within specification.

# Cylinder Bore Job Skill Practice Problems

Refer to the following diagram and tables to complete practice problems 48.1 through 48.4.

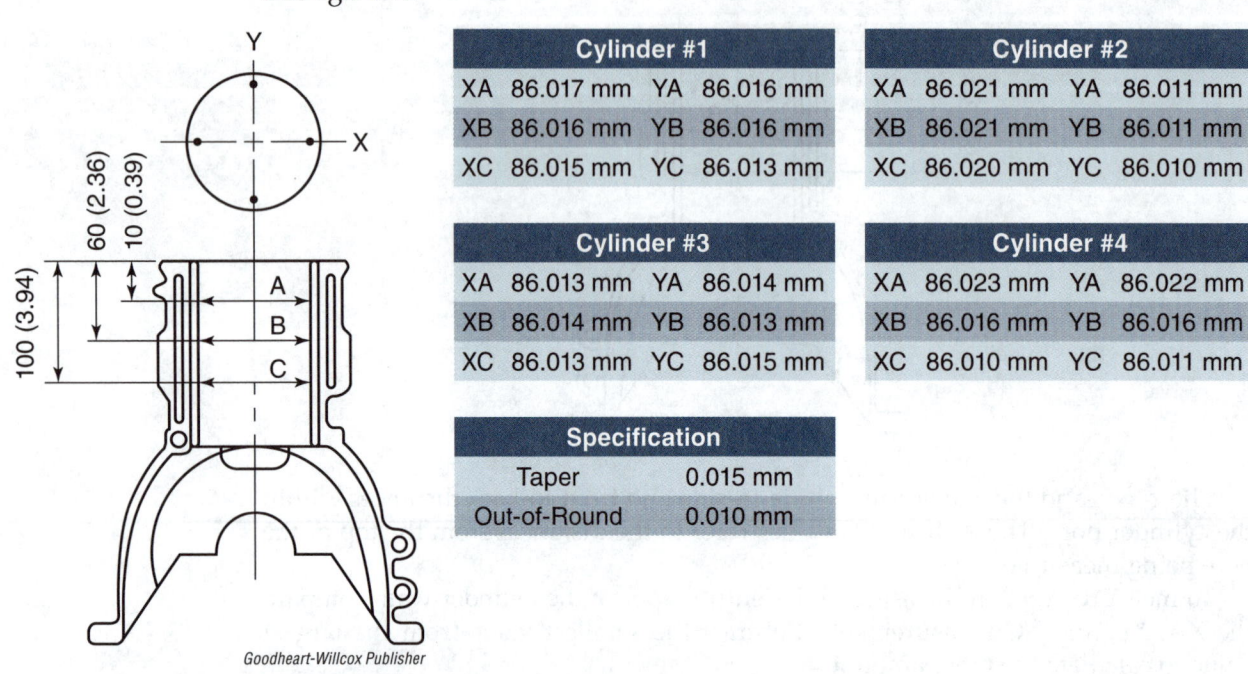

| Cylinder #1 | | | |
|---|---|---|---|
| XA 86.017 mm | YA 86.016 mm |
| XB 86.016 mm | YB 86.016 mm |
| XC 86.015 mm | YC 86.013 mm |

| Cylinder #2 | | | |
|---|---|---|---|
| XA 86.021 mm | YA 86.011 mm |
| XB 86.021 mm | YB 86.011 mm |
| XC 86.020 mm | YC 86.010 mm |

| Cylinder #3 | | | |
|---|---|---|---|
| XA 86.013 mm | YA 86.014 mm |
| XB 86.014 mm | YB 86.013 mm |
| XC 86.013 mm | YC 86.015 mm |

| Cylinder #4 | | | |
|---|---|---|---|
| XA 86.023 mm | YA 86.022 mm |
| XB 86.016 mm | YB 86.016 mm |
| XC 86.010 mm | YC 86.011 mm |

| Specification | |
|---|---|
| Taper | 0.015 mm |
| Out-of-Round | 0.010 mm |

*Goodheart-Willcox Publisher*

48.1 Calculate the amount of out-of-round for cylinder #1. Determine if the out-of-round is within specification.

48.2 Calculate the amount of taper for cylinder #4. Determine if the taper is within specification.

48.3 Calculate the amount of out-of-round for cylinder #2. Determine if the out-of-round is within specification.

**Name** _____ **Date** _____ **Class** _____

48.4 Calculate the amount of taper for cylinder #3. Determine if the taper is within specification.

Refer to the following diagram and tables to complete practice problems 48.5 through 48.10.

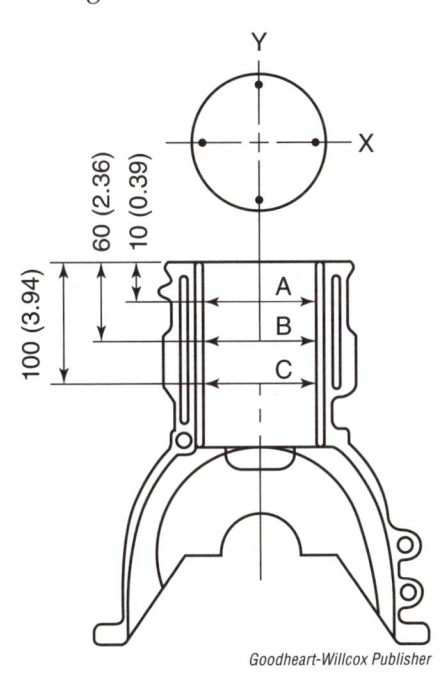

| Cylinder #1 | | | |
|---|---|---|---|
| XA | 3.5055" | YA | 3.5047" |
| XB | 3.5051" | YB | 3.5046" |
| XC | 3.5045" | YC | 3.5045" |

| Cylinder #2 | | | |
|---|---|---|---|
| XA | 3.5046" | YA | 3.5047" |
| XB | 3.5045" | YB | 3.5046" |
| XC | 3.5045" | YC | 3.5045" |

| Cylinder #3 | | | |
|---|---|---|---|
| XA | 3.5055" | YA | 3.5046" |
| XB | 3.5055" | YB | 3.5045" |
| XC | 3.5054" | YC | 3.5045" |

| Cylinder #4 | | | |
|---|---|---|---|
| XA | 3.5041" | YA | 3.5043" |
| XB | 3.5041" | YB | 3.5043" |
| XC | 3.5040" | YC | 3.5042" |

| Cylinder #5 | | | |
|---|---|---|---|
| XA | 3.5061" | YA | 3.5046" |
| XB | 3.5060" | YB | 3.5045" |
| XC | 3.5057" | YC | 3.5042" |

| Cylinder #6 | | | |
|---|---|---|---|
| XA | 3.5047" | YA | 3.5046" |
| XB | 3.5045" | YB | 3.5045" |
| XC | 3.5044" | YC | 3.5043" |

| Specification | |
|---|---|
| Taper | 0.0020" |
| Out-of-Round | 0.0010" |

*Goodheart-Willcox Publisher*

48.5 Calculate the amount of out-of-round for cylinder #3. Determine if the out-of-round is within specification.

48.6 Calculate the amount of taper for cylinder #1. Determine if the taper is within specification.

**Name** _____ **Date** _____ **Class** _____

48.7 Calculate the amount of out-of-round for cylinder #5. Determine if the out-of-round is within specification.

48.8 Calculate the amount of taper for cylinder #2. Determine if the taper is within specification.

48.9 Calculate the amount of out-of-round for cylinder #4. Determine if the out-of-round is within specification.

48.10 Calculate the amount of taper for cylinder #6. Determine if the taper is within specification.

# UNIT 6
# Electrical

Case Study 49 **Voltage Drop—Addition**
Case Study 50 **Reference Voltage—Subtraction**
Case Study 51 **Ohm's Law Part 1—Multiplication**
Case Study 52 **Ohm's Law Part 2—Division**
Case Study 53 **Applying Ohm's Law—Decimal Arithmetic**
Case Study 54 **Wire Gage Sizes—Greater Than and Less Than**
Case Study 55 **Wire Length—Fractions**
Case Study 56 **Temperature—Conversion**
Case Study 57 **Graphing Ohm's Law—Graphs and Tables**
Case Study 58 **Electrical Circuit Resistance—Formulas**
Case Study 59 **Digital Multimeter—Measurement**
Case Study 60 **Electrical System Specifications—Analyzing Specifications**

## CAREER PROFILE

Daniel Addie works as a service technician at Porsche Bellevue. During high school, automotive classes were not available to Daniel, but he worked at a regional quick-lube chain store throughout high school to gain experience. After graduating high school, he relocated to Arizona for training at Universal Technical Institute. Following his core training program, Daniel was seeking a challenge, and continued his training in Easton, Pennsylvania, in the Porsche Apprenticeship Training Program. This specialized training enabled Daniel to become a service technician at a world-class Porsche dealership.

On the job, Daniel uses math to track his flat-rate time, measure brakes and tires, and perform wheel alignments. He also applies his skills to calculate unit conversions and torque specifications. Reading gauges and coolant capacity specifications when servicing and refilling the cooling system found on rear-engine Porsche sports cars also requires math skills. Daniel works with numbers and solves problems throughout each day as a technician.

When diagnosing a vehicle issue, Daniel says, "Keep it simple. Don't overthink the problem and make it more difficult in your head." He recommends technicians have a thorough understanding of how the vehicle systems work and advises them to read the directions and follow procedures. This is especially important as technology continues to evolve on all cars, including sports cars. A strong math background is essential to understanding and diagnosing hybrid and electric vehicle technology.

*Goodheart-Willcox Publisher*
Daniel Addie—Service Technician, Porsche Bellevue.

# CASE STUDY 49

# Voltage Drop

## OBJECTIVES

*After studying this case study, you will be able to:*
- Identify Kirchhoff's voltage law.
- Apply Kirchhoff's voltage law to voltage drop circuit testing.

## TECHNICAL TERMS

Kirchhoff's voltage law    voltage    voltage drop

## MATH SKILLS
- Addition of whole and decimal numbers.
- Analyze circuits to compute voltage drop testing.

*Voltage* is the electrical potential as measured between the positive pole and the negative pole of a power source. *Voltage drop* is the measurement of how the energy is reduced at each electrical load in the circuit. These values are related based on *Kirchhoff's voltage law*.

*Goodheart-Willcox Publisher*

source voltage = voltage drop$_1$ + voltage drop$_2$ + voltage drop$_n$

The source voltage is the amount of voltage available at the power source. In each closed circuit, the voltage energy reduced at each electrical load will add up to the amount of source voltage. Review the following examples.

**Example:** An electrical circuit has three electrical loads within the series circuit. These electrical loads each have a voltage drop of exactly 3 volts. Calculate the source voltage.

source voltage = 3 volts + 3 volts + 3 volts
source voltage = 9 volts

**Example:** An electrical circuit has a power source of 20 volts. Within the series circuit, there are two electrical loads. The first electrical load measures 12 volts for voltage drop. Calculate the amount of voltage drop at the second load.

$$20 \text{ volts} = 12 \text{ volts} + x \text{ volts}$$
$$20 \text{ volts} - 12 \text{ volts} = x \text{ volts}$$
$$8 \text{ volts} = x \text{ volts}$$

## Voltage Drop Job Skill Practice Problems

49.1 An electrical circuit has three electrical loads in series. These loads measure 6 volts, 4 volts, and 3 volts. Calculate the source voltage.

49.2 An electrical circuit has four electrical loads in series. These loads measure 4.00 volts, 3.25 volts, 6.50 volts, and 7.75 volts. Calculate the source voltage.

49.3 An electrical circuit has four electrical loads in series. These loads measure 3.25 volts, 2.35 volts, 6.40 volts, and 3.00 volts. Calculate the source voltage.

49.4 An electrical circuit has a power source voltage of 14.5 volts. Within the series circuit, there are two electrical loads. The first load measures 9.6 volts. Calculate the voltage of the second load in the circuit.

49.5 An electrical circuit has a power source voltage of 12.6 volts. Within the series circuit, there are three electrical loads. The first load measures 4.1 volts and the second load measures 3.7 volts. Calculate the voltage of the third load in the circuit.

**Name** _____ **Date** _____ **Class** _____

49.6 A technician is diagnosing an electrical circuit issue. The source voltage is 12.6 volts. There is only one electrical load built into the circuit, and it has a voltage drop of 11.4 volts. This voltage drop test indicates unwanted resistance in the circuit. Calculate the voltage drop caused by the unwanted resistance in the circuit.

49.7 A technician is diagnosing an electrical circuit issue. The source voltage is 14.7 volts. There is only one electrical load built into the circuit, and it has a voltage drop of 12.9 volts. This voltage drop test indicates unwanted resistance in the circuit. Calculate the voltage drop caused by the unwanted resistance in the circuit.

49.8 A technician is diagnosing an electrical circuit issue. The source voltage is 5.0 volts. There is only one electrical load built into the circuit, and it has a voltage drop of 4.8 volts. This voltage drop test indicates unwanted resistance in the circuit. Calculate the voltage drop caused by the unwanted resistance in the circuit.

# CASE STUDY 50

# Reference Voltage

## OBJECTIVES

*After studying this case study, you will be able to:*
- Identify the purpose of electrical sensor reference voltage.
- Calculate signal voltage values based on reference voltage values.

## TECHNICAL TERMS

reference voltage        signal voltage

## MATH SKILLS

- Subtraction of whole number and decimal numbers.
- Analyze reference voltage values and signal voltage values.

---

Many sensors throughout the vehicle rely on a reference voltage value to function properly and generate a return signal for the control module. A *reference voltage* value is created by a fixed resistor in the control module that is in series with the sensor resistor. As the sensor resistance changes, the voltage drop across both resistors changes, and a *signal voltage* is calculated. Review the formula.

*Goodheart-Willcox Publisher*

signal voltage = reference voltage − sensor voltage drop

Typically, sensors have different resistance values based on the condition, and this will vary by temperature, pressure, or movement. Examples of these sensors are temperature sensors, fluid pressure sensors, and fluid level sensors. As the engine conditions change, the sensor voltage-drop and signal voltage change.

**Example:** A fuel level sensor uses a 5-volt reference signal. The voltage drop at the sensor is 1.3 volts. Calculate the signal voltage read by the engine control module.

signal voltage = 5.0 volts − 1.3 volts
signal voltage = 3.7 volts

Name _____  Date _____  Class _____

# Reference Voltage Job Skill Practice Problems

50.1  An engine coolant temperature sensor uses a 5-volt reference signal. The voltage drop at the sensor is 3.89 volts. Calculate the signal voltage read by the engine control module.

50.2  An oil pressure sensor uses a 5-volt reference signal. The voltage drop at the sensor is 2.45 volts. Calculate the signal voltage read by the engine control module.

50.3  A fuel level sensor uses a 12.6-volt reference signal. The voltage drop at the sensor is 9.78 volts. Calculate the signal voltage read by the engine control module.

50.4  A cylinder head temperature sensor uses a 5-volt reference signal. At start-up, the voltage drop at the sensor is 4.12 volts. At operating temperature, the voltage drop is 1.29 volts. Calculate the change in voltage drop between start-up and operating temperature.

Name _____ Date _____ Class _____

50.5 An oil pressure sensor uses a 5-volt reference signal. At start-up, the voltage drop at the sensor is 3.89 volts. At operating temperature, the voltage drop is 2.65 volts. Calculate the change in voltage drop between start-up and operating temperature.

50.6 A fuel level sensor uses a battery voltage and a reference voltage value. When the engine is running, this voltage is measured to be 14.3 volts. When the fuel level is full, the voltage drop at the sensor is 1.04 volts. When the fuel level is at the half full point, the voltage drop at the sensor is 6.89 volts. Calculate the change in voltage drop between the full fuel level and the half full fuel level.

50.7 A truck with a diesel engine uses a turbocharger exhaust temperature sensor with a reference voltage of 5 volts. The voltage drop at the sensor is 4.07 volts. Calculate the signal voltage read by the engine control module.

50.8 A hybrid car uses a high-voltage battery temperature sensor with a reference voltage of 5 volts. The data parameters for this sensor are 1.0 volts (194°F) to 4.8 volts (–40°F). The sensor has a voltage drop of 2.38 volts. Calculate the signal voltage and determine if the signal voltage is within the data parameters.

CASE STUDY 51

# Ohm's Law Part 1

## OBJECTIVES
*After studying this case study, you will be able to:*
- Calculate electrical circuit values using Ohm's law.
- Solve for unknown voltage values using Ohm's law.

## TECHNICAL TERMS
amperage          Ohm's law          resistance

## MATH SKILL
- Multiplication of whole and decimal numbers.

---

*Ohm's law* is the mathematical relationship between three electrical conditions: voltage, amperage, and resistance. If two of these values are known, the third value can be calculated using Ohm's law.

- *Voltage (v)*—The electrical potential as measured between the positive side and the negative side of a power source or within an electrical circuit.

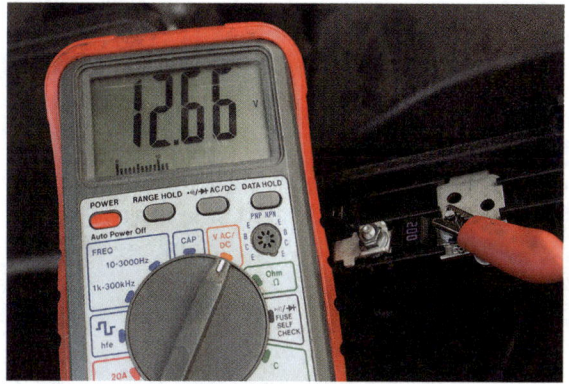

Goodheart-Willcox Publisher

- *Amperage (a)*—The number of electrons (electricity) flowing past a certain point over a certain period of time, described as electric current.
- *Resistance ($\Omega$)*—The opposition to current flow, necessary for a load to transfer the electricity into another form of energy (light, heat, motion).

The mathematical relationship between these values starts with the basic formula to solve for voltage. To solve for voltage, multiply amperage by resistance.

$$voltage = amperage \times resistance$$

**Example:** A technician is using a multimeter to make electrical measurements. The resistance of a taillight circuit is 4 $\Omega$ and the amperage measures 3.65 amps. Calculate the voltage of this circuit.

$$4 \, \Omega \times 3.65 \text{ amps} = 14.6 \text{ volts}$$

The voltage of the circuit is 14.6 volts.

Name _____ Date _____ Class _____

# Ohm's Law Part 1 Job Skill Practice Problems

51.1 A technician is using a multimeter to make electrical measurements. The resistance of a fuel pump is 7.2 Ω and the amperage measures 1.75 amps. Calculate the voltage of this circuit.

51.2 A technician is using a multimeter to make electrical measurements. The resistance of a headlight circuit is 3.5 Ω and the amperage measures 4.05 amps. Calculate the voltage of this circuit.

51.3 A technician is using a multimeter to make electrical measurements. The resistance of a heated side mirror circuit is 0.9 Ω and the amperage measures 16.1 amps. Calculate the voltage of this circuit.

51.4 A technician is using a multimeter to make electrical measurements. The resistance of a brake light circuit is 5.1 Ω and the amperage measures 2.80 amps. Calculate the voltage of this circuit.

**Name** _____ **Date** _____ **Class** _____

51.5 A technician is using a multimeter to make electrical measurements. The resistance of a license plate light circuit is 3.9 Ω and the amperage measures 3.2 amps. Calculate the voltage of this circuit.

51.6 A technician is using a multimeter to make electrical measurements. The resistance of a horn circuit is 2.15 Ω and the amperage measures 5.8 amps. Calculate the voltage of this circuit.

51.7 A technician is using a multimeter to make electrical measurements. The resistance of a reverse light circuit is 6.3 Ω and the amperage measures 2.3 amps. Calculate the voltage of this circuit.

51.8 A technician is using a multimeter to make electrical measurements. The resistance of an engine coolant temperature sensor circuit is 11.1 Ω and the amperage measures 0.450 amps. Calculate the voltage of this circuit.

# CASE STUDY 52

# Ohm's Law Part 2

## OBJECTIVES

*After studying this case study, you will be able to:*
- Calculate electrical circuit values using Ohm's law.
- Solve for unknown voltage values using Ohm's law.

## TECHNICAL TERMS

amperage    resistance

## MATH SKILL

- Division of whole and decimal numbers.

---

Ohm's law is the mathematical relationship between three electrical conditions: voltage, amperage, and resistance. If two of these values are known, the third value can be calculated using Ohm's law.

- *Voltage (v)*—The electrical potential as measured between the positive side and the negative side of a power source or within an electrical circuit.
- *Amperage (a)*—The number of electrons (electricity) flowing past a certain point over a certain period of time, described as electric current.
- *Resistance (Ω)*—The opposition to current flow, necessary for a load to transfer the electricity into another form of energy (light, heat, motion).

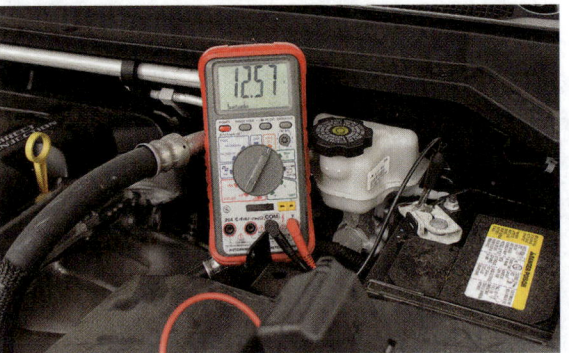

The mathematical relationship between these values and algebraic reasoning allows solving for an unknown amperage or resistance value.

$$amperage = \frac{voltage}{resistance}$$

$$resistance = \frac{voltage}{amperage}$$

**Example:** A technician is using a multimeter to make electrical measurements. The resistance of a taillight bulb is 3.3 Ω and the voltage is 14.6 volts. Calculate the amperage of this circuit. Round to the nearest hundredth.

14.6 volts ÷ 3.3 Ω = 4.42 amps

The taillight bulb circuit has a current flow of 4.42 amps.

Name _____ Date _____ Class _____

# Ohm's Law Part 2 Job Skill Practice Problems

52.1  A technician is using a multimeter to make electrical measurements. The resistance of a power seat motor is 1.3 Ω and the voltage is 14.5 volts. Calculate the amperage of this circuit. Round to the nearest hundredth.

52.2  A technician is using a multimeter to make electrical measurements. The amperage of a starter motor during cranking is 215 amps and the voltage is 11.4 volts. Calculate the resistance of the starter motor. Round to the nearest hundredth.

52.3  A technician is using a multimeter to make electrical measurements. The resistance of a power amplifier for a stereo is 0.6 Ω and the voltage is 14.8 volts. Calculate the amperage of this circuit. Round to the nearest hundredth.

52.4  A technician is using a multimeter to make electrical measurements. The resistance of a fuel pump is 2.1 Ω and the voltage is 14.6 volts. Calculate the amperage of this circuit. Round to the nearest hundredth.

**Name** _____ **Date** _____ **Class** _____

52.5 A technician is using a multimeter to make electrical measurements. The resistance of an engine coolant temperature sensor is 380 Ω and the voltage is 5.0 volts. Calculate the amperage of this circuit. Round to the nearest hundredth.

52.6 A technician is using a multimeter to make electrical measurements. The amperage of a fuel level sensor is 0.15 amps and the voltage is 14.6 volts. Calculate the resistance of this circuit. Round to the nearest hundredth.

52.7 A technician is using a multimeter to make electrical measurements. The amperage of an interior dome lamp is 0.65 amps and the voltage is 12.6 volts. Calculate the resistance of this circuit. Round to the nearest hundredth.

52.8 A technician is using a multimeter to make electrical measurements. The amperage of a power window motor is 1.3 amps and the voltage is 14.7 volts. Calculate the resistance of this circuit. Round to the nearest hundredth.

# CASE STUDY 53

# Applying Ohm's Law

## OBJECTIVES

*After studying this case study, you will be able to:*
- Identify how a variable resistance control switch is affected by Ohm's law.
- Identify how a variable resistance sensor is affected by Ohm's law.

## MATH SKILLS
- Arithmetic of decimal numbers.
- Analyze job skill problems using arithmetic of decimal numbers.

---

Ohm's law indicates that amperage and resistance values are inversely related. If resistance increases, amperage decreases; if resistance decreases, amperage increases. This concept of Ohm's law is the basis for variable resistance switches and sensors. Review the figure.

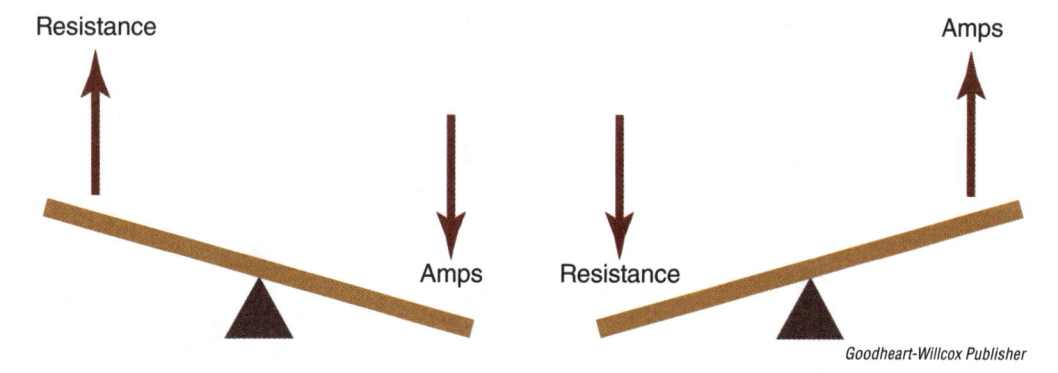

*Goodheart-Willcox Publisher*

The most basic example of a variable resistance switch is a climate control fan-motor switch. The fan speed is controlled by the amount of current flow through the fan motor. The variable resistance switch changes the amount of resistance in the electrical circuit to the motor, changing the amperage and speed of the fan motor. Review the following examples.

**Example:** A climate control fan-motor switch has three speeds: low, medium, and high. The voltage of the circuit is 14.5 volts. The fan motor has 6 Ω of resistance. The low-speed switch has 8 Ω of resistance, the medium switch has 4 Ω of resistance, and the high-speed switch has 0 Ω of resistance. Using Ohm's law, calculate the current draw in the circuit for all three speeds.

High speed = 14.5 volts ÷ (6 Ω + 0 Ω) = 2.417 amps
Medium speed = 14.5 volts ÷ (6 Ω + 4 Ω) = 1.45 amps
Low speed = 14.5 volts ÷ (6 Ω + 8 Ω) = 1.036 amps

**Example:** A fuel level sending unit uses a variable resistance sensor. The resistance changes as the fuel level float moves up and down. The engine control module (ECM) uses a 38 Ω resistor to create a reference voltage, and vehicle battery power is 14.5 volts. Refer to the table for some of the resistance values of the fuel level and use Ohm's law to calculate the amperage and voltage drop at the ECM and the sensor.

| Fuel Level Sensor | | | | |
|---|---|---|---|---|
| **Resistance** | 20 Ω | 200 Ω | 550 Ω | 780 Ω |
| **Fuel Level** | Full | Half | Low | Empty |

Amperage at full level = 14.5 volts ÷ (38 Ω + 20 Ω) = 0.25 amps
Full level voltage drop (ECM) = 38 Ω × 0.25 amps = 9.5 volts
Full level voltage drop (sensor) = 20 Ω × 0.25 amps = 5.0 volts
Total voltage = 9.5 volts + 5.0 volts = 14.5 volts
Amperage at low level = 14.5 volts ÷ (38 Ω + 550 Ω) = 0.0247 amps
Low level voltage drop (ECM) = 38 Ω × 0.0247 amps = 0.9386 volts
Low level voltage drop (sensor) = 550 Ω × 0.0247 amps = 13.585 volts
Total voltage = 0.9386 volts + 13.585 volts = 14.5 volts

Name _____ Date _____ Class _____

# Applying Ohm's Law Job Skill Practice Problems

53.1 A climate control fan motor has four speeds: low, medium-low, medium, and high. The voltage of the circuit is 14.5 volts. The fan motor has 9 Ω of resistance. The low speed switch has 14 Ω of resistance, the medium-low switch has 10 Ω of resistance, the medium speed switch has 6 Ω of resistance, and the high speed switch has 0 Ω of resistance. Using Ohm's law, calculate the current draw in the circuit for all four speeds and complete the table. Round to the nearest hundredth.

| Switch Range | Voltage | Switch Resistor | Motor Resistor | Amperage |
|---|---|---|---|---|
| Low | 14.5 | 14 Ω | 9 Ω | |
| Medium-Low | 14.5 | 10 Ω | 9 Ω | |
| Medium | 14.5 | 6 Ω | 9 Ω | |
| High | 14.5 | 0 Ω | 9 Ω | |

53.2 The throttle position sensor uses a variable resistance sensor to calculate throttle position. The voltage to the ECM is regulated to 10.0 volts. The ECM reference voltage signal resistor for this circuit is 35 Ω. The throttle position sensor resistance varies, from 35 Ω at wide-open-throttle (WOT) to 950 Ω at idle. Refer to the table for the resistance values of the throttle position sensor and use Ohm's law to calculate the amperage and voltage drop at the ECM and the sensor.

| Throttle Position Sensor ||||| 
|---|---|---|---|---|
| Resistance | 35 Ω | 250 Ω | 600 Ω | 950 Ω |
| Throttle Position | WOT | 75% Open | 50% Open | Idle |

53.3 A heated seat system uses a variable resistance sensor to calculate three seat temperature thresholds: low, medium, and high. This electrical circuit uses a 5-volt reference voltage signal from the body control module (BCM). The BCM reference voltage signal resistor is 7.6 Ω. Refer to the table for the resistance values of the seat temperature sensor and use Ohm's law to calculate the amperage and voltage drop at the BCM and the sensor.

| Heated Seat Temperature Sensor |   |   |   |
|---|---|---|---|
| Resistance | 4 Ω | 90 Ω | 370 Ω |
| Temperature Range | Low | Medium | High |

53.4 A rear-zone climate control fan motor has six speeds (Speed 1 to Speed 6, low to high). The voltage of the circuit is 14.5 volts. The fan motor has 12 Ω of resistance. Refer to the table for the resistance values of each fan speed. Using Ohm's law, calculate the current draw in the circuit for all six speeds and complete the table. Round to the nearest thousandth.

| Switch Range | Voltage | Switch Resistor | Motor Resistor | Amperage |
|---|---|---|---|---|
| Speed 1 | 14.5 | 45 Ω | 12 Ω | |
| Speed 2 | 14.5 | 36 Ω | 12 Ω | |
| Speed 3 | 14.5 | 27 Ω | 12 Ω | |
| Speed 4 | 14.5 | 18 Ω | 12 Ω | |
| Speed 5 | 14.5 | 9 Ω | 12 Ω | |
| Speed 6 | 14.5 | 0 Ω | 12 Ω | |

# CASE STUDY 54

# Wire Gage Sizes

## OBJECTIVES

*After studying this case study, you will be able to:*
- Identify wire gage sizes, wire diameters, and ampacity of wires.
- Compare wires to identify greater than and less than values.

## TECHNICAL TERM

ampacity

## MATH SKILLS

- Analyze greater than and less than values.
- Calculate arithmetic problems related to greater than and less than.

Automotive wire is designed to connect the circuit components and provide a path for electricity to flow. Wire size, the thickness of the wire, is determined based on the amount of current flowing through the wire and the length of the wire. The largest current draw on a gasoline powered non-hybrid vehicle is the starter motor. This circuit requires a larger diameter wire to handle the large current draw compared to a small amperage draw accessory like a single light bulb.

*Goodheart-Willcox Publisher*

The American Wire Gage (AWG) system has been established to provide a uniform scale for identifying different wire diameters. The AWG scale ranges from 0000 to 40, but most automotive wiring is between 4-AWG to 6-AWG for battery cables and 14-AWG to 20-AWG for circuit wiring. The AWG scale is unique in that the smaller the AWG value, the larger the wire diameter. Review the table.

*Ampacity* is the amperage capacity of a wire. There are many factors that affect wire ampacity, including wire length, temperature, insulation, and other related factors. *The ampacity values in the chart are listed for the purpose of demonstration, and should not be used as a reference to modify stock wiring or create electrical circuits.* Review the table and the following examples.

| Wire Gage Chart ||||| 
| AWG # | Diameter Inch | Diameter Metric | 10′ Ampacity | 3′ Ampacity |
|---|---|---|---|---|
| 4 | 0.2043 | 5.189 | 100 amps | 350 amps |
| 6 | 0.1620 | 4.115 | 60 amps | 225 amps |
| 8 | 0.1285 | 3.264 | 40 amps | 140 amps |
| 10 | 0.1019 | 2.588 | 27 amps | 90 amps |
| 12 | 0.0808 | 2.053 | 15 amps | 55 amps |
| 14 | 0.0641 | 1.628 | 10 amps | 35 amps |
| 16 | 0.0508 | 1.291 | 6 amps | 20 amps |
| 18 | 0.0403 | 1.024 | 4 amps | 10 amps |
| 20 | 0.0320 | 0.812 | 2 amps | 6 amps |

**Example:** A technician is comparing wire diameters. Determine which wire has a larger diameter, a 12-gage wire or a 20-gage wire.

12-gage wire = 0.0808″

20-gage wire = 0.0320″

0.0808″ > 0.0320″, so the 12-gage wire has a larger diameter.

**Example:** A technician is comparing wire ampacity values. Determine which wire has a smaller ampacity value, a 3′ 16-gage wire or a 10′ 14-gage wire.

3′ 16-gage wire = 20 amps

10′ 14-gage wire = 10 amps

10 amps < 20 amps, so the 10′ 14-gage wire has the smaller ampacity value.

Name _____  Date _____  Class _____

# Wire Gage Sizes Job Skill Practice Problems

Use the Wire Gage Chart to complete the following practice problems.

54.1  A technician is comparing wire diameters. Determine which wire has a larger diameter, a 10-gage wire or a 14-gage wire.

54.2  A technician is comparing wire diameters. Determine which wire has a smaller diameter, a 16-gage wire or an 18-gage wire.

54.3  A technician is comparing wire diameters. Determine which wire has a larger diameter, a 20-gage wire or a 4-gage wire.

54.4  A technician is comparing wire ampacity values. Determine which wire has a smaller ampacity value, a 3′ 10-gage wire or a 10′ 14-gage wire.

**Name** _____ **Date** _____ **Class** _____

54.5 A technician is comparing wire ampacity values. Determine which wire has a larger ampacity value, a 3′ 6-gage wire or a 3′ 4-gage wire.

54.6 A technician is comparing wire ampacity values. Determine which wire has a smaller ampacity value, a 10′ 16-gage wire or a 10′ 20-gage wire.

54.7 A technician is running a 3′ wire that will be protected with a 30-amp fuse. Determine the best wire gage for this wire.

54.8 A technician is running a 10′ wire that will be protected with a 15-amp fuse. Determine the best wire gage for this wire.

# CASE STUDY 55

# Wire Length

## OBJECTIVES

*After studying this case study, you will be able to:*
- Calculate total wire length after a solder repair.
- Calculate remaining wire length after a section of wire has been removed.

## MATH SKILLS
- Addition of fractions and mixed number fractions.
- Subtraction of fractions and mixed number fractions.

A solder wire repair is performed by stripping the ends of the wire insulation, carefully twisting the copper strands together, heating the wire with a solder iron, and allowing the solder to flow into the metal wire section. Once cooled, this wire joint is covered with shrink tube. A correctly performed solder repair is strong and conducts electricity.

When wire lengths are soldered together, the individual lengths are added together to determine the total length. When wire is cut from an exsisting piece of wire, the amount is subtracted from the total length. Review the following examples.

*Goodheart-Willcox Publisher*

**Example:** Two lengths of wire are being soldered together. One wire is 3 5/8″ and the other wire is 6 1/4″. Calculate the total length after these wires are soldered together.

$$3\ 5/8″ + 6\ 1/4″ =$$
$$3\ 5/8″ + 6\ 2/8″ = 9\ 7/8″$$

The total length is 9 7/8″.

**Example:** A length of wire is being cut from a spool of wire. The spool of wire is 36″. The length of wire being cut off is 9 3/16″. Calculate the remaining wire on the spool.

$$36″ = 35\ 16/16″$$
$$35\ 16/16″ - 9\ 3/16″ = 26\ 13/16″$$

The remaining length is 26 13/16″.

Name _____ Date _____ Class _____

# Wire Length Fraction Job Skill Practice Problems

55.1 Two lengths of wire are being soldered together. One wire is 4 1/2" and the other wire is 2 7/8". Calculate the total length after these wires are soldered together.

55.2 Three lengths of wire are being soldered together. One wire is 12 1/2", one wire is 2 5/8", and the other wire is 7 3/8". Calculate the total length after these wires are soldered together.

55.3 Two lengths of wire are being soldered together. One wire is 7 3/16" and the other wire is 8 7/8". Calculate the total length after these wires are soldered together.

55.4 Three lengths of wire are being soldered together. One wire is 10 11/16", one wire is 12 1/16", and the other wire is 7 3/4". Calculate the total length after these wires are soldered together.

**Name** _____  **Date** _____  **Class** _____

55.5  A length of wire is being cut from a spool of wire. The spool of wire is 96″. The length of wire being cut off is 14 11/16″. Calculate the remaining wire on the spool.

55.6  A length of wire is being cut from a spool of wire. The spool of wire is 48″. The length of wire being cut off is 5 7/8″. Calculate the remaining wire on the spool.

55.7  Two lengths of wire are being cut from a spool of wire. The spool of wire is 126″. The lengths of wire being cut off are 17 5/8″ and 19 7/16″. Calculate the remaining wire on the spool.

55.8  Two lengths of wire are being cut from a spool of wire. The spool of wire is 58″. The lengths of wire being cut off are 11 1/4″ and 20 9/16″. Calculate the remaining wire on the spool.

Copyright Goodheart-Willcox Co., Inc. May not be reproduced or posted to a publicly accessible website.

# CASE STUDY 56

# Temperature

## OBJECTIVES

*After studying this case study, you will be able to:*
- Identify the function of a k-type thermocouple.
- Calculate temperature conversion between Celsius and Fahrenheit.

## TECHNICAL TERMS

k-type thermocouple      thermocouple

## MATH SKILLS

- Conversion of whole and decimal numbers.
- Analyze job skill problems with temperature conversion factors.

---

A *thermocouple* is a junction of two metals that converts a temperature difference into a voltage signal. This voltage can be measured and converted into a temperature value on the Celsius and Fahrenheit scales. A common type of thermocouple used in automotive applications, especially in automotive research and development, is a k-type thermocouple.

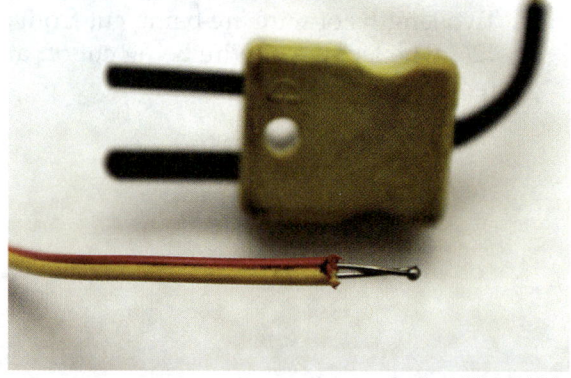

*Goodheart-Willcox Publisher*

A *k-type thermocouple* generally has an electrical connector that allows it to be plugged into a standard digital multimeter. The multimeter has a temperature setting, and can read both Celsius and Fahrenheit temperature values.

Conversion between Celsius and Fahrenheit is often required in automotive applications. The conversion formulas for these scales require entering the known temperature value into the formula to solve the unknown temperature value. Review the formulas and examples.

$$°F = °C \times 1.8 + 32$$
$$°C = (°F - 32) \div 1.8$$

**Example:** A cooling system thermostat is rated at 90.5°C. Convert this temperature value to Fahrenheit.

$$°F = 90.5°C \times 1.8 + 32$$
$$°F = 194.9$$

**Example:** A thermocouple is being used to measure the outside temperature of a catalytic converter. The multimeter reads 784°F. Convert this temperature value to Celsius.

$$°C = (784°F - 32) \div 1.8$$
$$°C = 417.8$$

Name _____ Date _____ Class _____

## Temperature Job Skill Practice Problems

56.1 A pressurized cooling system raises the boiling point of the engine coolant to 245°F. Convert this temperature value to Celsius. Round to the nearest tenth.

56.2 Radiator efficiency is being tested with a thermocouple and multimeter. The upper radiator hose measures 165°F. The lower radiator hose measures 58°C. Calculate the temperature difference between the upper and lower radiator hoses.

56.3 Exhaust header tube temperatures are being measured with a thermocouple and multimeter. The average temperature for Bank 1 is 275°F. The average temperature for Bank 2 is 141°C. Determine which cylinder bank is running hotter.

56.4 A tire technician is measuring tire tread temperature using a pyrometer-type thermocouple. The left front tire measures 136°F and the right front tire measures 56°C. Calculate the difference in temperature between the left and right front tires. Round to the nearest tenth.

Name _____ Date _____ Class _____

56.5 A vehicle research technician is monitoring high-voltage battery cells in a hybrid-electric vehicle during a testing cycle. Battery Cell #1 measures 90°C, Battery Cell #2 measures 89°C, and Battery Cell #3 measures 94°C. The testing limit for battery temperature is 200°F. Determine if each of these battery cells remained below 200°F during the testing cycle.

56.6 A technician suspects a faulty ambient air temperature sensor. A thermocouple connected to a digital multimeter is placed next to the ambient air temperature sensor. The sensor reading is 19.4°C. The multimeter reading is 67°F. Determine if the sensor is making an accurate ambient air temperature reading.

56.7 A transmission fluid temperature sensor is reading 57.2°C with a stock transmission fluid cooler. With an aftermarket transmission fluid cooler added to the system, the transmission fluid temperature drops to 127°F. Calculate the change in temperature with the aftermarket transmission fluid cooler.

56.8 An air conditioning (A/C) system is being performance tested for proper operation. With the A/C system in MAX COOL mode, the thermocouple connected to the center vent reads 8°C. The repair manual specifies the A/C output temperature should be below 42°F. Determine if this air conditioning system passes the performance test.

# CASE STUDY 57

# Graphing Ohm's Law

## OBJECTIVES
*After studying this case study, you will be able to:*
- Identify how changes in resistance and voltage effect changes in amperage.
- Identify how a short circuit causes a spike in amperage values.

## MATH SKILLS
- Analyze and interpret graphs and tables.
- Solve job skill problems based on data from graphs and tables.

The mathematical relationship between voltage, amperage, and resistance can be plotted on a graph as a visual representation of the values. Changes to these values on the graph correspond directly to the changes in the values found in the table. The graph can clearly show Ohm's law basics, such as when resistance decreases, the amperage increases, and when voltage increases, amperage also increases.

*Goodheart-Willcox Publisher*

The occurrence of when resistance becomes almost zero, known as a short circuit, can also be viewed on an Ohm's law graph. A fuse is designed to protect a circuit from an excessive amount of amperage, which occurs when the resistance is near zero.

**Example:** Shown are various resistance values applied to Ohm's law at 12.6 volts. Use the table and graph to answer the questions.

| Volts | Ohms | Amps |
|---|---|---|
| 12.6 | 10 | 1.26 |
| 12.6 | 8 | 1.58 |
| 12.6 | 6 | 2.10 |
| 12.6 | 4 | 3.15 |
| 12.6 | 2 | 6.30 |
| 12.6 | 1 | 12.60 |
| 12.6 | 0.5 | 25.20 |

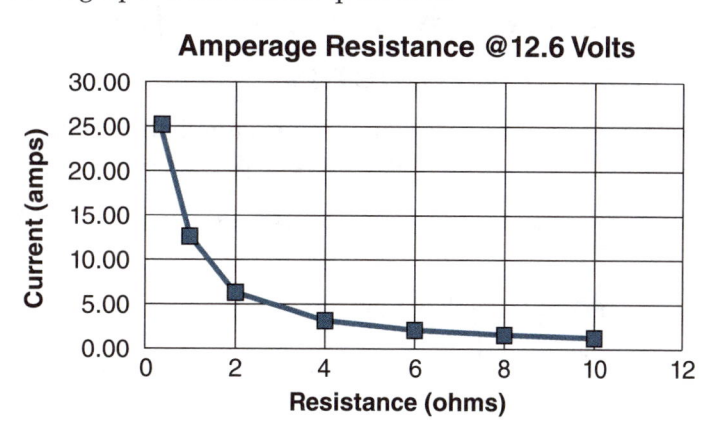

As resistance decreases, amperage (increases/decreases).

Increases

Calculate the change in current from 6 Ω to 2 Ω.

6.30 amps – 2.10 amps = 4.20 amps

4.20 amps

Estimate the current (amps) if the resistance is 0.25 Ω.

≈50 amps

Name _____ Date _____ Class _____

# Graphing Ohm's Law Job Skill Practice Problems

Shown are various resistance values applied to Ohm's law at 14.7 volts. Use the table and graph to complete practice problems 57.1 through 57.5.

| Volts | Ohms | Amps |
|-------|------|------|
| 14.7  | 10   | 1.47 |
| 14.7  | 8    | 1.84 |
| 14.7  | 6    | 2.45 |
| 14.7  | 4    | 3.68 |
| 14.7  | 2    | 7.35 |
| 14.7  | 1    | 14.70 |
| 14.7  | 0.5  | 29.40 |
| 14.7  | 0.25 | 58.80 |

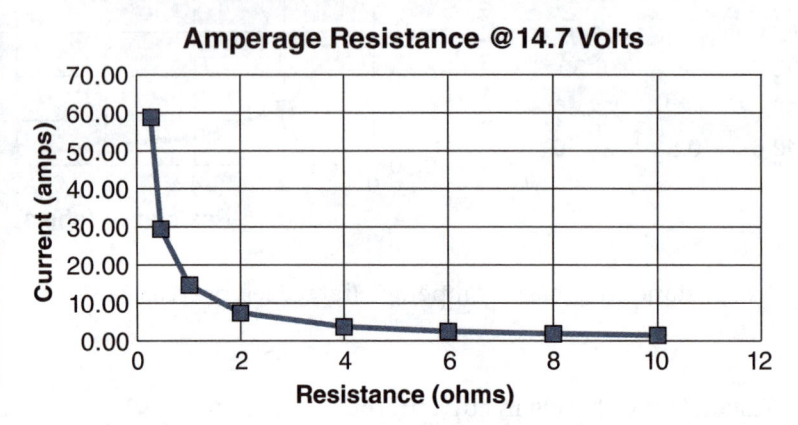

**Amperage Resistance @ 14.7 Volts**

57.1 If an electrical circuit had a resistance value of 5 Ω, estimate the amperage value.

57.2 Calculate the difference in amperage between 2 Ω and 8 Ω.

57.3 Estimate the amperage value if the resistance is 20 Ω.

57.4 If a circuit usually has around 2 Ω of resistance, but a short occurs causing the resistance to drop to 0.01 Ω, describe the effect on amperage.

**Name** _____ **Date** _____ **Class** _____

57.5 As resistance decreases, amperage (increases/decreases).

Shown are various resistance values applied to Ohm's law at 9.6 volts. Use the table and graph to complete practice problems 57.6 through 57.8.

| Volts | Ohms | Amps |
|-------|------|------|
| 9.6 | 10 | 0.96 |
| 9.6 | 8 | 1.20 |
| 9.6 | 6 | 1.60 |
| 9.6 | 4 | 2.40 |
| 9.6 | 2 | 4.80 |
| 9.6 | 1 | 9.60 |
| 9.6 | 0.5 | 19.20 |

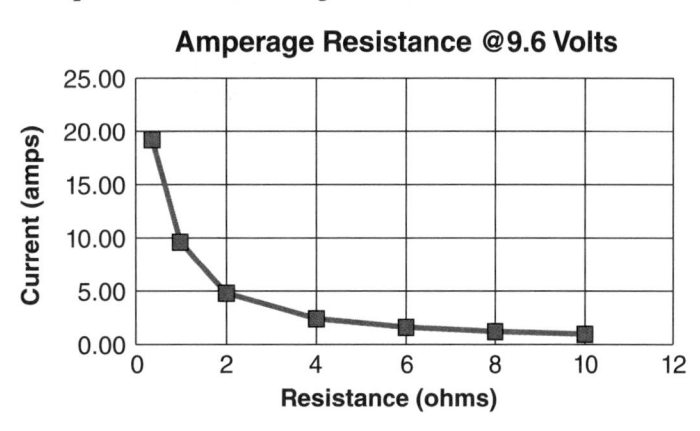

57.6 If an electrical circuit had a resistance value of 7 Ω, estimate the amperage value.

57.7 Calculate the difference in amperage between 0.5 Ω and 2 Ω.

57.8 Estimate the amperage value if the resistance is 50 Ω.

Shown are various voltage values applied to Ohm's law at a resistance value of 0.5 Ω. Use the table and graph to complete practice problems 57.9 through 57.12.

| Volts | Ohms | Amps |
|---|---|---|
| 14.7 | 0.5 | 29.40 |
| 12.6 | 0.5 | 25.20 |
| 10 | 0.5 | 20.00 |
| 9.6 | 0.5 | 19.20 |
| 5 | 0.5 | 10.00 |
| 0 | 0.5 | 0.00 |

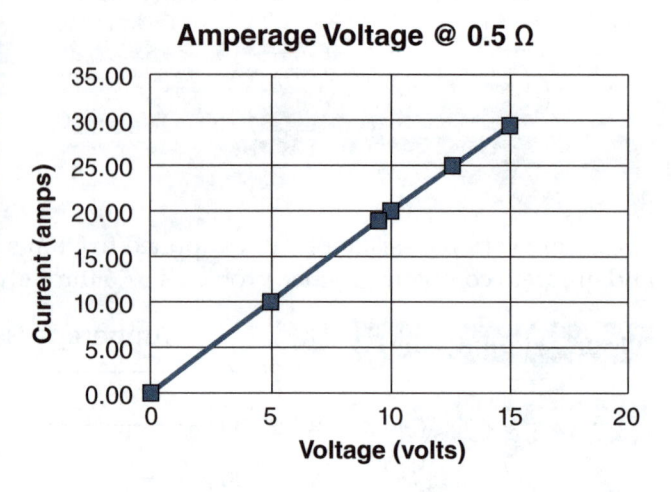

**Amperage Voltage @ 0.5 Ω**

57.9 As the voltage decreases, the amperage (increases, decreases).

57.10 Calculate the amperage difference between 5 volts and 10 volts.

57.11 Estimate the amperage at 20 volts.

57.12 Describe how a weak battery, low voltage, affects current output.

# CASE STUDY 58

# Electrical Circuit Resistance

## OBJECTIVES

*After studying this case study, you will be able to:*
- Calculate total resistance in a series circuit.
- Calculate total resistance in a parallel circuit.

## TECHNICAL TERMS

parallel circuit      series circuit

## MATH SKILLS

- Calculate values according to a formula.
- Analyze job skill problems to calculate electrical resistance.

Electrical circuits are designed to connect the power source to electrical loads controlled by a switch. The circuit requires a complete path in order for current to flow. Circuits can be designed as series circuits or parallel circuits.

*Series circuit*—An electrical circuit where all electrical loads are on the same path and share the total voltage.

To calculate total resistance in a series circuit, use the following formula:

$$R_t = R_1 + R_2 + R_n$$

*Goodheart-Willcox Publisher*

*Parallel circuit*—An electrical circuit where all electrical loads are on separate circuits and do not share the voltage, but all have equal total voltage.

To calculate total resistance in a parallel circuit, use the following formula:

$$R_t = \dfrac{1}{\dfrac{1}{R_1} + \dfrac{1}{R_2} + \dfrac{1}{R_n}}$$

**Example:** A series circuit has four resistors: $R_1 = 7\,\Omega$, $R_2 = 6\,\Omega$, $R_3 = 4\,\Omega$, and $R_4 = 2\,\Omega$. Create a series circuit with four resistors and calculate the total circuit resistance.

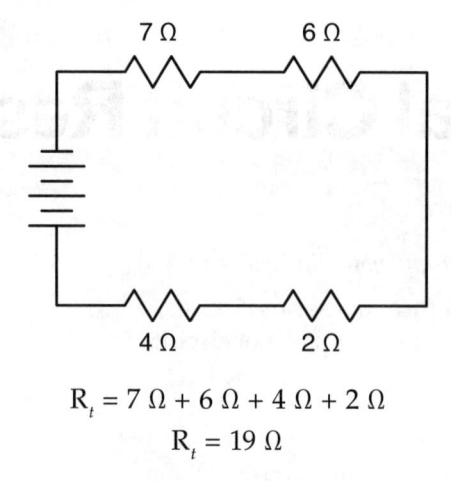

$$R_t = 7\,\Omega + 6\,\Omega + 4\,\Omega + 2\,\Omega$$
$$R_t = 19\,\Omega$$

**Example:** A parallel circuit has four resistors: $R_1 = 7\,\Omega$, $R_2 = 6\,\Omega$, $R_3 = 4\,\Omega$, and $R_4 = 2\,\Omega$. Create a parallel circuit with four resistors and calculate the total circuit resistance.

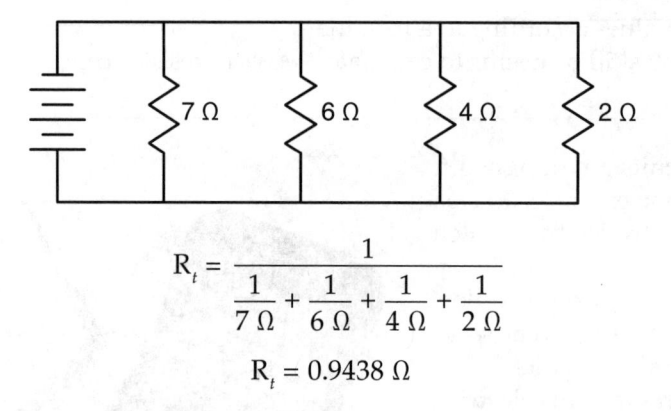

$$R_t = \dfrac{1}{\dfrac{1}{7\,\Omega} + \dfrac{1}{6\,\Omega} + \dfrac{1}{4\,\Omega} + \dfrac{1}{2\,\Omega}}$$

$$R_t = 0.9438\,\Omega$$

Name _____  Date _____  Class _____

# Electrical Circuit Resistance
# Job Skill Practice Problems

58.1 Create a series circuit with three resistors. Solve for total resistance.
    $R_1$: 5 Ω      $R_2$: 6 Ω      $R_3$: 4 Ω

58.2 Create a series circuit with five resistors. Solve for total resistance.
    $R_1$: 0.4 Ω      $R_3$: 0.7 Ω      $R_5$: 1.85 Ω
    $R_2$: 0.2 Ω      $R_4$: 0.25 Ω

58.3 Create a parallel circuit with three resistors. Solve for total resistance. Round to the nearest hundredth.
    $R_1$: 3 Ω      $R_2$: 5 Ω      $R_3$: 4 Ω

58.4 Create a parallel circuit with four resistors. Solve for total resistance. Round to the nearest hundredth.
$R_1$: 0.45 Ω     $R_2$: 0.12 Ω     $R_3$: 0.75 Ω     $R_4$: 0.35 Ω

58.5 Create a parallel circuit with four resistors. Solve for total resistance. Round to the nearest hundredth.
$R_1$: 12 Ω     $R_2$: 14 Ω     $R_3$: 18 Ω     $R_4$: 10 Ω

58.6 Create a parallel circuit with two series branches, four resistors total. Solve for total resistance. Round to the nearest hundredth.
Series Branch 1     $R_1$: 4 Ω     $R_2$: 3 Ω
Series Branch 2     $R_3$: 7 Ω     $R_4$: 8 Ω

# CASE STUDY 59

# Digital Multimeter

## OBJECTIVES

*After studying this case study, you will be able to:*
- Identify and analyze voltage measurements using a digital multimeter.
- Identify and analyze resistance measurements using a digital multimeter.
- Identify and analyze amperage measurements using a digital multimeter.

## MATH SKILLS
- Observe measured values using a digital multimeter.
- Analyze job skill problems related to voltage, amperage, and resistance.

The digital multimeter is designed to measure voltage, amperage, and resistance. An autoranging meter is able to analyze the electrical signal and adjust the place value on the screen. The electrical test leads at the bottom of the meter must be moved to different terminals when switching between volts, amps, and ohms.

*Goodheart-Willcox Publisher*

**To measure voltage**—Set the dial to voltage DC and insert the test leads in the V and COM (ground). Connect the test leads to the circuit in parallel to measure the potential difference between the two measurements points.

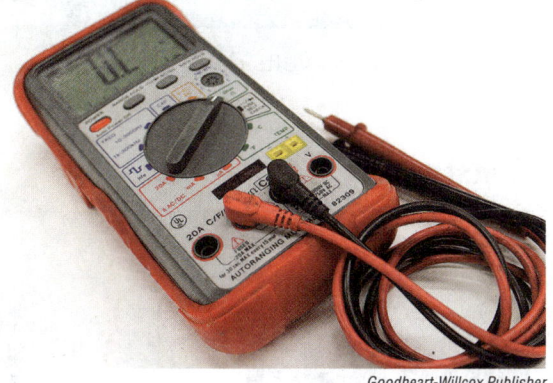

**To measure resistance**—Set the dial to the ohms (Ω) setting and insert the test leads in the Ω and COM (ground). On some meters, this is the same test lead port as voltage. Connect the test leads to the component or section of circuit to be measured *after* the circuit has been disconnected from the power source.

**To measure amperage**—Set the dial to the 20 amp setting and insert the test leads in the 20 amp and COM (ground). Open the circuit and connect the test lead in series to the circuit, so the meter becomes part of the circuit.

Review the following examples.

## Voltage

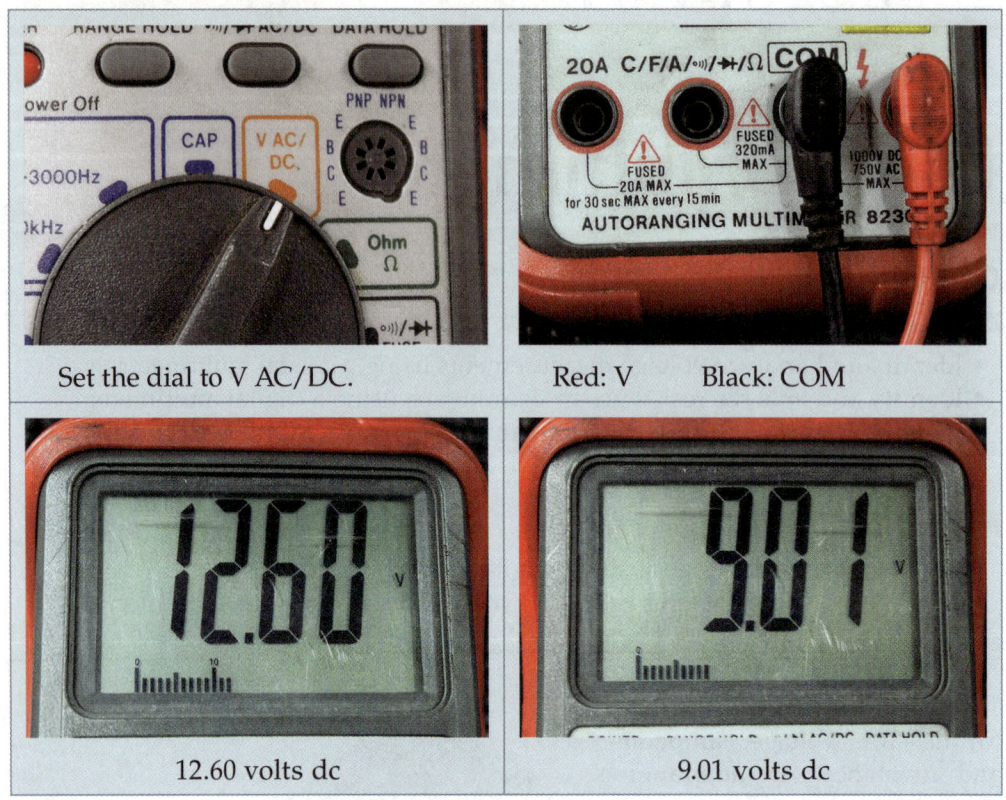

| Set the dial to V AC/DC. | Red: V  Black: COM |
|---|---|
| 12.60 volts dc | 9.01 volts dc |

## Resistance

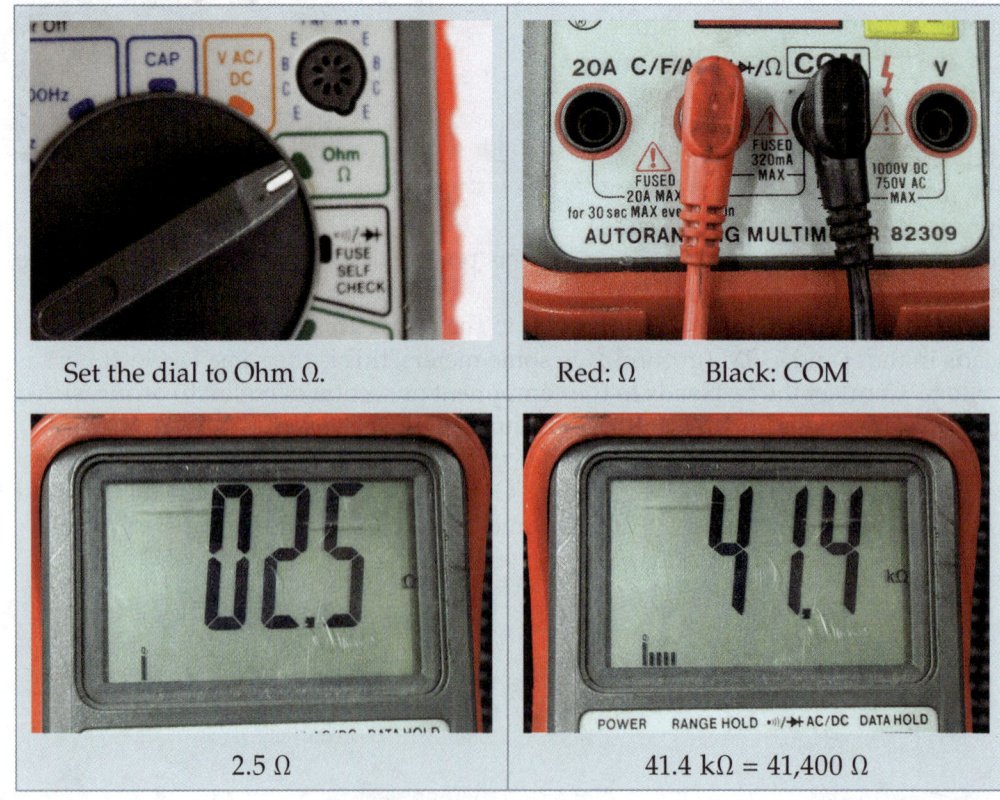

| Set the dial to Ohm Ω. | Red: Ω  Black: COM |
|---|---|
| 2.5 Ω | 41.4 kΩ = 41,400 Ω |

*Goodheart-Willcox Publisher*

## Amperage (Current)

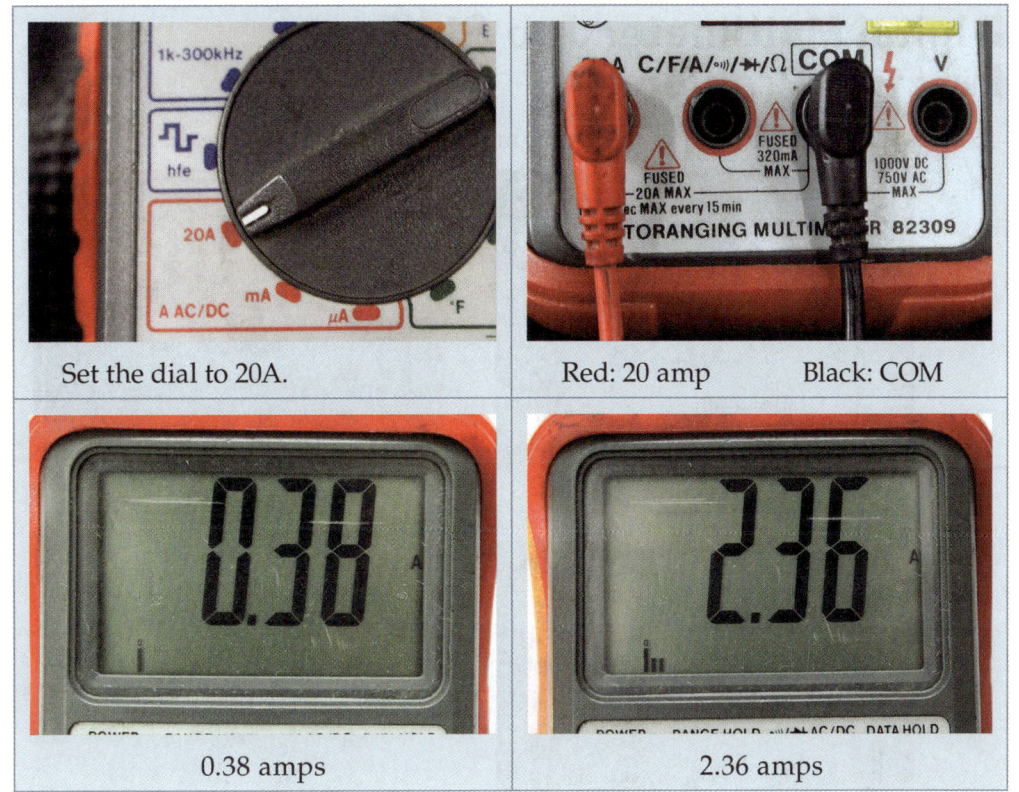

| | |
|---|---|
| Set the dial to 20A. | Red: 20 amp     Black: COM |
| 0.38 amps | 2.36 amps |

*Goodheart-Willcox Publisher*

Name _____ Date _____ Class _____

## Digital Multimeter Job Skill Practice Problems

59.1 Identify the reading on the digital multimeter. Label the answer.

1. _____   2. _____

3. _____

59.2 Identify the reading on the digital multimeter. Label the answer.

1. _____   2. _____

3. _____

Name _____ Date _____ Class _____

59.3 A technician is measuring open-circuit voltage across the battery terminals. Analyze the multimeter reading to determine if the engine is running or turned off.

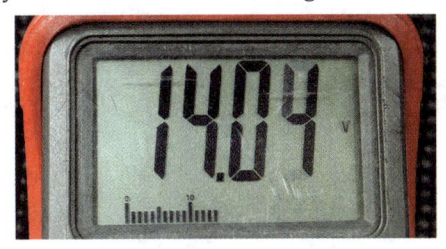

Multimeter reading: _____

59.4 A technician is measuring resistance of a ground wire connection. The desired resistance is 0.1 Ω or less. Analyze the multimeter reading to determine if the ground wire has excessive resistance or is within the desired resistance.

Multimeter reading: _____

59.5 A technician is measuring voltage of two electrical loads wired in series. Analyze the multimeters shown to calculate the total source voltage.

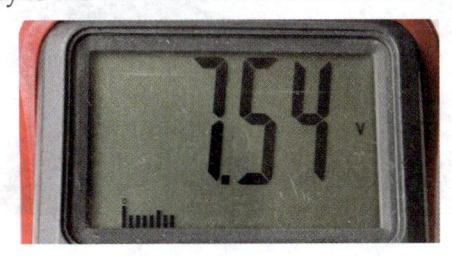

Multimeter reading: _____    Multimeter reading: _____

Total source voltage: _____

59.6 A technician is measuring current flow in a circuit using a digital multimeter. Analyze the multimeter reading and use Ohm's law to calculate the resistance of the circuit if the voltage is 12.6 volts.

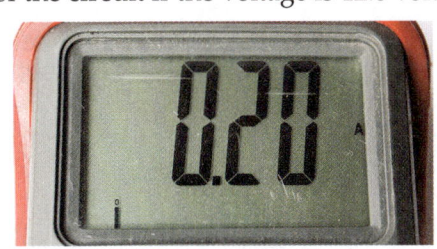

Multimeter reading: _____

Circut resistance: _____

# CASE STUDY 60

# Electrical System Specifications

## OBJECTIVES

*After studying this case study, you will be able to:*
- Identify electrical system specifications.
- Analyze battery, starting, charging, and other electrical system specifications.

## MATH SKILL
- Analyze and solve job skill problems related to electrical system specifications.

Modern vehicles are now equipped with electrical systems throughout the entire vehicle, from the windshield to the tires. Most vehicles have a dozen or more computers that communicate over a network to control most vehicle functions. The electrical capabilities have also evolved, allowing for electronic steering control, brake and traction control, collision avoidance systems, and fuel efficient engine management systems. More traditional vehicle electrical systems, such as battery, starting, and charging systems, have also evolved to be more functional and reliable. All of these systems have electrical specifications that may need to be located and considered by a technician during vehicle diagnosis and service.

Refer to the provided specification tables to solve the problems relating to electrical specifications.

*Goodheart-Willcox Publisher*

**Example:**

| Specifications | 3.5 L V6 |
|---|---|
| Cold Cranking Amps (CCA) | 590 A |
| Amp Hour Rating | 54 Ah |
| Reserve Capacity Rating | 90–100 minutes |
| Replacement Battery Number | 90-6YR |

A technician is testing a battery in a vehicle with a 3.5 L V6 using a handheld capacitance tester. The tester requires cold cranking amps (CCA) as a data input. Identify the CCA for this vehicle.

The battery in this vehicle is rated at 590 CCA.

# Electrical System Specifications
# Job Skill Practice Problems

Use the following table to complete problems 60.1 through 60.3.

| Specifications | 3.5 L V6 | 7.0 L V8 | 1.6 L L4 |
|---|---|---|---|
| Cold Cranking Amps (CCA) | 590 A | 630 A | 550 A |
| Amp Hour Rating | 54 Ah | 59 Ah | 50 Ah |
| Reserve Capacity Rating | 100 minutes | 110 minutes | 90 minutes |
| Replacement Battery Number | 90-6YR | 95C-84 | 85B-60 |

60.1  A technician has tested a battery from a vehicle with a 1.6 L L4 engine and determined the battery needs to be replaced. Identify the replacement battery part number.

60.2  Determine which engine requires the highest cold cranking amps rated battery.

60.3  Determine which battery has the lowest reserve capacity rating.

Use the following table to complete problems 60.4 through 60.6.

| Charging System Specifications - 2010 V6 - 3.8 L ||
|---|---|
| Application | Specification |
| Model: D.SC11 ||
| Generator | SC11 |
| Rated Output | 135 amps |
| Load Tested Output | 94 amps |
| Model: B.LZ44 ||
| Generator | LZ44 |
| Rated Output | 125 amps |
| Load Tested Output | 87 amps |
| Battery 34H-7RN ||
| Cold Cranking Amps | 625 amps |
| Amp Hour Rating | 66 Ah |
| Reserve Capacity Rating | 110 minutes |

Name _____ Date _____ Class _____

60.4 A ZL44 alternator is being replaced with an SC11 alternator. Calculate the increase in load tested output.

60.5 This vehicle is built with two trim levels, base model and limited model. The limited model has extra electrical system features and requires a higher rated output alternator. Determine with which alternator the limited model is equipped.

60.6 A technician is testing a battery in this vehicle using a handheld capacitance tester. The tester requires cold cranking amps as a data input. Identify the CCA for this vehicle.

Use the following table to complete problems 60.7 and 60.8.

| Electric Water Pump Specifications | |
|---|---|
| Characteristic | Specification |
| Construction | Motor-Driven |
| Voltage | 9–16 volts |
| Operation Condition | ON/OFF Control |
| Capacity | Above 8 LPM (12 volts) |
| Rated Current | Below 2.2A (12 volts) |
| Location | Engine Bay Front |

60.7 A technician is servicing a hybrid vehicle with an electric water pump. Identify the rated current of the electric water pump motor.

60.8 A technician is diagnosing a hybrid vehicle for fluid flow rate of an electric water pump. The technician measures a flow rate of 4 LPM maximum. Determine the percentage of actual flow rate compared to flow rate capacity.

Name _____ Date _____ Class _____

Use the following table to complete problems 60.9 and 60.10.

| Electric Power Steering Pinout Values / Parameters ||||
|---|---|---|---|
| Terminal Number | Wire Color | Description | Specified Condition |
| A75-2 | W-B | Power Ground | Below 1 Ω |
| A2-1 (M1) | R | Steering Motor Output Signal 1 | L: 11 to 14 volts R: Below 1 volt |
| E32-7 | SB-W | CAN Line | 54–70 Ω |
| A3-5 | W | Torque Sensor (wheel turned L) | 0.3 to 2.5 volts |
| A3-5 | W | Torque Sensor (wheel not turned) | 2.3 to 2.7 volts |
| A3-5 | W | Torque Sensor (wheel turned R) | 2.6 to 4.7 volts |

60.9 A technician is analyzing electric power steering pinout values on a hybrid vehicle equipped with electric power steering. The voltage drops from 2.5 volts to 0.5 volts when the steering wheel is turned left. Determine if this data signal is a normal condition.

60.10 A technician is measuring ground side resistance to diagnose a system-wide issue on a hybrid vehicle equipped with electric power steering. The power ground circuit measures 1.7 Ω using a digital multimeter. Determine if this resistance reading is within normal specification.

# UNIT 7
# Engine Performance

Case Study 61 **Electronic Throttle Controls—Addition**
Case Study 62 **Mass Airflow—Subtraction**
Case Study 63 **Ignition Coil Voltage—Multiplication**
Case Study 64 **Analyzing Compression Tests—Division**
Case Study 65 **Fuel Trim—Decimal Arithmetic**
Case Study 66 **Spark Plug Gap—Greater Than and Less Than**
Case Study 67 **Fuel Tank Capacity—Fractions**
Case Study 68 **Pressure—Conversions**
Case Study 69 **Engine Sensors—Graphs and Tables**
Case Study 70 **Lambda—Formulas**
Case Study 71 **Vacuum/Pressure Gauge Reading—Measurement**
Case Study 72 **Module Pinout Diagrams—Analyzing Specifications**

## CAREER PROFILE

John Dascher works as a diagnostic specialist and a lead technician at Lexus of Bellevue in Bellevue, Washington. John started his automotive career in high school, where he worked in the garage of a local gas station. Today, John solves driveability issues and difficult diagnostic problems. As a lead technician, he also oversees and mentors other technicians in the shop.

As a diagnostic specialist, John enjoys "solving puzzles, and the job satisfaction that comes with solving a difficult problem." A recent example of his using math to solve an automotive problem was the process of calibrating the blind spot monitor sensor. Setting up the calibration required using measurement and geometric reasoning to locate and position the sensor calibration tool. John also uses an oscilloscope as a diagnostic tool to identify electrical problems that are intermittent or only partial. "Reading a scope pattern and being able to analyze the graph is very important to diagnosis," John explains.

*Goodheart-Willcox Publisher*
John Dascher—Diagnostic Specialist, Lexus of Bellevue.

When mentoring other technicians, John is always encouraging them to stay organized, both with their tools and parts, and with the repair process. "Being organized saves time and helps prevent mistakes." John also teaches that understanding how vehicle systems are designed to work correctly is the first step in diagnosing a system that has failed. John agrees that the logical thinking required to solve math problems is the same logical thinking required to diagnose today's high-tech, computerized vehicle systems.

## CASE STUDY 61

# Electronic Throttle Controls

### OBJECTIVES

*After studying this case study, you will be able to:*
- Identify electronic throttle control system operation.
- Analyze electronic throttle control inputs and outputs related to engine speed.

### TECHNICAL TERMS

accelerator pedal position (APP)   electronic throttle control

### MATH SKILLS
- Addition of whole numbers.
- Analyze and solve job skill problems related to addition of whole numbers.

---

Modern fuel injection and throttle control systems have evolved from a cable linkage to *electronic throttle control*. This type of system uses an accelerator position sensor to send a signal to the control module. The control module regulates the actual throttle position with an output control signal to an actuator connected to the throttle plate.

The *accelerator pedal position (APP)* sensor output can be viewed as a voltage value and converted into a percentage. For instance, a closed throttle would be 0% APP and wide-open-throttle would be 100% APP. As the accelerator pedal is moved to open, the throttle opens. This allows more air to flow into the engine, resulting in more fuel in the engine, more powerful combustion, and more engine speed. As the APP sensor input values change, the control module changes the electronic throttle accordingly.

On engines with cable throttle linkage, the throttle is equipped with a throttle position sensor (TPS) that provides a voltage signal to the control module. This signal is interpreted and changed into a throttle position percentage on the scan tool as live data.

**Example:** A technician is monitoring throttle percentage using scan tool data. The throttle started at 7% and increased 15%. Calculate the new throttle percentage.

$$7\% + 15\% = 22\%$$

The new throttle percentage is 22%.

**Name** _____ **Date** _____ **Class** _____

# Electronic Throttle Controls
# Job Skill Practice Problems

61.1 A technician is testing an engine for an internal noise and holds the throttle around 18% open. The engine idle speed is 835 rpm and the engine speed increases by 730 rpm when the throttle is opened. Calculate the total engine speed with the throttle at 18%.

61.2 A technician is monitoring throttle percentage using scan tool data while on a test-drive. At 24 mph the throttle was at 13%, and at 52 mph the throttle increased by 19%. Calculate the new throttle percentage.

61.3 A technician is monitoring scan tool data during a test-drive. The engine has a shudder around 1,125 rpm and has a shudder again when the engine speed is increased by 760 rpm from when the first shudder occurred. Calculate the engine speed of the second engine shudder.

61.4 The engine idle speed is set at 6% throttle open. To prevent over-revving the engine in *Neutral*, the electronic throttle system is designed to only open 25% throttle above idle speed. Calculate the maximum throttle opening percentage in *Neutral*.

61.5 A technician is monitoring scan tool data during a test-drive. The engine has a harsh vibration around 1,045 rpm and has a harsh vibration again when the engine speed is increased by 940 rpm from when the first shudder occurred. Calculate the engine speed of the second harsh vibration.

61.6 A technician is monitoring throttle percentage using scan tool data while on a test-drive. At 13 mph the throttle was at 9%, and at 37 mph the throttle increased by 13%. Calculate the new throttle percentage.

# CASE STUDY 62

# Mass Airflow

## OBJECTIVES

*After studying this case study, you will be able to:*
- Identify mass airflow sensor values.
- Calculate changes in mass airflow and mass airflow sensor values.

## TECHNICAL TERM

mass airflow (MAF) sensor

## MATH SKILLS

- Subtraction of whole numbers.
- Analyze and solve job skill problems related to subtraction of whole numbers.

The amount of air entering an engine is calculated by a signal from the *mass airflow (MAF) sensor*. This sensor is typically located in the air intake tubing before the throttle, and the sensor signal ranges between near 0 volts and 5 volts. The changing voltage value is calculated into an air volume amount, listed as grams per second. The engine control module needs this information in order to determine how to control other engine outputs, such as fuel injector controls.

*Goodheart-Willcox Publisher*

| Mass Airflow (grams per second) | 0 | 3 | 6 | 9 | 16 | 32 | 56 | 90 | 115 | 155 | 185 |
|---|---|---|---|---|---|---|---|---|---|---|---|
| Sensor Voltage | <0.35 | 0.75 | 1.00 | 1.50 | 2.00 | 2.50 | 3.00 | 3.50 | 4.00 | 4.50 | 4.90 |

**Example:** A technician is monitoring scan tool data. The MAF sensor voltage changed from 3.00 volts to 2.00 volts. Calculate the difference in actual airflow.

$$3.00 \text{ volts} = 56 \text{ g/s}$$
$$2.00 \text{ volts} = 16 \text{ g/s}$$
$$56 \text{ g/s} - 16 \text{ g/s} = 40 \text{ g/s}$$

The mass airflow decreased by 40 g/s.

Name _____ Date _____ Class _____

## Mass Airflow Job Skill Practice Problems

62.1  A technician is monitoring scan tool data. The MAF sensor voltage changed from 4.00 volts to 3.50 volts. Calculate the difference in actual airflow.

62.2  A technician is monitoring scan tool data. The MAF sensor voltage changed from 2.50 volts to 2.00 volts. Calculate the difference in actual airflow.

62.3  A technician is monitoring scan tool data. The airflow volume changed from 115 g/s to 9 g/s. Calculate the difference in sensor voltage.

62.4  A technician is monitoring scan tool data. The airflow volume changed from 155 g/s to 56 g/s. Calculate the difference in sensor voltage.

62.5  A mass airflow sensor is very dirty and this is affecting the output of the sensor by reducing the voltage by 1.00 volt through the entire sensor range. If the sensor desired voltage is 3.00 volts but is reduced by 1.00 volt, calculate the effect on airflow volume.

62.6  A mass airflow sensor is very dirty and this is affecting the output of the sensor by reducing the voltage by 1.00 volt through the entire sensor range. If the sensor desired voltage is 2.50 volts but is reduced by 1.00 volt, calculate the effect on airflow volume.

# CASE STUDY 63

# Ignition Coil Voltage

## OBJECTIVES
*After studying this case study, you will be able to:*
- Identify ignition coil primary and secondary voltage values.
- Calculate secondary voltage based on ignition coil winding ratio.

## TECHNICAL TERMS
ignition coil       primary winding       secondary winding

## MATH SKILLS
- Multiplication of whole numbers.
- Multiplication based on a ratio value.

---

The *ignition coil* functions as a step-up transformer, designed to take automotive battery voltage (12–15 volts) and step up the voltage to the 12,000–60,000+ volts needed to cross the gap of a spark plug. The required voltage depends on the spark plug gap, cylinder pressures, air-fuel ratio, and engine load. Although the coil output voltage is only the necessary amount to arc at the gap, the coil must be capable of higher voltages when engine conditions change.

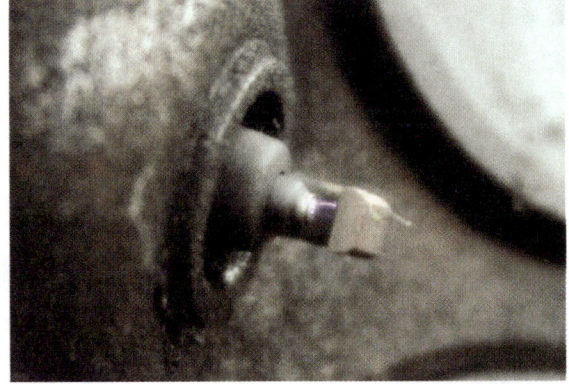

*Goodheart-Willcox Publisher*

   Inside the ignition coil are two coils of wire, a primary winding and a secondary winding. The *primary winding* is thicker wire with fewer turns. The *secondary winding* is much thinner wire with many thousands more windings. This ratio of windings is necessary to increase the voltage output of the coil. Most ignition coil winding ratios are typically between 70:1 and 100:1.

   When the ignition coil is "fired," the primary winding side is opened using mechanical points or an electrical transistor, causing a voltage spike between 150 and 600+ volts. The electromagnetic field of this voltage spike is induced in the primary winding and then multiplied by the winding ratio to create the high voltage output to arc to ground across the spark plug.

**Example:** An ignition coil has a primary winding voltage spike of 250 volts applied to an ignition coil with a winding ratio of 100:1. Calculate the maximum output voltage of this coil.

$$250 \text{ volts} \times 100 = 25{,}000 \text{ volts}$$
Coil output: 25,000 volts

Name _____ Date _____ Class _____

## Ignition Coil Voltage Job Skill Practice Problems

63.1 An ignition coil has a primary winding voltage spike of 230 volts applied to an ignition coil with a winding ratio of 90:1. Calculate the maximum output voltage of this coil.

63.2 An ignition coil has a primary winding voltage spike of 350 volts applied to an ignition coil with a winding ratio of 90:1. Calculate the maximum output voltage of this coil.

63.3 An ignition coil has a primary winding voltage spike of 295 volts applied to an ignition coil with a winding ratio of 70:1. Calculate the maximum output voltage of this coil.

63.4 An ignition coil has a primary winding voltage spike of 380 volts applied to an ignition coil with a winding ratio of 100:1. Calculate the maximum output voltage of this coil.

Copyright Goodheart-Willcox Co., Inc. May not be reproduced or posted to a publicly accessible website.

63.5 An ignition coil has a primary winding voltage spike of 550 volts applied to an ignition coil with a winding ratio of 90:1. Calculate the maximum output voltage of this coil.

63.6 An ignition coil has a primary winding voltage spike of 450 volts applied to an ignition coil with a winding ratio of 85:1. Calculate the maximum output voltage of this coil.

63.7 An ignition coil has a primary winding voltage spike of 395 volts applied to an ignition coil with a winding ratio of 70:1. Calculate the maximum output voltage of this coil.

63.8 An ignition coil has a primary winding voltage spike of 235 volts applied to an ignition coil with a winding ratio of 100:1. Calculate the maximum output voltage of this coil.

# CASE STUDY 64

# Analyzing Compression Tests

## OBJECTIVES

*After studying this case study, you will be able to:*
- Identify engine compression test pressure and variance specifications.
- Calculate engine compression values to determine engine cylinder integrity.

## TECHNICAL TERM

cylinder compression test

## MATH SKILLS

- Division of whole numbers.
- Conversion of decimal values to percentage values.

---

A *cylinder compression test* is performed to determine the static pressure that each engine cylinder can produce. The causes of lower compression pressures include leaking valves, leaking piston rings, or a leaking cylinder head gasket. Typically, all cylinders are tested for compression pressure, and the pressure values are compared once the test is completed. Compression test specifications commonly include a minimum pressure value and a percentage of variation from the lowest cylinder to the highest cylinder.

*Goodheart-Willcox Publisher*

$$variation\ \% = 100 - \frac{lowest\ pressure\ value}{highest\ pressure\ value}$$

**Example:**

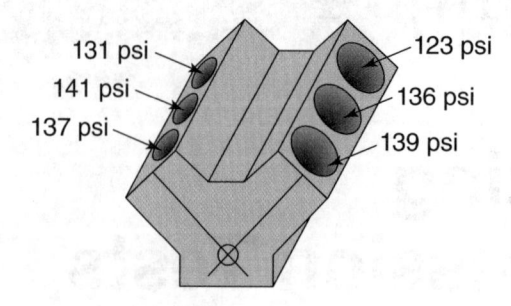

131 psi
141 psi
137 psi
123 psi
136 psi
139 psi

*Goodheart-Willcox Publisher*

A technician has performed a cylinder compression test on a V6 engine and obtained the results shown. The minimum pressure value is 100 psi and the pressure variation is <15%. Identify the lowest and highest pressure values and calculate the percentage of variation between highest and lowest.

Highest pressure value: 141 psi
Lowest pressure value: 123 psi
123 psi ÷ 141 psi = 0.87234
100 − 87.2 = 12.8

12.8% variation between highest and lowest pressure values.

# Analyzing Compression Tests
# Job Skill Practice Problems

64.1 A technician has performed a cylinder compression test on a V8 engine and obtained the results shown. The minimum pressure value is 932 kilopascals (kPa) and the pressure variation is <15%. Identify the lowest and highest pressure values and calculate the percentage of variation between highest and lowest.

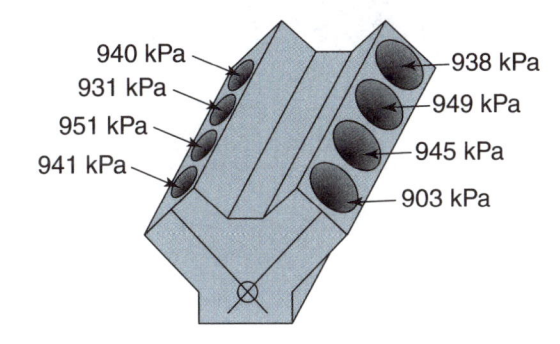

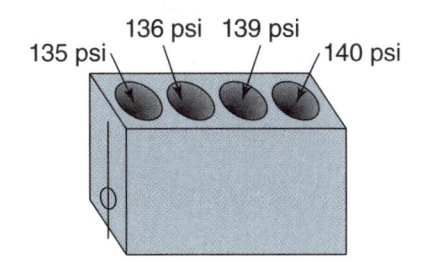

940 kPa
931 kPa
951 kPa
941 kPa
938 kPa
949 kPa
945 kPa
903 kPa

*Goodheart-Willcox Publisher*

64.2 A technician has performed a cylinder compression test on an inline 4-cylinder engine and obtained the results shown. The minimum pressure value is 128 psi and the pressure variation is <10%. Identify the lowest and highest pressure values and calculate the percentage of variation between highest and lowest.

135 psi   136 psi   139 psi   140 psi

*Goodheart-Willcox Publisher*

**Name** _____ **Date** _____ **Class** _____

64.3 A technician has performed a cylinder compression test on an inline 4-cylinder engine and obtained the results shown. The minimum pressure value is 7.0 bar and the pressure variation is <30%. Identify the lowest and highest pressure values and calculate the percentage of variation between highest and lowest.

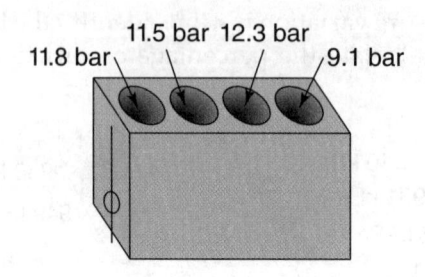

64.4 A technician has performed a cylinder compression test on a V6 engine and obtained the results shown. The minimum pressure value is 120 psi and the pressure variation is <20%. Identify the lowest and highest pressure values and calculate the percentage of variation between highest and lowest.

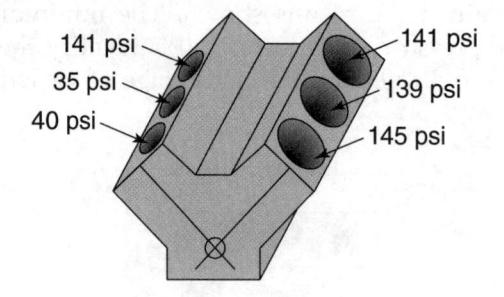

**Name** _____ **Date** _____ **Class** _____

64.5 A technician has performed a cylinder compression test on a V6 engine and obtained the results shown. The minimum pressure value is 690 kPa and the pressure variation is <12%. Identify the lowest and highest pressure values and calculate the percentage of variation between highest and lowest.

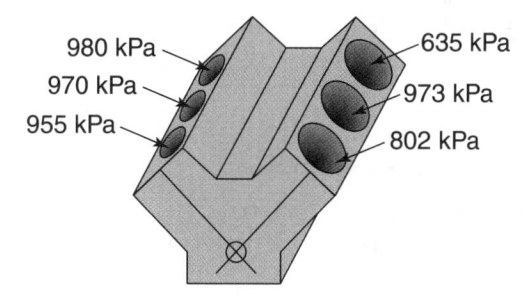

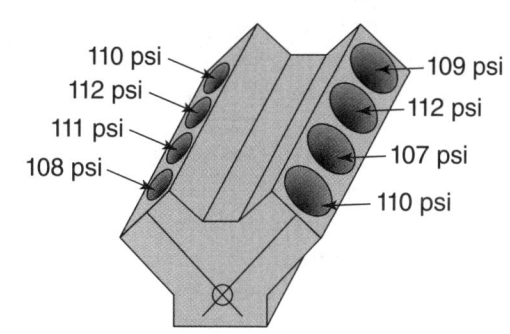

980 kPa
970 kPa
955 kPa
635 kPa
973 kPa
802 kPa

*Goodheart-Willcox Publisher*

64.6 A technician has performed a cylinder compression test on a V8 engine and obtained the results shown. The minimum pressure value is 120 psi and the pressure variation is <20%. Identify the lowest and highest pressure values and calculate the percentage of variation between highest and lowest.

110 psi
112 psi
111 psi
108 psi
109 psi
112 psi
107 psi
110 psi

*Goodheart-Willcox Publisher*

# CASE STUDY 65

# Fuel Trim

## OBJECTIVES
*After studying this case study, you will be able to:*
- Identify short-term and long-term fuel trim values.
- Calculate changes in short-term and long-term fuel trim values.

## TECHNICAL TERMS
fuel trim values      long-term fuel trim (LTFT)      short-term fuel trim (STFT)

## MATH SKILLS
- Calculate decimal arithmetic, including negative numbers.
- Analyze job skill problems related to decimal arithmetic.

*Fuel trim values* represent the changes made by the engine management system to maintain a targeted air-fuel ratio. The fuel trim values are displayed as a percentage, with a positive percentage indicating the system is more often running lean, and a negative percentage indicating the system is more often running rich. These values range from –25% to 25% and have an optimal range of 0%±3%.

If the fuel trim values exceed the range, a related diagnostic trouble code is set and the check engine light is turned on. A wide variety of factors could cause out-of-range fuel trim values. *Short-term fuel trim (STFT)* is immediate feedback based on current operating conditions. *Long-term fuel trim (LTFT)* is a cumulative average of fuel trim over a long period of time. Review the table and example.

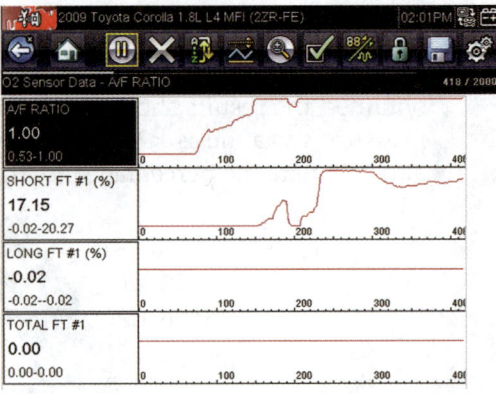

*Goodheart-Willcox Publisher*

| Fuel Trim Values – Long-Term/Short-Term ||||||||
|---|---|---|---|---|---|---|
| DTC | –25% | –3 | 0% | 3% | 25% | DTC |
| | Rich Exhaust || Perfect | Lean Exhaust |||
| | Lean A/F Commanded || 14.7:1 | Rich A/F Commanded |||
| | Fuel Trim Rich DTCs ||| Fuel Trim Lean DTCs |||
| | P0172 – Bank 1 ||| P0171 – Bank 1 |||
| | P0175 – Bank 2 ||| P0174 – Bank 2 |||

**Example:** A technician is reviewing scan tool data. The LTFT is –12.3% and the STFT is 3.6%. Calculate the difference between the LTFT and the STFT.

$$-12.3\% - 3.6\% = 15.9\%$$

The difference between LTFT and STFT is 15.9%.

Name _____ Date _____ Class _____

## Fuel Trim Job Skill Practice Problems

65.1 A technician is reviewing scan tool data. The LTFT Bank 1 is 9.3% and the LTFT Bank 2 is 1.6%. Calculate the difference of LTFT between Bank 1 and Bank 2.

65.2 A technician repaired a vacuum leak caused by a cracked vacuum hose. The STFT before the repair was 16.3%. The STFT after the repair was 2.8%. Calculate how much the repair changed the STFT.

65.3 A technician is reviewing scan tool data and notices –18.9% STFT for Bank 2. The technician identifies and repairs a leaking fuel injector. After the repair, the STFT for Bank 2 is –0.7%. Calculate how much the repair changed the STFT.

65.4 A technician is reviewing scan tool data and notices 9.9% STFT for Bank 1. The technician identifies and repairs a faulty mass airflow sensor. After the repair, the STFT for Bank 1 is –1.3%. Calculate how much the repair changed the STFT.

65.5 A technician is diagnosing a P0172 code. When reviewing the scan tool data, the LTFT for Bank 1 is –25%. The technician identifies and replaces the fuel pressure regulator. After performing the repair, the LTFT for Bank 1 is 2.4%. Calculate how much the repair changed the LTFT.

65.6 A technician is reviewing scan tool data for a V8 engine. The LTFT Bank 1 is –18.7%. The LTFT for Bank 2 is –1.3%. The technician identifies a rich condition on Bank 1. Calculate the difference between the LTFT for Bank 1 and the LTFT for Bank 2.

# CASE STUDY 66

# Spark Plug Gap

## OBJECTIVES

*After studying this case study, you will be able to:*
- Compare the spark plug gap to specification.
- Determine the variation of the measured gap value to the specified gap value.

## TECHNICAL TERM

spark plug gap

## MATH SKILLS

- Determine greater than, less than, and equal to specified gap values.
- Add and subtract to solve for the variance from the specified value.

The *spark plug gap* is the space between the center electrode and the ground electrode. This gap has a specified value, and it must be set to this value in order for the ignition system to function as designed. The spark plug gap can be measured using a plug gap tool or by using feeler gauges. Use caution with the electrodes of platinum and iridium spark plugs, as the center electrode is much finer and can be damaged when measuring.

*Goodheart-Willcox Publisher*

**Example:** A technician is inspecting the spark plugs on a 4-cylinder 1.8 L engine. Once the spark plugs are removed using a spark plug socket, the spark plug gap is measured. Review the measurements below, and use the table to answer the questions.

Measured spark plug gap size:

Cylinder #1: 0.046 in     Cylinder #2: 0.043 in
Cylinder #3: 0.039 in     Cylinder #4: 0.051 in

| Spark Plugs ||
|---|---|
| NGK: | ILZKR7B-11S |
| DENSO: | SXU22HCR11S |
| Electrode Gap ||
| Standard (new): | 1.1 mm (0.043 in) |

Determine if the spark plug gap is correct, too large, or too small for each cylinder.

>    Cylinder #1: 0.046 in > 0.043 in, so the spark plug gap is too large.
>    Cylinder #2: 0.043 in = 0.043 in, so the spark plug gap is correct.
>    Cylinder #3: 0.039 in < 0.043 in, so the spark plug gap is too small.
>    Cylinder #4: 0.051 in > 0.043 in, so the spark plug gap is too large.

Determine how far out of adjustment each spark plug is from the correct gap size.

>    Cylinder #1: 0.046 in − 0.043 in = 0.003 in
>    Cylinder #2: Gap is correct.
>    Cylinder #3: 0.039 in − 0.043 in = −0.004 in
>    Cylinder #4: 0.051 in − 0.043 in = 0.008 in

Name _____ Date _____ Class _____

# Spark Plug Gap Job Skill Practice Problems

A technician is inspecting the spark plug on a 3.9 L V6 engine. Once the spark plugs are removed using a spark plug socket, the spark plug gap is measured. Review the measurements below, and use the table to complete practice problems 66.1 and 66.2.

Measured spark plug gap size:

Cylinder #1: 0.054 in   Cylinder #2: 0.057 in   Cylinder #3: 0.051 in
Cylinder #4: 1.35 mm    Cylinder #5: 1.39 mm    Cylinder #6: 1.37 mm

| Spark Plugs ||
|---|---|
| Part Number: | MC-8411-7b |
| Electrode Gap ||
| Standard (new): | 1.37 mm (0.054 in) |

66.1 Determine if the spark plug gap for each cylinder is correct, too large, or too small for each cylinder.

Cylinder #1: _____   Cylinder #4: _____

Cylinder #2: _____   Cylinder #5: _____

Cylinder #3: _____   Cylinder #6: _____

66.2 Calculate how far out of adjustment each spark plug is from the correct gap size.

Cylinder #1: _____   Cylinder #4: _____

Cylinder #2: _____   Cylinder #5: _____

Cylinder #3: _____   Cylinder #6: _____

A technician is inspecting the spark plug on an inline 4-cylinder, 2.4 L engine. Once the spark plugs are removed using a spark plug socket, the spark plug gap is measured. Review the measurements below, and use the table to complete practice problems 66.3 and 66.4.

Measured spark plug gap size:

Cylinder #1: 0.048 in   Cylinder #2: 0.045 in
Cylinder #3: 0.037 in   Cylinder #4: 0.050 in

| Spark Plugs ||
|---|---|
| K24Z1: | SKJ20DR-M11 |
| K24Z6: | SXU22HCR11S |
| Electrode Gap ||
| Standard (new): | 1.0–1.1 mm (0.039–0.043 in) |

66.3 Determine if the spark plug gap for each cylinder is correct, too large, or too small for each cylinder.

Cylinder #1: _____   Cylinder #3: _____

Cylinder #2: _____   Cylinder #4: _____

66.4 Calculate how far out of adjustment each spark plug is from the correct gap size.

Cylinder #1: _____   Cylinder #3: _____

Cylinder #2: _____   Cylinder #4: _____

A technician is inspecting the spark plug on an inline 4-cylinder, 1.6 L turbocharged engine. Once the spark plugs are removed using a spark plug socket, the spark plug gap is measured. Review the measurements below, and use the table to complete practice problems 66.5 and 66.6.

Measured spark plug gap size:

Cylinder #1: 0.047 in   Cylinder #2: 0.035 in
Cylinder #3: 0.80 mm    Cylinder #4: 1.1 mm

| Spark Plugs | |
|---|---|
| MR16DT | NJ384-3G |
| MR18DE | NC578-7R |
| Electrode Gap | |
| Standard (new): | 0.9–1.1 mm (0.035–0.043 in) |

66.5 Determine if the spark plug gap for each cylinder is correct, too large, or too small for each cylinder.

Cylinder #1: _____   Cylinder #3: _____

Cylinder #2: _____   Cylinder #4: _____

66.6 Calculate how far out of adjustment each spark plug is from the correct gap size.

Cylinder #1: _____   Cylinder #3: _____

Cylinder #2: _____   Cylinder #4: _____

# CASE STUDY 67

# Fuel Tank Capacity

## OBJECTIVES

*After studying this case study, you will be able to:*
- Identify fuel tank capacity in gallons and liters.
- Calculate percentage of fuel remaining based on fraction gauge readings.

## MATH SKILLS

- Calculate a fraction of a whole number.
- Analyze job skill problems with fractions of whole numbers.

The amount of fuel tank capacity varies by vehicle type. Often, smaller compact cars have low capacity fuel tanks. Larger vehicles, including pickup trucks, typically have larger fuel tanks, and some may have two separate fuel tanks. The fuel gauge typically shows fuel level in fractions, but does not provide the actual number of gallons of fuel remaining in the tank.

*Goodheart-Willcox Publisher*

Calculations using fractions and whole numbers can determine the amount of fuel in gallons remaining in the tank, if the tank capacity is known. Review the example and the formula.

$$\frac{full\ capacity\ (gal)}{1} \times \frac{gauge\ numerator}{gauge\ denominator} = gallons\ remaining$$

**Example:** A midsize sedan has a fuel tank capacity of 14 gallons. The fuel gauge indicates the tank is 3/4 full. Calculate the amount of fuel remaining in the tank.

14/1 gallons × 3/4 = 42/4 gallons

42/4 gallons = 42 ÷ 4 = 10.5 gallons

There are 10.5 gallons of fuel remaining in the tank.

## Fuel Tank Capacity Job Skill Practice Problems

67.1 A midsize SUV has a fuel tank capacity of 13 gallons. The fuel gauge indicates the tank is 7/8 full. Calculate the amount of fuel remaining in the tank. Round to the nearest hundredth.

67.2 A compact sedan has a fuel tank capacity of 15 gallons. The fuel gauge indicates the tank is 11/20 full. Calculate the amount of fuel remaining in the tank.

67.3 A pickup truck has a fuel tank capacity of 18 gallons. The fuel gauge indicates the tank is 1/8 full. Calculate the amount of fuel remaining in the tank.

67.4 A series hybrid car has a fuel tank capacity of 9 gallons. The fuel gauge indicates the tank is 7/8 full. Calculate the amount of fuel remaining in the tank. Round to the nearest hundredth.

67.5 A pickup truck has dual gas tanks. One tank has a capacity of 19 gallons and the other tank has a capacity of 21 gallons. The fuel gauge indicates the 19-gallon tank is 3/4 full and the 21-gallon tank is 1/8 full. Calculate the total amount of fuel remaining in the tanks. Round to the nearest hundredth.

67.6 A pickup truck has dual gas tanks. One tank has a capacity of 20 gallons and the other tank has a capacity of 24 gallons. The fuel gauge indicates the 20-gallon tank is 1/4 full and the 24-gallon tank is 3/8 full. Calculate the total amount of fuel remaining in the tanks.

# CASE STUDY 68

# Pressure

## OBJECTIVES

*After studying this case study, you will be able to:*
- Identify pressure units used on various engine performance systems.
- Calculate pressure conversions between psi, bar, kPa, and in Hg.

## MATH SKILLS
- Conversion of whole and decimal numbers.
- Analyze job skill problems with pressure conversion factors.

Engine performance systems use both pressurized fluid and pressurized air to function. Gasoline and diesel fuel is pumped from the tank to the engine, and some systems use a low pressure tank pump and a high pressure engine pump. Pressurized air is measured as engine vacuum or boost pressure on turbocharged and supercharged engines. Cylinder compression tests, engine vacuum testing, and exhaust backpressure testing also rely on pressure values. Pressure can be identified as psi, bar, kPa, and in Hg. Conversion between units is often needed during diagnosis and service of engine performance systems.

*Goodheart-Willcox Publisher*

| Unit of Pressure | 1 = | psi | bar | kPa | in Hg |
|---|---|---|---|---|---|
| Pounds per square inch | 1 psi = | x | 0.068 | 6.894 | 14.73 |
| Bar | 1 bar = | 14.5 | x | 100 | 29.53 |
| Kilopascal | 1 kPa = | 0.145 | 0.01 | x | 0.295 |
| Inches of mercury | 1 in Hg = | 0.491 | 0.033 | 3.386 | x |

**Example:** A technician is monitoring fuel pressure using a fuel pressure gauge connected to the fuel rail. The pressure reading is 47 psi. Convert the pressure reading to kPa.

$$1 \text{ psi} = 6.894 \text{ kPa}$$
$$47 \text{ psi} \times 6.894 = 324.02 \text{ kPa}$$

The fuel pressure value is 324.02 kPa.

**Name** _____ **Date** _____ **Class** _____

## Pressure Job Skill Practice Problems

68.1 A turbocharger is providing 9.0 psi of boost pressure. Convert this value to in Hg.

68.2 A diesel common rail high pressure fuel pump provides 26,000 psi of fuel pressure. Convert this pressure value to bar.

68.3 An intake manifold-mounted barometric pressure sensor is reading 9.83 in Hg. Convert this pressure value to kPa. Round to the nearest hundredth.

68.4 A gasoline engine with direct injection has a fuel rail pressure of 2,150 psi. Convert this pressure value to bar.

68.5 A cooling system is pressurized to 1.0 bar. Convert this pressure value to psi.

**Name** _____ **Date** _____ **Class** _____

68.6 A carbureted fuel system with a block-mounted mechanical fuel pump has a fuel pressure of 8.5 psi. Convert this pressure value to kPa. Round to the nearest hundredth.

68.7 A cylinder compression test has a minimum pressure reading of 7.0 bar. Convert this pressure value to kPa.

68.8 A supercharged engine has a boost pressure of 7 psi. Convert this pressure value to in Hg.

68.9 A gasoline fuel system has a measured pressure of 395 kPa of fuel pressure. Convert this value to psi. Round to the nearest hundredth.

68.10 A cooling system pressure test indicates a leak at 5 psi. Convert this pressure value to bar.

# CASE STUDY 69

# Engine Sensors

## OBJECTIVES

*After studying this case study, you will be able to:*
- Identify engine sensor data in table and graph form.
- Analyze data in table and graph form to calculate related problems.

## MATH SKILLS
- Analyze and interpret graphs and tables.
- Solve jobs skill problems based on data from graphs and tables.

Modern engines require sensor data input to continuously monitor engine conditions and control engine output and performance. When a sensor fails, or the signal becomes inaccurate, the engine control module will no longer be able to maintain optimal control over the engine function. This will cause a diagnostic trouble code to set and the vehicle will require service. The technician is able to monitor the engine data and use the data to determine if the sensors are operating as designed. These sensors can be shown on a graph, and that graph can be used to determine sensor function or malfunction.

*Goodheart-Willcox Publisher*

**Example:** A technician is reviewing the function of a throttle position sensor. Shown is a graph of how the sensor is designed to function.

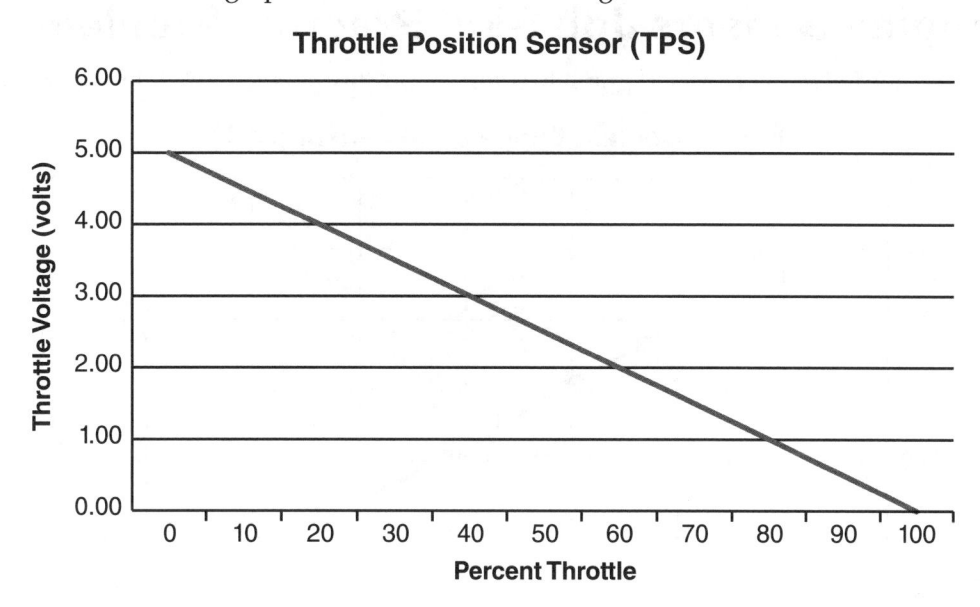

**Throttle Position Sensor (TPS)**

Determine the sensor voltage with the throttle closed.

The throttle closed is 0%, which is 5.0 volts.

Identify the voltage change from 20% throttle to 60% throttle.

The throttle voltage at 20% is 4.0 volts and at 60% is 2.0 volts.

The difference is 4 volts − 2 volts = 2 volts.

# Engine Sensors Job Skill Practice Problems

Use the the following table and graph to complete practice problems 69.1 through 69.4.

| Engine Coolant Temperature Sensor (ECT) | |
|---|---|
| °F | Voltage |
| −40 | 4.95 |
| −10 | 4.23 |
| 20 | 3.65 |
| 50 | 3.10 |
| 80 | 2.55 |
| 110 | 2.05 |
| 140 | 1.65 |
| 170 | 1.25 |
| 200 | 0.90 |
| 230 | 0.48 |
| 260 | 0.20 |

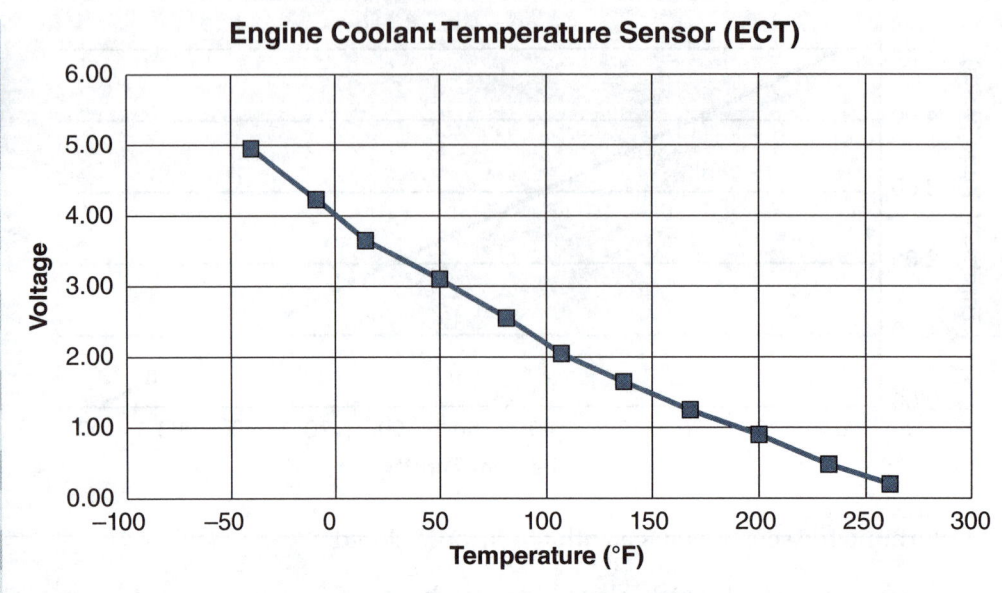

**Engine Coolant Temperature Sensor (ECT)**

69.1 Identify the ECT temperature (°F) value if the voltage reading is 2.05 volts.

69.2 The temperature value changes from 50°F to 170°F. Calculate the change in sensor voltage.

69.3 The thermostat opens at 200°F. Determine the voltage value of the sensor when the thermostat opens.

69.4 An engine has an overheating condition. What sensor voltage values would a technician observe under an overheating condition?

Name _____  Date _____  Class _____

Use the following table and graph to complete practice problems 69.5 through 69.8.

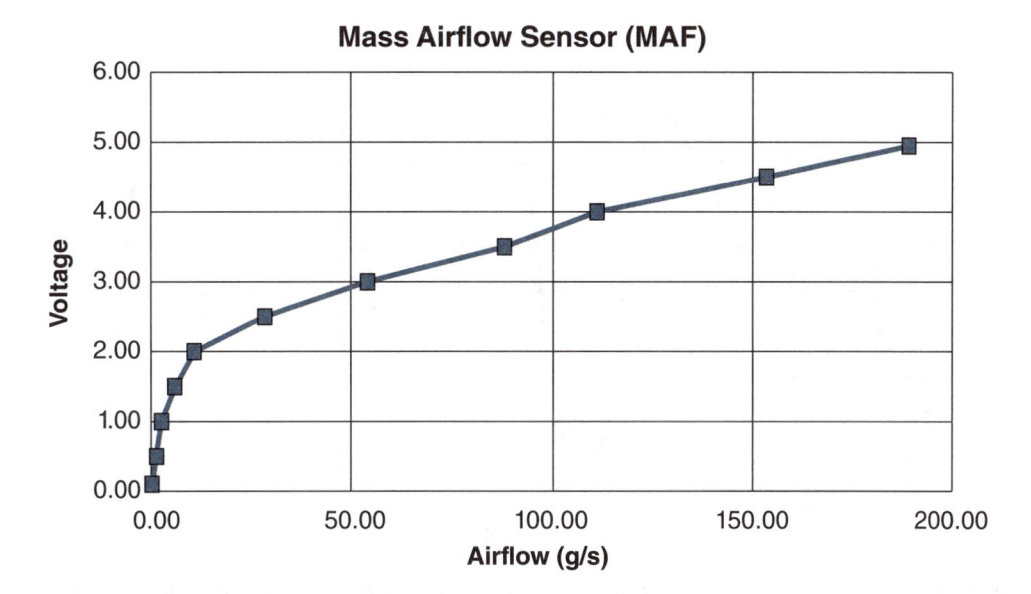

**Mass Airflow Sensor (MAF)**

| Airflow (g/s) | Voltage |
|---|---|
| 185.00 | 4.95 |
| 155.00 | 4.50 |
| 115.00 | 4.00 |
| 88.00 | 3.50 |
| 55.00 | 3.00 |
| 32.00 | 2.50 |
| 15.00 | 2.00 |
| 8.00 | 1.50 |
| 4.00 | 1.00 |
| 2.00 | 0.50 |
| 0.00 | 0.10 |

69.5 Identify the grams per second airflow reading if the sensor voltage is 2.50 volts.

69.6 If the voltage value changes from 2.00 volts to 4.00 volts, calculate the change in airflow.

69.7 Determine the most likely MAF sensor voltage value if the engine is idling.

69.8 Determine the most likely MAF airflow rate value if the engine is at wide-open-throttle (WOT).

Use the following graph to complete practice problems 69.9 and 69.10.

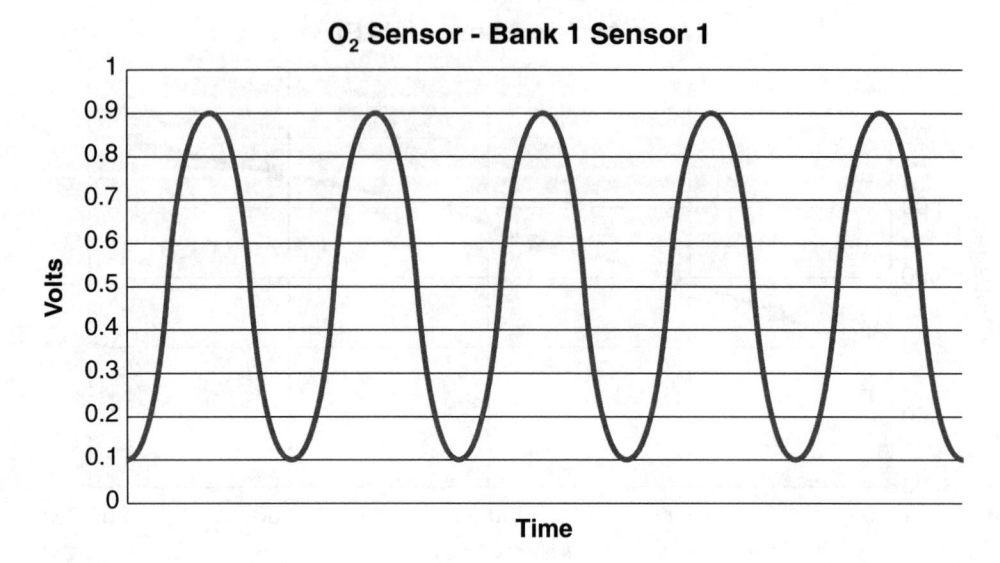

**O₂ Sensor - Bank 1 Sensor 1**

69.9 Determine the value range (minimum to maximum) of the sensor voltage.

69.10 If a voltage value > 0.5 volts is considered a rich air-fuel mixture, determine the voltage values of a lean air-fuel mixture.

# CASE STUDY 70

# Lambda

## OBJECTIVES

*After studying this case study, you will be able to:*
- Identify rich and lean stoichiometric air-fuel ratios.
- Calculate the lambda (λ) value and the rich or lean air-fuel ratio value.

## TECHNICAL TERM

stoichiometric air-fuel (A/F) ratio

## MATH SKILLS

- Calculate a value using a formula.
- Analyze job skill problems based on formula calculations.

---

Air and gasoline are combined in the combustion chamber and become the source of power to run the engine. This air-fuel mixture requires specific amounts of air and fuel, known as the **stoichiometric air-fuel (A/F) ratio**. This ratio is 14.71 pounds of air to 1 pound of fuel. More or less air to 1 pound of fuel results in a rich or lean air-fuel ratio. For example, 12.5:1 is a rich A/F ratio, with less air per pound of fuel. A 15.9:1 A/F ratio is a lean ratio, with more air per pound of fuel.

*Goodheart-Willcox Publisher*

The Greek letter lambda (λ) refers to the actual air-fuel ratio divided by the stoichiometric air-fuel ratio. The lambda value is calculated by the downstream exhaust oxygen sensor. A lambda value of 1.0 means there is a perfect stoichiometric ratio. A lambda value below 1.0 indicates a rich A/F mixture and a value above 1.0 indicates a lean A/F mixture. Review the formulas and the following examples.

$$\text{lambda } (\lambda) = \frac{\text{air-fuel ratio actual}}{\text{air-fuel ratio stoichiometric}}$$

$$\text{air-fuel actual} = 14.71 \times \text{lambda } (\lambda)$$

**Example:** A technician is reviewing data of a running engine to determine the lambda value. The actual A/F ratio is monitored at 13.9:1 and the stoichiometric ratio is 14.71:1. Calculate the lambda value and determine if the engine is running rich or lean.

$$13.9 \div 14.71 = 0.945$$
$$\text{lambda} = 0.945$$
$$0.945 < 1.0$$

The mixture is rich.

**Example:** A technician is monitoring the lambda value using a scan tool on a running engine. The lambda value is 1.095. Calculate the A/F ratio and determine if the engine is running rich or lean.

$$14.71 \times 1.095 = 16.10$$

The A/F ratio is 16.10:1

The mixture is lean.

Name _____  Date _____  Class _____

# Lambda Job Skill Practice Problems

70.1 A technician is reviewing data of a running engine to determine the lambda value. The actual A/F ratio is monitored at 15.1:1 and the stoichiometric ratio is 14.71:1. Calculate the lambda value and determine if the engine is running rich or lean. Round to the nearest hundredth.

70.2 A technician is monitoring the lambda value using a scan tool on a running engine. The lambda value is 0.976. Calculate the A/F ratio and determine if the engine is running rich or lean. Round to the nearest hundredth.

70.3 A technician is reviewing data of a running engine to determine the lambda value. The actual A/F ratio is monitored at 11.9:1 and the stoichiometric ratio is 14.71:1. Calculate the lambda value and determine if the engine is running rich or lean. Round to the nearest hundredth.

70.4 A technician is monitoring the lambda value using a scan tool on a running engine. The lambda value is 1.058. Calculate the A/F ratio and determine if the engine is running rich or lean. Round to the nearest hundredth.

70.5 A technician is monitoring the lambda value of a V8 engine using a scan tool. The lambda value for Bank 1 is 1.031 and the lambda value for Bank 2 is 1.020. Calculate the A/F ratio of each bank and determine if the engine is running rich or lean. Round to the nearest hundredth.

70.6 A technician is monitoring the lambda value of a V6 engine using a scan tool. The lambda value for Bank 1 is 0.945 and the lambda value for Bank 2 is 0.928. Calculate the A/F ratio of each bank and determine if the engine is running rich or lean. Round to the nearest hundredth.

70.7 A technician is monitoring the lambda value of an engine using a scan tool. At idle, the lambda value is 1.010. During hard acceleration on a test-drive, the lambda value changes to 0.897. Calculate the A/F ratio for idle and acceleration, and determine if the engine runs rich or lean during acceleration. Round to the nearest hundredth.

70.8 A technician is monitoring the lambda value of an engine using a scan tool. At idle, the lambda value is 1.003. During hard acceleration on a test-drive, the lambda value changes to 1.501. Calculate the A/F ratio for idle and acceleration, and determine if the engine runs rich or lean during acceleration. Round to the nearest hundredth.

# CASE STUDY 71

# Vacuum/Pressure Gauge Reading

## OBJECTIVES

*After studying this case study, you will be able to:*
- Identify vacuum and pressure readings on a gauge.
- Calculate changes in gauge readings.

## MATH SKILLS
- Interpret measurement tool readings.
- Analyze job skill problems related to measurement tool readings.

A compound gauge capable of reading pressure and vacuum is useful when analyzing and diagnosing engine control systems. The vacuum gauge can be connected to the intake manifold and used to measure vacuum as the engine cranks, idles, and runs at higher rpm. The vacuum gauge can also be used to check if vacuum is available to vacuum-operated engine control systems, such as EGR valves or intake manifold runner flaps. The pressure gauge can be used to measure boost pressure on forced-induction engines as well as measure fuel pressure on low pressure mechanical fuel systems found on carbureted vehicles.

*Goodheart-Willcox Publisher*

The compound vacuum/pressure gauge indicates vacuum to the left of the zero and pressure to the right of the zero. The vacuum scale has two units of measurement: cm Hg and in Hg. The pressure scale has two units of measurement: psi and kPa. Review the following examples.

**Example:**

The needle is to the left of the zero, indicating 12 in Hg *or* 30 cm Hg of vacuum.

**Example:**

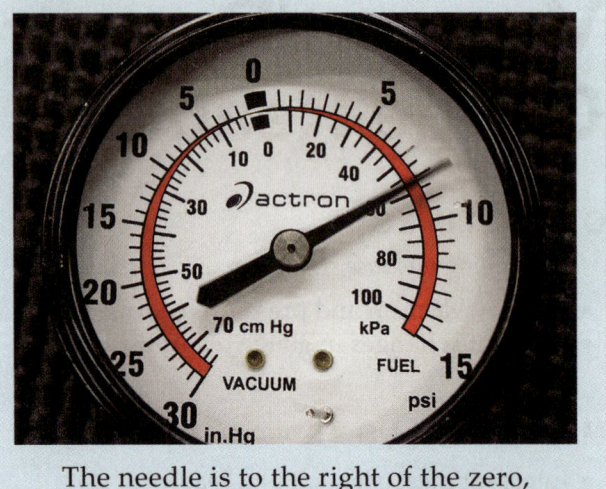

The needle is to the right of the zero, indicating 8 psi *or* 57 kPa of pressure.

*Goodheart-Willcox Publisher*

Name _____  Date _____  Class _____

# Vacuum/Pressure Gauge Reading Job Skill Practice Problems

71.1 Read the gauge and identify the correct unit label.

1. Standard gauge reading: _____

2. Metric gauge reading: _____

3. Standard gauge reading: _____

4. Metric gauge reading: _____

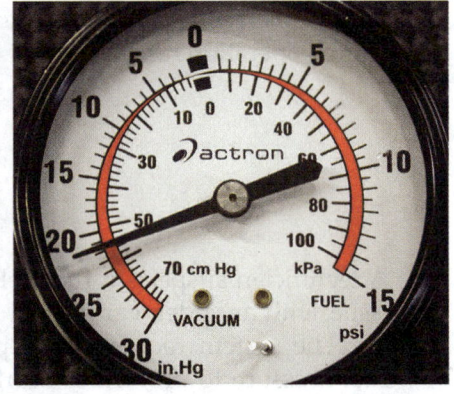

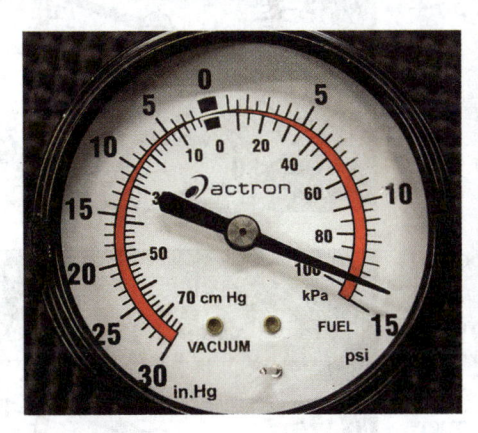

5. Standard gauge reading: _____

6. Metric gauge reading: _____

Name _____ Date _____ Class _____

7. Standard gauge reading: _____  8. Metric gauge reading: _____

71.2 A vacuum gauge is connected to the intake manifold on a naturally aspirated engine. The normal engine vacuum range is 17 in Hg to 21 in Hg. Analyze the gauge shown and determine if the vacuum is within normal engine operation range.

71.3 A technician suspects a fuel delivery issue with an older, carbureted vehicle. The system requires 8–10 psi of fuel pressure to prevent the carburetor from starving. Analyze the gauge shown and determine if the fuel pressure is within specification.

71.4 A vacuum-operated blend door located within the HVAC unit requires a minimum of 55 cm Hg to operate correctly. Analyze the gauge shown to determine if the vacuum measured at the blend door line is within specification to operate the door.

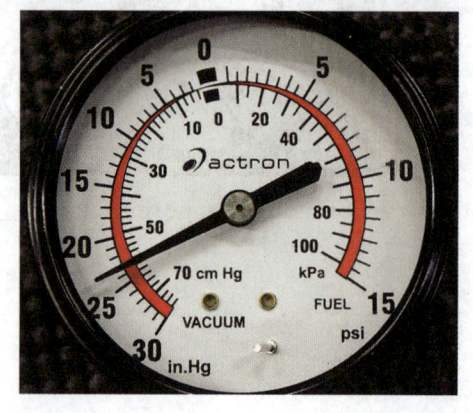

# CASE STUDY 72

# Module Pinout Diagrams

## OBJECTIVES

*After studying this case study, you will be able to:*
- Analyze module pinout diagrams.
- Determine pin number, pin location, and circuit function.

## MATH SKILLS
- Interpret and analyze specification diagrams.
- Analyze job skill problems related to specification diagrams.

The modern vehicle is equipped with an increasing number of control modules. These modules are computers that analyze sensor data and send out control signals to various actuators around the vehicle. Each module has one or more wire terminal connections that include a large number of wires. During diagnosis, it may be necessary to locate specific wires on these terminal connections for electrical testing.

*Goodheart-Willcox Publisher*

**Example:**

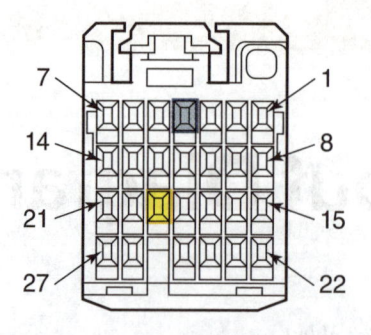

| Pin | Wire Color | Circuit Number | Function | Pin | Wire Color | Circuit Number | Function |
|---|---|---|---|---|---|---|---|
| 1 | - | - | Not Used | 15 | BU/WH | 1414 | LF Turn Signal |
| 2 | WH | 1390 | Off/Run/Crank Voltage | 16 | D-BU/WH | 1415 | RF Turn Signal |
| 3 | GY | 1884 | Cruise Control Signal | 17 | PU | 1375 | Radio Supply Voltage |
| 4 | WH/BK | 1073 | 5-Volt Reference | 18 | PU | 524 | High Beam Signal |
| 5 | L-GN | 1715 | Windshield Wiper Switch | 19 | OG | 192 | Front Fog Lamp Switch Signal |
| 6 | D-BU | 1796 | Steering Wheel Controls | 20 | PU | 5526 | Up/Down Window Signal |
| 7 | YE | 1996 | Remote Shift Selector | 21 | BN | 4 | Accessory Voltage |
| 8 | TN/BK | 6009 | Wiper Low Switch Signal | 22 | - | - | Not Used |
| 9 | L-BU | 1714 | Wiper High Switch Signal | 23 | D-GN | 306 | Headlamp Off Signal |
| 10 | - | - | Not Used | 24 | PK | 94 | Washer Switch Signal |
| 11 | - | - | Not Used | 25 | BN | 1356 | Flash To Pass Signal |
| 12 | - | - | Not Used | 26 | PU/WH | 5905 | Key Capture Signal |
| 13 | - | - | Not Used | 27 | - | - | Not Used |
| 14 | PK | 3 | Battery Positive Voltage | | | | |

*Goodheart-Willcox Publisher*

Identify the function of pin 14.

Pin 14 is battery positive voltage.

Determine the circuit number of the pin shaded blue.

The blue-shaded pin is circuit number 1073.

Determine the function of the pin shaded yellow.

The function of the circuit with the yellow-shaded pin is front fog lamp switch signal.

Name _____ Date _____ Class _____

# Module Pinout Diagrams
# Job Skill Practice Problems

Use the following diagram and table to complete practice problems 72.1 through 72.5.

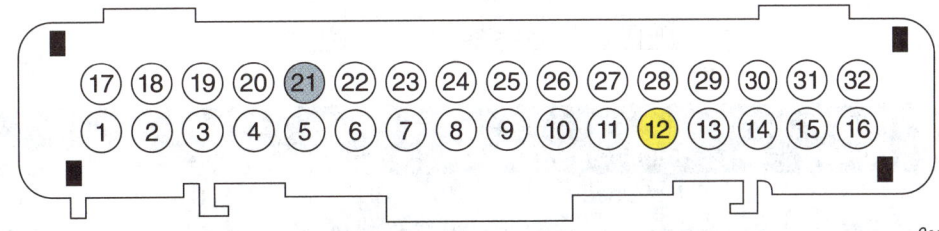

*Goodheart-Willcox Publisher*

| Pin | Wire Color | Circuit Number | Function | Pin | Wire Color | Circuit Number | Function |
|-----|-----------|----------------|----------|-----|-----------|----------------|----------|
| 1 | - | - | Not Used | 17 | - | - | Not Used |
| 2 | - | - | Not Used | 18 | GRY | 435 | EGR Control |
| 3 | BRN/WHT | 633 | CMP Signal | 19 | PPL/WHT | 1660 | HO2S High B1 S1 |
| 4 | PNK | 539 | Ignition Feed | 20 | PPL | 1665 | HO2S High B1 S2 |
| 5 | YEL/BLK | 846 | Injector #6 Control | 21 | PPL | 1670 | HO2S High B2 S1 |
| 6 | - | - | Not Used | 22 | PPL/WHT | 1668 | HO2S High B2 S2 |
| 7 | TAN | 1667 | HO2S B2 S1 | 23 | - | - | Not Used |
| 8 | PNK/BLK | 632 | CMP Low | 24 | TAN | 1671 | Brake Signal |
| 9 | - | - | Not Used | 25 | TAN/WHT | 1653 | Shift Control Lamp |
| 10 | TAN/BLK | 422 | TCC Solenoid | 26 | BRN | 441 | Fuel Pump Relay |
| 11 | - | - | Not Used | 27 | - | - | Not Used |
| 12 | GRN/WHT | 426 | EVAP Purge Control | 28 | PPL | 574 | CKP Low |
| 13 | WHT | 687 | 3-2 Control | 29 | GRN/BLK | 822 | VSS Low |
| 14 | BRN | 436 | AIR Relay Control | 30 | PPL/WHT | 821 | VSS Signal |
| 15 | WHT | 696 | VSS Output Signal | 31 | YEL | 573 | CKP Signal |
| 16 | - | - | Not Used | 32 | - | - | Not Used |

72.1 Identify the function of pin 8.

72.2 Identify the function of the yellow-shaded pin.

72.3 Identify the wire color for the fuel pump relay circuit.

72.4 Identify the pin number for circuit 696.

72.5 Identify the wire color, circuit number, and function of the blue-shaded pin.

Name _____ Date _____ Class _____

Use the following diagram and table to complete practice problems 72.6 through 72.10.

```
 1  2  3  4 [5]    6  7  8  9 10
11 12 13          14 15 16
17 18 19 20 21 22 23 24 25 26 27 28
```

*Goodheart-Willcox Publisher*

| Pin | Wire Color | Circuit Number | Function | Pin | Wire Color | Circuit Number | Function |
|---|---|---|---|---|---|---|---|
| 1 | - | - | Not Used | 15 | BU/WH | 1414 | Driver Side Inflator |
| 2 | WH | 456 | Driver Seat Position Sensor | 16 | D-BU/WH | 1415 | Passenger Side Inflator |
| 3 | GY | 234 | Front Pass Airbag Signal | 17 | PU | 1476 | Driver First Inflator |
| 4 | WH/BK | 678 | OPDS Sensor | 18 | BU/WH | 1477 | Driver Second Inflator |
| 5 | L-GN | 346 | Front Pass Weight Sensor | 19 | D-BU/WH | 1498 | Passenger First Inflator |
| 6 | D-BU | 768 | Left Front Impact Sensor | 20 | PU | 1499 | Passenger Second Inflator |
| 7 | YE | 54 | Right Front Impact Sensor | 21 | PU | 321432 | Driver Seat Belt Tensioner |
| 8 | TN/BK | 578 | Left Side Impact Sensor | 22 | - | - | Not Used |
| 9 | L-BU | 1714 | Right Side Impact Sensor | 23 | PU | 306 | Passenger Seat Belt Tensioner |
| 10 | - | - | Not Used | 24 | BN | 1436 | Left Side Curtain Inflator |
| 11 | D-BU/WH | 123 | Power Supply | 25 | OG | 1437 | Right Side Curtain Inflator |
| 12 | PU | 543 | Front Impact Sensor | 26 | D-GN | 5905 | SRS Indicator |
| 13 | BN | 345 | Rear Impact Sensor | 27 | PK | 513 | Side Airbag Cutoff Signal |
| 14 | RD | 985 | Battery Positive Voltage | 28 | BN | 27 | Data Link Connector |

72.6 Identify the function of pin 15.

72.7 Determine the wire color for the pin shaded yellow.

72.8 Identify the wire color of the SRS indicator circuit.

72.9 Identify the pin number for the driver seat belt tensioner.

72.10 Identify the function of the pin shaded blue.

# UNIT 8

# Driveline

Case Study 73 **Multi-Disc Clutch Adjustments—Addition**
Case Study 74 **Driveline Angle Calculation—Subtraction**
Case Study 75 **Gear Ratio Torque—Multiplication**
Case Study 76 **Differential Gear Ratios—Division**
Case Study 77 **Hydraulic Pressure—Decimal Arithmetic**
Case Study 78 **Planetary Gear Set Ratios—Greater Than and Less Than**
Case Study 79 **Manual Gear Set Ratios—Fractions**
Case Study 80 **Odometer Distance Values—Conversions**
Case Study 81 **Shift Solenoids—Graphs and Tables**
Case Study 82 **Driveline Speed—Formulas**
Case Study 83 **Gear Backlash—Measurement**
Case Study 84 **Differential Backlash—Analyzing Specifications**

## CAREER PROFILE

Amber Avery works as a technician at Toyota of Kirkland in Kirkland, Washington. She is an ASE Master Certified Technician and a Toyota T-Ten graduate. She started her automotive career as a technician at a local quick-lube oil change shop and as a community college student. When she learned about the apprenticeship-style Toyota T-Ten program, she knew it was the type of program that would help her into the career she wanted. She said, "I felt accomplished when I learned to fix my own car, and now I fix other people's cars all day."

On the job, Amber uses math to calculate air conditioning fluid conversions, measure and analyze brake system parts, and measure driveline angles. In addition, she often uses her knowledge of calculating voltage and amperage related to Ohm's law when diagnosing electrical concerns. Amber is confident when diagnosing tough electrical problems using her training and digital multimeter skills. According to Amber, "Knowing how to measure voltage drop is so important for electrical problems."

Strong analytical skills are helping Amber become a successful diagnostic technician. When asked about learning the automotive trade, Amber encourages students to "keep an open mind, be a sponge, and learn everything you can." She also encourages students to trust their training and not just try to guess through a problem. Amber is excited about her career opportunities and values the math skills and diagnostics training she has received.

*Goodheart-Willcox Publisher*
Amber Avery—Technician, Toyota of Kirkland.

# CASE STUDY 73

# Multi-Disc Clutch Adjustments

## OBJECTIVES
*After studying this case study, you will be able to:*
- Identify the function of the multi-plate clutch.
- Calculate shim adjustments for measured wear on multi-plate clutch assemblies.

## TECHNICAL TERMS
multi-disc clutch         standard clutch

## MATH SKILLS
- Addition of decimal numbers.
- Analyze job skill problems related to whole number and decimal arithmetic.

---

A *standard clutch* uses a pressure plate and friction disc to connect the engine flywheel to the input shaft of the manual transmission. A high performance clutch is designed to increase grip power between the engine and transmission by adding additional friction discs and creating a "clutch pack."

On a standard clutch, once the friction disc material wears out, the entire clutch assembly is replaced. A *multi-disc clutch* allows for the addition of various shims to compensate as the clutch material wears down. In order to determine the correct shim to add, the entire clutch pack assembly must be taken apart and each friction disc measured. Once all of the measurements are added together, the correct shim can be added to bring the clutch into specification. Review the following examples.

*Goodheart-Willcox Publisher*

**Example:** A three-disc clutch is made with 3 friction discs and 4 steel discs. The friction discs are 0.308″ thick and the steel discs are 0.367″ thick. Calculate the total installed thickness of the clutch discs.

$$(0.308″ \times 3) + (0.367″ \times 4) = \text{total thickness}$$
$$0.924″ + 1.468″ = 2.392″$$

The installed thickness of the clutch pack is 2.392″.

**Example:** A three-disc clutch pack has a new installed height of 2.425″. The clutch is disassembled, inspected, and measured. The maximum allowable wear before shims are required is 0.030″. Review the measurements and determine the total height of shims needed to return the clutch to specification.

| Disc | Thickness (in) |
|---|---|
| Steel Disc 1 | 0.371 |
| Friction Disc 1 | 0.311 |
| Steel Disc 2 | 0.369 |
| Friction Disc 2 | 0.309 |
| Steel Disc 3 | 0.370 |
| Friction Disc 3 | 0.312 |
| Steel Disc 4 | 0.368 |

$$0.371″ + 0.311″ + 0.369″ + 0.309″ + 0.370″ + 0.312″ + 0.368″ = 2.410″$$
$$2.425″ - 0.030″ = 2.395″ \text{ minimum height}$$
$$2.410″ > 2.395″$$

The clutch wear is within specification and no shim is needed.

# Multi-Disc Clutch Adjustments
# Job Skill Practice Problems

73.1 A three-disc clutch is made with 3 friction discs and 4 steel discs. The friction discs are 0.316" thick and the steel discs are 0.347" thick. Calculate the total installed thickness of the clutch discs.

73.2 A four-disc clutch is made with 4 friction discs and 5 steel discs. The friction discs are 0.292" thick and the steel discs are 0.325" thick. Calculate the total installed thickness of the clutch discs.

73.3 A three-disc clutch is made with 3 friction discs and 4 steel discs. The friction discs are 0.319" thick and the steel discs are 0.383" thick. Calculate the total installed thickness of the clutch discs.

73.4 A three-disc clutch pack has a new installed height of 2.595". The clutch is disassembled, inspected, and measured. The maximum allowable wear before shims are required is 0.030". Review the measurements and determine the total height of shims needed to return the clutch to specification.

| Disc | Thickness (in) |
|---|---|
| Steel Disc 1 | 0.391 |
| Friction Disc 1 | 0.330 |
| Steel Disc 2 | 0.389 |
| Friction Disc 2 | 0.331 |
| Steel Disc 3 | 0.390 |
| Friction Disc 3 | 0.334 |
| Steel Disc 4 | 0.389 |

Name _____  Date _____  Class _____

73.5 A three-disc clutch pack has a new installed height of 2.210". The clutch is disassembled, inspected, and measured. The maximum allowable wear before shims are required is 0.020". Review the measurements and determine the total height of shims needed to return the clutch to specification.

| Disc | Thickness (in) |
|---|---|
| Steel Disc 1 | 0.335 |
| Friction Disc 1 | 0.290 |
| Steel Disc 2 | 0.332 |
| Friction Disc 2 | 0.289 |
| Steel Disc 3 | 0.328 |
| Friction Disc 3 | 0.287 |
| Steel Disc 4 | 0.327 |

73.6 A three-disc clutch pack has a new installed height of 2.390". The clutch is disassembled, inspected, and measured. The maximum allowable wear before shims are required is 0.025". Review the measurements and determine the total height of shims needed to return the clutch to specification.

| Disc | Thickness (in) |
|---|---|
| Steel Disc 1 | 0.365 |
| Friction Disc 1 | 0.299 |
| Steel Disc 2 | 0.362 |
| Friction Disc 2 | 0.298 |
| Steel Disc 3 | 0.364 |
| Friction Disc 3 | 0.301 |
| Steel Disc 4 | 0.365 |

# CASE STUDY 74

# Driveline Angle Calculation

## OBJECTIVES

*After studying this case study, you will be able to:*
- Identify the required measurements for calculating driveline angles.
- Calculate the operating angle of universal joints based on driveline angles.

## MATH SKILLS
- Whole number subtraction.
- Analyze job skill problems related to whole number subtraction.

The driveshaft connects the transmission to the rear axle or the transfer case to the front and rear axles. The angle of the driveshaft compared to the level ground is only one thing to consider. When analyzing driveline angles, it is critical to calculate the operation angle of the universal joints. The universal joints connect the center section of the driveshaft to the yoke and allows the driveshaft operating angle to change while the driveshaft spins.

*Goodheart-Willcox Publisher*

To calculate the operation angle of the universal joints, it is necessary to know the angle of the transmission output shaft and the angle of the rear axle pinion, in addition to the driveshaft angles. A digital angle gauge is used to measure these angles, and many are designed to be accurate to 0.1°. Most driveline manufacturers recommend that universal joint operating angles do not exceed 3.0°.

To calculate the operating angle of the front universal joint, first measure the angle of the output shaft of the transmission, then the angle of the driveshaft. Next, subtract the smaller angle from the larger angle to calculate the operating angle of the universal joint.

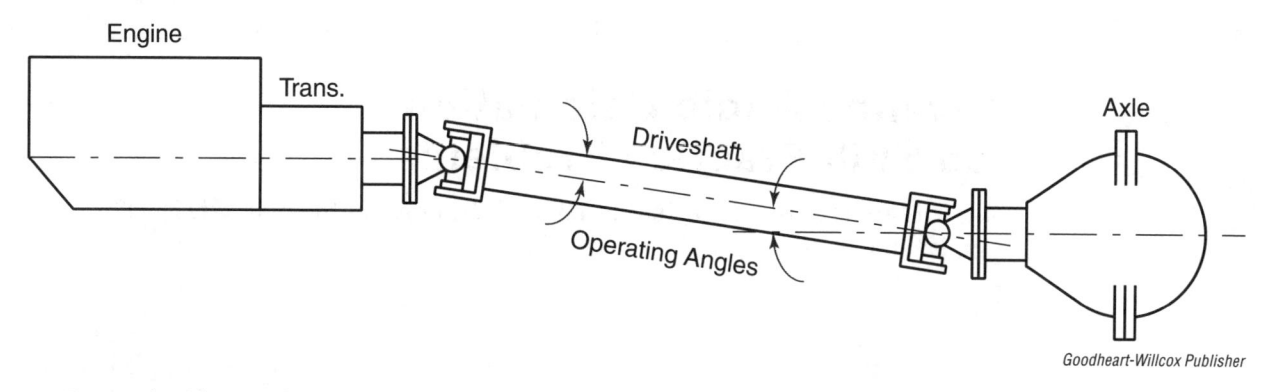

**Example:** The angle of the transmission is 4° and the angle of the driveshaft is 3°. Calculate the operating angle of the universal joint.

$$4° - 3° = 1°$$

The front universal joint has an operating angle of 1°.

# Driveline Angle Calculation
# Job Skill Practice Problems

74.1 The angle of the driveshaft is 4.3° and the angle of the rear axle is 3.1°. Calculate the operating angle of the universal joint.

74.2 The angle of the driveshaft is 2.1° and the angle of the rear axle is 3.2°. Calculate the operating angle of the universal joint.

74.3 The angle of the transfer case is 2.7° and the angle of the front driveshaft is 4.1°. Calculate the operating angle of the universal joint.

74.4 The angle of the transfer case is 1.9° and the angle of the front driveshaft is 3.4°. Calculate the operating angle of the universal joint.

74.5 A truck is being equipped with a suspension lift kit that changes the driveshaft angle from 2.0° to 4.0°. If the transmission angle is 1.3° and the rear axle angle is 2.1°, calculate the stock and lifted operating angles of each universal joint.

74.6 An SUV is being equipped with a suspension lift kit that changes the driveshaft angle from 2.3° to 4.5°. If the transmission angle is 1.8° and the rear axle angle is 2.8°, calculate the stock and lifted operating angles of each universal joint.

# CASE STUDY 75

# Gear Ratio Torque

## OBJECTIVES

*After studying this case study, you will be able to:*
- Identify the multiplication factor of gear ratios.
- Calculate the multiplication of engine torque through transmission and differential gears.

## TECHNICAL TERMS

direct-drive
gear ratios
overdrive
underdrive

## MATH SKILLS

- Multiplication of whole and decimal numbers.
- Analyze and solve job skill problems related to multiplication.

The engine creates torque, but the driveline uses the mechanical advantage of gear ratios to multiply engine torque to much greater amounts. *Gear ratios* multiply engine torque in the transmission and in the axle differential. In a manual transmission, sets of gears with a different number of teeth on each gear establish a gear ratio for that gear set. In the differential, the gear ratio is established by the number of teeth on the ring gear compared to the number of teeth on the pinion gear. Gear ratios can be an underdrive ratio, a direct-drive ratio, or an overdrive ratio.

*Goodheart-Willcox Publisher*

*Underdrive* uses a ratio higher than 1:1. This ratio multiplies torque but has a much slower output speed compared to an input speed. This high torque, low speed gear is needed to get the vehicle moving from a stop.

*Direct-drive* uses a ratio of 1:1. This ratio transfers torque and speed without increasing or decreasing either. In some transmissions, this is the highest gear.

*Overdrive* uses a ratio lower than 1:1. This ratio transfers less engine torque, but transfers an increase of speed. This low torque, high speed gear is used for high speed cruising.

**Example:** A truck equipped with a manual transmission has a first gear ratio of 3.75:1 and a differential gear ratio of 4.10:1. The engine is producing 210 foot-pounds of torque. Calculate the torque multiplication of the driveline.

210 foot-pounds × 3.75 × 4.10 = 3,228.75 foot-pounds
The output torque is 3,228.75 foot-pounds.

Name _____ Date _____ Class _____

# Gear Ratio Torque Job Skill Practice Problems

75.1 A modern muscle car is producing 295 foot-pounds of torque and is equipped with a 3.40:1 differential gear. Calculate the torque multiplication of each gear in the driveline.

Gear Ratios:
- 1st: 3.06
- 2nd: 1.62
- 3rd: 1.00
- 4th: 0.70

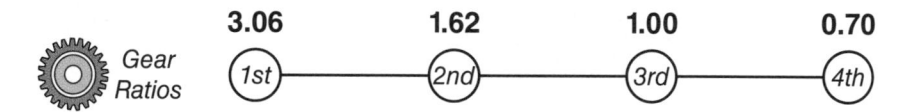

75.2 A truck is producing 195 foot-pounds of torque and is equipped with a 3.05:1 differential gear. Calculate the torque multiplication of each gear in the driveline.

Gear Ratios:
- 1st: 2.48
- 2nd: 1.48
- 3rd: 1.00
- 4th: 0.75

75.3 A sedan is producing 245 foot-pounds of torque and is equipped with a 3.60:1 differential gear. Calculate the torque multiplication of each gear in the driveline.

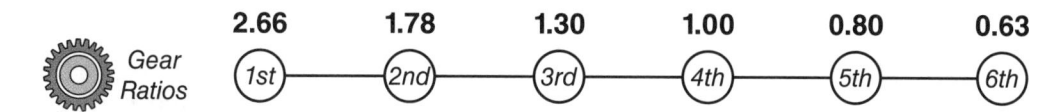

Gear Ratios:
- 1st: 2.66
- 2nd: 1.78
- 3rd: 1.30
- 4th: 1.00
- 5th: 0.80
- 6th: 0.63

**Name** _____  **Date** _____  **Class** _____

75.4 A 4X4 truck is producing 325 foot-pounds of torque and is equipped with a 3.20:1 differential gear ratio. Calculate the torque multiplication of each gear in the driveline.

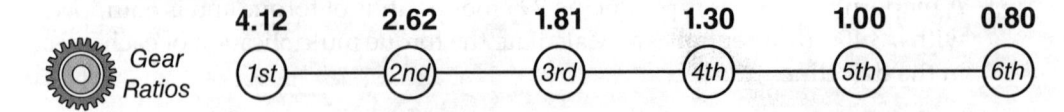

Gear Ratios:
- 1st: 4.12
- 2nd: 2.62
- 3rd: 1.81
- 4th: 1.30
- 5th: 1.00
- 6th: 0.80

75.5 A pickup truck is producing 369 foot-pounds of torque and is equipped with a 3.42:1 differential gear ratio. Calculate the torque multiplication of each gear in the driveline.

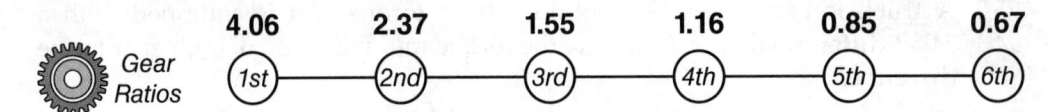

Gear Ratios:
- 1st: 4.06
- 2nd: 2.37
- 3rd: 1.55
- 4th: 1.16
- 5th: 0.85
- 6th: 0.67

75.6 A compact sedan is producing 126 foot-pounds of torque and is equipped with a 5.045:1 differential gear ratio. The vehicle is also equipped with a CVT automatic transmission that has a forward and reverse gear ratio range. Calculate the torque multiplication of each gear range minimum and maximum in the driveline.

Forward minimum: 2.480         Reverse minimum: 2.604
Forward maximum: 0.396         Reverse maximum: 1.680

# CASE STUDY 76

# Differential Gear Ratios

## OBJECTIVES

*After studying this case study, you will be able to:*

- Identify ring and pinion gear set ratios.
- Calculate the relationship between final drive gear ratio and acceleration.

## TECHNICAL TERMS

differential gear set
final drive gear ratio
pinion gear
ring gear

## MATH SKILLS

- Calculate problems using whole number and decimal division.
- Analyze word problems with whole number and decimal division.

---

The *differential gear set* is designed to use a pinion gear and a ring gear. These specially cut gears allow for driveshaft rotation to be transferred in a 90° angle to the axle shafts or half shafts and the wheels. The *pinion gear* is the drive gear, and the *ring gear* is the driven gear. The different number of teeth on the gears establishes a *final drive gear ratio*. This gear ratio can be calculated by dividing the number of ring gear teeth by the number of pinion gear teeth.

*Goodheart-Willcox Publisher*

Rear differential gear ratios can be modified to offer better acceleration or better top-end speed, depending on the application. Tall gear ratios are lower numbers, such as 3.00:1. Short gear ratios are higher numbers, such as 4.11:1. A tall gear ratio creates less torque multiplication, but allows for higher top-end speeds. A shorter gear ratio creates more torque multiplication and acceleration, but requires much higher engine speeds when cruising.

Review the following examples.

**Example:** A rear differential gear set has a pinion gear with 11 teeth and a ring gear with 37 teeth. Calculate the final drive gear ratio.

$$37 \text{ teeth} \div 11 \text{ teeth} = 3.36$$

The differential has a 3.36:1 gear ratio.

**Example:** A technician is changing a ring and pinion gear set to a set with a different ratio. The stock gears have 13 teeth on the pinion gear and 41 teeth on the ring gear. The new gears have 9 teeth on the pinion gear and 37 teeth on the ring gear. Determine if the new gears are taller or shorter compared to stock gears.

$$41 \text{ teeth} \div 13 \text{ teeth} = 3.15:1 \text{ stock}$$
$$37 \text{ teeth} \div 9 \text{ teeth} = 4.11:1 \text{ new}$$

4.11 > 3.15, so the gears are shorter and provide better acceleration.

Name _____ Date _____ Class _____

# Differential Gear Ratio Job Skill Practice Problems

76.1 A rear differential gear set has a pinion gear with 8 teeth and a ring gear with 37 teeth. Calculate the final drive gear ratio. Round to the nearest hundredth.

76.2 A rear differential gear set has a pinion gear with 10 teeth and a ring gear with 43 teeth. Calculate the final drive gear ratio. Round to the nearest hundredth.

76.3 A rear differential gear set has a pinion gear with 9 teeth and a ring gear with 35 teeth. Calculate the final drive gear ratio. Round to the nearest hundredth.

76.4 A rear differential gear set has a pinion gear with 11 teeth and a ring gear with 36 teeth. Calculate the final drive gear ratio. Round to the nearest hundredth.

76.5 A rear differential gear set has a pinion gear with 13 teeth and a ring gear with 39 teeth. Calculate the final drive gear ratio. Round to the nearest hundredth.

Copyright Goodheart-Willcox Co., Inc. May not be reproduced or posted to a publicly accessible website.

Name _____ Date _____ Class _____

76.6 A technician is changing a ring and pinion gear set to a set with a different ratio. The stock gears have 12 teeth on the pinion gear and 41 teeth on the ring gear. The new gears have 7 teeth on the pinion gear and 34 teeth on the ring gear. Calculate the final drive gear ratio of each set and determine if the new gears are taller or shorter compared to stock gears. Round to the nearest hundredth.

76.7 A technician is changing a ring and pinion gear set to a set with a different ratio. The stock gears have 10 teeth on the pinion gear and 35 teeth on the ring gear. The new gears have 11 teeth on the pinion gear and 41 teeth on the ring gear. Calculate the final drive gear ratio of each set and determine if the new gears are taller or shorter compared to stock gears. Round to the nearest hundredth.

76.8 A technician is changing a ring and pinion gear set to a set with a different ratio. The stock gears have 9 teeth on the pinion gear and 37 teeth on the ring gear. The new gears have 10 teeth on the pinion gear and 41 teeth on the ring gear. Calculate the final drive gear ratio of each set and determine if the new gears are taller or shorter compared to stock gears. Round to the nearest hundredth.

# CASE STUDY 77

# Hydraulic Pressure

## OBJECTIVES
*After studying this case study, you will be able to:*
- Identify Pascal's law of hydraulic pressure.
- Calculate the effects of piston size within a hydraulic system.

## TECHNICAL TERM
Pascal's law

## MATH SKILLS
- Calculate decimal arithmetic.
- Analyze job skill problems related to decimal arithmetic.

---

When pressure is applied to a noncompressible fluid in a contained space, that pressure is exerted completely throughout the fluid. This concept is known as **Pascal's law**. Fluid pressure is critical to the correct operation of a number of vehicle systems, including automatic transmissions and hydraulic clutch and brake systems.

Fluid pressure input may be generated through a piston, such as in a clutch or brake pedal. It may also be generated by a pump, such as an automatic transmission fluid pump. Force and motion are transmitted through the fluid to an output piston. Examples of output pistons include brake calipers, wheel cylinders, clutch slave cylinders, and valves within an automatic transmission. The transfer of motion and force through a hydraulic system can be calculated, and both motion and force can be increased or decreased, depending on the sizes of the input and output.

Review the following examples.

**Example:** A hydraulic system with an input piston area of 4 cm² is moved 2 cm. The output piston area is 4 cm². Calculate how far the output piston moves.

$$4 \text{ cm}^2 = 4 \text{ cm}^2$$

The output piston moves the same distance, 2 cm.

**Example:** A hydraulic system with an input piston area of 6 cm$^2$ is moved 2 cm. The output piston area is 3 cm$^2$. Calculate how far the output piston moves.

$$6 \text{ cm}^2 \div 3 \text{ cm}^2 = 2$$
$$2 \times 2 \text{ cm} = 4 \text{ cm of movement}$$

The output piston moves 4 cm, twice the distance of the input piston.

**Example:** A hydraulic system with an input piston area of 2 cm$^2$ is moved 3 cm. The output piston area is 4 cm$^2$. Calculate how far the output piston moves.

$$2 \text{ cm}^2 \div 4 \text{ cm}^2 = 0.5$$
$$0.5 \times 3 \text{ cm} = 1.5 \text{ cm}$$

The output piston moves 1.5 cm, half the distance of the input piston.

**Example:** A hydraulic system with an input piston area of 2 in$^2$ has an input force of 20 pounds. The output piston area is 4 in$^2$. Calculate the pressure applied to the output piston.

$$20 \text{ pounds of input force} \div 2 \text{ in}^2 = 10 \text{ psi}$$
$$10 \text{ psi} \times 4 \text{ in}^2 = 40 \text{ pounds of output force}$$

The pressure applied to the output piston is 40 pounds of force.

Name _____ Date _____ Class _____

# Hydraulic Pressure Job Skill Practice Problems

77.1 A hydraulic system with an input piston area of 8 cm² is moved 3 cm. The output piston area is 12 cm². Calculate how far the output piston moves.

77.2 A hydraulic system with an input piston area of 10 cm² is moved 6 cm. The output piston area is 7 cm². Calculate how far the output piston moves. Round to the nearest hundredth.

77.3 A hydraulic system with an input piston area of 3 cm² is moved 5 cm. The output piston area is 9 cm². Calculate how far the output piston moves. Round to the nearest hundredth.

77.4 A hydraulic system with an input piston area of 1.5 cm² is moved 4.5 cm. The output piston area is 2.75 cm². Calculate how far the output piston moves. Round to the nearest hundredth.

**Name** _____  **Date** _____  **Class** _____

77.5 A hydraulic system with an input piston area of 6 in² has an input force of 15 pounds. The output piston area is 3 in². Calculate the pressure applied to the output piston.

77.6 A hydraulic system with an input piston area of 1.5 in² has an input force of 45 pounds. The output piston area is 4 in². Calculate the pressure applied to the output piston.

77.7 A hydraulic system with an input piston area of 2 in² has an input force of 350 pounds. The output piston area is 5 in². Calculate the pressure applied to the output piston.

77.8 A hydraulic system with an input piston area of 0.75 in² has an input force of 120 pounds. The output piston area is 3 in². Calculate the pressure applied to the output piston.

# CASE STUDY 78

# Planetary Gear Set Ratios

## OBJECTIVES

*After studying this case study, you will be able to:*

- Identify basic planetary gear set operation.
- Calculate gear ratios of the various planetary gear set inputs and outputs.

## TECHNICAL TERM

planetary gear set

## MATH SKILLS

- Calculate planetary gear set gear ratios.
- Identify greater than and less than direct drive ratios.
- Order ratio values from least to greatest.

---

The planetary gear set is essential within an automatic transmission for the creation of various input and output ratios. Planetary gear sets are also found in many unique drivelines, from army tanks to hybrid electric vehicles.

The *planetary gear set* is made up of a single sun gear located in the center, a carrier bracket holding three or more planetary gears, and a single outer ring gear. To operate a planetary gear set, one gear is held (prevented from movement), one gear is the power input, and the final gear becomes the output gear. Technically, any combination of held, input, and output can be applied to the gears of a planetary gear set with different gear ratio output. If the planet gears are held, the direction of rotation of the output is *reversed* compared to the input.

*Goodheart-Willcox Publisher*

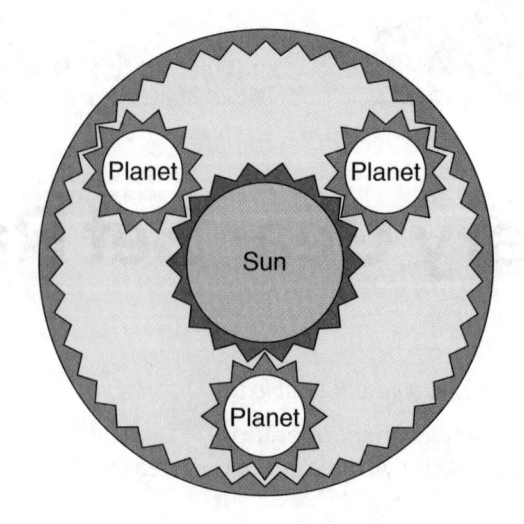

The number of teeth on the sun gear and the ring gear can be counted. When solving for gear ratios, the planet carrier gear value is calculated by adding the number of teeth on the sun and ring gears together.

To solve for gear ratio, use the formula:

*gear ratio = output gear ÷ input gear*

**Example:** A planetary gear set has 30 teeth on the ring gear and 12 teeth on the sun gear. This determines that the planet carrier gear set has a tooth value of 42. Calculate the gear ratio if the ring gear is the input gear, the sun gear is the held gear, and the planet carrier gear is the output gear.

42 teeth ÷ 30 teeth = 1.40

The gear ratio for ring gear input and sun gear held is 1.40:1.

**Example:** Using the same planetary gear set, calculate the gear ratio if the planet gear is the input gear, the sun gear is the held gear, and the ring gear is the output gear.

30 teeth ÷ 42 teeth = 0.71

The gear ratio for the sun gear input and the planet gear held is 0.71:1.

All of the input-output combination gear ratios can be solved. Gear ratios lower than 1.00:1 indicate overdrive and gear ratios higher than 1.00:1 indicate underdrive. Refer to the table (*indicates reverse output).

| Input | Held | Output | Gear Ratio |
|---|---|---|---|
| Sun | Ring | Planet | 3.50:1 |
| Ring | Sun | Planet | 1.40:1 |
| Planet | Ring | Sun | 0.29:1 |
| Planet | Sun | Ring | 0.71:1 |
| Sun | Planet | Ring* | 2.50:1 |
| Ring | Planet | Sun* | 0.40:1 |

# Planetary Gear Set Ratios
# Job Skill Practice Problems

78.1 A planetary gear set has 62 teeth on the ring gear and 28 teeth on the sun gear. This determines that the planet carrier gear set has a tooth value of 90. Calculate the six different gear ratio combinations and rank the gear ratios in order, from least to greatest. Round to the nearest hundredth.

| Input | Held | Output | Gear Ratio |
|---|---|---|---|
| Planet | Ring | Sun | |
| Planet | Sun | Ring | |
| Ring | Planet | Sun* | |
| Sun | Planet | Ring* | |
| Ring | Sun | Planet | |
| Sun | Ring | Planet | |

78.2 A planetary gear set has 70 teeth on the ring gear and 30 teeth on the sun gear. This determines that the planet carrier gear set has a tooth value of 100. Calculate the six different gear ratio combinations and rank the gear ratios in order, from least to greatest. Round to the nearest hundredth.

| Input | Held | Output | Gear Ratio |
|---|---|---|---|
| Planet | Ring | Sun | |
| Sun | Planet | Ring* | |
| Sun | Ring | Planet | |
| Planet | Sun | Ring | |
| Ring | Sun | Planet | |
| Ring | Planet | Sun* | |

**Name** _____  **Date** _____  **Class** _____

78.3 A planetary gear set has 55 teeth on the ring gear and 18 teeth on the sun gear. This determines that the planet carrier gear set has a tooth value of 73. Calculate the six different gear ratio combinations and rank the gear ratios in order, from least to greatest. Round to the nearest hundredth.

| Input | Held | Output | Gear Ratio |
|---|---|---|---|
| Ring | Planet | Sun* | _____ |
| Ring | Sun | Planet | _____ |
| Planet | Sun | Ring | _____ |
| Sun | Ring | Planet | _____ |
| Sun | Planet | Ring* | _____ |
| Planet | Ring | Sun | _____ |

# CASE STUDY 79

# Manual Gear Set Ratios

## OBJECTIVES
*After studying this case study, you will be able to:*
- Identify the number of teeth on the drive or driven gear.
- Calculate the number of teeth on a gear compared to another gear.

## MATH SKILLS
- Calculate a value using fractions.
- Analyze and solve fraction job skill problems.

A manual transmission is filled with gear sets connected and engaged by synchronizers. Each gear set has a different ratio, allowing the transmission to use lower gears to accelerate and higher gears to cruise at high speeds. The gear ratios of the helical cut gears inside the manual transmission can also be calculated using fractions. Review the following examples.

*Goodheart-Willcox Publisher*

**Example:** A drive gear has 12 teeth. The driven gear has 2/3 the number of teeth as the drive gear. Calculate the number of teeth on the driven gear.

12 teeth ÷ 3 = 4 teeth, then 4 teeth × 2 = 8 teeth

2/3 of 12 teeth is 8 teeth on the driven gear.

**Example:** A driven gear has 16 teeth. The drive gear has 1 3/4 the number of teeth as the driven gear. Calculate the number of teeth on the drive gear.

16 teeth ÷ 4 = 4 teeth, then 4 teeth × 3 = 12 teeth

12 teeth + 16 teeth = 28 teeth

1 3/4 of 16 teeth is 28 teeth on the drive gear.

Name _____  Date _____  Class _____

# Manual Gear Set Ratios Job Skill Practice Problems

79.1  A drive gear has 30 teeth. The driven gear has 2/5 the number of teeth as the drive gear. Calculate the number of teeth on the driven gear.

79.2  A driven gear has 18 teeth. The drive gear has 5/6 the number of teeth as the driven gear. Calculate the number of teeth on the drive gear.

79.3  A drive gear has 45 teeth. The driven gear has 4/9 the number of teeth as the drive gear. Calculate the number of teeth on the driven gear.

79.4  A driven gear has 28 teeth. The drive gear has 1/4 the number of teeth as the driven gear. Calculate the number of teeth on the drive gear.

**Name** _____  **Date** _____  **Class** _____

79.5 A drive gear has 56 teeth. The driven gear has 3/4 the number of teeth as the drive gear. Calculate the number of teeth on the driven gear.

79.6 A driven gear has 50 teeth. The drive gear has 1 3/5 the number of teeth as the driven gear. Calculate the number of teeth on the drive gear.

79.7 A driven gear has 96 teeth. The drive gear has 1 1/4 the number of teeth as the driven gear. Calculate the number of teeth on the drive gear.

79.8 A driven gear has 72 teeth. The drive gear has 1 7/12 the number of teeth as the driven gear. Calculate the number of teeth on the drive gear.

# CASE STUDY 80

# Odometer Distance Values

## OBJECTIVES

*After studying this case study, you will be able to:*
- Identify the conversion factors for distance values.
- Compute distance values using conversion factors based on word problems.

## MATH SKILLS
- Convert values using a conversion factor.
- Analyze job skill problems based on conversion factors.

The odometer is the gauge that records the distance a vehicle has been driven, in either miles or kilometers. The mile is the distance measurement used throughout the United States. Almost all other countries around the world use the kilometer as the distance measurement. The kilometer (km) is one thousand meters (the prefix *kilo-* indicates one thousand). The mile, which is based on the 1-foot measurement, is 5,280'. Refer to the table for distance conversion factors and review the following examples.

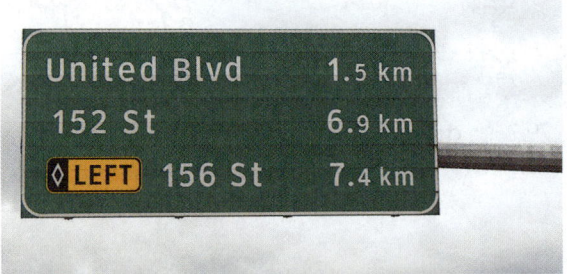

*Goodheart-Willcox Publisher*

| Distance Conversion Factors | | |
|---|---|---|
| 1 mile | = | 5,280' |
| 1 mile | = | 1.60934 km |
| 1 km | = | 0.621371 miles |
| 1 km | = | 3,280.84' |

**Example:** A vehicle travels from Calgary to Edmonton, a distance of about 298 km. Convert this distance to miles.

$$298 \text{ km} \times 0.621371 \text{ miles} = 185.2 \text{ miles}$$

The distance is about 185.2 miles.

**Example:** A vehicle travels from Bismarck to Pierre, a distance of about 210 miles. Convert this distance to kilometers.

$$210 \text{ miles} \times 1.60934 \text{ km} = 338.0 \text{ km}$$

The distance is about 338.0 km.

Name _____  Date _____  Class _____

## Odometer Distance Values
## Job Skill Practice Problems

80.1 Two technicians are taking turns driving from Duluth to Milwaukee to visit a motorcycle museum. The first technician drives the first 195 miles and the second technician drives the last 365 km. Calculate the total distance they drove to visit the motorcycle museum, in miles. Round to the nearest tenth.

80.2 A technician bought an intercooler on an Internet auction and chose to pick up the part in person. The technician lives in Riverside and the part is 269 km away in Bakersfield. Calculate how many miles away the part is located from the technician's home. Round to the nearest tenth.

80.3 A technician is considering two different job offers. One dealership is located 23 miles from his home. The other dealership is located 34 km from his home. Determine which job is located closer to the technician's home.

80.4 Two technicians are taking turns driving from Indianapolis to Detroit to visit the International Auto Show. The first technician drove the first 170 miles. The second technician drove the last 227 km. Determine which technician drove farther.

Name _____  Date _____  Class _____

80.5 A technician in Juneau drives 1179 km to Fairbanks to drop off some cylinder heads at the machine shop. The technician then drives 570 km to Anchorage to pick up some custom pistons and fuel injectors. Calculate the total distance driven, in miles. Round to the nearest tenth.

80.6 Two technicians are taking turns driving from Houston to Braselton to watch sports car racing. The first technician drove the first 920 km. The second technician drove the last 446 km. Calculate how many miles they drove altogether. Round to the nearest tenth.

80.7 A technician living in Santa Fe is looking at two different trucks for sale online. One truck is located 97 miles away and the other truck is located 148 km away. Calculate which truck is closer to Santa Fe.

80.8 Two technicians are driving 114 miles from Evansville to Bowling Green to visit the sports car museum. They stop for coffee after driving 90 km. Calculate how many miles remain after their stop. Round to the nearest tenth.

# CASE STUDY 81

# Shift Solenoids

## OBJECTIVES

*After studying this case study, you will be able to:*
- Interpret automatic transmission and transaxle shift solenoid tables.
- Analyze shift solenoid tables to identify when components are applied and released.

## MATH SKILLS
- Analyze tables and graphs to identify specific conditions.
- Solve job skill problems related to information on tables and graphs.

The electronically controlled automatic transmission and transaxle uses electrical solenoids to control internal shift components. Shift solenoids can either be applied or released, and are designated on shift solenoid tables as ON or OFF. The shift solenoids direct fluid flow, which controls different parts of the planetary gear sets, allowing the transmission to shift through the different gears. The shift solenoid valve controls for each gear of a basic 4-speed automatic transmission are shown in the table. Review the table and following examples.

*Goodheart-Willcox Publisher*

| Gear | Shift Solenoid 1 | Shift Solenoid 2 |
|---|---|---|
| Park, Reverse, Neutral | ON | OFF |
| First | ON | OFF |
| Second | OFF | OFF |
| Third (direct drive) | OFF | ON |
| Fourth (overdrive) | ON | ON |

**Example:** Identify the gear engaged when both solenoids are released (OFF).

Second gear is engaged when both shift solenoids are released.

**Example:** This electronically controlled transmission will not upshift from second gear. Analyze the table to determine which shift control solenoid is not operating correctly.

Shift Solenoid 2 is not applying (ON), causing third gear and fourth gear to not engage.

Name _____  Date _____  Class _____

## Shift Solenoids Job Skill Practice Problems

Use the following table to complete practice problems 81.1 through 81.4.

| Gear | Shift Solenoid 1 | Shift Solenoid 2 | Shift Solenoid 3 |
|---|---|---|---|
| Park, Reverse, Neutral | ON | ON | ON |
| First | ON | ON | ON |
| Second | OFF | ON | ON |
| Third | OFF | OFF | ON |
| Fourth | OFF | OFF | OFF |
| Fifth | ON | OFF | OFF |

81.1 Identify the gear selected when all shift solenoids are released (OFF).

81.2 A transmission will not upshift beyond first gear into second gear. Identify the shift solenoid that will not turn off.

81.3 If Shift Solenoid 3 will not release (OFF), identify the gears that the transmission will not engage.

81.4 Identify the gears selected when all shift solenoids are engaged (ON).

Name _____ Date _____ Class _____

Use the following table to complete practice problems 81.5 through 81.8.

| Gear | Park Pawl | Shift Solenoid A | Shift Solenoid B | Shift Solenoid C | Shift Solenoid D | Shift Solenoid E |
|---|---|---|---|---|---|---|
| P | ON | ON | OFF | OFF | OFF | OFF |
| N | OFF | ON | OFF | OFF | OFF | OFF |
| R | OFF | ON | ON | OFF | ON | OFF |
| 1 | OFF | ON | ON | ON | OFF | OFF |
| 2 | OFF | ON | ON | OFF | OFF | ON |
| 3 | OFF | OFF | ON | ON | OFF | ON |
| 4 | OFF | OFF | ON | OFF | ON | ON |
| 5 | OFF | OFF | ON | ON | ON | OFF |
| 6 | OFF | OFF | OFF | ON | ON | ON |
| 7 | OFF | ON | OFF | ON | ON | OFF |
| 8 | OFF | ON | OFF | OFF | ON | ON |

81.5 Identify the shift solenoids that are released (OFF) in first gear.

81.6 For each gear upshift, identify the shift solenoid that switches from engaged (ON) to released (OFF).

81.7 The transmission will not upshift out of first gear. Identify which shift solenoid will not engage (ON).

81.8 The transmission will not engage reverse from neutral or first gear. Identify which shift solenoid will not engage (ON).

# CASE STUDY 82

# Driveline Speed

## OBJECTIVES

*After studying this case study, you will be able to:*
- Calculate tire diameter using a formula.
- Calculate vehicle speed related to driveline changes using a formula.

## MATH SKILLS
- Solve job skill problems using a formula or series of formulas.
- Analyze results of a formula calculation to identify specific results.

Changes to gear ratio and tire size will have an effect on the overall speed of the vehicle. Changing either of these factors will have an effect on the vehicle speed, by either providing quicker acceleration or lower engine rpm and higher vehicle speeds. Calculating the cruising vehicle speed and tire diameter uses specific formulas. Cruising vehicle speed refers to a vehicle that has already accelerated to speed and is now maintaining the current speed.

*Goodheart-Willcox Publisher*

$$\text{tire diameter} = \frac{\text{section width} \times \text{aspect ratio} \times 2}{25.4 + \text{wheel diameter}}$$

$$\text{vehicle speed} = \frac{\text{tire diameter} \times \text{engine speed (rpm)}}{377 \times \text{gear ratio}}$$

**Example:** Solve for the diameter of a 215/65R16 tire.

$$\text{tire diameter} = \frac{215 \times 0.65 \times 2}{25.4 + 16}$$

$$\text{tire diameter} = 27.00''$$

**Example:** Solve for the vehicle speed of a vehicle with a tire diameter of 27.00″, at 2,500 rpm, and a gear ratio of 3.73.

$$\text{vehicle speed} = \frac{27.00 \times 2{,}500}{377 \times 3.73}$$

vehicle speed = 48 miles per hour

**Example:** Use the same vehicle, but change the gear ratio to 4.10:1 and calculate the change in speed.

$$\text{vehicle speed} = \frac{27.00 \times 2{,}500}{377 \times 4.10}$$

vehicle speed = 43.7 miles per hour

**Name** _____  **Date** _____  **Class** _____

## Driveline Speed Job Skill Practice Problems

82.1  A truck is equipped with P235/70R17 tires and a 3.73:1 differential gear ratio. Calculate the vehicle cruising speed at 3,000 rpm. Round to the nearest tenth for all calculations.

82.2  A sports car is equipped with P285/35R19 tires and a 2.41:1 differential gear ratio. Calculate the vehicle cruising speed at 3,500 rpm. Round to the nearest tenth for all calculations.

82.3  A compact car is equipped with P215/50R17 tires and a 4.10:1 differential gear ratio. Calculate the vehicle cruising speed at 2,350 rpm. Round to the nearest tenth for all calculations.

82.4  A truck is equipped with P275/65R18 tires and a 3.73:1 differential gear ratio. Calculate the change to vehicle cruising speed at 2,500 rpm if the differential gear ratio is changed to 3.00:1. Round to the nearest tenth for all calculations.

82.5 A compact car is equipped with P195/55R15 tires and a 3.50:1 differential gear ratio. Calculate the change to vehicle cruising speed at 2,500 rpm if the differential gear ratio is changed to 4.10:1. Round to the nearest tenth for all calculations.

82.6 A sedan is equipped with P215/55R17 tires and a 3.90:1 differential gear ratio. Calculate the change to vehicle cruising speed at 2,800 rpm if the tire size is changed to P235/45R17. Round to the nearest tenth for all calculations.

82.7 An AWD sport-utility vehicle is equipped with P205/65R18 tires and a 3.55:1 differential gear ratio. Calculate the change to vehicle cruising speed at 2,000 rpm if the tire size is changed to P215/55R18. Round to the nearest tenth for all calculations.

82.8 A classic muscle car is equipped with P235/65R16 tires and a 3.73:1 differential gear ratio. Calculate the change to vehicle cruising speed at 2,800 rpm if the tire size is changed to P255/65R16 and the rear differential gear ratio is changed to 4.10:1. Round to the nearest tenth for all calculations.

# CASE STUDY 83

# Gear Backlash

## OBJECTIVES
*After studying this case study, you will be able to:*
- Analyze dial indicator readings to measure ring and pinion gear backlash.
- Calculate total backlash using a dial indicator.

## TECHNICAL TERM
backlash

## MATH SKILLS
- Interpret measurements using a dial gauge.
- Analyze job skill problems related to measurements.

---

The amount of space between the gear teeth in a ring and pinion gear set is *backlash*. This can be measured using a dial indicator, with the dial needle placed on a ring gear tooth. With the pinion gear held firm, the ring gear can be moved back and forth within the pinion gear teeth. With a dial indicator set up on the ring gear, the movement of the dial indicator gauge shows the movement between the teeth, the gear backlash.

**Example:** Shown are the dial indicator readings of the ring gear movement. Calculate the backlash.

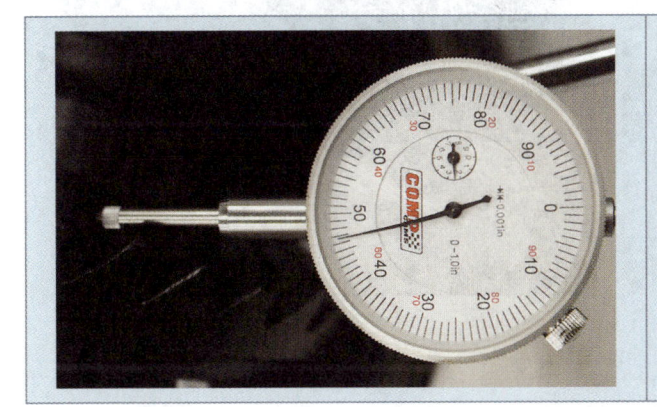

Goodheart-Willcox Publisher

The dial indicator ranges from 0.047″ to 0.067″.
0.067″ − 0.047″ = 0.020″
The gear backlash is 0.020″.

387

**388** Math for Automotive Technicians

Name _____ Date _____ Class _____

# Gear Backlash Job Skill Practice Problems

83.1 Shown are the dial indicator readings of the ring gear movement. Calculate the backlash.

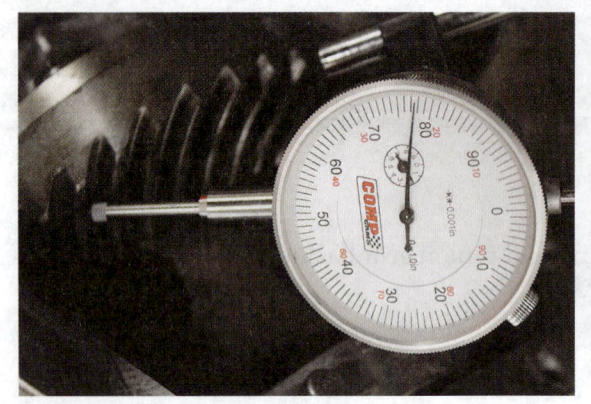

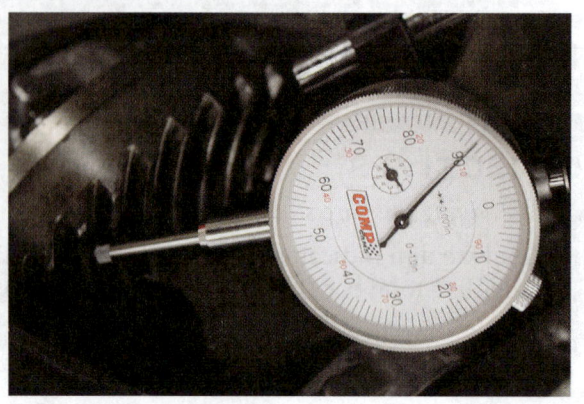

Backlash: _____

83.2 Shown are the dial indicator readings of the ring gear movement. Calculate the backlash.

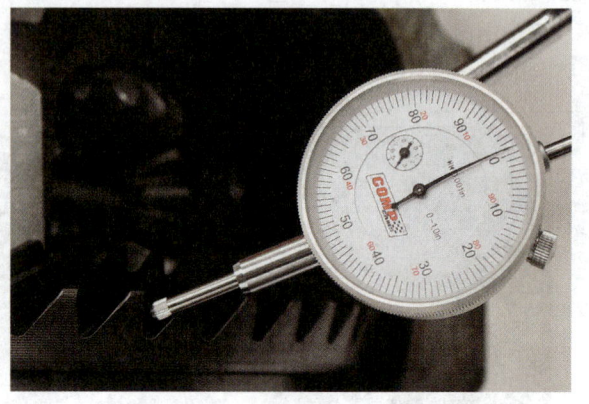

Backlash: _____

Name _____ Date _____ Class _____

83.3 Shown are the dial indicator readings of the ring gear movement. Calculate the backlash.

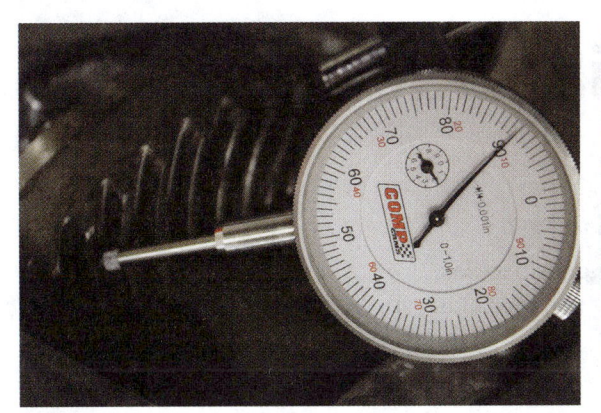

Backlash: _____

83.4 Shown are the dial indicator readings of the ring gear movement. Calculate the backlash.

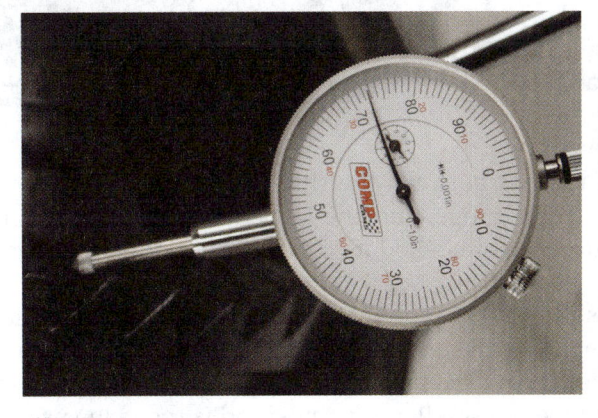

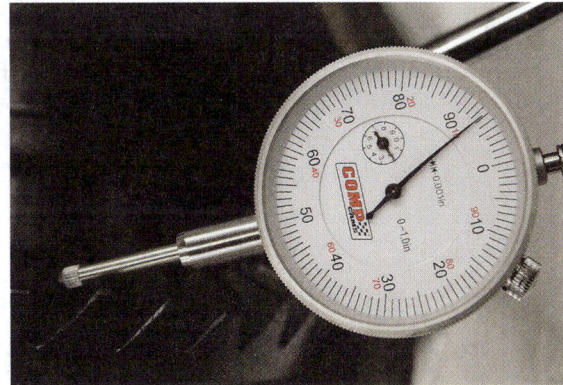

Backlash: _____

# CASE STUDY 84

# Differential Backlash

## OBJECTIVES

*After studying this case study, you will be able to:*
- Identify differential ring gear backlash.
- Analyze differential ring gear backlash specifications.

## MATH SKILLS
- Compare actual readings to specification tables.
- Analyze job skill problems related to ring gear backlash specifications.

---

The ring and pinion gear of a differential may need to be rebuilt if the gear set has been damaged or a different gear ratio set is desired. Measuring and adjusting ring gear backlash is part of the installation and measurement process when servicing or inspecting a differential gear set.

Backlash is measured by placing a dial indicator on a ring gear tooth and measuring how far the ring gear moves relative to a held pinion gear. This measurement identifies how much "play" there is between the ring gear and pinion gear teeth. Backlash has a specification value range, and the standard specification range is used when measuring a differential installed as part of routine maintenance and inspection.

*Goodheart-Willcox Publisher*

The preferred backlash is the value range that should be used when building a new ring and pinion gear set, and adjusted with shims to obtain the optimal backlash value. Most manufacturers provide a backlash range value and a backlash preferred value. The preferred value is a smaller tolerance, and is the value used when building a gear set. The range value is the acceptable range when measuring a gear without rebuilding the gear.

Review the table and the following examples.

| Backlash Specifications | | |
|---|---|---|
| Backlash Range | 0.10–0.20 mm | 0.0039–0.0078" |
| Backlash Preferred | 0.13–0.18 mm | 0.005–0.007" |

**Example:** A technician is measuring backlash of the rear differential on a truck. The technician measures 0.0084″ of backlash using the dial indicator. Determine if this measurement is within the specification range or if service is needed.

$$0.0084″ > 0.0078″$$

The backlash measurement is greater than the specification, so service is required.

**Example:** A technician is rebuilding a differential with 3.73 gears on a truck. The technician measures 0.15 mm of backlash using the dial indicator. Determine if this measurement is within the preferred specification range or if more shims are required.

$$0.15 \text{ mm} > 0.13 \text{ mm and } 0.15 \text{ mm} < 0.18 \text{ mm}$$

The backlash measurement is within specification.

Name _____ Date _____ Class _____

# Differential Backlash Job Skill Practice Problems

Use the following table to complete practice problems 84.1 through 84.10.

| Truck "C" Backlash Specifications | | |
|---|---|---|
| Backlash Range | 0.08–0.25 mm | 0.003–0.010″ |
| Backlash Preferred | 0.13–0.18 mm | 0.005–0.007″ |
| **Truck "F" Backlash Specifications** | | |
| Backlash Range | 0.20–0.38 mm | 0.008–0.015″ |
| Backlash Preferred | 0.30–0.38 mm | 0.012–0.015″ |
| **Truck "T" Backlash Specifications** | | |
| Backlash Range | 0.10–0.20 mm | 0.0039–0.0078″ |
| Backlash Preferred | 0.13–0.18 mm | 0.0051–0.0070″ |
| **Truck "G" Backlash Specifications** | | |
| Backlash Range | 0.12–0.20 mm | 0.0050–0.0078″ |
| Backlash Preferred | 0.14–0.18 mm | 0.0055–0.0070″ |
| **Truck "D" Backlash Specifications** | | |
| Backlash Range | 0.15–0.203 mm | 0.006–0.008″ |
| Backlash Preferred | 0.17–0.19 mm | 0.0066–0.0075″ |

84.1 A technician is measuring backlash of the rear differential on a "T" truck. The technician measures 0.0061″ of backlash using the dial indicator. Determine if this measurement is within the specification range or if service is needed.

84.2 A technician is rebuilding a differential with 3.90 gears on a "C" truck. The technician measures 0.11 mm of backlash using the dial indicator. Determine if this measurement is within the preferred specification range or if more shims are required.

**Name** _____ **Date** _____ **Class** _____

84.3 A technician is measuring backlash of the rear differential on a "D" truck. The technician measures 0.210 mm of backlash using the dial indicator. Determine if this measurement is within the specification range or if service is needed.

84.4 A technician is rebuilding a differential with 4.10 gears on a "T" truck. The technician measures 0.010" of backlash using the dial indicator. Determine if this measurement is within the preferred specification range or if more shims are required.

84.5 A technician is measuring backlash of the rear differential on a "G" truck. The technician measures 0.0045" of backlash using the dial indicator. Determine if this measurement is within the specification range or if service is needed.

84.6 A technician is rebuilding a differential with 3.25 gears on a "C" truck. The technician measures 0.21 mm of backlash using the dial indicator. Determine if this measurement is within the preferred specification range or if more shims are required.

Name _____ Date _____ Class _____

84.7 A technician is measuring backlash of the rear differential on a "G" truck. The technician measures 0.0056" of backlash using the dial indicator. Determine if this measurement is within the specification range or if service is needed.

84.8 A technician is rebuilding a differential with 3.90 gears on an "F" truck. The technician measures 0.23 mm of backlash using the dial indicator. Determine if this measurement is within the preferred specification range or if more shims are required.

84.9 A technician is measuring backlash of the rear differential on an "F" truck. The technician measures 0.018" of backlash using the dial indicator. Determine if this measurement is within the specification range or if service is needed.

84.10 A technician is rebuilding a differential with 3.00 gears on a "D" truck. The technician measures 0.18 mm of backlash using the dial indicator. Determine if this measurement is within the preferred specification range or if more shims are required.

# UNIT 9

# Air Conditioning and Hybrid Technology

Case Study 85 **Air Conditioning System Oil—Addition**
Case Study 86 **Compressor Clutch Air Gap—Subtraction**
Case Study 87 **Hybrid Vehicle High-Voltage Battery—Multiplication**
Case Study 88 **Electric Car Speed and Acceleration—Division**
Case Study 89 **Cooling System Boiling Point—Decimal Arithmetic**
Case Study 90 **Hybrid Vehicle Payback—Greater Than and Less Than**
Case Study 91 **Evaporator and Condenser Area—Fractions**
Case Study 92 **Refrigerant Weight—Conversions**
Case Study 93 **Air Conditioning System Pressures—Graphs and Tables**
Case Study 94 **Miles per Gallon Equivalent—Formulas**
Case Study 95 **Air Conditioning Gauge Reading—Measurement**
Case Study 96 **Hybrid Electric Fuel Economy—Analyzing Specifications**

## CAREER PROFILE

Amandeep Singh is a Mopar CAP student and a service technician at Rairdon's Chrysler-Dodge-Jeep in Arlington, Washington. After high school, Amandeep studied nursing and worked as a nurse. Although it was rewarding to help people, Amandeep wanted to return to his high school passion of repairing cars. The apprenticeship training model works well for him, since he enjoys learning on the job in a fast-paced work environment.

As a technician, Amandeep uses math to diagnose vehicle systems by reading pressure gauges, using measurement tools, and analyzing electrical measurements. "Vehicle inspections are full of math—checking tires and brakes, and measuring fluids and other maintenance parts," says Amandeep. His experience as a nurse has helped him troubleshoot and diagnose symptom-based automotive problems. "Before, I used a stethoscope to listen to people; now I use one to listen to internal engine noises."

Amandeep encourages other people to find a career in something they enjoy doing. "I want to go to work; my job is not boring. I am always on my feet doing something new and never just sitting around," says Amandeep. The fast-paced learning and working environment requires critical-thinking and problem-solving skills that are developed through mathematical thinking.

Amandeep Singh—Technician and Mopar CAP Student, Rairdon's Chrysler-Dodge-Jeep.

# CASE STUDY 85

# Air Conditioning System Oil

## OBJECTIVES
*After studying this case study, you will be able to:*
- Identify the purpose of the correct oil amount and type.
- Calculate the correct amount of oil to add based on the components replaced.

## MATH SKILLS
- Addition of whole and decimal values.
- Solve job skill problems related to whole number and decimal addition.

Air conditioning systems require oil within the system to lubricate the compressor and seal the O-ring connections within the system. The correct type of oil is also critical; a low oil level will cause damage to the compressor and an overfilled system will cause weak air conditioning system performance. Most R-134a non-hybrid vehicle systems use a polyalkylene glycol (PAG) oil and hybrid vehicles typically require a nonconductive, polyol ester (POE) oil. Newer 1234-yf systems require manufacturer specific, specially designed oil.

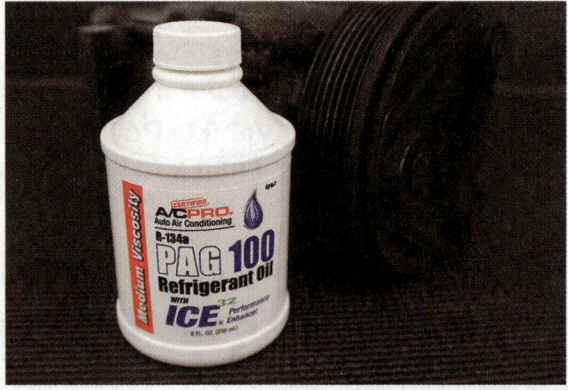

*Goodheart-Willcox Publisher*

When servicing an air conditioning system, most repairs require part replacement. Any type of part replacement requires evacuating the refrigerant and some of the oil from the system. When recharging the system, most procedures require replacing the oil removed and lost during service.

**Example:** A technician is replacing a damaged air conditioning condenser on a system with a capacity of 4.9 fluid ounces of PAG oil. During the recovery, 2.1 ounces of oil are removed. The manufacturer service information recommends adding 1.8 ounces of oil when replacing the condenser. Calculate how much oil the technician should add during system charging.

$$1.8 \text{ ounces} + 2.1 \text{ ounces} = 3.9 \text{ ounces}$$

The technician should add 3.9 ounces to the system during recharging.

Name _____ Date _____ Class _____

# Air Conditioning System Oil
# Job Skill Practice Problems

85.1 A technician is repairing an O-ring leak on an air conditioning system with a capacity of 4.2 fluid ounces of PAG oil. During the recovery, 1.8 ounces of oil are removed. The manufacturer service information recommends adding 0.9 ounces of oil when repairing an O-ring. Calculate how much oil the technician should add during system charging.

85.2 A technician is replacing a receiver/dryer cartridge on an air conditioning system with a capacity of 4.5 fluid ounces of POE oil. During the recovery, 2.9 ounces of oil are removed. The manufacturer service information recommends adding 0.7 ounces of oil when replacing the receiver/dryer cartridge. Calculate how much oil the technician should add during system charging.

85.3 A technician is replacing a compressor on an air conditioning system with a capacity of 4.2 fluid ounces of PAG oil. During the recovery, 2.6 ounces of oil are removed. The manufacturer service information recommends not adding oil when replacing a compressor with a new compressor, since the new compressor is prefilled with oil. Calculate how much oil the technician should add during system charging.

Copyright Goodheart-Willcox Co., Inc. May not be reproduced or posted to a publicly accessible website.

85.4 A technician is replacing a compressor on an air conditioning system with a capacity of 4.0 fluid ounces of PAG oil. During the recovery, 1.9 ounces of oil are removed. The replacement compressor is a functional used part from a local auto parts recycling yard, and the compressor is empty. The technician drains 1.1 ounces of oil from the inoperative compressor, and should use that amount to calculate the amount to add to the used part. Calculate how much oil the technician should add during system charging.

85.5 A technician is repairing an evaporator core on an air conditioning system with a capacity of 3.5 fluid ounces of POE oil. During the recovery, 1.1 ounces of oil are removed. The manufacturer service information recommends adding 1.5 ounces of oil when replacing an evaporator core. Calculate how much oil the technician should add during system charging.

85.6 A technician is replacing a compressor and two refrigerant lines on an air conditioning system with a capacity of 5.1 fluid ounces of PAG oil. During the recovery, 2.7 ounces of oil are removed. The manufacturer service information recommends adding 0.6 ounces of oil when replacing each refrigerant line and not adding any oil when replacing the compressor with a new part. Calculate how much oil the technician should add during system charging.

# CASE STUDY 86

# Compressor Clutch Air Gap

## OBJECTIVES

*After studying this case study, you will be able to:*
- Identify the compressor clutch air gap size using a feeler gauge set.
- Calculate the clutch air gap and compare values to specification.

## MATH SKILLS
- Subtraction of whole and decimal numbers.
- Analyze job skill problems related to subtraction of whole and decimal numbers.

---

The belt driven air conditioning compressor is designed to cycle on and off using an electromagnetic clutch during normal air conditioning operation. In the disengaged position, there is an "air gap" between the pulley and the clutch. If this air gap is too large due to clutch pulley wear, the electromagnetic field will not be strong enough to engage the clutch. Some compressors have the air gap set by installing shims when they are built at the factory.

*Goodheart-Willcox Publisher*

A technician can adjust the air gap later by removing or installing shims so that the gap is within specification. To do this, the technician would measure the current air gap, remove the compressor, and then measure the shims. Rebuild kits are used to calculate and install the correct shims to bring the air gap into specification.

**Example:** A technician measures the clutch air gap using feeler gauges and determines the gap to be 0.041". The gap specification is 0.016–0.033". The technician removes the clutch pulley and finds two 0.013" shims. The new shims kit includes 0.005" and 0.010" thick shims. Calculate the appropriate shims needed to adjust the air gap into the specification range.

Calculate gap:

$$\text{air gap total} - \text{shims} = \text{total wear}$$
$$0.041" - (0.013" \times 2) = 0.015"$$

The compressor has 0.015" of total wear.

Calculate shims:

desired clutch gap − total wear = shim amount needed
0.020″ − 0.015″ = 0.005″

Adding a single, 0.005″ shim will set the clutch gap at 0.020″, which is within specification.

Name _____ Date _____ Class _____

# Compressor Clutch Air Gap
# Job Skill Practice Problems

86.1 A technician measures the clutch air gap using feeler gauges and determines the gap to be 0.70 mm. The gap specification is 0.30–0.50 mm. The technician removes the clutch pulley and finds four 0.10 mm shims. The new shims kit includes 0.20 mm, 0.30 mm, and 0.10 mm thick shims. Calculate the appropriate shims needed to adjust the air gap into the specification range.

86.2 A technician measures the clutch air gap using feeler gauges and determines the gap to be 0.87 mm. The gap specification is 0.35–0.65 mm. The technician removes the clutch pulley and finds two 0.20 mm shims and one 0.10 mm shim. The new shims kit includes 0.1 mm, 0.2 mm, 0.4 mm, and 0.5 mm thick shims. Calculate the appropriate shims needed to adjust the air gap into the specification range.

86.3 A technician measures the clutch air gap using feeler gauges and determines the gap to be 0.031″. The gap specification is 0.014″–0.024″. The technician removes the clutch pulley and finds two 0.010″ shims. The new shims kit includes 0.005″ and 0.010″ thick shims. Calculate the appropriate shims needed to adjust the air gap into the specification range.

86.4 A technician measures the clutch air gap using feeler gauges and determines the gap to be 0.029″. The gap specification is 0.012″–0.024″. The technician removes the clutch pulley and finds three 0.005″ shims. The new shims kit includes 0.005″ and 0.010″ thick shims. Calculate the appropriate shims needed to adjust the air gap into the specification range.

# CASE STUDY 87

# Hybrid Vehicle High-Voltage Battery

## OBJECTIVES

*After studying this case study, you will be able to:*
- Identify the layout of the internal cells of a high-voltage hybrid vehicle battery.
- Calculate the total voltage output of the high-voltage hybrid vehicle battery.

## MATH SKILLS
- Multiplication of whole and decimal numbers.
- Solve job skill problems related to multiplication.

The automotive vehicle high-voltage battery, from the outside, looks like a large metal box with thick orange cables running in and out. Inside the battery, there are many battery cells connected in a series circuit that creates the high-voltage values. The manufacturers of hybrid and electric vehicles use different internal high-voltage battery designs to accomplish the total output voltage required for each specific vehicle. The voltage capability can be determined by multiplying the number of cells by the voltage production of each cell.

*Goodheart-Willcox Publisher*

**Example:** A hybrid vehicle uses a lithium ion battery made of 250 cells, each producing 1.3 volts. Calculate the total voltage capability of this high-voltage battery.

250 cells × 1.3 volts = 325 volts

The high-voltage capability of this battery is 325 volts.

Name _____ Date _____ Class _____

# Hybrid Vehicle High-Voltage Battery Job Skill Practice Problems

87.1 A hybrid vehicle uses a lithium ion battery made of 28 cells, each producing 8.4 volts. Calculate the total voltage capability of this high-voltage battery.

87.2 A hybrid vehicle uses a nickel-metal hydride battery made of 38 cells, each producing 8.4 volts. Calculate the total voltage capability of this high-voltage battery.

87.3 A hybrid vehicle uses a lithium polymer battery made of 120 cells, each producing 1.2 volts. Calculate the total voltage capability of this high-voltage battery.

87.4 A full electric vehicle uses a lithium ion battery made of 192 cells, each producing 3.8 volts. Calculate the total voltage capability of this high-voltage battery.

87.5 A full electric vehicle uses a lithium ion battery made of 72 cells, each producing 3.75 volts. Calculate the total voltage capability of this high-voltage battery.

87.6 A full electric vehicle uses a lithium ion battery made of 90 cells, each producing 2.25 volts. Calculate the total voltage capability of this high-voltage battery.

# CASE STUDY 88

# Electric Car Speed and Acceleration

## OBJECTIVES

*After studying this case study, you will be able to:*
- Identify the formula to calculate velocity and acceleration rates.
- Calculate the rate of acceleration of various vehicles.

## MATH SKILLS
- Division of whole and decimal numbers.
- Calculate a rate of change using division.

The design of an electric car allows for rapid acceleration compared to a gasoline engine. The electric traction motor is capable of almost immediately spinning at top speed and high torque, whereas a gasoline engine requires time to build up speed and torque. Some performance electric vehicles have been configured to offer very rapid acceleration rates. The cost to rapid acceleration with an electric car is a higher load and usage of the stored electricity. This shortens the already limited mileage range. Review the formulas and the following examples to calculate velocity and acceleration rates.

*Goodheart-Willcox Publisher*

$$velocity\ (speed) = \frac{distance}{time}$$

$$acceleration = \frac{final\ velocity - initial\ velocity}{change\ in\ time} = \frac{\Delta\ velocity}{\Delta\ time}$$

**Example:** An electric car travels 264′ in 4 seconds. Calculate the speed in miles per hour (1 mph = 1.4667 feet per second).

First:

$$264' \div 4 \text{ seconds} = 66 \text{ feet per second}$$

Then:

$$66 \text{ feet per second} \div 1.4667 \text{ feet per second} = 45 \text{ miles per hour}$$

Conclusion:

$$45 \text{ miles per hour}$$

**Example:** An electric car is stopped at 0 mph and accelerates to 60 mph in 4.1 seconds. Calculate the acceleration rate of the electric car.

First (convert 60 mph to feet per second):

$$60 \text{ mph} \times 1.4667 \text{ feet per second} = 88 \text{ feet per second}$$

Then:

$$\frac{\text{velocity}}{\text{time}} = \frac{88 \text{ feet per second}}{4.1 \text{ seconds}} = 21.46 \text{ ft/s}^2$$

Conclusion:

The acceleration rate is 21.46 ft/s$^2$.

# Electric Car Speed and Acceleration
# Job Skill Practice Problems

88.1 An electric car travels 330 feet in 3 seconds. Calculate the speed in miles per hour (1 mph = 1.4667 feet per second).

88.2 An electric car travels 440 feet in 5 seconds. Calculate the speed in miles per hour (1 mph = 1.4667 feet per second).

88.3 An electric car travels 39 meters in 2 seconds. Calculate the speed in kilometers per hour (1 km/h = 0.2778 meters per second).

88.4 An electric car travels 71 meters in 3 seconds. Calculate the speed in kilometers per hour (1 km/h = 0.2778 meters per second).

Name _____  Date _____  Class _____

88.5 An electric car is stopped at 0 mph and accelerates to 60 mph in 3.9 seconds. Calculate the acceleration rate of the electric car.

88.6 An electric car is traveling at 30 mph and accelerates to 65 mph in 1.8 seconds. Calculate the acceleration rate of the electric car.

88.7 An electric car is traveling at 27 mph and accelerates to 55 mph in 3.2 seconds. Calculate the acceleration rate of the electric car.

88.8 An electric car is stopped at 0 mph and accelerates to 90 mph in 4.3 seconds. Calculate the acceleration rate of the electric car.

# CASE STUDY 89

# Cooling System Boiling Point

## OBJECTIVES

*After studying this case study, you will be able to:*
- Identify factors that affect the boiling point of the liquid cooling system.
- Calculate the boiling point of the engine coolant related to mixture and system pressure.

## MATH SKILLS
- Calculate decimal arithmetic.
- Analyze job skill problems using decimal arithmetic.

The liquid cooling system is designed to control the heat created by the engine during combustion. Most hybrid vehicles have a secondary cooling system used to remove heat created by the high-voltage system. Although pure water is best at absorbing heat from the engine and electrical components, water has a low boiling point and causes corrosion inside metal parts. For this reason, a mixture of water and coolant is necessary. Adding coolant raises the boiling point of the fluid mixture.

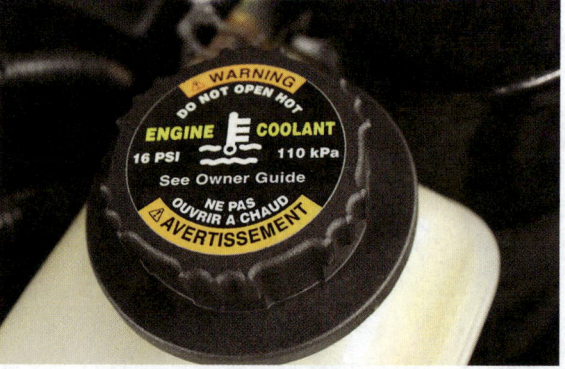

*Goodheart-Willcox Publisher*

The radiator cap also raises the boiling point of the fluid by sealing the system. Inside the sealed cooling system, the mixture's boiling point rises as pressure increases. The vent pressure of the cooling system is indicated on the radiator cap in psi or bar. The vent pressure determines the point at which the coolant will boil and vent from the cooling system into the overflow system. The overflow system and vented radiator cap are designed to maintain a proper coolant level.

Review the boiling point of the coolant-water mixtures in the following table.

| Effect of Coolant-Water Mixture on Boiling Point ||| 
|---|---|---|
| 100% Water | 50-50 Mixture | 70-30 Mixture |
| 100°C | 106°C | 113°C |
| 212°F | 223°F | 235°F |

The effect of pressurizing the cooling system raises the boiling point by 3°F for each 1 psi of pressure or 4.35°F for each 0.1 bar of pressure. Review the following examples. Note that in the examples and practice problems, the radiator caps are rated in psi or bar, but all of the temperatures are in Fahrenheit (°F).

**Example:** An engine cooling system is equipped with a 13 lb radiator cap and has a 50-50 coolant mixture. Calculate the expected boiling point (°F) of this cooling system.

$$223°F + (13 \text{ psi} \times 3°F) = 262°F$$

The cooling system boiling point is 262°F.

**Example:** An engine cooling system is equipped with a 0.9 bar radiator cap and has a 70-30 coolant mixture. Calculate the expected boiling point (°F) of this cooling system.

$$235°F + (9 \text{ bar} \times 4.35°F) = 274°F$$

The cooling system boiling point is 274°F.

## Cooling System Boiling Point
## Job Skill Practice Problems

Round answers to the nearest whole number.

89.1 An engine cooling system is equipped with a 16 lb radiator cap and has a 50-50 coolant mixture. Calculate the expected boiling point (°F) of this cooling system.

89.2 A technician pressure tests a radiator cap and finds that it only holds pressure to 6 lb. If this cap is used on a cooling system with a 50-50 coolant mixture, calculate the expected boiling point (°F) of this cooling system.

89.3 An engine with a 50-50 coolant mixture is equipped with a stock 13 lb radiator cap. The radiator cap is replaced with a 17 lb cap. Calculate the expected increase of the boiling point (°F) with the new radiator cap compared to the stock radiator cap.

89.4 An engine cooling system is equipped with a 0.9 bar radiator cap and has a 50-50 coolant mixture. Calculate the expected boiling point (°F) of this cooling system.

Name _____  Date _____  Class _____

89.5 A technician pressure tests a radiator cap and finds that it only holds pressure to 0.5 bar. If this cap is used on a cooling system with a 50-50 coolant mixture, calculate the expected boiling point (°F) of this cooling system.

89.6 An engine with a 50-50 coolant mixture is equipped with a stock 0.9 bar radiator cap. The radiator cap is replaced with a 1.1 bar cap. Calculate the expected increase of the boiling point (°F) with the new radiator cap compared to the stock radiator cap.

89.7 An engine with a 70-30 coolant mixture is equipped with a 1.0 bar radiator cap. Calculate the expected boiling point (°F) of this cooling system.

89.8 A technician pressure tests a radiator cap and finds that it only holds pressure to 8 lb. If this cap is used on a cooling system with a 70-30 coolant mixture, calculate the expected boiling point (°F) of this cooling system.

# CASE STUDY 90

# Hybrid Vehicle Payback

## OBJECTIVES

*After studying this case study, you will be able to:*
- Compare the purchase cost and fuel savings cost of hybrid and non-hybrid vehicle models.
- Calculate the amount of time for hybrid vehicle payback.

## MATH SKILLS

- Compare values as greater than and less than.
- Calculate whole number and decimal arithmetic.

The manufacturer suggested retail price (MSRP) of a hybrid vehicle is higher than the price of a comparable non-hybrid model. Some car lines offer gasoline-only and hybrid versions of the same model vehicle. Although consumers purchase hybrid vehicles for a variety of reasons, every hybrid vehicle has a payback point. The payback point is the time it takes to recuperate the additional cost of hybrid technology in the form of fuel savings costs. Most vehicle consumers keep a car for six years, so reaching the payback point before selling the hybrid car makes the purchase a good value.

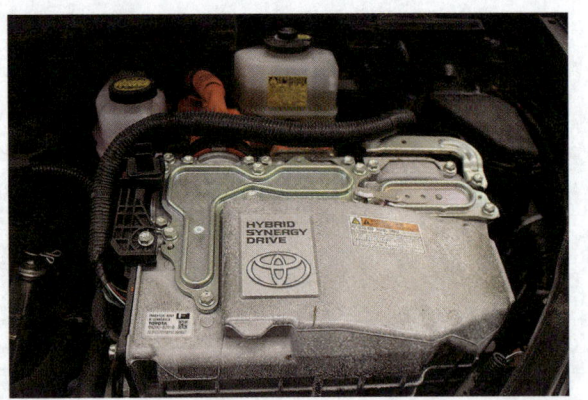

*Goodheart-Willcox Publisher*

**Example:** A vehicle manufacturer offers a gasoline-only and a hybrid model of the same vehicle. The MSRP of the gasoline-only model is $26,785 and the hybrid model is $31,403. The combined fuel mileage is 31 mpg for the gasoline-only model and 46 mpg for the hybrid model. If the vehicle is driven an average of 1,000 miles per month and gasoline averages $2.20 per gallon, calculate the payback point and determine if the payback point is before or after the 6-year average ownership point.

Find the price difference.

hybrid MSRP – gasoline-only MSRP = price difference
$31,403 – $26,785 = $4,618

The hybrid vehicle costs $4,618 more up front.

Find the number of gallons used by each model per month and calculate the difference.

miles per month ÷ mpg = gallons used per month

1,000 miles per month ÷ 46 mpg = 21.74 gallons per month for the hybrid model

1,000 miles per month ÷ 31 mpg = 32.26 gallons per month for the gasoline-only model

32.26 gallons − 21.74 gallons = 10.52 gallons per month difference
The hybrid vehicle uses 10.52 fewer gallons of gas per month.

Find the amount saved per month for the hybrid.

gallons per month difference × price per gallon = amount saved per month
10.52 gallons × $2.20 per gallon = $23.14 per month
The hybrid vehicle driver saves $23.14 per month on gasoline.

Find the payback point.

price difference ÷ amount saved per month = number of months to reach payback point

$4,618 ÷ $23.14 = 199.57 months
The payback point is 200 months, or 16 years and 8 months.
16 years, 8 months > 6 years of typical vehicle ownership

Name _____ Date _____ Class _____

# Hybrid Vehicle Payback Job Skill Practice Problems

90.1 A vehicle manufacturer offers a gasoline-only and a hybrid model of the same vehicle. The MSRP of the gasoline-only model is $23,120 and the hybrid model is $25,990. The fuel mileage combined is 27 mpg for the gasoline-only and 42 mpg for the hybrid. If the vehicle is driven an average of 1,000 miles per month and gasoline averages $2.20 per gallon, calculate the payback point and determine if the payback point is before or after the 6-year average ownership point.

90.2 A vehicle manufacturer offers a gasoline-only and a hybrid model of the same vehicle. The MSRP of the gasoline-only model is $23,050 and the hybrid model is $24,735. The fuel mileage combined is 31 mpg for the gasoline-only and 47 mpg for the hybrid. If the vehicle is driven an average of 1,200 miles per month and gasoline averages $2.20 per gallon, calculate the payback point and determine if the payback point is before or after the 6-year average ownership point.

**Name** _____ **Date** _____ **Class** _____

90.3 A vehicle manufacturer offers a gasoline-only and a hybrid model of the same vehicle. The MSRP of the gasoline-only model is $23,995 and the hybrid model is $28,640. The fuel mileage combined is 28 mpg for the gasoline-only and 43 mpg for the hybrid. If the vehicle is driven an average of 1,000 miles per month and gasoline averages $2.20 per gallon, calculate the payback point and determine if the payback point is before or after the 6-year average ownership point.

90.4 A vehicle manufacturer offers a gasoline-only and a hybrid model of the same vehicle. The MSRP of the gasoline-only model is $29,845 and the hybrid model is $32,340. The fuel mileage combined is 23 mpg for the gasoline-only and 36 mpg for the hybrid. If the vehicle is driven an average of 1,500 miles per month and gasoline averages $2.20 per gallon, calculate the payback point and determine if the payback point is before or after the 6-year average ownership point.

# CASE STUDY 91

# Evaporator and Condenser Area

## OBJECTIVES

*After studying this case study, you will be able to:*
- Identify the function and size of the evaporator and the condenser.
- Calculate the area of the evaporator and the condenser.

## TECHNICAL TERMS

condenser          evaporator

## MATH SKILLS

- Multiplication of fractional and mixed numbers.
- Calculate area of a rectangle.

The *evaporator* is located inside the passenger compartment and functions as a heat exchanger as part of the air conditioning system. The evaporator is where low pressure liquid is converted into low pressure gas. At the opposite side of the air conditioning system is the condenser, located under the hood in front of the radiator. The *condenser* releases heat as the refrigerant changes from a high pressure gas to a high pressure liquid.

*Goodheart-Willcox Publisher*

The area of an evaporator or a condenser can be calculated by measuring each dimension of the rectangle and multiplying one dimension by the other.

$$area = length \times width$$

**Example:** A condenser measures 21 5/8″ by 16 9/16″. Calculate the area of the condenser. Round to the nearest whole number.

Convert 21 5/8 to 173/8 and 16 9/16 to 265/16.
173/8 × 265/16 = 45,845/128
45,845 ÷ 128 = 358.164

The condenser has an area of 358 square inches.

# Evaporator and Condenser Area Job Skill Practice Problems

91.1 A condenser measures 19 3/16" by 5 7/16". Calculate the area of the condenser. Round to the nearest whole number.

91.2 An evaporator measures 11 1/8" by 9 11/16". Calculate the area of the evaporator. Round to the nearest whole number.

91.3 A condenser measures 20 5/8" by 13 13/16". Calculate the area of the condenser. Round to the nearest whole number.

91.4 An evaporator measures 10 1/8" by 14 1/4". Calculate the area of the evaporator. Round to the nearest whole number.

91.5 A plastic bag has blown into the front grill/fascia and is blocking half of the condenser. If the condenser measures 24 3/4" by 17 1/16", calculate the area of the condenser *not* blocked by the plastic bag. Round to the nearest whole number.

91.6 A clogged condensate drain is causing the evaporator to ice up and block half of the area of the evaporator. If the evaporator measures 8 3/8" by 6 5/8", calculate the area of the evaporator *not* blocked by the ice. Round to the nearest whole number.

91.7 A pile of leaves and pine needles have accumulated in the front grill and is blocking one-third of the condenser. If the condenser measures 20 9/16" by 18 1/4", calculate the area of the condenser blocked by the leaves and pine needles. Round to the nearest whole number.

91.8 A clogged condensate drain is causing the evaporator to ice up and block three-fourths of the area of the evaporator. If the evaporator measures 9 3/8" by 9 3/8", calculate the area of the evaporator blocked by the ice. Round to the nearest whole number.

# CASE STUDY 92

# Refrigerant Weight

## OBJECTIVES

*After studying this case study, you will be able to:*
- Identify mobile air conditioning refrigerant weight.
- Convert refrigerant quantities between metric and standard designations.

## MATH SKILLS
- Conversion of whole and decimal values.
- Analyze job skill problems related to conversion of quantity values.

The refrigerant in a mobile air conditioning system is continously changing from a liquid to gas state as it circulates through the system. When charging an air conditioning system, the refrigerant enters the system as a gas. Vehicles equipped with air conditioning will have a decal under the hood showing the recommended amount of refrigerant the system requires. Most full-service air conditioning machines will indicate how much refrigerant was removed during the vacuum/remove process and will require a charge value when refilling the system.

*Goodheart-Willcox Publisher*

The refrigerant value can be given in pounds, pounds and ounces, ounces only, or kilograms. Review the conversion table and the following examples.

| Gas Weight Conversion Factors | | |
|---|---|---|
| 1 lb | = | 16 oz |
| 0.1 lb | = | 1.6 oz |
| 1 lb | = | 0.4535 kg |
| 1 kg | = | 2.20 lb |

**Example:** A technician is charging the refrigerant in an air conditioning system. The system requires a charge of 1.8 kg. Calculate how many pounds of refrigerant this system requires.

$$1.8 \text{ kg} \times 2.20 \text{ lb} = 3.96 \text{ lb}$$

This system requires 3.96 lb of refrigerant.

**Example:** A technician is using an automatic air conditioning recovery machine to remove the refrigerant from the vehicle system. The machine indicates the recovery is complete and that it recovered 0.9 pounds of refrigerant. Calculate the number of ounces removed from the system.

$$0.9 \text{ lb} \times 16 \text{ oz} = 14.4 \text{ oz}$$

The system recovered 14.4 ounces.

Name _____ Date _____ Class _____

# Refrigerant Weight Job Skill Practice Problems

92.1 A technician is charging the refrigerant in an air conditioning system. The system requires a charge of 21 ounces. Calculate how many pounds of refrigerant this system requires. Round to the nearest tenth.

92.2 A technician is trying to determine how much refrigerant leaked out of the system. The factory fill specification is 1.2 lb. The recovery machine removed 0.49 kg from the system. Convert and calculate how much less the recovery amount was compared to the factory fill amount. Round to the nearest hundredth.

92.3 A technician is using an automatic air conditioning service machine to refill the system. The under-hood sticker indicates a charge of 0.77 kg is required. Calculate how many ounces are required to refill the system. Round to the nearest tenth.

92.4 A technician is using an automatic air conditioning service machine to recover the refrigerant from a vehicle. The machine indicates the recovery is complete and that it recovered 1.3 pounds of refrigerant. Calculate the number of ounces removed from the system.

**Name** _____ **Date** _____ **Class** _____

92.5 A technician is charging the refrigerant in an air conditioning system. The system requires a charge of 1.35 kg. Calculate how many pounds of refrigerant this system requires.

92.6 A technician is trying to determine how much refrigerant leaked out of the system. The factory fill specification is 1 lb 7 oz. The recovery machine removed 0.63 kg from the system. Convert and calculate how much less the recovery amount was compared to the factory fill amount. Round to the nearest hundredth.

# CASE STUDY 93

# Air Conditioning System Pressures

## OBJECTIVES

*After studying this case study, you will be able to:*
- Identify common high side and low side air conditioning system pressures.
- Analyze pressure readings and compare to common known values in a table.

## TECHNICAL TERMS

manifold gauge set  refrigerant cycle

## MATH SKILLS

- Analyze data from a table to identify values.
- Compare data in a table to known values.

---

During air conditioning operation, the refrigerant changes between liquid and gas and from low pressure to high pressure. These changes are known as the ***refrigerant cycle***, and allow heat and moisture to be removed from the passenger compartment and released under the hood. In order to test the system pressures, two service ports are located on the lines entering and leaving the air conditioning compressor. These service ports are the high side and low side service ports, and when a manifold gauge set is connected to the ports, the line pressures can be identified and monitored.

*Goodheart-Willcox Publisher*

There are a variety of factors that affect air conditioning system operation. Weather conditions, such as temperature and humidity, have a significant effect on the refrigerant cycle. When temperature and humidity are higher, the system pressures are higher and the system has to work harder to remove the heat. Other factors include system design, condenser airflow, and a correct fill level of refrigerant and oil.

The pressure chart shown is based on normal system operation under normal temperature and humidity conditions.

| R-134a Temperature Pressure Chart |||
|---|---|---|
| Ambient Temperature | Low Pressure Gauge | High Pressure Gauge |
| 65°F | 25–35 psi | 135–155 psi |
| 70°F | 35–40 psi | 145–160 psi |
| 75°F | 35–45 psi | 150–170 psi |
| 80°F | 40–50 psi | 175–210 psi |
| 85°F | 45–55 psi | 225–250 psi |
| 90°F | 45–55 psi | 250–270 psi |
| 95°F | 50–55 psi | 275–300 psi |
| 100°F | 50–55 psi | 315–325 psi |
| 105°F | 50–55 psi | 330–335 psi |
| 110°F | 50–55 psi | 340–345 psi |

**Example:** A technician is monitoring air conditioning system pressures. The ambient temperature is 75°F. The low pressure gauge is reading about 42 psi and the high pressure gauge is reading 165 psi. Determine if these pressures are within the normal range.

42 psi is in the 35–45 psi range for low pressure.

165 psi is in the 150–170 psi range for high pressure.

Both high and low pressure readings are within normal range.

The *manifold gauge set* allows a technician to analyze pressure readings and diagnose system issues. There are many unique system problems that may cause incorrect air conditioning system operation.

| General Diagnosis of A/C Pressure Readings |||
|---|---|---|
| Low Side | High Side | Diagnosis |
| Within Pressure Range | Within Pressure Range | Correct System Operation |
| High Pressure | High Pressure | Overcharged System |
| Low Pressure | Low Pressure | Undercharged System |
| Low or Normal | High | Faulty Component |
| High or Normal | Low | |
| No Change | No Change | Inoperative System |

**Example:** A technician is monitoring air conditioning system pressures. The ambient temperature is 85°F. The low pressure gauge is reading about 31 psi and the high pressure gauge is reading 143 psi. Determine the general system diagnosis.

31 psi is below the 45–55 psi range for low pressure.

143 psi is below the 225–250 psi range for high pressure.

Both high and low pressure readings are below normal range.

The general diagnosis would be an undercharged system.

**Name** _____ **Date** _____ **Class** _____

# Air Conditioning System Pressures
# Job Skill Practice Problems

Use the charts provided for the air conditioning diagnosis practice problems.

93.1 A technician is monitoring air conditioning system pressures. The ambient temperature is 105°F. The low pressure gauge is reading about 53 psi and the high pressure gauge is reading 330 psi. Determine the general system diagnosis.

93.2 A technician is monitoring air conditioning system pressures. The ambient temperature is 75°F. The low pressure gauge is reading about 35 psi and the high pressure gauge is reading 218 psi. Determine the general system diagnosis.

93.3 A technician is monitoring air conditioning system pressures. The ambient temperature is 80°F. The low pressure gauge is reading about 31 psi and the high pressure gauge is reading 143 psi. Determine the general system diagnosis.

Name _____  Date _____  Class _____

93.4 A technician is monitoring air conditioning system pressures. The ambient temperature is 95°F. The low pressure gauge is reading about 28 psi and the high pressure gauge is reading 136 psi. Determine the general system diagnosis.

93.5 A technician is monitoring air conditioning system pressures. The ambient temperature is 90°F. The low pressure gauge is reading about 54 psi and the high pressure gauge is reading 265 psi. Determine the general system diagnosis.

93.6 A technician is monitoring air conditioning system pressures. The ambient temperature is 70°F. The low pressure gauge is reading about 72 psi and the high pressure gauge is reading 78 psi. Determine the general system diagnosis.

# CASE STUDY 94

# Miles per Gallon Equivalent

## OBJECTIVES

*After studying this case study, you will be able to:*
- Identify the formula to determine the MPGe value.
- Calculate the MPGe based on input data.

## TECHNICAL TERM

miles per gallon equivalent (MPGe)

## MATH SKILLS

- Solve a formula using input data.
- Analyze data and a formula to compare results.

In 2010, the *miles per gallon equivalent (MPGe)* was introduced to help manufacturers provide fuel economy information for vehicles equipped with electric-only propulsion. The MPGe is calculated based on the energy content of one gallon of gasoline, equivalent to 33.70 kilowatt-hours (kWh). Review the formula.

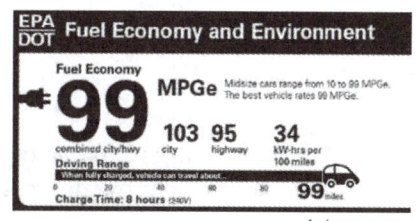

*fueleconomy.gov*

$$1\ MPGe = 1\ mile\ per\ 33.70\ kWh$$

$$MPGe = 3{,}370 \div kWh\ to\ drive\ 100\ miles$$

**Example:** An electric car is capable of driving 100 miles using 32.00 kWh. Calculate the MPGe.

$$3{,}370 \div 32 = 105.3$$

This vehicle has an MPGe value of 105.

## Miles per Gallon Equivalent
## Job Skill Practice Problems

94.1 An electric car is capable of driving 100 miles using 30.50 kWh. Calculate the MPGe. Round to the nearest whole number.

94.2 An electric car is capable of driving 100 miles using 28.00 kWh. Calculate the MPGe. Round to the nearest whole number.

94.3 An electric car is capable of driving 100 miles using 36.00 kWh. Calculate the MPGe. Round to the nearest whole number.

94.4 An electric car is capable of driving 100 miles using 38.50 kWh. Calculate the MPGe. Round to the nearest whole number.

**Name** _____ **Date** _____ **Class** _____

94.5 An electric car is capable of driving 100 miles using 30.75 kWh. Calculate the MPGe. Round to the nearest whole number.

94.6 An electric car is capable of driving 100 miles using 29.00 kWh. Calculate the MPGe. Round to the nearest whole number.

94.7 An electric car is capable of driving 100 miles using 18.00 kWh. Calculate the MPGe. Round to the nearest whole number.

94.8 An electric car is capable of driving 100 miles using 41.00 kWh. Calculate the MPGe. Round to the nearest whole number.

# CASE STUDY 95

# Air Conditioning Gauge Reading

## OBJECTIVES

*After studying this case study, you will be able to:*

- Identify high and low pressure readings on a manifold gauge set.
- Identify temperature readings on a manifold gauge set.

## MATH SKILLS

- Measurement of pressure values.
- Measurement of temperature values.

The manifold gauge set is designed to connect to the high pressure and low pressure sides of the air conditioning system. Once connected, the pressure values in each side of the system are shown on the gauges. Different gauge sets are required for different automotive refrigerant systems. The gauge set shown in this case study is designed for R-134a refrigerant. A different type of gauge is required for the newer refrigerant type, 1234-yf.

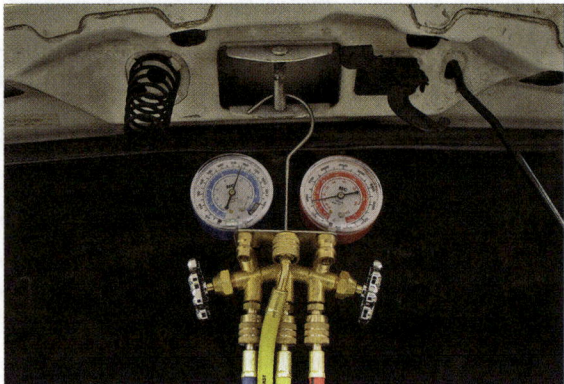

*Goodheart-Willcox Publisher*

The manifold gauge set uses the color blue to indicate low side pressure and the color red to indicate high side pressure. The low pressure gauge shows pressure ranging from 0 to 120 psi and vacuum to 30 in Hg on one scale. The high pressure gauge shows pressure ranging from 0 to 500 psi. Both gauges show the R-134a temperature on a separate scale.

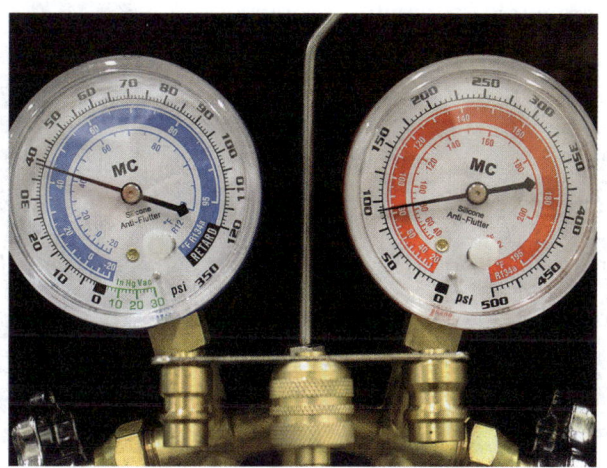

*Goodheart-Willcox Publisher*

**Example:**

Identify the low pressure gauge value.

        The low pressure gauge is reading 39 psi.

Identify the high pressure gauge value.

        The high pressure gauge is reading 93 psi.

# Air Conditioning Gauge Reading Job Skill Practice Problems

Use the gauges shown to record measurements for practice problems 95.1–95.8.

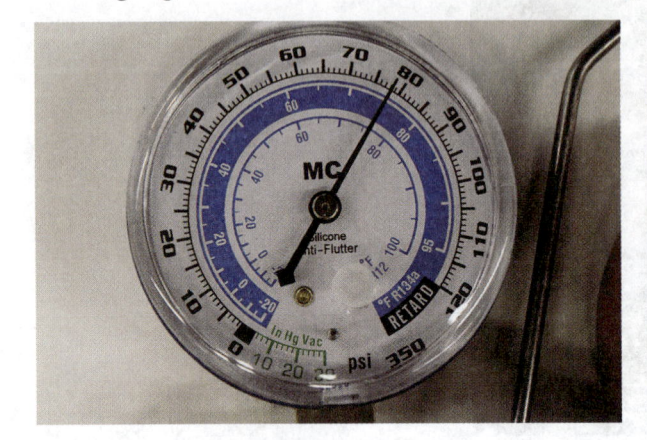

95.1. Pressure: _____

R-134a Temperature: _____

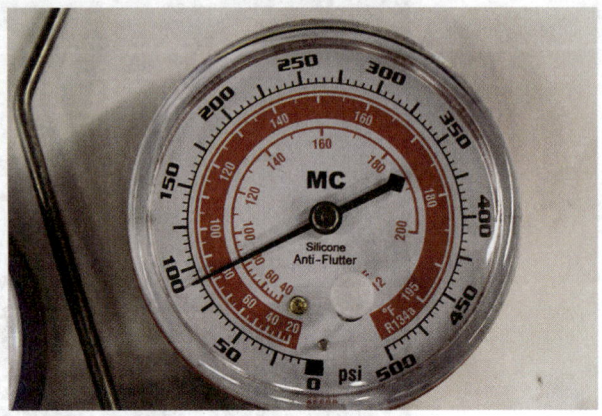

95.2. Pressure: _____

R-134a Temperature: _____

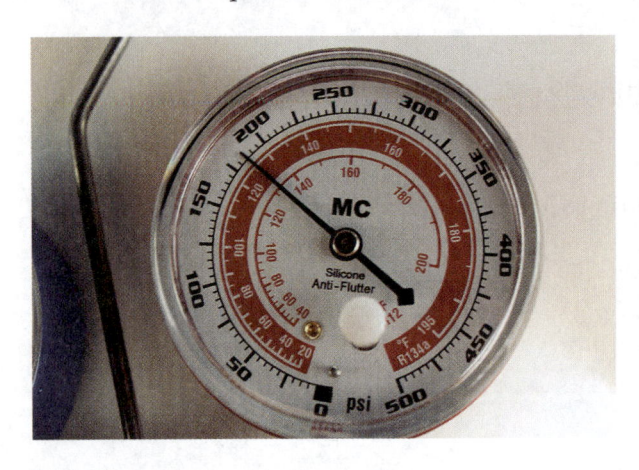

95.3. Pressure: _____

R-134a Temperature: _____

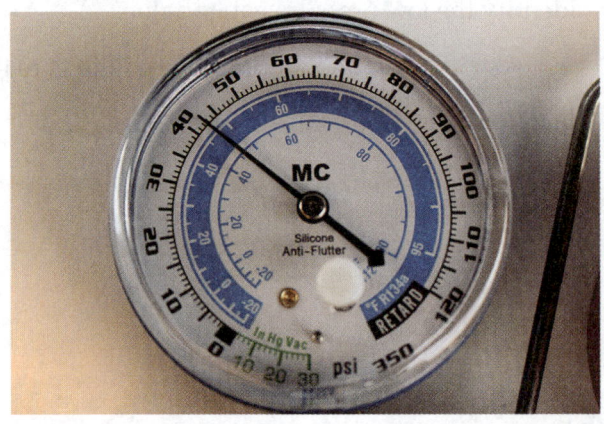

95.4. Pressure: _____

R-134a Temperature: _____

Unit 9    Air Conditioning and Hybrid Technology    **433**

Name _____    Date _____    Class _____

95.5.   Low Gauge Pressure: _____

High Gauge Pressure: _____

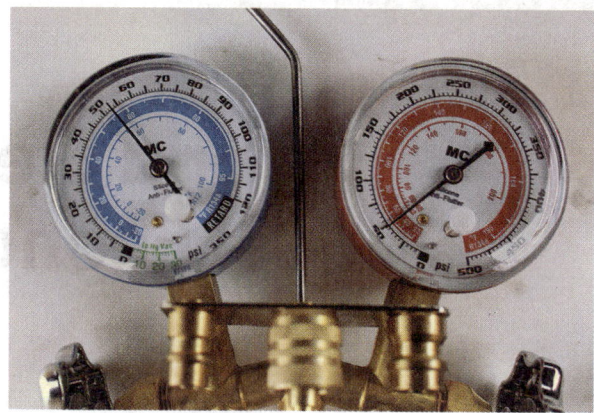

95.6.   Low Gauge Pressure: _____

High Gauge Pressure: _____

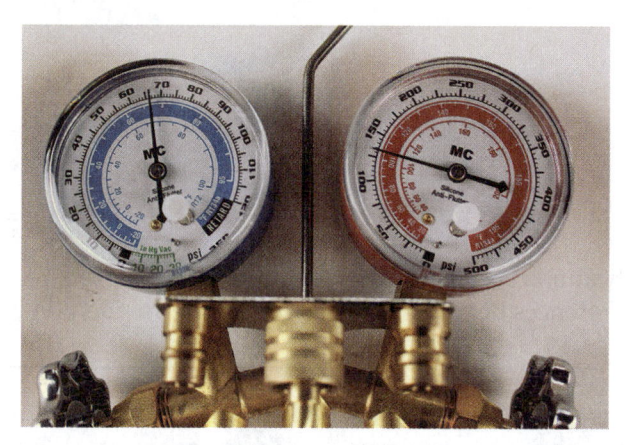

95.7.   Low Gauge Pressure: _____

High Gauge Pressure: _____

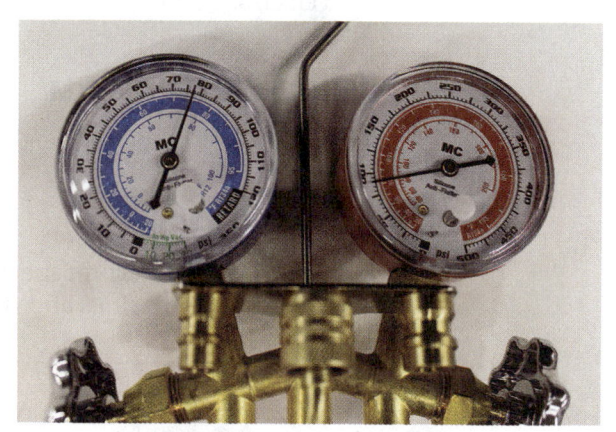

95.8.   Low Gauge Pressure: _____

High Gauge Pressure: _____

Copyright Goodheart-Willcox Co., Inc. May not be reproduced or posted to a publicly accessible website.

# CASE STUDY 96

# Hybrid Electric Fuel Economy

## OBJECTIVES

*After studying this case study, you will be able to:*
- Identify fuel economy information from specifications provided on the Monroney label.
- Compare fuel economy information between hybrid, plug-in, and full electric vehicles.

## TECHNICAL TERM

Monroney label

## MATH SKILLS

- Analyze and interpret specifications based on provided data.
- Calculate similarities and differences between vehicles based on provided data.

The *Monroney label* is a window sticker on all new vehicles intended to provide a full disclosure of information about the vehicle. The information provided on the Monroney label is regulated by federal legislation passed in 1958. In 2007, the fuel economy regulation section on the Monroney label was updated to provide better information about hybrid vehicles, plug-in hybrids, hydrogen fuel cell cars, and full electric cars.

*Goodheart-Willcox Publisher*

The Monroney label includes a section that details the fuel economy information for each vehicle. The example shown is the fuel economy section of a sample Monroney label. Review the example.

*fueleconomy.gov*

This label is an example of a gasoline-only midsize SUV. The city, highway, and combined miles per gallon are shown. The annual fuel cost is calculated based on 15,000 miles per year at $3.00 per gallon. The label also shows how many gallons of gasoline are required to drive the vehicle 100 miles and how much more the fuel costs will be compared to the average vehicle in one year.

Review the following examples.

**Example:** Identify the highway mpg.

The highway mpg is listed as 26 mpg.

**Example:** Describe the smog rating compared to the highest score possible.

The smog rating of 5 is in the middle of the rating scale.

**Example:** Compare this vehicle to a vehicle that uses 5.1 gallons of gas to drive 100 miles. Determine which vehicle is more fuel efficient.

5.1 gallons > 4.8 gallons, so the vehicle that uses 4.8 gallons is more efficient than the comparison vehicle.

## Hybrid Electric Fuel Economy Job Skill Practice Problems

Use the following label to complete practice problems 96.1 through 96.3.

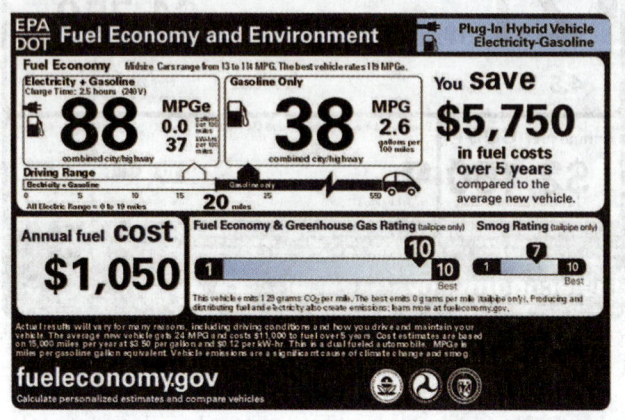

*fueleconomy.gov*

96.1 Determine the electricity + gasoline driving range.

96.2 Identify the gallons of fuel needed to drive 100 miles.

96.3 Determine the charge time using a 240-volt charging system.

Name _____ Date _____ Class _____

Use the following two labels to compare and analyze the vehicles in practice problems 96.4 through 96.8.

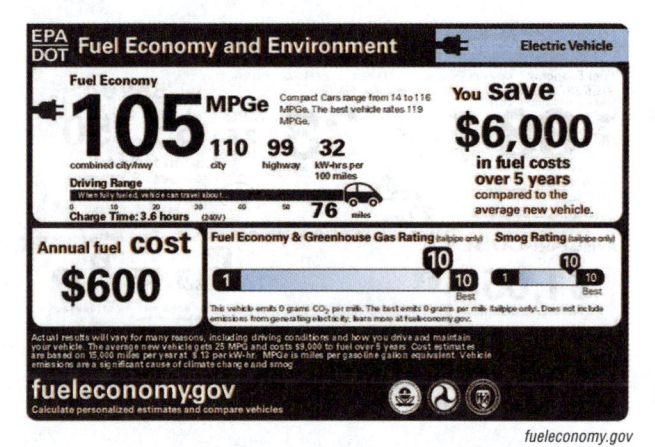

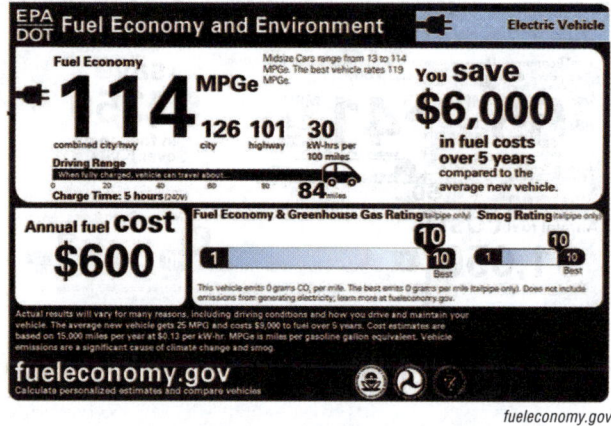

Full Electric Compact Vehicle #1

Full Electric Midsize Vehicle #2

96.4 Determine which vehicle uses fewer kWh per 100 miles.

96.5 Calculate the difference in driving range between the two vehicles.

96.6 Calculate how much shorter the charge time is for Vehicle #1 compared to Vehicle #2.

96.7 Determine which vehicle has a better (higher) smog rating.

96.8 The best vehicle rates 119 MPGe. Calculate how far below this rating each vehicle shown is rated.

Name _____ Date _____ Class _____

Use the following two labels to compare and analyze the vehicles in practice problems 96.9 through 96.13.

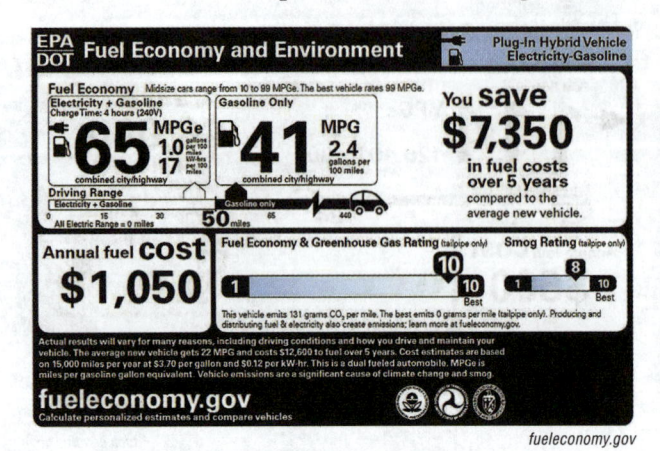

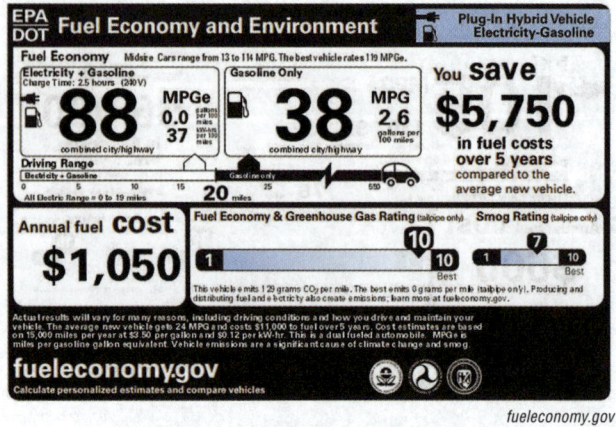

Plug-In Midsize Vehicle #1

Plug-In Midsize Vehicle #2

96.9 Calculate how much greater the electricity + gasoline range is for Vehicle #1 compared to Vehicle #2.

96.10 Determine which vehicle has a better gasoline-only combined mpg rating.

96.11 Determine which vehicle has a better electricity + gasoline MPGe rating.

96.12 Calculate the annual fuel cost difference if Vehicle #2 is purchased compared to Vehicle #1.

96.13 Determine which vehicle has a better smog rating.

# REFERENCE SECTION

## Units of Measure

| US Customary | Metric |
|---|---|
| **Length** | |
| 12 inches = 1 foot | 1 kilometer = 1000 meters |
| 36 inches = 1 yard | 1 hectometer = 100 meters |
| 3 feet = 1 yard | 1 dekameter = 10 meters |
| 5,280 feet = 1 mile | 1 meter = 1 meter |
| 16.5 feet = 1 rod | 1 decimeter = 0.1 meter |
| 320 rods = 1 mile | 1 centimeter = 0.01 meter |
| 6 feet = 1 fathom | 1 millimeter = 0.001 meter |
| **Weight** | |
| 27.34 grains = 1 dram | 1 tonne = 1,000,000 grams |
| 438 grains = 1 ounce | 1 kilogram = 1000 grams |
| 16 drams = 1 ounce | 1 hectogram = 100 grams |
| 16 ounces = 1 pound | 1 dekagram = 10 grams |
| 2000 pounds = 1 short ton | 1 gram = 1 gram |
| 2240 pounds = 1 long ton | 1 decigram = 0.1 gram |
| 25 pounds = 1 quarter | 1 centigram = 0.01 gram |
| 4 quarters = 1 cwt | 1 milligram = 0.001 gram |
| **Volume** | |
| 8 ounces = 1 cup | 1 hectoliter = 100 liters |
| 16 ounces = 1 pint | 1 dekaliter = 10 liters |
| 32 ounces = 1 quart | 1 liter = 1 liter |
| 2 cups = 1 pint | 1 deciliter = 0.1 liter |
| 2 pints = 1 quart | 1 centiliter = 0.01 liter |
| 4 quarts = 1 gallon | 1 milliliter = 0.001 liter |
| 8 pints = 1 gallon | 1000 milliliters = 1 liter |
| **Area** | |
| 144 sq inches = 1 sq foot | 100 sq millimeters = 1 sq centimeter |
| 9 sq feet = 1 sq yard | 100 sq centimeters = 1 sq decimeter |
| 43,560 sq ft = 160 sq rods | 100 sq decimeters = 1 sq meter |
| 160 sq rods = 1 acre | 10,000 sq meters = 1 hectare |
| 640 acres = 1 sq mile | |

### Temperature

| Fahrenheit | | Celsius |
|---|---|---|
| 32° F | Water freezes | 0° C |
| 68° F | Reasonable room temperature | 20° C |
| 98.6° F | Normal body temperature | 37° C |
| 173° F | Alcohol boils | 78.34° C |
| 212° F | Water boils | 100° C |

# Useful Conversions

| WHEN YOU KNOW: | MULTIPLY BY: | TO FIND: |
|---|---|---|
| **Torque** | | |
| pound-inch | 0.11298 | newton-meters (N•m) |
| pound-foot | 1.3558 | newton-meters |
| **Light** | | |
| foot candles | 1.0764 | lumens/meters$^2$ (lm/m$^2$) |
| **Fuel Performance** | | |
| miles/gallon | 0.4251 | kilometers/liter (km/L) |
| **Speed** | | |
| miles/hour | 1.6093 | kilometers/hr (km/h) |
| **Force** | | |
| kilogram | 9.807 | newtons (n) |
| ounce | 0.278 | newtons |
| pound | 4.448 | newtons |
| **Power** | | |
| horsepower | 0.746 | kilowatts (kw) |
| **Pressure or Stress** | | |
| inches of water | 0.2491 | kilopascals (kPa) |
| pounds/sq in | 6.895 | kilopascals |
| **Energy or Work** | | |
| btu | 1055.0 | joules (J) |
| foot-pound | 1.3558 | joules |
| kilowatt-hour | 3600000.0 | joules |

# Conversion Table: Metric to US Customary

| WHEN YOU KNOW: | Multiply By: * = Exact Very accurate | Multiply By: * = Exact Approximate | TO FIND: |
|---|---|---|---|
| **Length** | | | |
| millimeters | 0.0393701 | 0.04 | inches |
| centimeters | 0.3937008 | 0.4 | inches |
| meters | 3.280840 | 3.3 | feet |
| meters | 1.093613 | 1.1 | yards |
| kilometers | 0.621371 | 0.6 | miles |
| **Weight** | | | |
| grains | 0.00228571 | 0.0023 | ounces |
| grams | 0.03527396 | 0.035 | ounces |
| kilograms | 2.204623 | 2.2 | pounds |
| tonnes | 1.1023113 | 1.1 | short tons |
| **Volume** | | | |
| milliliters | 0.20001 | 0.2 | teaspoons |
| milliliters | 0.06667 | 0.067 | tablespoons |
| milliliters | 0.03381402 | 0.03 | fluid ounces |
| liters | 61.02374 | 61.024 | cubic inches |
| liters | 2.113376 | 2.1 | pints |
| liters | 1.056688 | 1.06 | quarts |
| liters | 0.26417205 | 0.26 | gallons |
| liters | 0.03531467 | 0.035 | cubic feet |
| cubic meters | 61023.74 | 61023.7 | cubic inches |
| cubic meters | 35.31467 | 35.0 | cubic feet |
| cubic meters | 1.3079506 | 1.3 | cubic yards |
| cubic meters | 264.17205 | 264.0 | gallons |
| **Area** | | | |
| square centimeters | 0.1550003 | 0.16 | square inches |
| square centimeters | 0.00107639 | 0.001 | square feet |
| square meters | 10.76391 | 10.8 | square feet |
| square meters | 1.195990 | 1.2 | square yards |
| square kilometers | 0.386102 | 0.4 | square miles |
| hectares | 2.471054 | 2.5 | acres |
| **Temperature** | | | |
| Celsius | *9/5 (then add 32) | *9/5 (then add 32) | Fahrenheit |

# Conversion Table: US Customary to Metric

| WHEN YOU KNOW: | Multiply By: * = Exact Very accurate | Multiply By: * = Exact Approximate | TO FIND: |
|---|---|---|---|
| \multicolumn{4}{c}{Length} ||||
| inches | * 25.4 | | millimeters |
| inches | * 2.54 | | centimeters |
| feet | * 0.3048 | | meters |
| feet | * 30.48 | | centimeters |
| yards | * 0.9144 | 0.9 | meters |
| miles | * 1.609344 | 1.6 | kilometers |
| \multicolumn{4}{c}{Weight} ||||
| grains | 15.43236 | 15.4 | grams |
| ounces | * 28.349523125 | 28.0 | grams |
| ounces | * 0.028349523125 | 0.028 | kilograms |
| pounds | * 0.45359237 | 0.45 | kilograms |
| short tons | * 0.90718474 | 0.9 | tonnes |
| \multicolumn{4}{c}{Volume} ||||
| teaspoons | * 4.97512 | 5.0 | milliliters |
| tablespoons | * 14.92537 | 15.0 | milliliters |
| fluid ounces | 29.57353 | 30.0 | milliliters |
| cups | * 0.236588240 | 0.24 | liters |
| pints | * 0.473176473 | 0.47 | liters |
| quarts | * 0.946352946 | 0.95 | liters |
| gallons | * 3.785411784 | 3.8 | liters |
| cubic inches | * 0.016387064 | 0.02 | liters |
| cubic feet | * 0.028316846592 | 0.03 | cubic meters |
| cubic yards | * 0.764554857984 | 0.76 | cubic meters |
| \multicolumn{4}{c}{Area} ||||
| square inches | * 6.4516 | 6.5 | square centimeters |
| square feet | * 0.09290304 | 0.09 | square meters |
| square yards | * 0.83612736 | 0.8 | square meters |
| square miles | * 2.589989 | 2.6 | square kilometers |
| acres | * 0.40468564224 | 0.4 | hectares |
| \multicolumn{4}{c}{Temperature} ||||
| Fahrenheit | *5/9 (after subtracting 32) | | Celsius |

# Decimal Equivalents of 8ths, 16ths, 32nds, and 64ths

| 8ths | 32nds | 64ths | 64ths |
|---|---|---|---|
| 1/8 = .125 | 1/32 = .03125 | 1/64 = .015625 | 33/64 = .515625 |
| 1/4 = .250 | 3/32 = .09375 | 3/64 = .046875 | 35/64 = .546875 |
| 3/8 = .375 | 5/32 = .15625 | 5/64 = .078125 | 37/64 = .578125 |
| 1/2 = .500 | 7/32 = .21875 | 7/64 = .109375 | 39/64 = .609375 |
| 5/8 = .625 | 9/32 = .28125 | 9/64 = .140625 | 41/64 = .640625 |
| 3/4 = .750 | 11/32 = .34375 | 11/64 = .171875 | 43/64 = .703125 |
| 7/8 = .875 | 13/32 = .40625 | 13/64 = .203125 | 45/64 = .671875 |
| **16ths** | 15/32 = .46875 | 15/64 = .234375 | 47/64 = .734375 |
| 1/16 = .0625 | 17/32 = .53125 | 17/64 = .265625 | 49/64 = .765625 |
| 3/16 = .1875 | 19/32 = .59375 | 19/64 = .296875 | 51/64 = .796875 |
| 5/16 = .3125 | 21/32 = .65625 | 21/64 = .328125 | 53/64 = .828125 |
| 7/16 = .4375 | 23/32 = .71875 | 23/64 = .359375 | 55/64 = .859375 |
| 9/16 = .5625 | 25/32 = .78125 | 25/64 = .390625 | 57/64 = .890625 |
| 11/16 = .6875 | 27/32 = .84375 | 27/64 = .421875 | 59/64 = .921875 |
| 13/16 = .8125 | 29/32 = .90625 | 29/64 = .453125 | 61/64 = .953125 |
| 15/16 = .9375 | 31/32 = .96875 | 31/64 = .484375 | 63/64 = .984375 |

# Rules Relative to the Circle

**To find circumference—**
Multiply diameter by                     3.1416        Or divide diameter by              0.03183

**To find diameter—**
Multiply circumference by            0.3183        Or divide circumference by    3.1416

**To find radius—**
Multiply circumference by            0.15915      Or divide circumference by    6.28318

**To find side of an inscribed square—**
Multiply diameter by                     0.7071
Or multiply circumference by        0.2251        Or divide circumference by    4.4428

**To find side of an equal square—**
Multiply diameter by                     0.8862        Or divide diameter by              1.1284
Or multiply circumference by        0.2821        Or divide circumference by    3.545

**Square—**
A side multiplied by        1.4142    equals diameter of its circumscribing circle.
A side multiplied by        4.443      equals circumference of its circumscribing circle.
A side multiplied by        1.128      equals diameter of an equal circle.
A side multiplied by        3.547      equals circumference of an equal circle.

**To find the area of a circle—**
Multiply circumference by 1/4 of the diameter
Or multiply the square of diameter by             0.7854
Or multiply the square of circumference by    0.07958
Or multiply the square of 1/2 diameter by      3.1416

# Grade Markings for Bolts

| Bolt Head Marking | SAE = Society of Automotive Engineers<br>ASTM = American Society for Testing and Materials | Bolt Material | Minimum Tensile Strength in Pounds per Square Inch (psi) |
|---|---|---|---|
| No Marks | SAE Grade 1<br>SAE Grade 2<br>Indeterminate quality | Low-carbon steel<br>Low-carbon steel | 65,000 psi |
| 2 Marks | SAE Grade 3 | Medium-carbon steel, cold worked | 110,000 psi |
| 3 Marks | SAE Grade 5<br>ASTM – A 325<br>Common commercial quality | Medium-carbon steel, quenched and tempered | 120,000 psi |
| Letters BB | ASTM – A 354 | Low-alloy steel or medium-carbon steel, quenched and tempered | 105,000 psi |
| Letters BC | ASTM – A 354 | Low-alloy steel or medium-carbon steel, quenched and tempered | 125,000 psi |
| 4 Marks | SAE Grade 6<br>Better commercial quality | Medium-carbon steel, quenched and tempered | 140,000 psi |
| 5 Marks | SAE Grade 7 | Medium-carbon alloy steel, quenched and tempered, roll-threaded after heat treatment | 133,000 psi |
| 6 Marks | SAE Grade 8<br>ASTM – A 345<br>Best commercial quality | Medium-carbon alloy steel, quenched and tempered | 150,000 psi |

# Bolt Torquing Chart

| Metric Standard ||||||
|---|---|---|---|---|---|
| Grade of Bolt | 5D | .8G | 10K | 12K | |
| Min. Ten. Strength | 71,160 psi | 113,800 psi | 142,200 psi | 170,679 psi | |
| Markings on Head | 5D | .8G | 10K | 12K | Size of Socket or Wrench Opening |
| **Metric** || Foot-Pounds ||| **Metric** |
| Bolt Dia. | US Dec. Equiv. | | | | Bolt Head |
| 6 mm | .2362 | 5 | 6 | 8 | 10 | 10 mm |
| 8 mm | .3150 | 10 | 16 | 22 | 27 | 14 mm |
| 10 mm | .3937 | 19 | 31 | 40 | 49 | 17 mm |
| 12 mm | .4720 | 34 | 54 | 70 | 86 | 19 mm |
| 14 mm | .5512 | 55 | 89 | 117 | 137 | 22 mm |
| 16 mm | .6299 | 83 | 132 | 175 | 208 | 24 mm |
| 18 mm | .7090 | 111 | 182 | 236 | 283 | 27 mm |
| 22 mm | .8661 | 182 | 284 | 394 | 464 | 32 mm |

| SAE Standard/Foot-Pounds ||||||
|---|---|---|---|---|---|
| Grade of Bolt | SAE 1 & 2 | SAE 5 | SAE 6 | SAE 8 | |
| Min. Ten. Strength | 64,000 psi | 105,000 psi | 133,000 psi | 150,000 psi | |
| Markings on Head | (plain) | (3 lines) | (4 lines) | (6 lines) | Size of Socket or Wrench Opening |
| **US Standard** | Foot-Pounds |||| **US Standard** ||
| Bolt Dia. | | | | | Bolt Head | Nut |
| 1/4 | 5 | 7 | 10 | 10.5 | 3/8 | 7/16 |
| 5/16 | 9 | 14 | 19 | 22 | 1/2 | 9/16 |
| 3/8 | 15 | 25 | 34 | 37 | 9/16 | 5/8 |
| 7/16 | 24 | 40 | 55 | 60 | 5/8 | 3/4 |
| 1/2 | 37 | 60 | 85 | 92 | 3/4 | 13/16 |
| 9/16 | 53 | 88 | 120 | 132 | 7/8 | 7/8 |
| 5/8 | 74 | 120 | 167 | 180 | 15/16 | 1 |
| 3/4 | 120 | 200 | 280 | 296 | 1 1/8 | 1 1/8 |

# GLOSSARY

## A

**accelerator pedal position (APP).** A sensor signal that can be viewed as a voltage value and converted into a percentage. A closed throttle is 0% APP, and a wide-open-throttle is 100% APP. (7)

**addend.** A value that is combined with one or more separate values to form a total value, or sum, in an addition problem. (1)

**addition.** The process of combining two or more separate values, or addends, to form a total value, or sum. (1)

**ampacity.** The amperage capacity of a wire. (6)

**amperage.** The number of electrons (electricity) flowing past a certain point over a certain period of time. (6)

**aspect ratio.** A value that indicates the height of the tire sidewall based on a percentage of the tire width. (4)

## B

**backlash.** The amount of space between the gear teeth in a ring and pinion gear set. (8)

**bar graph.** A visual representation of data using bars to represent values. (1)

**bore.** The diameter of the cylinder, machined into the engine block. (5)

**bottom-dead-center (BDC).** The end of piston travel in the down position. (5)

## C

**charging battery.** The "recovery" stage of the battery, with voltage around 13.6 to 14.6 volts. (3)

**clean metal.** A metal not mixed with any other types of metal. (2)

**clearance.** The small space between two parts, such as the cylinder bore and the piston. (5)

**combustion chamber volume.** The volume in the cylinder head and the thickness of the cylinder head gasket when the piston is at top-dead-center. (5)

**condenser.** Part of an air conditioning system that releases heat as the refrigerant changes from a high pressure gas to a high pressure liquid. (9)

**conversion factor.** A value used to convert from one unit to another, typically by multiplying or dividing. (1)

**cranking battery.** The "work" stage of the battery, with voltage at its lowest measured value, typically 10 or 11 volts. (3)

**cross-camber.** The difference between the camber angle from one side to the other. (4)

**cross-caster.** The difference between the caster angle from one side to the other. (4)

**cylinder compression test.** A test performed to determine the static pressure that each engine cylinder can produce. (7)

## D

**decimal number.** A number that represents a value between whole numbers. (1)

**decimal point.** Part of a decimal number that locates the place value of the whole number and indicates the value on the right side of the decimal point. (1)

**denominator.** In a fraction, the value that represents the whole being considered. (1)

**dial caliper.** A measurement tool that typically divides ten inches into 1/1,000 of an inch. (1)

**dial indicator.** A compound gauge used to measure round or rotating items, such as crankshafts and brake discs, and to measure end-play. (1)

**difference.** The value determined when one value, the subtrahend, is removed from another value, the minuend, in a subtraction problem. (1)

**differential gear set.** A gear set designed to use a pinion gear and a ring gear that allows for the driveshaft rotation to be transferred in a 90° angle to the axle shafts or half shafts and the wheels. (8)

**digital dial caliper.** A tool similar to an analog dial caliper, but it uses a digital readout indicating the measurement value automatically. (1)

**direct-drive.** A gear ratio of 1:1. This ratio transfers torque and speed without increasing or decreasing either. (8)

**dirty metal.** A metal with small amounts of other, cheaper metals mixed in with the higher value metal. (2)

**dividend.** The value being divided in a division problem. The dividend is separated into groups based on the divisor. (1)

**division.** The process of separating a single quantity into smaller groups of an equal, lesser quantity. (1)

**divisor.** The value that divides the dividend in a division problem. The divisor separates the dividend into equal groups. (1)

## E

**electronic throttle control.** A type of throttle control system that uses an accelerator position sensor to send a signal to the control module to control the actual throttle plate position. (7)

**equal.** A term to describe when one value is the exact same as another value. (1)

**evaporator.** Part of an air conditioning system that functions as a heat exchanger, where low pressure liquid is converted into low pressure gas. (9)

**exhaust duration.** The total number of degrees from when the exhaust valve opens to when it closes. (5)

## F

**factor.** A value multiplied in a multiplication problem. One factor is the quantity in each set and the other factor is the number of sets. (1)

**feeler gauge.** A tool designed to compare the thickness of a metal tab gauge to the gap being measured. (1)

**final drive gear ratio.** A ratio calculated by dividing the number of ring gear teeth by the number of pinion gear teeth in a differential gear set. (8)

Note: The number in parentheses following each definition indicates the chapter in which the term can be found.

**flat-rate labor time system.** A time system based on one-tenth of an hour used to estimate repairs, bill customers, and pay technicians. (2)
**formula.** A mathematical sentence that can be used to determine a result based on inputs. (1)
**fraction.** A numerical representation of a part of a whole. (1)
**fuel trim value.** A percentage that represents the changes made by the engine management system to maintain a targeted air-fuel ratio. (7)

# G

**gear ratios.** A ratio determined by the number of teeth on gears within a gear set. (8)
**graph.** A visual representation of a relationship between multiple sets of data. (1)
**greater than.** A term to describe when one value is larger than another value. (1)
**gross pay.** The total amount of pay received for work, before any deductions have been taken out. (2)

# H

**horsepower.** A calculation of the rate of work produced. (5)

# I

**ignition coil.** A coil that functions as a step-up transformer, designed to take automotive battery voltage (12–15 volts) and step up the voltage to the 12,000–16,000+ volts needed to cross the gap of a spark plug. (7)
**improper fraction.** A fraction with a numerator that is larger than the denominator. (1)
**intake duration.** The total number of degrees from when the intake valve opens to when it closes. (5)

# K

**Kirchloff's voltage law.** A law stating that the source voltage is equal to the sum of voltage drops in the circuit. (6)
**k-type thermocouple.** A common type of thermocouple used in automotive applications that generally has an electrical connector that allows it to be plugged into a standard digital multimeter. (6)

# L

**less than.** A term to describe when one value is smaller than another value. (1)
**long-term fuel trim (LTFT).** Fuel trim value based on a cumulative average of fuel trim over a long period of time. (7)
**lowest terms.** A numerator and denominator of a fraction that cannot be reduced. (1)
**lug spacing gauge.** A tool designed to identify the exact size of lug nut spacing. (3)

# M

**manifold gauge set.** A gauge set used to measure and monitor line pressures in an air conditioning system. (9)
**mass airflow (MAF) sensor.** A sensor that calculates the amount of air entering an engine. (7)
**mean value.** A value found by adding all of the values in a data set and dividing the sum by the quantity of values in the set. Often referred to as the "average." (2)

**micrometer.** A precision measurement tool that can be used to measure outside diameter in inches and metric. (1)
**miles per gallon equivalent (MPGe).** A value calculated based on the energy content of one gallon of gasoline, used to convey fuel economy information for vehicles equipped with electric-only propulsion. (9)
**minuend.** The value in a subtraction problem from which the subtrahend is removed. (1)
**mixed number.** A whole number followed directly with a fraction. (1)
**Monroney label.** A window sticker on all new vehicles that provides a full disclosure of information about the vehicle. (9)
**multi-disc clutch.** A clutch with more than one friction and steel disc that may require the addition of various shims to compensate as the clutch material wears down. (8)
**multiplication.** The process of combining sets of a value into a total, or product, where one factor is the quantity in each set and the other factor is the number of sets. (1)

# N

**net pay.** The total amount of pay on the employee's paycheck, after all required and optional deductions have been taken out. (2)
**numerator.** In a fraction, the value that represents the part of the whole being considered. (1)

# O

**Ohm's law.** The mathematical relationship between three electrical conditions: voltage, amperage, and resistance. (6)
**order of operations.** The sequence in which different mathematical operations must be performed. (1)
**out-of-round.** A value determined by comparing the X-Y measurements, such as crankshaft and camshaft journals. (5)
**overdrive.** A gear ratio lower than 1.0. This ratio transfers less engine torque, but transfers an increase of speed. (8)

# P

**parallel circuit.** An electrical circuit where all electrical loads are on separate circuits and do not share the voltage, but all have equal total voltage. (6)
**Pascal's law.** A law that states that when pressure is applied to a non-compressible fluid in a contained space, the pressure is exerted completely throughout the fluid. (8)
**pinion gear.** The drive gear in a differential gear set. (8)
**piston displacement.** The volume of air the piston displaces during the stroke from bottom-dead-center to top-dead-center. This value is the total engine displacement divided by the number of cylinders. (5)
**planetary gear set.** A gear set made up of a single sun gear located in the center, a carrier bracket holding three or more planetary gears, and a single outer ring gear. During operation, one gear is held, one is the input, and one is the output. (8)
**plus or minus symbol.** A symbol used to indicate a range of values. (1)
**primary winding.** One of two coils of wire in an ignition coil. The primary winding is the thicker wire with fewer turns. (7)
**product.** The total value in a multiplication problem. (1)

## Q

**quotient.** The value in a division problem determined by separating the dividend into groups based on the divisor. (1)

## R

**reference voltage.** A value created by a fixed resistor in the control module that is in series with the sensor resistor. (6)
**refractometer.** A tool used to measure the concentration of a mixture. This can help determine the freeze level of coolant mixtures. (3)
**refrigerant cycle.** The changes made by the refrigerant between liquid and gas and from low pressure to high pressure during air conditioning operations. (9)
**resistance.** The opposition to current flow, necessary for a load to transfer the electricity into another form of energy (light, heat, motion). (6)
**ride height.** The position of the vehicle body relative to the wheel and compared to the ground. (4)
**ring gear.** The driven gear in a differential gear set. (8)
**rocker arm ratio.** A multiplier of the camshaft lobe that increases the total valve movement in the cylinder head. (5)
**rounding.** The process of simplifying a number to a larger or a smaller value that makes calculations easier. (1)

## S

**secondary winding.** One of two coils of wire in an ignition coil. The secondary winding is the thinner wire with many thousands more windings. (7)
**series circuit.** An electrical circuit where all loads are on the same path and share the total voltage. (6)
**service interval.** The mileage at which a part or fluid should be replaced or serviced. (3)
**short-term fuel trim (STFT).** Fuel trim value based on current operating conditions. (7)
**signal voltage.** The value calculated by subtracting the sensor voltage drop from the reference voltage. (6)
**source voltage.** The amount of voltage available at the power source, such as the automotive battery. (6)
**spark plug gap.** The space between the center electrode and the ground electrode. (7)
**specifications.** Set requirements for different parts and systems determined by automotive manufacturers. (1)
**stabilized battery.** The neutral state of the battery indicating the vehicle is shut down and in "sleep mode." The voltage should read 12.6 volts. (3)
**standard clutch.** A clutch that uses a pressure plate and friction disc to connect the engine flywheel to the input shaft of the manual transmission. (8)
**steel ruler.** A more precise type of tape measure, typically only six or twelve inches long. (1)
**stoichiometric air-fuel (A/F) ratio.** A ratio of 14.71 pounds of air to 1 pound of fuel. This is the targeted ratio of the air-fuel mixture needed for combustion in an internal combustion gasoline engine. (7)
**stroke.** The distance the piston travels within the cylinder, from top-dead-center to bottom-dead-center. (5)
**subtraction.** The process of removing one value from another value to obtain a difference value. (1)
**subtrahend.** The value in a subtraction problem that is removed from the minuend. (1)
**sum.** The total value of two or more separate values, or addends, added together. (1)
**surface charge.** The battery stage directly after the running engine is shut off. This higher voltage value will slowly drop to 12.6 volts. (3)
**suspension springs.** Springs that support the weight of most of the vehicle. (4)

## T

**tape measure.** A compact measurement tool designed to measure from 1/16 inch to 12 feet or greater, depending on the length of the tape measure. (1)
**taper.** A value determined by comparing the A-B measurements of a shaft, such as crankshaft and camshaft journals. (5)
**thermocouple.** A junction of two metals that converts a temperature difference into a voltage signal. (6)
**timing belt.** A belt that connects the crankshaft to the camshaft and is responsible for rotating both shafts in sync with each other. (3)
**tire pressure gauge.** A tool used to measure tire pressure. (1)
**tire tread.** The patterned section around the outside of the tire that contacts the road. (3)
**tire tread depth gauge.** A tool used to measure tire tread depth. (1)
**top-dead-center (TDC).** The end of piston travel in the up position. (5)
**torque.** The measurement of rotational force. (3)
**torque value.** The level of rotational force used to tighten a bolt or nut with a torque instrument. (3)

## U

**underdrive.** A gear ratio higher than 1.0. This ratio multiplies torque but has a much slower output speed compared to input speed. (8)
**Uniform Tire Quality Grading (UTQG) system.** A system used to rate tires on temperature, treadwear, and traction. (4)
**unit conversion.** Converting between different units of measurement. (1)
**unsprung weight.** The parts of a vehicle not supported by the suspension springs. (4)

## V

**valve overlap.** A period during the engine operating cycle when a cylinder's intake and exhaust valves are open at the same time. (5)
**Vehicle Identification Number (VIN).** A 17-digit alphanumeric code that provides critical information about a vehicle, including a production sequence. (2)
**voltage.** The electrical potential as measured between the positive pole and the negative pole of a power source. (6)
**voltage drop.** The measurement of how the energy is reduced at each electrical load in the circuit. (6)
**volumetric efficiency (VE).** The calculated value of airflow efficiency of an engine. (5)

# INDEX

## A

A/F ratio. *See* stoichiometric air-fuel ratio
acceleration, 361
    electric car, 404–405
accelerator pedal position (APP), 306
addends, 2
adding
    decimal numbers, 24
        air conditioning system oil problems, 397–398
        alignment angles problems, 180–181
        brake system problems, 207–208
        disc brake micrometer problems, 204
        flat-rate labor time problems, 87–90
        multi-disc clutch adjustments problems, 352–353
        voltage drop problems, 260–261
    fractions, 38
        hose length calculation problems, 96–97
        ride height problems, 188–189
        tread depth problems, 141–142
    mixed numbers
        wire length problems, 280–281
    whole numbers, 2–6, 72–74
        air conditioning system oil problems, 397–398
        electric throttle problems, 307–308
        repair order problems, 120–122
        unsprung weight problems, 166–168
        valve overlap and duration problems, 213–214
        voltage drop problems, 260–261
        work uniform problems, 73–74
addition, 2–4
air conditioning system
    gauge reading, 430–431
        problems, 432–433
    oil, 396
        problems, 397–398
    pressure, 423–424
    pressure reading, 424
        problems, 425–426
    refrigerant, 419
    servicing, 396
    temperature pressure chart, 424
air-fuel ratio
    lambda, 337–338
    stoichiometric air-fuel (A/F) ratio, 337
air gap, 399
    compressors, 399–400
air pressure, 329
alignment angles, 178–179
    cross-camber, 178–179
    cross-caster, 178–179
    measurements, 179
    specifications, 178
American Wire Gage (AWG), 275
ampacity, 275

amperage, 265, 268
APP. *See* accelerator pedal position
area
    condenser and evaporator area problems, 417–418
    square footage, 110
        problems, 111–112
arithmetic
    decimal numbers
        cooling system boiling point problems, 410–411
        hybrid vehicle payback problems, 414–415
        hydraulic pressure problems, 367–368
        manual gear set ratio problems, 374–375
    whole numbers
        hybrid vehicle payback problems, 414–415
aspect ratio, 172
automatic transmission and transaxle, 378–379
    table, 379
average. *See* mean value
AWG. *See* American Wire Gage

## B

backlash, 387
    differential, 390–391
    gear, 387
    pinion gear, 390–391
    ring gear, 390–391
    specifications, 390
bar, 329
bar graph, 47
battery, 132–133
    cycle, 132–133
    high-voltage, hybrid vehicle, 402
    voltage, 132–133
        problems, 134–135
BDC. *See* bottom dead center
boiling point, 408
    cooling system, 408–409
bore, 226
borrowing, in subtraction, 8
bottom dead center (BDC), 210, 226
brake
    disc, 191, 203
        measuring problems, 204
    drum, 190–191
    fluid, 194
        testing, 194–195
    inspection, 129
    pads, 129
        pad life, 129
        problems, 130–131
    system, 205–206
        functions, 205
        specifications, 206

brake drums, 190–191
brake micrometer, 203

## C

camshaft, 215
    exhaust duration, 210
    intake duration, 210
    specifications, 210
    valve overlap, 210
camshaft and crankshaft journal, 248–249
    problems, 250–251
camshaft lobe, 215
    exhaust valve, 215
    intake valve, 215
career profile
    crew chief assistant, 1
    diagnostic specialist, 305
    diagnostic technician, 71
    engine builder and machinist, 209
    entry-level apprentice technician, 117
    race technician, 71
    sales and service technician, 163
    service technician, 257, 395
    technician, 349
carrying
    in addition, 3
    in multiplication, 12
Celsius, 282
charging battery, 132
clean metal, 78
clearance, 230
clutch gap, 399–400
    multi-disc, 350–351
    standard, 350
combustion chamber volume, 222–223
comeback, 91
common denominator, 38
compression ratio, 222–223
compression test, 315–316
    problems, 317–319
compressor clutch air gap, 399–400
    problems, 401
condenser, 416
    area, 416
control module, 306, 345
    module pinout diagram, 345
conversion factor, 43
converting units. *See* unit conversion
coolant, 408
    coolant-water mixture, 408
coolant freeze level, 48, 147–148
    problems, 149–150
cooling system, 408–409
    boiling point, 408–409
        problems, 410–411
cranking battery, 132
crankshaft rotation, 210
crew chief assistant, 1
cross-camber, 178–179

cross-caster, 178–179
customary tape measure, 38
customer service survey, 91–92
    comeback, 91
cylinder bore, 230, 252–253
    measuring problems, 254–256
    out-of-round, 252–253
    size specifications, 230
    taper, 252–253
cylinder compression test, 315–316

## D

data analysis
    A/C pressure reading, 424
        problems, 425–426
    brake fluid data, 195
        problems, 196–198
    brake system specifications problems, 207–208
    engine cooling system, 240
        problems, 241–243
    mean value, 91–92
    module pinout diagrams, 345–346
        problems, 347–348
    temperature pressure chart, 424
    vehicle identification number, 113
        problems, 115–116
dealership service centers, 75
decimal numbers
    adding, 24–25
        alignment angles problems, 180–181
        air conditioning system oil problems, 397–398
        brake system problems, 207–208
        disc brake micrometer problems, 204
        flat-rate labor time problems, 87–90
        multi-disc clutch adjustments problems, 352–353
        voltage drop problems, 260–261
    arithmetic
        applying Ohm's law problems, 273–274
        cooling system boiling point problems, 410–411
        fuel trim, 320–321
        fuel trim problems, 322
        hybrid vehicle payback problems, 414–415
        hydraulic pressure problems, 367–368
    converting to percentage, 315
        compression test problems, 317–319
    converting to whole numbers
        pressure problems, 330–331
    dividing, 24–29
        compression ratio problems, 224–225
        differential gear ratio problems, 363–364
        electric car speed and acceleration problems, 406–407
        Ohm's law problems, 269–270
    fractional equivalency, 233
        engine parts problems, 234–235
    multiplying, 24
        battery voltage problems, 134–135
        flat-rate labor time problems, 87–90
        gear ratio torque problems, 359–360
        hybrid vehicle, high-voltage battery, 403
        linear brake measurement problems, 182–183
        maintenance parts problems, 127–128
        Ohm's law problems, 266–267
        rocker arm ratio problems, 220–221
        tire size aspect ratio problems, 173–174
    number value, 23
    rounding, 24
    subtracting, 24
        alignment angles problems, 180–181
        battery voltage problems, 134–135
        brake system problems, 207–208
        camshaft lobe problems, 216–217
        compressor clutch air gap problems, 401
        reference voltage problems, 263–264
decimal point, 23
    placement in product, 24
    placement in quotient, 24
denominator, 37
diagnostic specialist, 305
diagnostic technician, 71
dial caliper, 59–60
dial indicator, 59, 61
difference, 7
differential backlash, 390–391
    problems, 392–394
differential gear ratio, 361–362
    problems, 363–364
differential gear set, 361
    final drive gear ratio, 361
    gear ratio problems, 363–364
    pinion gear, 361–362
    ring gear, 361–362
digital multimeter, 282, 295–297
    measuring amperage, 295, 297
    measuring resistance, 295–296
    measuring voltage, 295–296
    problems, 298–299
direct-drive, 357
dirty metal, 78
disc brake, 190, 203
    measuring problems, 204
distance conversion factors, 376
    odometer distance values problems, 377–378
dividend, 17
dividing
    decimal numbers, 24
        compression ratio problems, 224–225
        differential gear ratio problems, 363–364
        electric car speed and acceleration problems, 406–407
        Ohm's law problems, 269–270
    whole numbers, 17–22
        brake pad life problems, 130–131
        compression ratio problems, 224–225
        compression test problems, 317–319
        differential gear ratio problems, 363–364
        electric car speed and acceleration problems, 406–407
        Ohm's law problems, 269–270
        stopping distance problems, 176–177
        tool payment problems, 83–84
division 17–19
divisor, 17
drive gear, 373–374
driveline, 354, 357
    angle, 354–355
    problems, 356
driveline speed, 383–384
    problems, 385
    tire diameter, 383–384
    vehicle speed, 383–384
driven gear, 373–374
driveshaft, 354
drum brake, 191, 203

## E

electrical circuit, 258–259
    resistance, 291–292
        problems, 293–294
    voltage drop, voltage drop problems, 260–261
electrical system specifications, 300–301
    problems, 302–304
electric car, 404
    acceleration and speed, 404–405
        problems, 406–407
electronic throttle control system, 306
    problems, 307–308
engine
    compression test, 315–316
    control module, 306
    cooling system, 239–240
        problems, 241–243
    fuel pressure, 136
    oil pressure, 136
    parts, 233–234
        problems, 234–235
    power, 244–245
        horsepower, 244
    rpm, 244
    sensor, 332–333
        pressure sensor, 136
        problems, 334–336
    size, 236
        problems, 237–238
        unit values, 236
    tune-up, 159–160
        problems, 161–162
        specifications, 160
engine block, 226
    calculations, 226–227
    problems, 228–229
    size value, 226–227
engine builder and machinist, 209
engine displacement, 226
entry-level apprentice technician, 117
equal, 31
evaporator, 416
    area, 416
exhaust duration, 210

## F

factor, 11
Fahrenheit, 282
fasteners, 143
feeler gauge, 59, 62, 399
final drive gear ratio, 361
flat-rate labor time system, 85–86
    chart, 86
    problems, 87–90
fluid service, 98
fluid volume, 98
    conversion, 98
        problems, 99–100
formula, 53
formula calculation
    driveline speed problems, 385
    electrical circuit resistance problems, 293–294
    engine power and efficiency problems, 246–247
    lambda problems, 339–340
    miles per gallon equivalent problems, 428–429
    tire diameter problems, 201–202
    torque problems, 153–154
    wage earning problems, 108–109
four-stroke engine
    bottom dead center, 210
    camshaft, 210–211
        exhaust duration, 210
        intake duration, 210
        specifications, 210
        valve overlap, 210
    crankshaft rotation, 210
    operating cycle, 210–212
    piston stroke, 210
    top dead center, 210
    valve overlap, 210
    valve overlap angle, 211–212
fractional equivalency, 233
fractions
    adding, 38
        hose length calculation problems, 96–97
        ride height problems, 188–189
        tire tread depth problems, 141–142
    common denominators, 38
    decimal equivalency, 233
        engine parts problems, 234–235
    fraction of a whole number
        fuel tank capacity problems, 328
    improper fractions, 37
    lowest terms, 38
    mixed numbers, 37
        adding, wire length problems, 280–281
        multiplying, condenser and evaporator area problems, 417–418
    parts of, 38
    subtracting, 38
        hose length calculation problems, 96–97
        ride height problems, 188–189
        tire tread depth problems, 141–142
        wire length problems, 280–281
fuel economy, 434–435
    Monroney label, 434–435
    specifications, 435
fuel gauge, 327
fuel pressure, 136
fuel tank, 327
fuel tank capacity, 327
    problems, 328
fuel trim, 320–321

## G

gauge types
    feeler gauge, 59, 62, 399
    fuel gauge, 327
    lug spacing gauge, 155–156
    odometer, 276
    pressure gauge, 341–342
    tire pressure gauge, 59, 62, 156–157
    tire tread depth gauge, 59, 62, 139–140, 156–157
    vacuum gauge, 341–342
gear backlash, 387
    problems, 388–389
gear components
    drive, 373–374
    driven, 373–374
    number of teeth, 373–374
gear ratio, 357–358, 361–362
    direct-drive, 357
    final drive, 361
    overdrive, 357
    torque, 357–358
        problems, 359–360
    underdrive, 357
gear set, manual, 373
graph, 47–48
    bar graph, 47
    interpreting data sets, 47–48
        brake fluid problems, 196–198
        coolant freeze levels, 147–150
        engine cooling system problems, 241–243
        engine sensor problems, 334–336
        Ohm's law problems, 287–290
        shift solenoid problems, 381–382
        workplace productivity problems, 103–105
    line graph, 48
gross pay, 106

## H

horsepower, 244
    engine power and efficiency problems, 246–247
    rpm, 244
hose length, 95
hybrid electric fuel economy, 434–435
    problems, 436–438
hybrid vehicle
    cooling system, 408–409
    cost savings, 412–413
    fuel economy, 434–435
    fuel savings, 412–413
    high-voltage battery, 402–403
    payback, 412–413
hydraulic pressure, 365–366
    Pascal's law, 365–366
    problems, 367–368
hydraulic system, 365–366
    piston size, 365–366
    pressure, 365–366
        problems, 367–368

## I

ignition coil, 311–312
ignition coil voltage, 311–312
    problems, 313–314
improper fractions, 37
    converting to mixed numbers, 37
    hose length calculation problems, 96–97
in Hg. *See* inches of mercury
inches of mercury (in Hg), 329
inequalities, 31–32
    alignment angles problems, 180–181
    fractions, 31
    greater than, 31
    hybrid vehicle payback problems, 414–415
    less than, 31
    mixed numbers, 31
    piston bore clearance problems, 231–232
    planetary gear set ratio problems, 371–372
    pressure sensor data, 136
    pressure sensor problems, 137–138
    spark plug gap problems, 325–326
    wire gage problems, 277–278
input values, 53
intake duration, 210
internal combustion engine, 244

## K

kilometer (km), 276
kilopascal (kPa), 329, 342
Kirchhoff's voltage law, 259
km. *See* kilometer
kPa. *See* kilopascal
k-type thermocouple, 282
    multimeter, 282

## L

labor time, flat-rate, 85–86
    chart, 86
lambda, 337–338
    problems, 339–340
line graph, 48
long division, 18
long-term fuel trim (LTFT), 320–321
lowest terms, 38
low pressure fuel systems, 95
LTFT. *See* long-term fuel trim
lug spacing gauge, 155–156

## M

MAF. *See* mass airflow sensor
maintenance parts, 126
    problems, 127–128
    vehicle maintenance, 126

manifold gauge set, 424
   pressure reading, 430–431
   temperature reading, 430–431
manual gear set ratio, 373
   drive and driven gears, 373–374
   problems, 374–375
mass airflow, 309
   problems, 310
mass airflow (MAF) sensor, 309
mean value, 91
   customer service survey, 91
   problems, 93–94
measurement
   dial caliper, 60
   dial gauge, 387
      gear backlash problems, 388–389
   dial indicator, 61
   digital dial caliper, 61
   digital multimeter, 295–297
      problems, 298–299
   feeler gauge, 61
   manifold gauge set, 431
      problems, 432–433
   micrometer, 59, 61, 215, 248–249
      brake, 203
      cam and crank journal problems, 250–251
      disc brake micrometer problems, 204
   steel ruler, 60
   tape measure, 60
   tire pressure gauge, 62
   tires and wheels problems, 158
   tire tread depth, 139–140
   tire tread depth gauge, 62, 139
   vacuum/pressure gauge, 341–342
      problems, 343–344
micrometer, 59, 61, 214, 248–249
   brake, 203
mile, 276
miles per gallon, 427
miles per gallon equivalent (MPGe), 427
   problems, 428–429
miles per hour (mph), 405
minuend, 7
mixed numbers, 37
   adding, wire length problems, 280–281
   multiplying, condenser and evaporator area problems, 417–418
   subtracting, wire length problems, 280–281
module pinout diagram, 345–346
   problems, 347–348
Monroney label, 434–435
   hybrid electric fuel economy problems, 436–438
MPGe. *See* miles per gallon equivalent
mph. *See* miles per hour
multi-disc clutch, 350–351
   adjustment problems, 352–353
multimeter. *See* digital multimeter
multiplication 11–13
   table, 12
multiplying
   decimal numbers, 24
      battery voltage problems, 134–135
      flat-rate labor time problems, 87–90
      gear ratio torque problems, 359–360
   hybrid vehicle, high-voltage battery, 403
   linear brake measurement problems, 182–183
   maintenance parts problems, 127–128
   Ohm's law problems, 266–267
   rocker arm ratio problems, 220–221
   tire size aspect ratio problems, 173–174
fractions, condenser and evaporator area problems, 417–418
mixed numbers, condenser and evaporator area problems, 417–418
whole numbers, 11–16
   flat-rate labor time problems, 87–90
   gear ratio torque problems, 359–360
   hybrid vehicle, high-voltage battery, 403
   ignition coil voltage problems, 313–314
   linear brake measurement problems, 182–183
   maintenance parts problems, 127–128
   Ohm's law problems, 266–267
   rocker arm ratio problems, 220–221
   tire size aspect ratio problems, 173–174

# N

net pay, 106
number line
   addition, 2
   subtraction, 7
numerator, 37

# O

odometer, 276
   distance values problems, 377–378
Ohm's law, 265
   amperage, 265, 268
   applying, 271–272
   graphing problems, 288–290
   graphs, 287
   problems, 266–267, 269–270, 273–274
   resistance, 265, 268
   resistance and amperage relationship, 271
   resistance, voltage, and amperage relationship, 286–287
   voltage, 265
oil
   air conditioning systems, 396
   oil pressure, engine, 136
order of operations, 54
   wage earning problems, 108–109
out-of-round, 248–249
   measuring, 253
output values, 53
overdrive, 357–358

# P

parallel circuit, 291–292
Pascal's law, 365–366
payback, hybrid vehicle, 412–413
percentage, fuel trim value, 320–321
pie graph, 47
pinion gear, 361–362
   backlash, 390–391
pin location, module pinout diagram, 346
pin number, module pinout diagram, 346
piston, 230
piston displacement, 222–223
   crankshaft rotation, 210
   displacement, 222–223
   size, hydraulic system, 365–366
   size specifications, 230
   stroke, bottom dead center, 210
   stroke, top dead center, 210
piston bore clearance, 230
   problems, 231–232
place value, 23
planetary gear set, 369
   sun gear, 370–371
planetary gear set ratio, 369–370
   formula, 370
   inputs and outputs, 370
   problems, 371–372
plus or minus symbol, 31
pounds per square inch (psi), 329, 342
pressure, 329
   cooling system boiling point, 408–409
pressure gauge, 341–342
   vacuum/pressure gauge problems, 343–344
pressure reading
   A/C, 424
   manifold gauge set, 430–431
   manifold gauge set reading problems, 432–433
pressure sensor, 136
   data, 136
   problems, 137–138
primary winding, 311–312
product, 11
productivity, workplace data, 102
psi. *See* pounds per square inch

# Q

quotient, 17

# R

race technician, 1
ratio
   ignition coil voltage problems, 313–314
   rocker arm, 218–219
   rocker arm ratio problems, 220–221
   windings, 311
reducing fractions, 38
   hose length calculation problems, 96–97
reference voltage, 262
   formula, 262
   problems, 263–264
refractometers, 147
refrigerant, 419
refrigerant cycle, 423
refrigerant weight, 419–420
   problems, 421–422
remainder, 18

repair orders, 118–119
  labor section, 119
  parts/fees section, 119
  problems, 120–122
resistance, 265, 268
resistors, 291–292
ride height, 187
  measurements, 187
ring gear, 361–362
  backlash, 390–391
    specifications, 390–391
rocker arm, 218–219
rocker arm ratio, 218–219
  definition, 218
rounding, 24
  decimal numbers, 24
  decimal number to fractional value, 233
    engine parts problems, 234–235
  square footage and area, 110
    problems, 111–112
rpm, 244

## S

sales and service technician, 163
scrap metal, 78
  clean metal, 78
  dirty metal, 78
  estimated weight, 79
  pricing, 78–79
secondary winding, 311–312
sensor, 262
  engine, 332–333
    problems, 334–336
  resistance value, 262
  throttle position sensor (TPS), 333
  voltage, 309
  voltage-drop, 262
series circuit, 291–292
service information, 65
service interval, 123, 169
  table, 169
service technician, 257, 395
shift solenoids, 379–380
  problems, 381–382
shims, 399–400
shop equipment, 110
  square footage and area, 110
shop inventory, 75
short-term fuel trim (STFT), 320–321
signal voltage, 262
solder repair, 279
solenoid, shift, 379–380
source voltage, 258
spark plug gap, 323–324
  problems, 325–326
specifications, 65
  analyzing, 65–66
  backlash, 390–391
    differential backlash problems, 392–394
  brake system, 206
  compression test, 315
  control modules, 345–346

module pinout diagram problems, 347–348
cylinder bore, 230, 252–253
  problems, 254–256
electrical systems, 300–301
  electrical specifications problems, 302–304
engine tune-up, 160
  problems, 161–162
exhaust duration, 210
fuel economy, 435
  hybrid electric fuel economy problems, 436–438
intake duration, 210
piston size, 230
  differential backlash problems, 392–394
spark plug gap, 323
  problems, 325–326
speed, 404–405
square footage and area, 110
  problems, 111–112
  rounding, 110
stabilized battery, 132
standard clutch, 350
steel ruler, 59–60
step-up transformer, 311
  ignition coil, 311
STFT. See short-term fuel trim
stoichiometric air-fuel (A/F) ratio, 337–338
stopping distance, 175
stroke engine, 226
subtracting
  decimal numbers, 24
    alignment angles problems, 180–181
    battery voltage problems, 134–135
    brake system problems, 207–208
    camshaft lobe problems, 216–217
    compressor clutch air gap problems, 401
    reference voltage problems, 263–264
  fractions, 38
    hose length calculation problems, 96–97
    mixed numbers, wire length problems, 280–281
    ride height problems, 188–189
    tire tread depth problems, 141–142
  whole numbers, 7–10
    camshaft lobe problems, 216–217
    compressor clutch air gap problems, 401
    driveline angle problems, 356
    mass airflow problems, 310
    reference voltage problems, 263–264
    service interval problems, 170–171
    shop inventory problems, 76–77
    timing belt service interval problems, 124–125
subtraction, 7–8
subtrahend, 7
sum, 2
sun gear, planetary gear set, 370–371
suspension springs, 164

## T

tape measure, 59–60
  customary, 38
  fractions, 38
    ride height problems, 188–189
taper, 248–249
  measuring, 253
TDC. See top dead center
technician, 349
temperature
  Celsius and Fahrenheit, 282–283
  conversion, 282–283
  k-type thermocouple, 282
  pressure chart, 424
  problems, 284–285
  thermocouple, 282–283
thermocouple, 282–283
throttle
  cable, 306
  closed, 306
throttle position sensor (TPS), 333
timing belt, 123
timing belt service interval, 123
  problems, 124–125
tire diameter, 199–200, 383–384
  problems, 201–202, 385–386
tire gauge, 59, 62
tire pressure gauge, 59, 62, 156–157
tires, 155–157
  analyzing, 182–183
    temperature rating, 182
    traction rating, 182
    treadwear rating, 182
    Uniform Tire Quality Grading (UTQG) system, 182–183
  diameter, 199–200, 383–384
  driveline, formula, 199
  problems, 158
  sidewall, 172
  size, 199–200
    formula, 199
  tread depth gauge, 59, 62, 139–140, 156–157
tire sidewall, 172
tire size, aspect ratio, 172
tire tread, 139
tire tread depth, 139–140
  gauge, 59, 62, 139–140, 156–157
  problems, 141–142, 158
top dead center (TDC), 210, 226
torque, 151
  gear ratio, 357–358
  measuring, 151–152
  problems, 153–154
torque value, 143–144
  conversion values, 144
  problems, 145–146
TPS. See throttle position sensor
traction rating, 182
tread depth gauge, 59, 62, 139–140, 156–157
treadwear rating, 182

## U

underdrive, 357–358

Uniform Tire Quality Grading (UTQG)
    system, 182–183
unit conversion, 43–46
    automotive-related unit designation
        labels, 43
    Celsius and Fahrenheit, 282–283
        temperature problems, 284–285
    decimal numbers, temperature
        problems, 284–285
    distance values, 376
        odometer distance values
            problems, 377–378
    engine components, 236
        engine size problems, 237–238
    fluid volume values, 98
        fluid volume problems, 99–100
    length values, 44
    linear break measure, 190
        problems, 182–183
    refrigerant
        problems, 421–422
        weight values, 419–420
    temperature, 282–283
    torque value, 144
        problems, 145–146
    units of pressure, 329
        problems, 330–331
    weight values, 44
    whole numbers, temperature
        problems, 284–285
unsprung weight, 164–165
    problems, 166–168
UTQG. See Uniform Tire Quality Grading
    system

## V

vacuum gauge, 341–342
    problems, 343–344
vacuum/pressure gauge, compound,
    341–342
    problems, 343–344
valve, shift solenoid, 379–380
valve duration, 210–212
valve lash value, 219

rocker arm ratio, 219
valve overlap, 210–212
variance, spark plug gap problems, 325–326
VE. See volumetric efficiency
vehicle identification number (VIN), 113
    designation, 114
    problems, 115–116
vehicle speed, calculating, 383–384
velocity, 404–405
VIN. See vehicle identification number
voltage, 259
    battery, 132–133
    hybrid vehicle high-voltage battery, 402
        problems, 403
    ignition coil, 311–312
    source voltage, 258
    thermocouple, 282
voltage drop, 258–259
volumetric efficiency (VE), 245
    engine power and efficiency problems,
        246–247

## W

wage earnings, 106
    gross pay, 106–107
    net pay, 106–107
    problems, 108–109
wheels, 155–157
    lug spacing size, 155–156
    problems, 158
whole numbers
    adding
        air conditioning system oil
            problems, 397–398
        electric throttle problems, 307–308
        unsprung weight problems,
            166–168
        valve overlap and duration
            problems, 213–214
        voltage drop problems, 260–261
    arithmetic, hybrid vehicle payback
        problems, 414–415
    converting to decimal numbers,
        pressure problems, 330–331

dividing, 17–22
    brake pad life problems, 130–131
    compression ratio problems,
        224–225
    compression test problems, 317–319
    differential gear ratio problems,
        363–364
    electric car speed and acceleration
        problems, 406–407
    Ohm's law problems, 269–270
    stopping distance problems, 176–177
multiplying
    gear ratio torque problems, 359–360
    hybrid vehicle, high-voltage
        battery, 403
    ignition coil voltage problems,
        313–314
    linear brake measurement
        problems, 182–183
    maintenance parts problems,
        127–128
    Ohm's law problems, 266–267
    rocker arm ratio problems, 220–221
    tire size aspect ratio problems,
        173–174
subtracting
    camshaft lobe problems, 216–217
    compressor clutch air gap
        problems, 401
    driveline angle problems, 356
    mass airflow problems, 310
    reference voltage problems, 263–264
    service interval problems, 170–171
windings, ratio, 311
wire, 275
    ampacity, 275
    gage size, 275–276
        chart, 276
        problems, 277–278
    length, 279
    solder repair, 279
workplace productivity, 101–102
    problems, 103–105
work uniforms, 72

# ANSWERS TO ODD-NUMBERED QUESTIONS

## Unit 1—Basic Math Skills

### Lesson 1: Addition

1.1 a. 7
   c. 8
   e. 5
   g. 13
   i. 14
   k. 10
1.2 a. 22
   c. 23
   e. 27
   g. 46
   i. 30
   k. 55
1.3 a. 15
   c. 90
   e. 26
   g. 235
   i. 30
   k. 226
1.4 a. 19 vehicles
   c. 131 vehicles
   e. 406 batteries

### Lesson 2: Subtraction

2.1 a. 7
   c. 3
   e. 1
   g. 3
   i. 4
   k. 3
2.2 a. 7
   c. 205
   e. 58
   g. 176
   i. 27
   k. 39
2.3 a. –5
   c. –3
   e. –15
   g. –2
   i. –15
2.4 a. $232.00
   c. 42°
   e. $28.00

### Lesson 3: Multiplication

3.1 a. 12
   c. 42
   e. 0
   g. 28
   i. 35
   k. 24
3.2 a. 170
   c. 87
   e. 8,132
   g. 1,134
   i. 2,835
3.3 a. $760.00
   c. $268.00
   e. 1,350 towels per case

### Lesson 4: Division

4.1 a. 2
   c. 7
   e. 3
   g. 8
   i. 4
   k. 4
   m. 10
   o. 9
4.2 a. 3 r 1
   c. 3 r 2
   e. 4 r 1
   g. 7 r 1
   i. 4 r 3
4.3 a. 25 4/5

c. 65 1/7
e. 93 2/6 or 93 1/3
g. 34 5/7
4.4 a. $314.00
c. 37 hp/cylinder
e. 2 volts
g. 8,969 5/15 miles or 8,969 1/3 miles

## Lesson 5: Decimal Arithmetic

5.1 a. four tenths
c. three ten-thousandths
e. four thousand eight hundred seventy-nine
g. 350
i. 0.201
5.2 a. 1
c. 46
e. 352
g. 70
i. 50
k. 130
5.3 a. 14.6
c. 775.31
e. 90.56
g. 17
i. 1,469.05
5.4 a. 15.75
c. 44.6524
e. 80.1515
g. 106.396
5.5 a. 3.5
5.6 a. $44.34
c. 0.037 mm
e. 0.372 mm

## Lesson 6: Greater Than and Less Than

6.1 a. <
c. =
e. >
g. >
i. <
k. <
m. <
o. >
6.2 a. <
c. <
e. =
6.3 a. 1 to 7
c. 18.5 to 31.5
e. 1.5 to 2
6.4 a. February
c. Economy semimetallic brake pads
e. The technicians completed the same number of jobs.
g. Option 2
i. 0.9° to 1.7°

## Lesson 7: Fractions

7.1 a. 6/15
c. 9/15 or 3/5
e. 8/9
g. 10/15 or 2/3
i. 11/15
7.2 a. 2 1/7
c. 8 3/4
e. 6 1/4
7.3 a. 3/4
c. 1/2
e. 3/4
g. 3/7
i. 2/9
7.4 a. 1/2
c. 7/16
e. 7/8
g. 1 1/4
i. 1/8
k. 1 1/2
7.5 a. Common denominator: 32, sum: 27/32
c. Common denominator: 32, difference: 15/32
7.6 a. 5 2/8 inches or 5 1/4 inches
c. 9/32 inches
e. 74 11/16 inches

## Lesson 8: Conversion

8.1 a. 6437.2 meters

c. 15,840 feet

e. 15.157 inches (rounded to 3 decimal places)

8.2 a. 340.2 grams

c. 2.172 pounds (rounded to 3 decimal places)

e. 187.638 pounds (rounded to 3 decimal places)

g. 4.536 metric tons

## Lesson 9: Graphs and Tables

9.1 a. Oil change – 4

Tire rotation – 5

Brake service – 2

Alternator replacement – 1

Spark plug service – 3

9.2 a. July

c. 7 months

e. 26 batteries

9.3 a. 325

c. 5,500 rpm

e. HP before at 6,500

## Lesson 10: Formulas

10.1a. Set 1: 21

Set 2: 2,100

Set 3: 65

10.2a. 25.5

c. 2,503

10.3a. 18.6 miles per gallon

c. 22.1 miles per gallon

e. $17.42

g. $20.44

## Lesson 11: Measurement

11.1a. 12 7/8 inches

c. 20 3/8 inches

e. 1 5/8 inches

g. 2 9/16 inches

i. 2 7/8 inches

11.2a. 3.263 inches

c. 3.238 inches

e. 1.010 inches

11.3a. 0.154 inches

c. 0.297 inches

e. 0.089 inches

g. 2.05 mm

i. 4.62 mm

k. 18.86 mm

11.4a. 0.831

c. 0.39

e. 38 psi

## Lesson 12: Analyzing Specifications

12.1a. 0.885 cu in

c. Clockwise

12.2a. 26.0 mm

c. 25.0 mm

e. 10.5 mm

12.3a. 3.16:1

c. Third

e. 6T71-MH3

# Unit 2—Around the Shop

## Case Study 1: Work Uniforms

1.1  160 shirts

120 pants

1.3  81 shirts

1.5  50 shirts

50 pants

1.7  157 shirts

102 pants

## Case Study 2: Shop Inventory

2.1  29 cans

2.3  18 quarts

2.5  28 gallons

2.7  14 gallons

## Case Study 3: Scrap Metal Pricing

3.1  1,244 pounds

3.3  939 pounds

3.5  $229.44

3.7  $228.75

## Case Study 4: Paying for Professional Tools

4.1 8 weeks
4.3 8 weeks
4.5 19 weeks
4.7 $78.25

## Case Study 5: Flat-Rate Labor Times

5.1 3.8 hours
5.3 1.9 hours
5.5 $54.15
5.7 2.3 hours
5.9 $71.88
5.11 6.9 hours
5.13 $190.79
5.15 5.5 hours
5.17 $141.63
5.19 $20.62

## Case Study 6: Customer Service Surveys

6.1 5.8
6.3 315.6
6.5 3.33
6.7 Technician A = 3.83
    Technician B = 4.67

## Case Study 7: Hose Length Calculations

7.1 62 1/4"
7.3 16 13/16"
7.5 No, the vehicle requires 27 3/4" of fuel line.
7.7 33 5/8"

## Case Study 8: Fluid Volume

8.1 220 quarts
8.3 2.9484 gallons
8.5 2.226 quarts
8.7 2.914 quarts

## Case Study 9: Workplace Productivity

9.1 Week 4
9.3 Week 4
9.5 Lube Tech 1
9.7 $60.00
9.9 Line Tech 1
9.11 Electrical diagnosis
     Drivability diagnosis
9.13 49

## Case Study 10: Wage Earnings

10.1 $1,110.00
10.3 $1,060.88
10.5 $1,028.00
10.7 $634.18
10.9 $745.35

## Case Study 11: Shop Equipment

11.1 2 ft by 8 ft
11.3 4 ft by 5 ft
11.5 288 square feet
11.7 8,064 square inches
11.9 24.1 square feet

## Case Study 12: Vehicle Identification Number

12.1 CU0H9
12.3 1C4
12.5 4
12.7 YV1MH1748X1589687
12.9 Volkswagen, Germany

# Unit 3—Vehicle Maintenance

## Case Study 13: Repair Orders

**13.1**

| Parts/Fees |||
|---|---|---|
| Quantity | Part Number / Description | Cost |
| 1 | AKB5864 Ceramic Brake Pads Front | $58.33 |
| 2 | TEK9871 Front Brake Disc | $34.93 ea. |
| 2 | BST183-2 Front Struts | $123.59 ea. |
| 1 | Environmental Impact Fee | $15 |

Used Parts? Discard: ___ Return: ___

Total Parts Cost: **$390.37**

**Labor** — Concern, Cause, Correction

| Labor Task | Flat-Rate Time |
|---|---|
| Replace front brake pads | 1.3 hours |
| Replace front brake discs | 0.4 hours |
| Replace front struts | 2.4 hours |

Labor Rate/hour: **$105**

Total Flat-Rate Time: **4.1 hours**

**13.3**

| Parts/Fees |||
|---|---|---|
| Quantity | Part Number / Description | Cost |
| 1 | IF4832 Window Switch | $139.59 |
| 1 | IF88695-1 Rear Back Window Motor | $319.79 |

Used Parts? Discard: ___ Return: ___

Total Parts Cost: **$459.38**

**Labor** — Concern, Cause, Correction

| Labor Task | Flat-Rate Time |
|---|---|
| Electrical diagnosis | 1.5 hours |
| Replace left window switch | 0.4 hours |
| Replace back window motor | 1.8 hours |

Labor Rate/hour: **$115**

Total Flat-Rate Time: **3.7 hours**

## Case Study 14: Timing Belt Service Intervals

14.1 10,752 miles
14.3 47,962 miles
14.5 22,331 miles
14.7 792 miles
14.9 70,013 miles

## Case Study 15: Maintenance Parts

15.1 $54
15.3 26 blades
15.5 Brand G = $335
    Brand Y = $365
15.7 $34.36
15.9 $3,032

## Case Study 16: Brake Pad Life

16.1 22,563 miles
16.3 9,304 miles
16.5 Front brakes = 23,616 miles remaining
    Rear brakes = 36,736 miles remaining
    Front brakes will reach the 2 mm limit first.
16.7 11,540 miles

## Case Study 17: Analyzing Battery Voltage

17.1  0.7 volts
17.3  2.1 volts
17.5  0 volts
17.7  1.3 volts

## Case Study 18: Pressure Sensor Data Analysis

18.1  Within specifications
18.3  Not within specifications
18.5  Not within specifications
18.7  Not within specifications

## Case Study 19: Tire Tread Depth

19.1  4/32"
19.3  Right front tire
19.5  9/32"
19.7  42,750 miles

## Case Study 20: Torque Values

20.1  3.237 foot-pounds
20.3  408 inch-pounds
20.5  Overtightened
20.7  21.696 Newton-meters

## Case Study 21: Coolant Freeze Levels

21.1  36% ethylene-glycol, 64% water
21.3  25% ethylene-glycol, 75% water
21.5  3.5 gallons of each
21.7  8°F

## Case Study 22: Torque

22.1  39 Newton-meters
22.3  180 foot-pounds
22.5  25 pounds
22.7  3 feet
22.9  7 inches

## Case Study 23: Tires and Wheels

23.1  12 mm
23.3  28 psi
23.5  9 1/2"

## Case Study 24: Engine Tune-Up

24.1  Within specification
24.3  0.2 mm larger
24.5  Intake valve clearance out of specification by 0.02 mm
24.7  Information not provided.

# Unit 4—Chassis

## Case Study 25: Unsprung Weight

25.1  206 pounds
25.3  197 pounds
25.5  141 kg

## Case Study 26: Service Intervals

26.1  27,011 miles
26.3  7,991 miles
26.5  2,541 miles
26.7  2,551 miles

## Case Study 27: Tire Size Aspect Ratio

27.1  101.25 mm
27.3  133.25 mm
27.5  132.75 mm
27.7  129.25 mm
27.9  213.75 mm

## Case Study 28: Stopping Distance Factors

28.1  76.3 ft/s and 97.4 ft/s
28.3  120 ft/s and 94.7 ft/s
28.5  109 ft/s and 101 ft/s

## Case Study 29: Alignment Angles

29.1  0.9° to 1.5°
29.3  0.4° to 1.2°
29.5  4.25° − 0.75° = 3.50°       3.5° < 3.87°
      Within specification
29.7  5.75° + 0.25° = 6.00°       6.12° > 6.00°
      Out of specification
29.9  0.3°                        0.3° > 0.2°
      Out of specification
29.11 0.7°                        0.7° > 0.5°
      Out of specification

## Case Study 30: Analyzing Tires

30.1  Tires A, B, C, and D are within budget. Tire E is not within budget ($103 x 4 = $412 > $400).
30.3  Tire B
30.5  Tire B
30.7  Tires C, D, and E
30.9  Tire C
30.11 Tire B
30.13 Tires A and C
30.15 Tire C

## Case Study 31: Ride Height Measurements

31.1  Front: 3/8″
      Rear: 1/8″
31.3  Front: 1/16″
      Rear: 3/16″
31.5  Left front: 42 1/2″
      Right front: 42 1/2″
      Left rear: 43 1/4″
      Right rear: 43 5/16″

## Case Study 32: Linear Measurement

32.1  25.0698 mm or 25.070 mm rounded
32.3  26.3398 mm or 26.340 mm rounded
32.5  22.3266 mm or 22.327 mm rounded
32.7  278.8158 mm or 278.816 mm rounded
32.9  267.843 mm
32.11 263.6266 mm or 263.627 mm rounded

## Case Study 33: Brake Fluid Testing

33.1  3 cars
33.3  3 cars
33.5

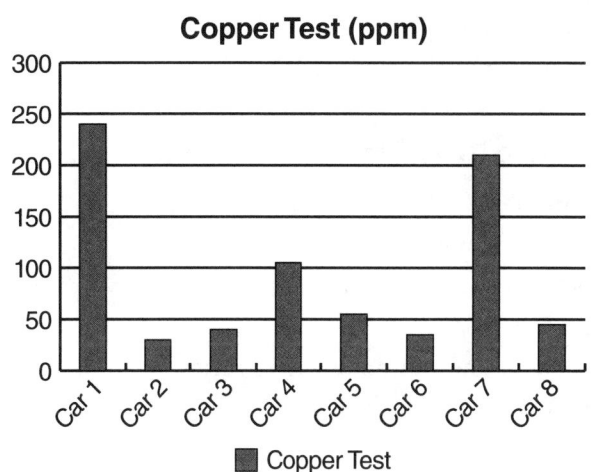

**Copper Test (ppm)**

| Car | ppm |
|---|---|
| Car 1 | 240 |
| Car 2 | 30 |
| Car 3 | 40 |
| Car 4 | 105 |
| Car 5 | 55 |
| Car 6 | 35 |
| Car 7 | 210 |
| Car 8 | 45 |

33.7  4 cars
33.9

**Moisture Test (%)**

| Car | % |
|---|---|
| Car 1 | 2% |
| Car 2 | 3% |
| Car 3 | 3% |
| Car 4 | 4% |
| Car 5 | 2% |
| Car 6 | 1% |
| Car 7 | 1% |
| Car 8 | 3% |
| Car 9 | 1% |
| Car 10 | 1% |

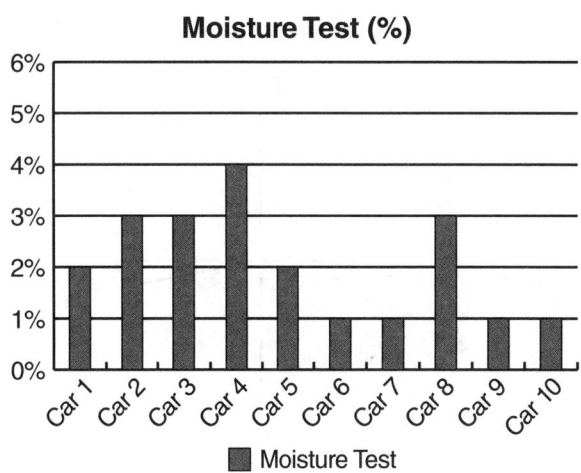

33.11 Car 10
33.13 Cars 2, 3, 4, and 8

## Case Study 34: Tire Diameter

34.1  Stock tire diameter: 31.6″
      New tire diameter: 33.7″
      Change in tire diameter: 2.1″
34.3  Stock tire diameter: 30.0″
      New tire diameter: 26.5″
      Change in tire diameter: 3.5″
34.5  Original tire diameter: 30.5″
      New tire diameter: 30.6″
      New total driveline ratio: 3.90:1

## Case Study 35: Disc Brake Micrometer

35.1  0.977″
35.3  1.113″
35.5  0.937″
35.7  1.138″

## Case Study 36: Brake System

36.1  Yes, within service limit
36.3  Yes, within service limit
36.5  Both are within service limit.
36.7  0.017″
36.9  No, not within limit, requires service
36.11 0.09″

# Unit 5—Engine Mechanical

## Case Study 37: Valve Overlap and Duration

37.1

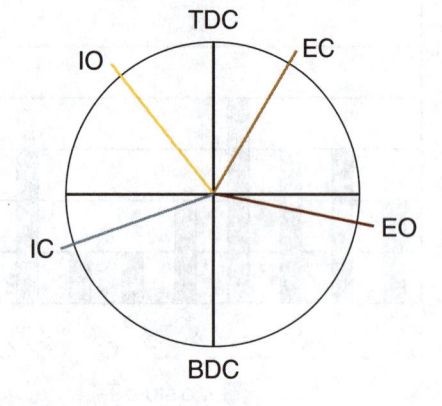

Valve Overlap: 70°
Intake Valve Duration: 290°
Exhaust Valve Duration: 290°

37.3

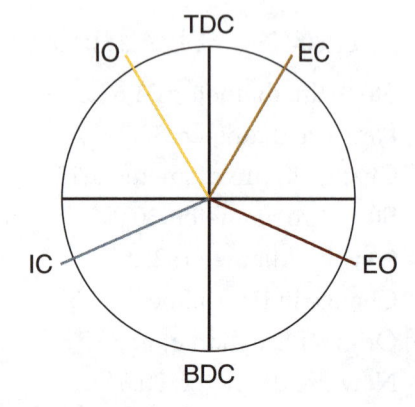

Valve Overlap: 62°
Intake Valve Duration: 278°
Exhaust Valve Duration: 278°

## Case Study 38: Camshaft Lobe

38.1  Cylinder 1    0.35″
      Cylinder 2    0.351″
      Cylinder 3    0.349″
      Cylinder 4    0.352″
38.3  4.65 mm
38.5  0.564″
38.7  Intake    0.05″
      Exhaust  0.051″

## Case Study 39: Rocker Arm Ratio

39.1  1.85:1
39.3  1.70:1
39.5  0.602″
39.7  Intake    0.057″
      Exhaust  0.066″

## Case Study 40: Compression Ratio

40.1  10.33:1
40.3  10.31:1
40.5  10.01:1

## Case Study 41: Engine Block Calculations

41.1  244.1 cubic inches
41.3  223.2 cubic inches
41.5  651.5 cubic inches
41.7  496.0 cubic inches

## Case Study 42: Piston Bore Clearance

42.1  Cylinder 1:    0.0015; Yes
      Cylinder 2:    0.0015; Yes
      Cylinder 3:    0.0012; No
      Cylinder 4:    0.0012; No
      Cylinder 5:    0.0016; Yes
      Cylinder 6:    0.0015; Yes
42.3  Cylinder 1:    0.00103; Yes
      Cylinder 2:    0.00101; Yes
      Cylinder 3:    0.00099; Yes
      Cylinder 4:    0.00092; Yes

## Case Study 43: Engine Parts
43.1  13.8125"
43.3  1.875"
43.5  1.375"
43.7  1 1/6"
43.9  2 7/16"

## Case Study 44: Engine Size
44.1  7.4 liters
44.3  152.6 cubic inches
44.5  116 cubic inch 4-cylinder engine has a smaller volume per cylinder
44.7  5.0 L V8 has a larger volume per cylinder
44.9  1000 cubic centimeter 3-cylinder engine has a smaller total volume

## Case Study 45: Cooling System
45.1  4°F
45.3  Engine #1
45.5  Engine #1    198°F
      Engine #2    200°F
45.7  50°F
45.9  No, the engine temperature does not exceed the thermostat maximum.

## Case Study 46: Engine Power and Efficiency
46.1  158.5 hp
46.3  188.5 hp
46.5  0.96 or 96%
46.7  71.4 hp
46.9  6% increase

## Case Study 47: Cam and Crank Journal
47.1  A: 36.00 mm
      B: 36.02 mm
      Taper: 0.02 mm
47.3  X: 91.05 mm
      Y: 90.98 mm
      Out of round: 0.07 mm
47.5  X: 76.41 mm
      Y: 76.45 mm
      Out of round: 0.04 mm, not within specification

## Case Study 48: Cylinder Bore
48.1  0.001 mm, within specification
      0.001 < 0.010
48.3  0.01 mm, not within specification
      0.01 = 0.01
48.5  0.0009", within specification
      0.0009 < 0.0010
48.7  0.0015", not within specification
      0.0015 > 0.0010
48.9  0.0002", within specification
      0.0002 < 0.0010

# Unit 6—Electrical

## Case Study 49: Voltage Drop
49.1  13 volts
49.3  15.00 volts
49.5  4.8 volts
49.7  1.8 volts

## Case Study 50: Reference Voltage
50.1  1.11 volts
50.3  2.82 volts
50.5  1.24 volts
50.7  0.93 volts

## Case Study 51: Ohm's Law Part 1
51.1  12.6 volts
51.3  14.49 volts
51.5  12.48 volts
51.7  14.49 volts

## Case Study 52: Ohm's Law Part 2
52.1  11.15 amps
52.3  24.67 amps
52.5  0.01 amps
52.7  19.38 Ω

## Case Study 53: Applying Ohm's Law

53.1 Low speed: 0.63 amps
Medium-low speed: 0.76 amps
Medium speed: 0.97 amps
High speed: 1.61 amps

53.3 Amperage at low level: 0.431 amps
Low level BCM voltage drop: 3.276 volts or 3.3 volts
Low level sensor voltage drop: 1.724 volts or 1.7 volts
Amperage at medium level: 0.051 amps
Medium level BCM voltage drop: 0.39 volts or 0.4 volts
Medium level sensor voltage drop: 4.59 volts or 4.6 volts
Amperage at high level: 0.013 amps
High level BCM voltage drop: 0.099 volts or 0.1 volts
High level sensor voltage drop: 4.81 volts

## Case Study 54: Wire Gage sizes

54.1 10-gage wire is larger
54.3 4-gage wire is larger
54.5 3′ 4-gage wire is larger
54.7 14-gage wire

## Case Study 55: Wire Length

55.1 7 3/8″
55.3 16 1/16″
55.5 81 5/16″
55.7 88 15/16″

## Case Study 56: Temperature

56.1 118.3°C
56.3 Bank 2
56.5 No, battery cell #3 was 201.2°F.
56.7 7.96°F or 4.42°C

## Case Study 57: Graphing Ohm's Law

57.1 Around 3 amps
57.3 Around 0.75 amps
57.5 Increases
57.7 14.4 amps
57.9 Decreases
57.11 40 amps

## Case Study 58: Electrical Circuit Resistance

58.1 15 Ω

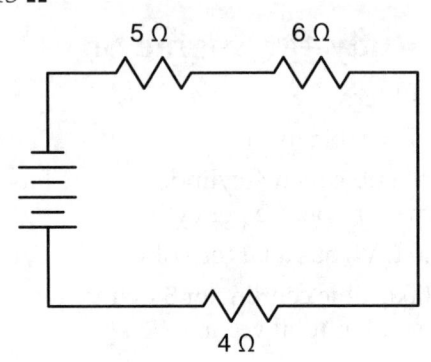

58.3 1.28 Ω

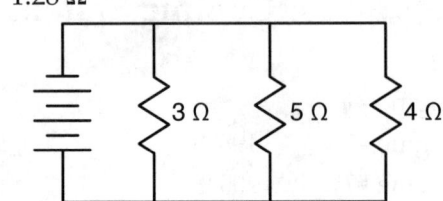

58.5 3.22 Ω

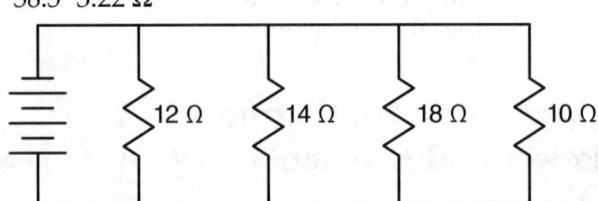

## Case Study 59: Digital Multimeter

59.1.1 15.24 volts
59.1.2 0.85 amps
59.1.3 14.26 Ω
59.3 14.07 volts; engine turned on
59.5 13.61 volts

## Case Study 60: Electrical System Specifications

60.1 85B-60
60.3 1.6 L L4
60.5 D.SC11
60.7 2.2 amps
60.9 Within specified condition

# Unit 7—Engine Performance

## Case Study 61: Electronic Throttle Controls

61.1 1,565 rpm
61.3 1,885 rpm
61.5 1,985 rpm

## Case Study 62: Mass Airflow

62.1 25 g/s
62.3 2.50 volts
62.5 Decreased by 40 g/s

## Case Study 63: Ignition Coil Voltage

63.1 20,700 volts
63.3 20,650 volts
63.5 49,500 volts
63.7 27,650 volts

## Case Study 64: Analyzing Compression Tests

64.1 Highest pressure value: 951 kPa
Lowest pressure value: 903 kPa
5.0% variation between highest and lowest
64.3 Highest pressure value: 12.3 bar
Lowest pressure value: 9.1 bar
26.0% variation between highest and lowest
64.5 Highest pressure value: 980 kPa
Lowest pressure value: 635 kPa
35.2% variation between highest and lowest

## Case Study 65: Fuel Trim

65.1 7.7%
65.3 18.2%
65.5 27.4%

## Case Study 66: Spark Plug Gap

66.1 Cylinder 1: correct
Cylinder 2: too large
Cylinder 3: too small
Cylinder 4: too small
Cylinder 5: too large
Cylinder 6: correct
66.3 Cylinder 1: too large
Cylinder 2: too large
Cylinder 3: too small
Cylinder 4: too large
66.5 Cylinder 1: too large
Cylinder 2: correct
Cylinder 3: too small
Cylinder 4: correct

## Case Study 67: Fuel Tank Capacity

67.1 11.38 gallons
67.3 2.25 gallons
67.5 Total: 16.88 gallons

## Case Study 68: Pressure

68.1 132.57 in Hg
68.3 33.28 kPa
68.5 14.5 psi
68.7 700 kPa
68.9 57.28 psi

## Case Study 69: Engine Sensors

69.1 110°F
69.3 0.90 volts
69.5 32.00 g/s
69.7 0.10 volts
69.9 0.1 to 0.9

## Case Study 70: Lambda

70.1 1.03; running lean
70.3 0.81; running rich
70.5 Bank 1: 15.17:1; running lean
Bank 2: 15.00:1; running lean
70.7 Idle: 14.86:1
Hard acceleration: 13.19:1; running rich

## Case Study 71: Vacuum/Pressure Gauge Reading

71.1.1 23 in Hg
71.1.2 75 kPa

71.1.3  7 in Hg
71.1.4  54 cm Hg
71.1.5  14 psi
71.1.6  40 kPa
71.1.7  11 psi
71.1.8  58 cm Hg
 71.3   9.5 psi is within normal range.

## Case Study 72: Module Pinout Diagrams

72.1  CMP Low
72.3  Brown
72.5  Purple/White; 1668; HO2S High B2 S2
72.7  Light Green
72.9  21

# Unit 8—Driveline

## Case Study 73: Multi-Disc Clutch Adjustments

73.1  2.336″
73.3  2.489″
73.5  0.002″

## Case Study 74: Driveline Angle Calculation

74.1  1.2°
74.3  1.4°
74.5

|        | Transmission | Rear |
|--------|--------------|------|
| Stock  | 0.7°         | 0.1° |
| Lift   | 2.7°         | 1.9° |

## Case Study 75: Gear Ratio Torque

75.1  1st: 3,069.18 foot-pounds
      2nd: 1,624.86 foot-pounds
      3rd: 1,003 foot-pounds
      4th: 702.1 foot-pounds
75.3  1st: 2,346.12 foot-pounds
      2nd: 1,569.96 foot-pounds
      3rd: 1,146.6 foot-pounds
      4th: 882 foot-pounds
      5th: 705.6 foot-pounds
      6th: 555.66 foot-pounds
75.5  1st: 5,123.6 foot-pounds
      2nd: 2,990.8 foot-pounds
      3rd: 1,956 foot-pounds
      4th: 1,463.8 foot-pounds
      5th: 1,072.6 foot-pounds
      6th: 845.5 foot-pounds

## Case Study 76: Differential Gear Ratios

76.1  4.63:1
76.3  3.89:1
76.5  3.00:1
76.7  Stock: 3.5:1
      New: 3.73:1
      New gear set is shorter.

## Case Study 77: Hydraulic Pressure

77.1  2 cm
77.3  1.67 cm
77.5  7.5 pounds of force
77.7  875 pounds of force

## Case Study 78: Planetary Gear Set Ratios

78.1

| Input  | Held   | Output | Gear Ratio |
|--------|--------|--------|------------|
| Planet | Ring   | Sun    | 0.31:1     |
| Planet | Sun    | Ring   | 0.69:1     |
| Ring   | Planet | Sun*   | 0.45:1     |
| Sun    | Planet | Ring*  | 2.21:1     |
| Ring   | Sun    | Planet | 1.45:1     |
| Sun    | Ring   | Planet | 3.21:1     |

From least to greatest:
0.31:1
0.45:1
0.69:1
1.45:1
2.21:1
3.21:1

78.3

| Input | Held | Output | Gear Ratio |
|---|---|---|---|
| Ring | Planet | Sun* | 0.33:1 |
| Ring | Sun | Planet | 1.33:1 |
| Planet | Sun | Ring | 0.75:1 |
| Sun | Ring | Planet | 4.06:1 |
| Sun | Planet | Ring* | 3.06:1 |
| Planet | Ring | Sun | 0.25:1 |

From least to greatest:
0.25:1
0.33:1
0.75:1
1.33:1
3.06:1
4.06:1

## Case Study 79: Manual Gear Set Ratios

79.1 12 teeth
79.3 20 teeth
79.5 42 teeth
79.7 120 teeth

## Case Study 80: Odometer Distance Values

80.1 421.8 miles
80.3 34 km is closer
80.5 1,086.8 miles
80.7 Truck at 148 km is closer.

## Case Study 81: Shift Solenoids

81.1 Fourth
81.3 Fourth and Fifth
81.5 Shift Solenoid D + E
81.7 Shift Solenoid E

## Case Study 82: Driveline Speed

82.1 64.0 miles per hour
82.3 38.8 miles per hour
82.5 Decrease 6.5 miles per hour
82.7 Decrease 1.6 miles per hour

## Case Study 83: Gear Backlash

83.1 0.012″
83.3 0.012″

## Case Study 84: Differential Backlash

84.1 Within specification range
84.3 Service needed
84.5 Service needed
84.7 Within specification range
84.9 Service needed

# Unit 9—Air Conditioning and Hybrid Technology

## Case Study 85: Air Conditioning System Oil

85.1 2.7 ounces
85.3 2.6 ounces
85.5 2.6 ounces

## Case Study 86: Compressor Clutch Air Gap

86.1 0.10 mm shim
86.3 0.005″ shim

## Case Study 87: Hybrid Vehicle High-Voltage Battery

87.1 235.2 volts
87.3 144 volts
87.5 270 volts

## Case Study 88: Electric Car Speed and Acceleration

88.1 75 miles per hour
88.3 70.2 kilometers per hour
88.5 22.56 ft/s$^2$
88.7 12.83 ft/s$^2$

## Case Study 89: Cooling System Boiling Point

89.1  271°F
89.3  12°F
89.5  245°F
89.7  279°F

## Case Study 90: Hybrid Vehicle Payback

90.1  Payback point is 99 months or 8 years 3 months.
      8 years 3 months > 6-year average ownership
90.3  Payback point is 170 months or 14 years 2 months.
      14 years 2 months > 6-year average ownership

## Case Study 91: Evaporator and Condenser Area

91.1  104 sq in
91.3  285 sq in
91.5  211 sq in
91.7  125 sq in

## Case Study 92: Refrigerant Weight

92.1  1.3 lb
92.3  27.1 oz
92.5  2.97 lb

## Case Study 93: Air Conditioning System Pressures

93.1  Correct system operation
93.3  Undercharged system
93.5  Correct system operation

## Case Study 94: Miles per Gallon Equivalent

94.1  111 MPGe value
94.3  94 MPGe value
94.5  110 MPGe value
94.7  187 MPGe value

## Case Study 95: Air Conditioning Gauge Reading

95.1  Pressure: 78 psi
      Temperature: 75°F
95.3  Pressure: 185 psi
      Temperature: 125°F
95.5  Low Gauge Pressure: 42 psi
      High Gauge Pressure: 172 psi
95.7  Low Gauge Pressure: 67 psi
      High Gauge Pressure: 135 psi

## Case Study 96: Hybrid Electric Fuel Economy

96.1   0–20 miles
96.3   2.5 hours
96.5   8 miles
96.7   They are equal at 10.
96.9   30 miles
96.11  Vehicle #2
96.13  Vehicle #1